Dr Darold Treffert has been Director of several major American psychiatric hospitals, and since 1979 has divided his time between private practice and a position as Executive Director of the Fond du Lac County Health Care Center in Wisconsin. His research on the Savant Syndrome has appeared in many journals including *Time* and *Newsweek* and he travels and lectures frequently.

EXTRAORDINARY PEOPLE

DAROLD A. TREFFERT

BLACK SWAN

EXTRAORDINARY PEOPLE

A BLACK SWAN BOOK 0 552 994049

Originally published in Great Britain
by Bantam Press a division of
Transworld Publishers Ltd.

PRINTING HISTORY

Bantam Press edition published 1989
Black Swan edition published 1990

Copyright © Darold A. Treffert 1989

Black Swan Books are published by
Transworld Publishers Ltd, 61–63 Uxbridge
Road, Ealing, London W5 5SA, in Australia
by Transworld Publishers (Australia) Pty
Ltd, 15–23 Helles Avenue, Moorebank,
NSW 2170, and in New Zealand by
Transworld Publishers (N.Z.) Ltd, Cnr
Moselle and Waipareira Avenues,
Henderson, Auckland.

Made and printed in Great Britain by
Cox & Wyman Ltd, Reading, Berkshire.

This book
about extraordinary people I have
been privileged to work with
is dedicated to
the special people I have been
privileged to live with

Dorothy M.
Jon, Joni, Jill & Jay

Contents

Acknowledgments   ix
Introduction   xi
Prologue   xvii
Savant Syndrome: Defining the Condition   xxvi

ONE: GENIUS AMONG US
1. The Genius of Earlswood Asylum and Other Early Savants   3
2. Music: Language for an Endless Infancy   16
3. If This is June 6th, It Must Be Friday: The Calendar Calculators   36
4. The Brilliant and the Backward: The Lightning Calculators   55
5. "An Exaltation of Memory": the Mnemonists   68
6. The Cats' Raphael and Other "Rara Avis"   79
7. From Mr. A to Mr. Z: Other Savant Skills   92

TWO: PORTRAITS
8. Leslie   103
9. Ellen   116
10. Alonzo   123

THREE: GENIUS WITHIN US
11. Explaining the Inexplicable   131
12. "Great Vigor of Memory" — in the Savant and in the Rest of Us   165
13. New Savants and New Findings   187
14. How Do They Do It?   215
15. And What of the Future?   226
16. A Smoother Pebble   250

Bibliography   275
Appendix   283
Index   285

Acknowledgments

Twenty-five years of interest in any topic generates indebtedness to innumerable persons. I can only acknowledge some of those for their help with this book.

I wish to thank the extraordinary families of these extraordinary people for sharing them with me and teaching me as much about inspiration as illness. Appreciation goes especially to May and Joe Lemke; Mary Parker Larsen and the Miracle of Love Ministries; Mrs. Pat Smith; Evelyn and Ollie Clemons; Ory and Barbara Boudreaux; and the many other families I have had the privilege of meeting in person or through correspondence.

Graditude extends to Ruth Czoschke, my long-time secretary, for transposing my illegible notes to a typed manuscript; Sister Sharon and the St. Agnes Hospital Medical Library for helping trace some rather obscure references; Pam Driscol, Driscol Gallery; Dr. Bernard Rimland of the Institute for Child Behavior Research; Dr. Laurence Becker of Creative Learning Environments; Suzanne St. Pierre and Morley Safer of *60 Minutes* for giving Savant Syndrome visibility and thus putting me in touch with so many more families and researchers interested in this condition; Peter Livingston for his interest and encouragement; and Margaret Wimberger of Harper & Row for her constructive suggestions and editing help.

Finally, thank you to my wife, Dorothy, for her enthusiasm about this book and her understanding tolerance while I was working on it; my partners for their coverage when I was away from my practice; Elaine and my office staff for helping to meet deadlines; and my patients for their patience about this project.

Introduction

Jeremy can stand at the side of the railroad tracks and give you the cumulative total of the numbers on the boxcars, however many, as the end of the train rolls by. But he is severely autistic and cannot count.

George and his identical twin brother Charles can tell you all the years in which your birthday fell on a Thursday. They can also tell you, within a span of 40,000 years backward or forward, the day of the week on which any date you choose fell or will fall. In their spare time George and Charles swap 20-digit prime numbers for amusement. Yet they cannot add simple figures or even tell you what a formula is, let alone write one out.

Leslie has never had any formal musical training. Yet upon hearing Tchaikovsky's Piano Concerto No. 1 on the piano for the first time in his teen years, he played it back flawlessly and without hesitation. He can do the same with any other piece of music, no matter how long or complex. Yet he cannot hold a utensil to eat and merely repeats in monotone fashion that which is spoken to him. Leslie is blind, is severely mentally handicapped and has cerebral palsy.

Ellen is also blind, with an I.Q. of less than 50. She too is a musical genius. She constructs complicated chords to accompany music of any type she hears on the radio or television. She sang back the entire soundtrack of the Broadway musical *Evita* after one hearing of the album, transposing orchestra and chorus to the piano with her complex, precise chords including intense dissonances to reproduce mob and crowd noises. In addition she has a remarkable spatial sense and a phenomenal memory.

Kenneth is 38 years old but has a mental age of 11 years. His entire vocabulary consists of 58 words. Yet he can give the population of every city and town in the United States with a population over 5,000; the names, number of rooms and locations of 2,000 leading hotels in America; the distance from each city and town to the largest city in its state; statistics concerning 3,000 mountains and rivers; and the dates and essential facts of over 2,000 leading inventions and discoveries.

Jedediah, with a mental age of 10, unable to write his name, answered the question "In a body whose three sides are 23,145,789 yards, 5,642,732 yards and 54,965 yards, how many cubicle ⅛ths of an inch exist?" with the correct 28-digit figure after a five-hour computation. "Would you like the answer backwards or forwards?" he inquired. "I can give it either way."

Alonzo has an I.Q. of 50 and a vocabulary of about that many words. Like Leslie, he only parrots back what is said to him and rarely initiates speech. But his animal sculptures are magnificent. He can complete a horse and colt in absolutely perfect anatomic detail in less than an hour. One fleeting glance at a picture is all he requires for a model that he will then reproduce in three-dimensional detail.

David is mentally ill, requiring long-term hospitalization because of his dangerous and devastating rage attacks. While seriously impaired in a number of other areas, he has memorized the bus system of Milwaukee, Wisconsin. Give him the number of the bus pulling up in front of you and the time of day and he will tell you on what corner you are standing anywhere in the city.

These, and all the other cases described in this book, are examples of the fascinating "idiot savant," a term coined by Dr. J. Langdon Down of London exactly 100 years ago, when the word "idiot" did not have the negative, comical implication it now carries.[1] At that time, "idiot" was an accepted medical and psychological term referring to a specific level of intellectual functioning—an I.Q. level of less than 25. The word "savant" was derived from a French word meaning "to know" or "man of learning." Observing persons with severe mental handicap displaying advanced levels of learning, even though in very narrow ranges, led to the then descriptive, still colorful juxtaposition of the two words "idiot savant."

Understandably, some people object to that term now because the word "idiot" gives the condition a connotation that is neither deserved nor fair. Therefore, the terms "savant" and "Savant Syndrome" will be used hereafter in referring to these remarkable people and the astonishing phenomenon they present.

Savant Syndrome is a condition in which persons with major mental illness or major intellectual handicap have spectacular islands of ability and brilliance that stand in stark, startling contrast to those handicaps.

In some savants—those we call "talented savants"—the skills are remarkable simply in contrast to the handicap, but in other, more rare savants, those I call "prodigious," the abilities and skills would be remarkable even if viewed in normal persons.

Until now, the scientific articles and media presentations describing the several hundred savants known of over this past century have been isolated, anecdotal accounts of single individuals and their truly extraordinary stories. But there is much more to Savant Syndrome than interesting stories. Within this group of remarkable people, diverse as they at first appear, is a commonality that deserves study, for it may provide a key to understanding not just how they—handicapped but with uncommon talent—function, but how we—without handicap but with common talent—function as well.

The significance of Savant Syndrome lies in our inability to explain it. The savants stand as a clear reminder of our ignorance about ourselves, especially about how our brains function. For no model of brain function, particularly memory, will be complete until it can include and account for this remarkable condition.

So many questions leap up. How can this be? How can extremely handicapped persons possess these islands of genius? What do they share in common? Why, with all the skills in the human repertoire, do the skills of the savant fall in such constant and recurrent narrow ranges? Why does the obscure skill of calendar calculating occur in so many of the savants?

Why is it that phenomenal memory is seen in all the savants, no matter what particular individual skill they exhibit? Is that memory different in the savant than in the rest of us? Is the genius a direct result of the deficiency or do the two factors simply coexist coincidentally?

What can we learn about this dysfunction, albeit a spectacular dysfunction, of mind and memory in the savant that might provide clues to normal function of mind and memory? Might the existence of these geniuses among us suggest that some such genius lies within each of us, waiting to be tapped?

These are the questions that Savant Syndrome raises. And the savants provide an opportunity to answer these questions with study and inquiry. Their extraordinary brain function—their abnormality—can allow us to understand ordinary brain function and normality. In learning how they work we can learn how we work. Technology only now available allows study not just of brain structure, but of brain function as well. Information from the study of this unusual brain capacity, in contrast to normal brain function, may stimulate inquiry about ways to channel and harness memory, and perhaps, conceivably, lead to expanded memory ability in all humans—for example, the enhanced retrieval of the tremendous store of information we each have within us but are so poorly able to recall.

What I have tried to do in this book is to tell these remarkable stories, balancing what is scientifically astonishing and noteworthy with that which is, from a human interest standpoint, equally as astonishing and equally as noteworthy. For these are stories not just of unique brain function and unique brain circuitry; these are stories also of love, warmth, hope, belief, incredible perseverance and indefatigable determination. This book will look not only at the condition the savant has, but also at the savant who has that condition. And it will look at the families, teachers and caretakers—the believers and the cheerleaders— who also play such a crucial and admirable role in the development and fulfillment of the savants.

The time has come to take savants out of the "Gee Whiz" category and learn what we can about them, and from them, not just about memory and brain function, but about human potential and possibilities as well. Beyond any scientific significance is the inspiration and hope that these stories provide for other handicapped persons and their caretakers.

So this book, and the study of the savant, may do something for us but I hope it will do something for the savant as well. In his introduction to Dostoyevsky's book *The Idiot*, Harold Rosenberg points out that "idiot" in the original and classical sense of the word meant "a private and unrelated person, an outsider."[2] In the many accounts I have read, so many of the savants, strange and wonderful as they are, are viewed as somewhat strange, as outsiders. By better understanding them and their condition, perhaps we can come to see savants as less strange, less private and less unrelated to us.

The savants I have been privileged to meet are neither strange to me nor strangers. They are geniuses to be sure, paradoxes of handicap and brilliance. If we get to know them carefully, they may provide some clues to the genius that resides, I believe, within each of us. In that we all have much in common. We can learn from, and contribute to, each other.

Learning from, and contributing to, each other is the purpose of this book. It is dedicated to these remarkable persons and their remarkable families, who not only care for them but care about them as well. It is a glimpse at them and, from that, a glimpse at ourselves. It is a look at talent, creativity, intelligence and the interfaces among them. It is a study in adversity and overcoming adversity.

Savant Syndrome can teach us a lesson in producing superiority from deficiency and in appreciating what is present rather than regretting what is absent. In learning about the savant's uniqueness, in witnessing what unconditional belief in someone, even though handicapped, can do and in using the savant's determination as an inspiration, we can use this curious and fortuitous mix of scientific possibilities and human interest to propel us further ahead than we have ever been before in understanding both science *and* human potential.

I met my first savant on July 1, 1959. I was 26 years old and had just completed a residency in psychiatry at University Hospitals in Madison, Wisconsin.

My first professional assignment was to direct and develop a 30-bed Children's Unit, which had just been established, at Winnebago State Hospital near Oshkosh, Wisconsin. The time had come to set up a separate unit for children. Winnebago was one of two psychiatric institutes in Wisconsin and received patients from 32 counties in the north and east halves of the state. These were patients with major mental illness or other severe mental handicaps. The child and adolescent population of that facility, which at that time had about 1,000 patients, had grown to 30, in keeping with a surge in that population in all of the psychiatric facilities around the country. The need for a separate unit was obvious.

As I walked onto the unit that first day I noticed David. He stood there with a rolled-up scroll-like device on which perhaps a hundred names were neatly written. As David turned the pencil on which the scroll had been wound each name came into view, one at a time, in a cardboard opening over the scroll. It looked just like a window on the front of a bus where the destinations are listed and are changed as the bus route changes. And that's just what it was. The names on David's scroll were the names of streets—Capitol Drive, State Street, Lincoln Avenue. David had memorized the bus system of Milwaukee, Wisconsin. If you gave him the number of a bus and the time of day he could tell you at which corner the bus was then stopping.

David was a very disturbed boy. His rage episodes and serious mental illness necessitated continuous hospitalization. His overall functioning was substantially impaired except for this particular area of exceptional ability. He would have been a great cab dispatcher.

There were other savants on the unit. Billy could make free-throws. Could he ever make free-throws! He was like a baseball pitching machine, only with a basketball. He always stood in exactly the same place at the free-throw line with his feet in exactly the same position and his body in the same stance. On each throw his arm motions were identical, as was the arc of the ball, as was his accuracy—perfect. He never missed. He showed no emotion, no over-correction or under-correction. There was nothing to correct. He was a basketball robot. Unfortunately he had that same robot-like approach to everything. His mutism and his inability to communicate were evidence of his profound disturbance which required his hospitalization on a long-term basis.

Then there was Tony. Unlike Billy, Tony used language. But he too had a very serious behavioral condition and would make vicious attacks toward himself, and sometimes at others. Tony knew history. He delighted each day in approaching visitors or staff, including new young doctors, asking them the significance of that particular day in history. Usually eliciting no answer, or a few wild guesses, Tony would spout off a long list of events that occurred on that day in history, much like the radio announcer on the morning show I listened to each day on my way to work—except that the announcer read it from an almanac he used each day. Tony was an almanac.

There were other cases like David, Billy and Tony on the unit. I was struck by the islands of intelligence, even genius, that existed in what otherwise was a sea of severe handicap and disability and I began to be interested particularly in this paradox of ability and disability so striking when seen side by side in the same patient.

This phenomenon—islands of intelligence—was particularly frequent in the unit's patients with Early Infantile Autism. These were handsome children who appeared quite normal physically. But they acted differently. They were profoundly withdrawn, looked completely preoccupied and had an intense desire for sameness. Either they were mute or had language with no useful interpersonal communication value, consisting of peculiar use of pronouns, neologisms and metaphors. They seemed to be in worlds of their own. They did not respond when you spoke to them, and seemed to look through you rather than at you. On first meeting them you would think they were deaf.

These patients were born that way. Dr. Leo Kanner, in 1944, named this condition "Early Infantile Autism" and it is this condition that is generally meant when the term "autistic child" is used in the media and in the press.[3] Typically this is the child portrayed on some television special—hopelessly withdrawn, mute and cowering in a fetal position under a bed until, in the final scene, the new, young therapist crawls under the bed and utters the magic word that releases the frightened child from the theretofore hidden trauma. It is usually then that the child falls into the arms of the therapist, half-sobbing and half-talking in a veritable cascade of dammed up words. In reality, it simply never works this way.

We know this condition now to be biologic, not psychologic, in origin. It is a developmental disability that manifests itself in this very stereotypical fashion. For a time parents were cruelly, and wrongly, blamed as if they had somehow done this to the child. The callous term "refrigerator mother" grew out of this horrendously mistaken theory.

In this group of children with this condition—Early Infantile Autism—some savant characteristics appear with a frequency as high as 10 percent.[4] We certainly had our share of such patients at Winnebago. In some the island of ability was fairly simple but still noticeable, for example, the ability to make exceedingly intricate string puzzles and pictures. In others, though, the ability stood out much more strikingly, particularly in contrast to their severe handicap and disability. One child, for example, had the ability to put jigsaw puzzles together methodically and mechanically, viewing the shapes of the pieces in an uncanny manner, seemingly with no attention to the picture itself, and then picking them up one by one and laying them into the proper place, one against the other, robot-like, until the puzzle was quickly completed. In still others the skill would have been noticeable, like the free-throws and the bus system memorization, even if it had been present in a normal child.

These autistic patients represented about one third of the children and adolescents on the unit. A second third was a group of patients who, unlike the autistic children, seemed quite normal at birth and seemed to be progressing normally throughout the first years of their lives, perhaps even to adolescence. Often then there had been some event in their lives—a severe physical illness, an operation or a near drowning—following which the child or adolescent took on many of the same characteristics, in a rapid regression, as the autistic children in the first group. These cases represent Childhood Schizophrenia or the onset of schizophrenia, a major mental illness, in the child-adolescent years. While savant skills are seen in some of these patients, the incidence is not nearly as high in this group as in the autistic group.

The final third of the children and adolescents on the unit were patients with clear organic brain damage that occurred either before or at birth, or resulted from subsequent injury or illness. It is to this group that the term "developmentally disabled" or "mentally retarded" would be applied. These patients were at Winnebago, a psychiatric hospital, because of severe behavioral problems superimposed on the basic mental retardation. If the retardation were the only problem they would have been placed elsewhere, either in the community or in a center specifically for persons with developmental disability.

(You will note, incidentally, that throughout this book I use the terms "developmental disability" and "mental retardation" interchangeably. I realize that some people object to the term "mental retardation" but I use it because it is more easily recognized, more easily understood and, frankly, easier to use. To me "mental retardation" is not the derogatory term some believe it to be, and with its meaning of slowing of development or progress, it is really quite descriptive and accurate. I use the term with all due respect.)

These three groups of patients—those with Early Infantile Autism, schizophrenia and developmental disability—are important in understanding Savant Syndrome and in analyzing the cases that follow. Likewise, the distinction between autism as a symptom and autism as an illness (as the term is popularly used) becomes important, as will be seen.

As I worked with the patients on the unit, those patients who had Early Infantile Autism were of special interest to me. The islands of intelligence that so many of them showed were particularly fascinating. Looking for any epidemiologic or etiologic factors that might provide some clue to the genesis of this disorder, I conducted a research project in which I was able to identify 69 such patients in Wisconsin over a five-year time span, out of 280 children with the broader diagnosis of childhood schizophrenia.[5]

I found that the disorder was rare—only about 7 cases occurred per 100,000 children, an incidence very near the one found by another researcher in England.[6] Like Kanner before me, I found that the parents of these children had a higher educational level than did the parents of childhood psychiatric patients with other disorders. I found the male-female ratio in this disorder to be about 4:1; there were few firstborn males, however, with this disorder, and the age of the mother at the time of the child's birth was older than other matched control groups with different diagnoses.

This study accomplished several things for me. By careful classification based on specific symptoms it separated the conditions of Early Infantile Autism, Childhood Schizophrenia and developmental disability into the three different entities they are. Second, it verified a number of findings in earlier studies, including the rarity of Early Infantile Autism, the predominance of males among those with this disorder and the interesting finding of higher educational levels in the parents of children with this disorder. Thirdly, by carefully defining and limiting the term "Early Infantile Autism" to a specific set of symptoms it clarified the distinction between autism as a symptom and autism as a separate disorder. The study found characteristics of Early Infantile Autism that are very similar in some ways to some characteristics of Savant Syndrome and may explain, in part, portions of that condition.

This study put me in touch with other investigators throughout the world interested in this rather rare disorder. It further heightened my interest in the islands of intelligence that this population presented. And it left me with some lingering questions about Early Infantile Autism, questions which interest me still and which loom up regarding Savant Syndrome.

After two years on the Children's Unit I became Superintendent of Winnebago in 1964. Obviously I had much more to do then than to ponder the intriguing questions that the fascinating illness of Early Infantile Autism raised. But I did not forget those questions. I was busied, however, with many other things, like trying to run the hospital itself. Fifteen years later, in 1979, I left Winnebago to divide my time between the private practice of psychiatry at Brookside Medical Center in Fond du Lac and being the Executive Director of the Fond du Lac County Health Care Center, a 150-bed community mental health center. Though I had filed away the data on the autistic children I had seen, and on the savant phenomenon present in some of them, it still intrigued me.

I didn't see many autistic children in my Fond du Lac practice. What I did see, though, were a number of adult patients on whom I was doing sodium amytal interviews to enhance recall of buried memories and sometimes hidden traumas. Occasionally that seemed like the best approach where repressed memories were hidden, but crucial. In those interviews patients recalled in extraordinarily minute detail a whole variety of experiences they thought they had forgotten. In some instances a whole journey down a particular street on a particular night would be recalled with exquisite attention to particulars—changing stop and go lights, street signs and passing autos. Both the patients and I were often startled at the voluminous amount of material stored but out of access in the patient's waking state, as if a tape recorder of sorts were running all the time, recording all our experiences. The memories were there. What was missing was access and recall.

Simultaneously, reports were constantly cropping up in scientific literature about the neurosurgical studies of brain mapping, especially the use of tiny electrical probes to determine epileptogenic foci—the seizure trigger—in the exposed cortex of patients who suffered certain kinds of seizures. The brain itself has no pain fibers within it. The pain fibers are in the surrounding capsule of the brain, the dura mater. Once the dura is numbed with a local anesthetic the patient can remain awake while the surgeon uses a tiny electrical probe to find the site where certain kinds of seizures are triggered. This site can then be surgically removed and some seizure disorders corrected. In the random search for these foci the probe hits a variety of spots on the cortex and when it does, memories flood the patient's consciousness. These memories, long forgotten, or seemingly so—the birthday party the day you turned 5, and the guests present; a day in class 20 years earlier; a walk on a particular path on a particular day complete with the accompanying aromas and sounds—are the kinds of "random" memories we all often experience in our dreams and dismiss in the morning, if we remember them at all, wondering "where did that come from?" In these studies, the probe activated a circuit or a pathway not available to us in ordinary life on an ordinary day.

I had filed away the accounts of these studies, too, along with my observations of the savants I had known, as I was busy with many other things.

Then Leslie Lemke came to Fond du Lac. It was June 1980. The Department of Social Services had invited May Lemke and her remarkable foster son Leslie to give a concert honoring the foster parents of the county, hoping to interest other families in becoming foster parents. I did not go to the concert but my daughter Joni did. She came home that evening and said she had seen a "miracle." She found it almost impossible to believe. She described a totally blind, retarded boy with cerebral palsy who hardly spoke at all, sitting mutely at a piano, hunched over the keyboard, looking exceedingly handicapped until he began to play and sing in a most marvelous manner. His spasticity, which was so evident when he was just sitting, disappeared when he played, in much the same way a stutterer's speech clears when he rises to talk to an audience. I told Joni that what she had just seen was an example of Savant Syndrome.

Joni was not the only one to raise questions about what she had just seen. Personnel from one of the television stations, who had decided to cover what they thought would be another fairly routine event, also found what they saw very difficult to believe. In fact, they wondered if it was "for real." They wanted me to review the tapes to make certain that this had not somehow been staged and, if it had not, to provide some kind of explanation of how this was possible. The tapes, while certainly startling, were eminently believable to me. Leslie was simply, but marvelously, demonstrating his "island of genius," which was like the ones I had seen so many times before in children on the unit at Winnebago. Without doubt, however, this island of genius was the biggest island I had ever seen.

There was a reporter from one of the wire services with the television station personnel that day and the story of Leslie's "miracle" and his devoted foster mother May was carried in the newspapers that night, while that astonishing concert was broadcast on television. On December 19, 1980, *The CBS Evening News with Walter Cronkite* used Leslie as part of its Christmas season message telling the story of "a young man, his handicaps, his foster mother, a piano and a miracle." Leslie was a celebrity.

In January 1981 *That's Incredible* broadcast their version of the story. It showed May, her husband Joe and Leslie Lemke just as they lived every day in a modest little cottage on a small lake near Milwaukee, Wisconsin. The program was very well done, indeed, and was as much about May as it was about Leslie. The television crew came to Fond du Lac where I provided some commentary for the story and spoke of Savant Syndrome.

I discussed the striking combination of Savant Syndrome and a dedicated foster mother who worked with this youngster with so much love, care, hope and patience and how the final product was a melding of those two remarkable circumstances. The results, I said, serve as inspiration to other parents and foster parents, particularly those of handicapped youngsters.

May closed the program with a prognosis about Leslie when she commented: "A little retardation is still there because he cannot answer questions or converse on his own just yet. But there is more to come." She certainly was right; there was more to come, as you will see.

Numerous television programs, newspaper articles and magazine stories told the story of Leslie, May and Joe Lemke. Leslie and May appeared on *Donahue* in February 1983. In October of that year *60 Minutes* did what has become a very well-known program on Savant Syndrome featuring not only Leslie but George, a calendar calculator, and Alonzo Clemons, a sculptor. It was viewed by millions, and while it did not make Savant Syndrome a household word, it did give visibility to this astonishing condition and three astonishing individuals. Morley Safer lists it as one of his ten favorite pieces among all those that he has done. I provided some commentary on this program also and raised some questions as well. One question still intrigues me. Is it possible for the brain to understand itself? Perhaps it can understand the kidney, or the liver, or the heart. But can the brain transcend itself to figure itself out? I am still not sure about the answer to that question.

These exposures put me in touch with researchers and scientists around the country and around the world who shared an interest in this condition from a whole variety of perspectives, some very different from mine. They also brought many new cases to my attention, cases I would have never known about were it not for this sudden attention to and curiosity about the puzzling paradox of being backward and brilliant at the same time.

Cases from around the country and around the world, from the past one hundred years through to the present, form the basis for this book, which brings together in a single place all that we know about this obscure but wondrous condition. Savant Syndrome provides, I am convinced, a window to the brain like no other window available to us; it has the potential to explain the pathways of memory that exist in the savants I have seen, in the patients I have interviewed with Sodium Amytal, in neurosurgical patients who have undergone the electrical probe and in the rest of us. Suppose we understood these pathways of memory and could harness them? All our memories are stored in prodigious amount until the special circuitry of the savant, or the Amytal, or the probe, or our dreams allows us access. What links the rest of us to the savant is the tremendous storage of memories we have in common; what separates us is the deep but narrow access of the savant contrasted with the broader but more shallow access of the rest of us. But what if . . . ?

I was drawn to psychiatry as a specialty because it, unlike the other specialties I could have chosen, seemed so young in its knowledge, with so little known and so much to be discovered. Somehow knowledge about the eyeball, or the liver, or the kidney seems more available, less vague and more easily encapsulated and contained than information about the brain, the emotions and human potential. I suppose it is that same curiosity about the unknown, the seemingly unexplainable, that has stimulated my interest in the savants and their extraordinary condition. I look at the savant with the same burning inquisitiveness with which I looked at some of the psychotic patients I saw early in my medical school years and internship. We seemed to know so much about the liver and so little about the brain, so much about diabetes and so little about schizophrenia. We knew even less about autism. But like autism, Savant Syndrome does exist. Since it exists, it must have an explanation. We cannot simply look at the savant in wonderment and awe, then go on as if no explanation is due, or none possible. Savant Syndrome may be difficult to explain, but surely it cannot be unexplainable. In explaining and understanding it, we will, I am convinced, explain and understand more about ourselves.

This book, I hope, begins that explanation.

Savant Syndrome: Defining the Condition

The beginning of wisdom is to call things by their right name.

In trying to accurately describe Savant Syndrome, and then understand it, there needs to be agreement on certain definitions and terminology. What follows is the terminology that will be used in this book to attempt to bring some uniformity to the various reports and papers of the past on this topic.

Savant Syndrome is an exceedingly rare condition in which persons with serious mental handicaps, either from developmental disability (mental retardation) or major mental illness (Early Infantile Autism or schizophrenia), have spectacular islands of ability or brilliance which stand in stark, markedly incongruous contrast to the handicap. In some, savant skills are remarkable simply in contrast to the handicap *(talented savants* or *savant I)*. In others, with a much rarer form of the condition, the ability or brilliance is not only spectacular in contrast to the handicap, but would be spectacular even if viewed in a normal person *(prodigious savants* or *savant II)*.

The condition can be congenital and present at birth, or it can be acquired and develop in an otherwise normal person following injury or disease of the central nervous system. It occurs in males more frequently than in females in an approximate 6:1 ratio. The skills often appear suddenly, without explanation, and can disappear just as suddenly.

The ability or brilliance, while spectacular, occurs within a very narrow range considering all the skills in the human repertoire. It occurs generally in one of the following areas: calendar calculating; music, almost exclusively limited to the piano; lightning calculating and mathematics; art, including painting, drawing or sculpting; mechanical ability; prodigious memory (mnemonism); or very rarely, unusual sensory discrimination (smell or touch) or extrasensory perception.

A person with Savant Syndrome was called an "idiot savant" when the condition was first described in 1887—"idiot" referring to a specific level of I.Q. functioning (below 25) and "savant" meaning a learned or knowledgeable person. Actually, the idiot savant is not an idiot at all, even by that early definition, since in almost all cases, the I.Q. of a savant is above 25, usually in the range of 40 to 70.

Savant Syndrome is rare. Studies have placed the incidence at 1:2,-000 in an institutionalized developmentally disabled population.[7] The incidence of Savant Syndrome in patients with Early Infantile Autism is much higher; it occurs in as many as 9.8 percent of the cases.[4] However, Early Infantile Autism itself is very rare; its incidence is about 7 cases per 100,000 children.[5] Within those two groups, prodigious savants are extremely rare—less than 100 cases have been reported in all world literature on this topic during the past 100 years.

Over the last century cases have been reported in adults and children from around the world. The condition appears to be over-represented in the blind where a triad of blindness, mental retardation and exceptional musical ability occurs with some frequency and regularity. When blindness does exist it significantly and notably is most likely caused by *retrolental fibroplasia,* a loss of vision due, in almost all cases, to excess oxygen administered to prematurely born children. This practice of using high concentrations of oxygen in the newborn nursery has been stopped now that the association between it and blindness has been clearly established, but before that association was apparent many such cases did occur and an unusually high number of those cases now exhibit Savant Syndrome.

Common to all the savants with their various skills is phenomenal memory, sometimes, but not always, of the eidetic type. *Eidetic memory* is a term applied to an extremely vivid recall process in which an actual positively colored image persists in the visual field for as long as 40 seconds after scanning an object. Sometimes the term is applied as well to an allied process called "visual image memory," more commonly known as "photographic memory." The latter can be of either a visual or auditory type. Whether the memory in any particular case is purely eidetic in nature or not, the savant remembers with remarkable and minute detail and depth, but that "hi-fidelity" memory function exists within an extremely narrow and limited range.

Autism as an illness and autism (or autistic behavior) as a symptom need to be differentiated. *Autism as an illness* refers to the specific condition of Early Infantile Autism, which is present at birth and characterized by profound withdrawal, an obsessive desire for sameness, absence of affectionate relationships with others, islands of ability with retention of intelligence in specific areas of functioning and either mutism or language that does not seem to serve any useful interpersonal purpose, is bizarre and is filled with neologisms and a peculiar use of pronouns. Deafness is often erroneously suspected because of the autistic patient's inattentiveness. Early Infantile Autism is extremely rare, is an entity by itself and is not synonymous with Childhood Schizophrenia.

Autism as a symptom may include some of the above behaviors, but it is a much broader term and refers to the presence of autistic behaviors in patients with one of a variety of disorders, including developmental disability, schizophrenia and other forms of psychosis. Such autistic symptoms are quite frequently seen in all of these disorders. The term "autistic child" as used in the scientific literature often does not distinguish between those with Early Infantile Autism and those with these other disorders. In this book an attempt will be made, wherever possible, to differentiate Early Infantile Autism as a separate and distinct entity from autism or more widely defined autistic symptoms.

Developmental disability and *mental retardation* are used synonymously in this book. Both terms refer to biologically based intellectual defect from congenital, prenatal, birth or postnatal causes. Developmental disability is usually present at or just after birth, resulting in the latter case from birth injury, but it can begin later in life following injury or disease. Early Infantile Autism is considered a developmental disability by some, since both are biological in origin, but in this book the terms will be used to refer to separate and distinct entities. Mental retardation, or developmental disability, is defined as occurring when the I.Q. is below 70.

I.Q., or intelligence quotient, is a measure of intellectual capacity that arose from the work of Alfred Binet, a French psychologist, and Theodore Simon, a French psychiatrist, who were attempting to develop some uniform method of assessing mentally retarded persons for educability.[139] A measure ultimately evolved in which a ratio, or quotient, is determined by dividing mental age by chronological age (I.Q. = mental age [MA] ÷ chronological age [CA] × 100). There are a number of tests available to determine I.Q. The Stanford-Binet uses a variety of tasks at each age level from age 2 to adult. This age-level concept is particularly useful for determining the intellectual capacity of children and for evaluating mental retardation. Some examiners prefer the Wechsler Intelligence Scale for Children—Revised (WISC-R) for ages 6 through 16 and the Wechsler Preschool and Primary Scale of Intelligence (WPPSI) for ages 4 to 6. These two instruments depend on a series of subtests to yield verbal, performance and then full-scale I.Q. levels.

The most widely used and best standardized test for determining I.Q., however, is the WAIS (Wechsler Adult Intelligence Scale). The WAIS consists of eleven subtests, including six verbal (information, comprehension, arithmetic, similarities, digit memory and vocabulary) and five performance (digit symbol, picture completion, block design, picture arrangement and object assembly). The test is administered in a uniform manner and subtest scores are weighted so they are comparable. Intelligence levels are determined statistically following a normal curve of distribution producing the following ranges: very superior (130+); superior (120–129); bright normal (110–119); normal (90–109); dull normal (80–89); borderline (70–79); and mental deficiency (below 69). Using this normal curve distribution 2.2 percent of the population are designated as falling at either extreme, either very superior or mentally retarded; 50 percent of the population falls into the normal (90–109) range.

Mental retardation itself is further subclassified on the basis of I.Q. as follows: borderline (I.Q. 68 to 85); mild (I.Q. 52 to 67); moderate (I.Q. 36 to 51); severe (I.Q. 20 to 35); and profound (I.Q. below 20). This is a classification scheme accepted by the World Health Organization and the American Psychiatric Association. The American Association on Mental Deficiency scheme differs very slightly from these. These uniform designations have replaced, fortunately, the more archaic terms of "idiot," "moron" and "imbecile," although those words still have some general use in Europe.

The term *echolalia* appears frequently in descriptions of the savant. This is an abnormal form of speech in which a person merely repeats back, usually verbatim, whatever is said to him or her rather than initiating any independent conversation. The greeting "Hello, how are you today?," for example, would be answered by parroting back "Hello, how are you today?" instead of giving an original and spontaneous reply.

The terms *hydrocephalic* and *microcephalic* are used in some of the descriptions of the savant as well. Hydrocephalic refers to a condition in which, because of either congenital or acquired blockage of spinal fluid drainage in the brain, there is an increase in volume of such fluid in the brain, causing the head to enlarge and expand well beyond normal size. Microcephalic refers to a condition, congenital in nature, in which the head, and consequently the brain, is well below normal size. Both these conditions produce mental retardation of varying degrees.

ONE

GENIUS AMONG US

1

The Genius of
Earlswood Asylum
and other
Early Savants

Perhaps history does repeat itself. Dr. J. Langdon Down, like me, was a psychiatrist, was a mental hospital Superintendent and was fascinated by what he saw in some of the young patients on his units. But his hospital was in England, a century ago. In 1887 he was invited to give the prestigious Lettsomian Lectures before the Medical Society of London. In those lectures he outlined what he had seen in his 30 years as Superintendent of Earlswood Asylum, sharing with his fellow physicians his careful observations, descriptions and conclusions about the patients in his hospital.[1]

He found those lectures "a convenient place to treat an interesting class of cases for which the term 'idiots savants' has been given, and of which a considerable number have come under my observation." His definition is brief but useful: "Children who, while feebleminded, exhibit special faculties which are capable of being cultivated to a very great extent." Even he had reservations about the name. "I have no liking for the term 'idiot.' It is so frequently a name of reproach. No one likes the name, and no mother will admit that her child deserves the title," he cautioned. He suggested that the term "idiot" be "advantageously replaced by 'feebleminded'." I doubt that would have been an advance.

Interestingly, it is not for naming the idiot savant that Down is best known. He is remembered best for his classic description of a form of mental retardation that bears his name—Down's Syndrome. It was in those same Lettsomian Lectures that he described that condition so meticulously and so accurately, along with giving his equally classic description of the idiot savant. Those lectures were later published as

3

a textbook on developmental disability entitled *On Some Mental Affections of Childhood and Youth.*

Just as I was, a century later, Down was struck by the paradox of deficiency and superiority occurring in the same patient. One of his patients built exquisite ships and copied complicated texts verbatim but could not understand a single sentence of what he had copied. Another drew with remarkable skill but had "a comparative blank in all the higher faculties of mind." A third case was a boy who could "read an entire book and ever more remember it." On reading the *Rise and Fall of the Roman Empire* the boy skipped a line on the third page, found his mistake, retraced his steps and, ever after when reciting the work from memory word for word, which he did easily, would always skip the line, go back and correct the error with as much regularity as if it had been part of the text itself. Down coined the interesting and useful designation "verbal adhesion" for this memory without consciousness, a phenomenon that is integrally a part of Savant Syndrome.

He recounted more memory feats. One boy had memorized an entire hymn book. Other children remembered dates and past events. One child could remember the address of every candy shop in London and tell the date of his every visit. Another told the time of arrival of all the children at an institution and could supply accurate records if challenged. Another knew the home address of every resident.

Astonishingly well-developed arithmetical genius was evident in some children. One 12-year-old boy could multiply any three-digit figures by three-digit figures with perfect accuracy as quickly as the numbers could be written on paper. This skill is known as "lightning calculating." "None of them can explain how they do it, I mean, by what mental process," noted Down.

Music was another skill noted in Down's account of this condition. These savants readily acquired tunes and rarely forgot them. He had one boy in his care who, after attending an opera, would come away with perfect recollection of all the arias, and would continue to hum or sing them correctly and indefinitely.

The rather rare skill of perfect appreciation of past or passing time was documented. A 17-year-old boy who was unable to use a clock or tell time in any conventional manner could nonetheless tell time with perfect precision when tested on numerous occasions. Down noted that, sometimes, this patient's response was less accurate, particularly when he was a little excited. He then "had to be shaken like an old watch and then the time would be truly given." It was on this patient that Down ultimately did an autopsy and found "no difference in his cerebrum from an ordinary brain, except that he had two well-marked and distinct soft commissures." He did not elaborate on that finding but apparently meant that two areas of the brain, or two convolutions, connected together in a manner not typical or common, perhaps from some type of scarring.

Down made two other crucial observations that have been repeatedly confirmed in the subsequent century by others interested in this condition. One was that in none of these cases was he able to find a history of like skill in the patient's parents, brothers or sisters. Second, he found no female savant: "All these cases of idiot savants were males: I have never met with a female."

All of medicine is built on careful observation, meaningful sorting and then calling everything by its right name. Down may not have selected exactly the right name for this condition, but he certainly was an excellent observer and sorter. It is his meticulous observations and accurate classifications that mark the beginnings of our knowledge about Savant Syndrome.

SOME OTHER EARLY DESCRIPTIONS

While Down distinguished himself by naming the condition "idiot savant," he was not alone in noting the amazing paradox of ability and disability that existed in some developmentally disabled patients. In 1866 Dr. Edward Sequin wrote a book entitled *Idiocy: Its Treatment by the Physiological Method.* [8] This before-its-time holistic approach to the developmentally disabled gave a series of case reports on patients, some of whom clearly qualified as savants, although Sequin did not use that name. Rather, he used the term "idiotic genius." Even "idiot savant," it seems to me, is an improvement over Sequin's choice of words.

Sequin described several cases, including that of Blind Tom and that of James Henry Pullen, both of which are discussed in considerable detail later in this book. His categorization of the types of developmental disability and their causes is most insightful. He points to social isolation and sensory deprivation as being capable of producing sizable intellectual defects, along with purely biological or genetic causes, which were the only real etiologies being discussed in his day. He provides some optimism and hope for healing, as is consistent with most holistic approaches, and argues for understanding and compassion, not just categorization, when approaching these conditions. He notes:

> There is no knowing what an idiot can do till tried; and such who can be taught nothing in one way, may learn much in another. The youth just described (Pullen), with all his cleverness, could never be made to understand that an annual sum paid quarterly would equal in amount

the same paid weekly. Yet another child, stupid at all other things, will make arithmetical calculations mentally, of great extent, with perfect accuracy and marvelous readiness. Without phrenology, philosophy, or explanation of any sort, what better proof that idiots are exactly like all of us, incomplete beings, only more infirm?

Sequin closes his book with a touching "in memoriam" to three of his patients who, in spite of their handicap, "enlisted to defend the Republic" and were killed in battle. One was cited for his bravery at Gettysburg. Ironically, Sequin notes that in the case of one of these brave souls there was little interest on the part of the family until after his death when the "relatives who had never previously inquired for him, inquired for his money and divided it among themselves."

Sequin's tribute to these noble men is kinder: "By their life and death, these once abandoned children, reclaimed to society-life by science and practical Christianity, showed that the institution for idiots can already develop the noblest sentiments of man, Friendship, Gratitude, Love of Home, and Devotion to one's Country."

His final challenge is to those of us who would try to study and understand handicaps by carefully observing and then drawing conclusions from what we have seen and studied. His cases, he states, "are numerous enough to represent idiocy in its most important aspects; and incomplete enough to make them stand like a stimulus for the friends of idiots to do better. *Progress is in proportion to the thoroughness of observation.*"

Sequin was a keen and thorough observer. While he may not have used the terminology by which we know it, he certainly captured the essence of Savant Syndrome.

Alfred Binet, whose name is synonymous with I.Q. testing, was fascinated by calculating prodigies. His extremely intricate study of two such non-savant calculators, Jacques Inaudi and Pericles Diamandi, contains much of importance in relationship to savants and their unique abilities, particularly lightning and calendar calculations.[9] Binet and his collaborator in these studies, the famous neurologist Dr. Jean Martin Charcot, held a conference on calculating prodigies at a well-known mental hospital in France, the Salpetriere. Neither Inaudi nor Diamandi was retarded, certainly, but the study of them by Binet pointed out the crucial differences between auditory and visual calculators; raised questions about prenatal influences on lightning calculating abilities; and demonstrated that lightning calculating and calendar calculating are linked. One of his observations is particularly significant in trying to explain the savant who can calendar calculate but not understand the method or system by which he or she does it. As Binet con-

6

cludes in his 1894 treatise on this subject, "The unconscious which is within us, and which psychology has in recent years often succeeded in illuminating, is perhaps capable of foreseeing the solution to a problem or long arithmetic operation without carrying the details of the calculations."

Dr. William W. Ireland was another pioneer in the study of the savant although he, like Sequin, did not use that term. In his 1891 book, *The Mental Affections of Children: Idiocy, Imbecility, and Insanity,* Ireland, like Down, was struck by the remarkable memory and incongruous talent in some of the patients at his Scottish institution.[10] He comments on two patients in his hospital, one with special talent for drawing and carving wood and the other with special talent in architecture and construction. He describes another patient as having a gift of "mental arithmetic," being able to add and multiply with lightning rapidness. He documents a case of a very limited individual with an astonishing "power of reckoning," who was able to give the number of minutes lived when told a person's age.

Ireland describes his theory on the disparity, in some mentally handicapped persons, between what he calls "cultivated talents" and "weak, neglected other faculties." He notes that, in patients with "special talents," those talents often received "very careful cultivation, and while they have been cultivated the other faculties have been frequently neglected." He notes this same tendency to focus on special skills in persons of normal intelligence or even genius, sometimes to the exclusion of a balanced, overall adjustment. It was not surprising to Ireland, therefore, that skills or talents could be developed to a very high level, but with the trade-off of impaired development in other areas. As he notes, "If one considers that men of special genius are sometimes behind men in very commonplace qualities—of this Mozart is a striking instance—it will not be out of measure surprising that some imbeciles should be highly distinguished above other imbeciles by some special bent or talent."

He concludes that constructive or mechanical genius was more frequently seen in his population than any other gift.

Another early case report on Savant Syndrome appeared in the medical journal *Lancet* on June 5, 1909.[11] According to the journal, at a meeting of the Society for Psychiatry and Neurology in Vienna, Dr. A. Witzmann "showed a man, aged 20 years, who possessed an extraordinary memory for certain of the data recorded in calendars. This individual, who, moreover, was an inmate of an asylum for idiots, could with utmost readiness tell what day of the week it had been or would be on any given day of the month in any year during the long period from the year 1000 of the Christian era until the year 2000." The report goes on to indicate that Witzmann, even after considerable study, "has not yet succeeded in finding out by what means the young man has acquired this faculty, at once so marvelous and so rare."

Witzmann believed, however, that the patient had found some kind of code by which he worked because his arithmetic was faulty when asked to set down figures of a computation based on ordinary tables seen on some calendars. Some of the typical questions were: What day of the week was October 3rd, 1907? What was the day of the week on June 14, 1808? Witzmann noted that family history gave no assistance in trying to understand this phenomenon. Remarkable was the fact that the man's knowledge of the calendar did not extend beyond the year 2000, stopping suddenly at that point. In addition to knowing the day of the week for each day of the month, he also knew the patron saint of each day of that month. Witzmann comments that neurologists had previously seen persons who possessed a special ability to store in their brain and reproduce at will masses of figures such as the times on railroad timetables, budget statistics and entries in bank books. He uses the colorful term "brain athletes" to describe these remarkable people.

DR. ALFRED F. TREDGOLD'S CLASSIC TEXT

Every syndrome in medicine seems to have its classic description somewhere in medical literature. Kanner's article on Infantile Autism or Down's description of the syndrome that bears his name are two splendid examples.[1, 3] The classic description of the savant, which falls into my "I wish I had said that" category, is the chapter on idiot savants in a 1914 textbook *Mental Deficiency (Amentia)*, by Dr. Alfred F. Tredgold of London.[12] The titles that follow Tredgold's name on the cover of that book amount to his curriculum vitae: "Consulting Physician to the National Association for the Feeble-minded, and to the Littleton Home for Defective Children; Lecturer at the Medical Graduates' College, London; formerly Medical Expert to the Royal Commission on the Feeble-minded; Research Scholar in Insanity and Neuropathology of the London County Council and Assistant in the Claybury Pathological Laboratory; Late Resident Clinical Assistant in the Northcumberland County Asylum, etc."

The chapter on the idiot savant in his textbook is trailblazing and still endures. While newer theories have emerged, nowhere is there a more succinct, colorful and capturing description of the savant. Tredgold, like Down, devoted his entire practice to the care of the mentally deficient. His book, revised into as many as eleven later editions, still is a standard textbook throughout the British Commonwealth and the

United States in the field of developmental disability. The later editions of his work still contain this chapter in its original form. Few such medical chapters survive a near century of reproduction.

Tredgold makes several interesting and accurate observations. He points out that idiot savants are not, in fact, idiots because they are rarely of that lowest grade of mental defect (I.Q. 25 or below). Second, he points out that, almost invariably, they are males, with female savants being very rare. Third, he notes that the talents are chiefly in the direction of imitation and that there is little capacity for originating or for creativity. Fourth, he points out that the talents are frequently lost before adult life.

Turning to specific cases, he notes some patients with *special senses*. He describes instances of delicacy of smell or an increased development of visual sense. He also describes patients with a phenomenal sense of hearing and others with hyperdevelopment of the tactile sense as well.

He moves on then to a group of cases in which *motor functions* are the extraordinary talent. In that group, he includes the gift of drawing and particularly highlights the case of Gottfried Mind, who had such a marvelous capacity for drawing pictures of cats that he came to be known as "The Cats' Raphael." Mind was a cretin (hypothyroid) patient born in 1768 who died at age 46. At an early age he showed considerable talent for drawing. He could neither read nor write, he had no idea of the value of money and his hands were remarkably large and rough. Tredgold notes that this patient's general appearance was so obviously indicative of a mental defect that, when he walked through the city, he was accompanied by jeering children. In spite of all this, his drawings and watercolor sketches, not only of cats but of deer, rabbits, bears and groups of children, were so marvelously lifelike and so skillfully executed that he acquired fame throughout Europe. In fact, one of his pictures, of a cat and kittens, was purchased by King George IV.

Under motor skills, Tredgold also includes the "gift of tongues"—the extraordinary capacity for producing spoken words. He described a case of Dr. Martin W. Barr's, an epileptic patient, age 22, who was unable to read or write. This patient rarely spoke spontaneously and then in only short disconnected words or the simplest of sentences. Yet he had a remarkable capacity for repeating fluently and with proper intonation everything said to him, whether it was in his mother tongue or in a language such as Greek, Japanese, Danish, Spanish or the like. Tredgold also refers to, as being quite common, patients who would reel off cantos of poetry verbatim.

The third talent, *memory*, intrigued Tredgold as well. He described a 65-year-old patient whose penchant was biographical history. When any prominent person at any point in history was named there would flow forth from this patient a steady, unhesitating stream of information, including a full account of that person's birth, life and death. A second case of phenomenal memory was a younger man, age 56, whose memory related to dates and occurrences, but only those of his own life. He became a valuable resource on anything that had occurred at the institution while he was a patient there—among other things, he could repeat the year, month and day on which each medical officer had come and then gone.

Tredgold includes calendar calculating under memory and cites one of Down's cases who had "a pronounced sense of locality," being able to give complex directions to and from various points in the vicinity without the slightest hesitation. This particular savant was also a calendar calculator and a lightning calculator, being able to do multiplication "with the rapidity of a reflex movement." Tredgold also cites a case of Dr. Forbes Winslow's, a patient who could remember "the day when every person had been buried in the parish for 35 years, and could repeat with unvarying accuracy the name and age of the deceased and the mourners at the funeral. But he was a complete fool. Out of line of burials, he had not one idea, could not give an intelligible reply to a single question, nor be trusted to even feed himself." Tredgold observes that in the idiot savant the phenomenal memory was in its simplest automatic form. He refers to another of Down's cases, the boy who could read a book and recite the pages word for word; he also refers to two cases of a Dr. Maudsley's, one in which the patient could repeat verbatim a newspaper he had just read and another in which an even more remarkable patient could repeat *backwards* anything that he had just read.

Turning to *musical talent,* Tredgold describes a most striking example—a case of a Dr. Trelat's that involved, interestingly, a female. Trelat described the patient as follows:

> They had at the Salpetriere an imbecile born blind, affected with rickets and crippled, who had great musical talents. Her voice was very correct and whenever she had sung or heard some piece she knew perfectly well the words and the music. As long as she lived they came to her to correct the mistakes in singing of her companions; they asked her to repeat a passage which had gone wrong, which she always did admirably. One day, Geraldy Liszt and Meyerbeer came to the humble singing class of our asylum to bring her encouraging consolations.

Finally, Tredgold lists savants with "extraordinary capacity for *arithmetic and calculations."* Once again drawing on a case of Down's, Tredgold describes an "imbecile boy of twelve years who could multiply three figures by three other figures with lightning rapidity." He recounts a case of a Dr. Howe's, "a low-grade ament [mental retardate] who, if told the age of anyone, would in a very short time calculate the number of minutes he had lived." He refers to a case of Dr. D. Adam Wizel's, a female patient with an outstanding faculty for multiplication and division. She divided 576, 560 and 336 by 16 with "astonishing quickness" and could carry out multiplication functions such as 23 × 23, 45 × 18 and 78 × 78 "immediately and by a peculiar method of her own." Yet she did very poorly at simple arithmetic.

How does Tredgold view and explain all of this? He states:

> The condition is exceptional and relatively uncommon; on the other hand, it is not so rare but that a considerable number of cases have been recorded. Presumably the special aptitude is related to an increased development of certain cerebral neurones, but as to how and why this is brought about we can only conjecture. In many of the cases I have seen there has been a marked predilection (which, however, has rarely been marked in the ancestors), and I can only assume that this is the result of some primary developmental anomaly or of some fortuitous circumstance of early life which has aroused the child's interest in a particular direction, and thence led to the concentration of all his mental activities upon the one object. The talent, whatever it is, and however originating, certainly owes much of its development to constant exercise.

A most insightful analysis by a most careful observer.

Tredgold concludes his famous chapter with an account of an extremely interesting case, that of James Henry Pullen.

THE GENIUS OF EARLSWOOD ASYLUM

James Henry Pullen spent 66 years of his life at the Earlswood Asylum. He entered that facility at age 15 and stayed there until his death in 1916. At least three observers wrote fairly extensively about him—Sequin, Tredgold and Dr. F. Sano.[8, 12, 13] From those accounts comes a composite description of this skilled craftsman, this "deaf and dumb" handicapped man, a national celebrity and a character. I am not sure which of the three doctors first named Pullen the "Genius of Earlswood Asylum," but clearly they all considered him such. Even His Majesty King Edward, when Prince of Wales, took a tremendous interest in this marvelous yet peculiar man and sent him tusks of ivory to encourage him in producing beautiful carvings. It is Pullen who comes to mind when Dostoyevsky describes the idiot as a private, unrelated person, an outsider.[2]

Pullen's parents and grandparents were hard-working, normal people with no family history of mental illness or retardation. His parents were, however, first cousins. A brother was also deaf and dumb but had this same remarkable drawing ability; that brother died, also at Earlswood, at age 35 of cancer.

Pullen was deaf and nearly mute. At age 5 or 6, he was impressed by the small ships that his playmates tried to maneuver on narrow puddles in Dalston, his birthplace, and he became obsessed with making such toys. He became skilled in carving ships and reproducing them in penciled drawings. Because of his deafness and muteness, he was isolated, eccentric and alone. Until he was 7 years old, he spoke only one word, "muvver." He later learned some monosyllabic words. He entered the Earlswood Asylum at age 15. According to Sano, Pullen "was unable to give any intelligible answer, unless he could accompany his broken words by gestures."[13]

Pullen continued his skills as carpenter and cabinet maker and became a tremendous craftsman. From morning until night he worked constantly in his workshop, and after returning to his room in the evening, he would do drawings in dark and colored chalk which, according to Sequin,

> . . . are most meritorious; and many of them, framed and glazed by himself, adorn the corridor and other parts of the asylum. One was graciously approved and accepted by the Queen, who was kindly pleased to send the artist a present; and Mr. Sidney had the honor of showing some of them to the Prince Consort, no common judge of art, who expressed the greatest surprise that one so gifted was still to be kept in the category of idiots, or ever had been one. His Royal Highness was particularly astonished, not only by his copies of first rate engravings, but by an imaginary drawing made by him of the Siege of Sebastopol, partly from the illustrated London News and partly from his own ideas.

Because of his expert craftsmanship, Pullen became a bit of a celebrity at Earlswood. He was given two workshops, and freedom to pursue his talents. Those two workshops became museums of his art after his death, containing many of his drawings and carvings, including a very insightful drawing about himself depicting forty scenes of his life. Those museums can still be visited at the Earlswood Asylum today.

At age 26, Pullen made his first representation of the universe in the shape of a ship. Sano describes it thus:

> It is a large barge, half as wide as it is long. There is a well furnished room in the center. White ivory angels are outside of the prow and Satan (Neptunus?) is at the stern. A center rod acts on twelve oars and

fort lightning strikes the top of the construction. Thus there is partly traditional influence and partly genuine conception, the whole being a fine illustration as how men are inclined to accumulate in one general synthesis their knowledge of the world, as they have perceived and conceived it. For Pullen the world could only be a ship.

Pullen was 35 years old when he began his masterpiece, *The Great Eastern*. It was a model ship for which he fashioned every screw, pulley, anchor and paddle from drawings he made beforehand. The planks were attached to the ribs by wooden pins that numbered over one million. The model was 10 feet long and contained 5,585 rivets and had 13 lifeboats hoisted on complete davits. State cabins were complete with chairs, bunks, tables and decorations. Pullen constructed the ship so that the entire deck could be raised to view the intricate detail below. He spent seven years completing this complicated ship, but it attracted worldwide attention when exhibited at the prestigious Fisheries Exhibition in 1883 in England, where it won the first prize medal.

Sequin described Pullen, at age 19, as alternately wild and sullen. He was, in fact, "the pupil who was six months learning the difference between a dog's head and his tail. If spoken to, he uttered by no means pleasant sounds; and when corrected, he would run away and hide himself, if possible." He never learned to read or write.

The older Pullen was usually quiet and reserved, particularly if left alone to pursue his talents. But there was another side to him as well. He was intolerant of advice, suspicious of strangers and, at times, ill-tempered and violent. He once wrecked his workshop in a fit of anger and, another time, erected a guillotine-like instrument over a door, hoping that a staff member he particularly disliked might come through. Another time he threatened to blow up his workshops. He both impressed and frightened people with a giant mannequin in the center of his workshop, inside of which he would sit, directing movements of its arms and legs and talking through a concealed bugle fitted to its mouth. Pullen was remarkably sensitive to vibrations coming through the ground and devised an alarm system in his workshop, based on that sensitivity, that made him aware of any approaching visitor.

Pullen was egocentric, preoccupied and egotistical. His few words were boastful and proud such as "very clever" and "wonderful" (not an uncommon characteristic of many savants). A note in a casebook at Earlswood describes him as "the quintessence of self-conceit."

Tredgold sums up Pullen this way:

His powers of observation, comparison, attention, memory, will and pertinacity are extraordinary; and yet he is obviously too childish, and at the same time too emotional, unstable, and lacking in mental balance to make any headway, or even to hold his own, in the outside world. Without someone to stage-manage him, his remarkable gifts would never suffice to supply him with the necessities of life, or even if they did, he would easily succumb to his utter want for ordinary prudence and foresight and his defect of common sense. In spite of his delicacy of manipulation, he has never learned to read or write beyond the simplest words of one syllable. He can understand a little of what is said to him by lip reading, and more by signs, but, beyond a few words, nearly all that he says in reply is absolutely unintelligible.

Tredgold concludes that Pullen did not have "primary amentia" (congenital mental retardation) at all but had a mild secondary deficiency due to sense deprivation (deafness). He theorizes that Pullen's isolated condition caused "all the powers of his mind (which do not seem to me to have been intrinsically defective) to be devoted to, and concentrated upon, these occupations with the result that he developed a power of copying drawings, of carving wood (and later in ivory), and a general mechanical dexterity of the very highest order."

Sequin sums it up this way: "In short, he has seemingly just missed, by defect of some faculties, and the want of equilibrium in those he possesses, being a distinguished genius."

Sano has a different view. He concludes that if Pullen had simply been affected by sensory deprivation, like Helen Keller, "deprived of sight and hearing, and yet able to acquire every kind of knowledge that ennobles human understanding," Pullen should have been able to advance much further with the kind of attention and notoriety that he experienced because of his tremendous skill as a craftsman. Sano points out, however, "but Pullen with both his eyes wide open to the bright world of London, and his skilled ten fingers under complete sense control, Pullen, even after having been busy for months in the printer's shop at Earlswood, could not absorb, digest, or exteriorise the most ordinary sentence of politeness. To say, 'I am very much obliged you so' was strange to him in grammatical arrangement as well as in social meaning."

Sano carried his analysis of the case of Pullen one step further. For him, the case did not end with Pullen's death. Writing in the *Journal of Mental Science* in July 1918, Sano gives not only his view of Pullen's life, but an exhaustive description of Pullen's brain on which he did a postmortem examination. It is an amazingly detailed map of the brain, complete with actual drawings of each convolution and each fissure. While there are few autopsies available on savants at all (Down described one mentioned earlier), clearly there is no other with this meticulous detail. The brain showed only arteriosclerosis, not unusual at Pullen's age. There was a slightly larger-than-normal corpus callosum (the mass of fibers connecting the cerebral hemispheres) and a good preservation of the occipital lobes (the visual center of the brain). In other words, the pathway between the occipital lobes and central hemispheres was well developed, and Sano concludes from these findings that those pathways were "bound to have special capacity in the visual sphere of mental existence." There was some lack of cerebral development, in Sano's view, which confirmed his impression that Pullen's problems were not just a result of sensory deprivation but that Pullen did, in fact, have organically based defects which kept him from developing accelerated and generalized abilities as Helen Keller did. While Sano found evidence to explain Pullen's retardation from the autopsy, he concluded that any further explanation of Pullen's character "was not to be found in his convolutions." Sano concludes that the deaf mutism of Pullen did have a cortical origin, was biologically based and contributed to his retardation through more than sensory deprivation.

Sano sums up his puzzlement and awe of Pullen by quoting Carlyle's *Hero Worship* to capture the magic and mystery of the savant: "Science has done much for us, but it is a poor science that would hide from us the deep sacred infinitude of nescience, whither we can never penetrate, on which all science swims as a mere superficial film. This world, after all our science and sciences, is still a miracle—wonderful, inscrutable, magique, and more, to whosoever will think of it."

And so was Pullen. Like the other savants before and after him, Pullen was a paradox of ability and disability. He captured the interest of kings, doctors and the public. He was proud, even boastful, but with good reason given his prodigious ability. He capitalized on that ability with tremendous motivation and became the recipient of equally tremendous reinforcement. He was original, one of a kind, not soon to be duplicated.

Pullen, and the condition he had, is a remarkable mystery.

Music: Language
for an Endless
Infancy

The civil war had ended. "Cannon had ceased to be the orchestra," as Dr. Edward Sequin wrote, and a 16-year-old blind slave boy resumed his piano concert tour that had already taken him, at age 11, to the White House and now was to take him around the country and then the world.[8] His vocabulary was less than 100 words, but his musical repertoire was over 5,000 pieces. He was "idiotic for any other purpose," concluded Sequin, "and can accomplish nothing but gyrations and melodies." In Philadelphia a panel of 16 outstanding musicians of the day signed a statement with their conclusions about Blind Tom, as he had come to be known: "Whether in his improvisations of performances of compositions by Gottschalk, Verdi, and others; in fact, [in] every form of musical examination—and the experiments were too numerous to mention—[he] showed a capacity ranking him among the most wonderful phenomena in musical history."

The story of this memorable "idiotic musical genius" begins at a slave auction in Georgia in 1850[14, 15] where his mother was sold as a slave by one Perry Oliver to a Colonel Bethune of a nearby county. Her fourteenth child was included in the sale "for nothing" because he was completely blind and was thought, therefore, to be useless and of no value. He was named Thomas Greene Bethune by his new master. On the colonel's Georgia plantation Blind Tom was allowed to roam the rooms of the mansion. Fascinated with sounds of all types—rain on the roof, the grating of corn in the sheller, but most of all music—Tom would listen intensely to the colonel's daughters practicing their sonatas and minuets on the piano. He would follow the music with his body movements. "Till 5 or 6 years old he could not speak, scarce walk, and gave no other sign of intelligence than this everlasting thirst for music," notes Sequin, "but at 4 years already, if taken out from the corner where he lay dejected, and seated at the piano, he would play beautiful tunes; his little hands having already taken possession of the keys, and his wonderful ear of any combination of notes they had once heard."

Late one night Colonel Bethune, who had no idea of the boy's talent, heard music coming from the drawing room in the darkened house. Thinking it must be one of his daughters playing, although that would be odd at such a late hour, he ventured downstairs and was startled to find the 4-year-old blind boy, so limited in other ways, playing a Mozart sonata—with flourish and without error. He had learned it by listening to one of the colonel's daughters, who had mastered it after weeks of practice. The colonel was astonished.

Like any slave child, Tom never attended school, but he was incapable of learning in areas other than music. He was restless and explosive and required constant supervision. He seemed irresistibly drawn to the piano and within a few years, without any instruction whatsoever, he could listen to a piece of music once, then sit down at the piano and play it through note for note, accent for accent, without error and without interruption. At age 6, he began to improvise as well as repeat. Colonel Bethune hired professional musicians to play for the child and there developed an instant repertoire of concert quality.

Word of the "blind genius" spread, and at age 7, Tom gave a concert. It was a sellout, and the newspaper reports were enthusiastic, so the colonel and young Tom took to the road on a concert tour, performing almost daily. Tom is said to have earned $100,000 in the first year of giving concerts.

Every note of every piece Tom heard was indelibly imprinted on his mind, and he was able to reproduce any piece from beginning to end without a moment's hesitation. His repertoire included Beethoven, Mendelssohn, Bach, Chopin, Verdi, Rossini, Donizetti, Meyerbeer and many others. A program from one of his early concerts stated, "Blind Tom can only play what he has heard or what he has improvised. Until about two years ago, a list of pieces that Tom heard was kept, numbering nearly 2,000 pieces. Unfortunately, this catalog was lost. Since, he has heard perhaps 3,000 pieces, and his repertoire now numbers upwards of 5,000 entirely on his memory depending." Another newspaper reported, "His memory is so accurate that he can repeat, without the loss of a syllable, a discourse of 15 minutes length, of which he does not understand a word. Songs, too, in French or German, after a single hearing, he renders not only literally in words, but in notes, style, and expression."

At age 11 Tom played at the White House before President James

Buchanan. Several musicians, who felt Tom had tricked the public and the President, tested him at his hotel the following day. They played two completely new compositions. The first, 13 pages in length, Tom repeated from beginning to end without effort or error, and the second, 20 pages in length, he also played to perfection.

In 1862 he performed an even more amazing feat. Tom could not read music, obviously, but he was presented with a 14-page original composition and was asked to play secondo while the composer played the treble part. This meant he had to improvise the entire secondo part in step with the musician's execution of the first part. Never having heard the piece before, Tom sat beside the composer and played the first note to the last in the secondo part. Following that, he "fairly shoved the man from his seat and proceeded to play the treble with more brilliancy and power than its composer." A report of that event concludes "to play secondo to music never heard or seen infers the comprehension of the full drift of the symphony in its current—a capacity to create, in short."

Tom and Colonel Bethune then toured Europe. While there, Tom was subjected to a test to determine whether he had perfect pitch. As Tom listened, two pianos were hammered on noisily and haphazardly, while on a third, simultaneously, a run of 20 notes was played. Seated at one of the pianos immediately afterward, Tom was able to repeat the run of 20 notes perfectly. The fact that he could distinguish and reproduce those notes appeared to prove to the experimenters that he possessed absolute pitch. Following the European tour, Tom again played to capacity audiences in the United States.

Sequin provides a vivid picture of Blind Tom in concert:

He is led by the hand or sleeve before an audience, and begins by presenting himself in the third person, and in a few words thrown away, rather than spoken, saying, "Blind Tom will play this or that piece for you," etc., after which he begins the piano. His execution is sometimes sweet, oftener of an unknown force, which manifestly proceeds from powers higher up than his wrist. When he sends certain clangorous agonies his shoulder-blades bear as it were directly on the keys, his whole frame vibrates with the instrument. If some person of the company is invited to play a new tune that the sable artist will have to repeat, he being used to it, understands what is the matter, and shows his satisfaction by his countenance, a laughing, stooping, with various rubbings of the hand, alternating with an increase of the sideway swinging of his body, and some uncouth smiles. As soon as the new tune begins, Tom takes some ludicrous posture, expressive of listening, but soon lowering his body and raising on one leg, so that both are perfectly horizontal, and supported upon the other leg, representing the letter T, he moves upon that improvised axis like the pirouette dancer, but indefinitely. These long gyrations are interrupted by other spells of motionless listening, with or without change of posture, or persevered in and ornamented with spasmodic movements of the hands; this is his studying posture. When the stranger is through, Tom stops, seats himself at the piano, and reproduces the musical idea perfectly, if the piece was entirely new to him; but reproduces tune for tune, note for note, if he only heard it previously two or three times.

A newspaper account of Blind Tom, quoted by Edward Podolsky, describes his concert appearance thus:

Blind Tom seated himself at last before the piano, a full half-yard distant, stretching out his arms full length, like an ape clawing his food; his feet when not on the pedals, twisted incessantly; he answered some jokes of his master's with a loud "Yha! Yha!"

Nothing indexes the brain like a laugh; this was idiotic.

"Now, Tom, boy, something we like from Verdi!" the colonel commanded.

The head fell further back, the claws began to work, and those of the composer's harmonies which you could have chosen as the purest exponents of passion began to float through the room. Selections from Weber, Beethoven, and others whom I have forgotten followed. At the close of each piece, Tom, without waiting for the audience, would applaud himself violently, kicking, pounding his hands together, turning always to his master for the approving pat on the head.[14]

Tom continued to appear on the concert stage until age 53, when his career came to a close because of the death of Colonel Bethune. Tom had become so dependent upon the colonel that after the colonel's death he lost the urge to perform and "sank into a sullen belligerent state of mind." Blind Tom died in 1908, lonely and alone.

MUSIC, BLINDNESS AND MENTAL HANDICAP—
A MYSTERIOUS TRIAD

Blind Tom gives credence to Tredgold's observation that "most aments are fond of music."[12] Ireland concurs when he states "the power of musical performance sometimes escapes in insanity; it seems to me that the musical faculty is localized in both sides of the brain and that it may still survive after extensive injuries to the brain, which have impaired or destroyed more complex mental capabilities."[10]

The association of musical ability and mental retardation is frequent throughout the literature on the savant. Of particular interest, beyond that, is the frequently occurring triad of blindness, mental defect and musical genius. While not all musical savants are blind, this triad occurs with startling regularity in the century-old literature; witness the stories of Blind Tom and Dr. Trelat's case at the Salpetriere in the 1800s, and the present-day cases of Leslie Lemke and Ellen Boudreaux, about whom we will learn more later. (The similarity between Blind Tom and Leslie Lemke, who lived a century apart in time but who were strikingly similar in their histories, even in the manner in which their talents were discovered, is uncanny. Trelat's case of a girl with blindness, retardation, musical genius *and* physical handicap resembles Leslie's case even more closely since he has those same *four* features, the only difference being the type of physical handicap.[1] Trelat's patient had rickets, Leslie has cerebral palsy.)

David C. Rife and Lawrence H. Snyder cite Henry H. Goddard's case of "a blind, imbecile girl" in a New Jersey institution who possessed unusual musical ability:[16]

> "She could play a new, difficult piece on the piano after having heard it only once. On one occasion a rather noted musician was visiting the Institution, and when told about the girl, requested that he might see for himself what she could do. When she appeared he played an unpublished composition of his own, and then asked her if she could play it. She asked to hear it once more, and after it had been played the second time, she played the piece perfectly."

These authors refer as well to a "Blind Joe" who, like Blind Tom, was "a musician of the same type and used to appear in Keith's vaudeville." Finally, they list a case at the Wrentham Massachusetts State School of a 19-year-old blind male who played the piano by ear. He could play anything he heard, and had perfect pitch. Interestingly, he had a brother who, like himself, was retarded but who had no musical ability and a blind sister, of normal intelligence, who played the piano and composed music.

MUSIC, MEMORY AND MENINGITIS

Musical genius in severely damaged individuals sometimes appears only after injury or disease rather than being present at birth. One of the earliest cases of acquired savantism, where a spectacular talent developed after illness in a previously normal individual, was presented by Blanche M. Minogue in 1923.[17]

This was the case of a 23-year-old individual with a mental age of 7 but with marked ability as a pianist. Born in 1900, X., as he was called by Minogue, was a healthy child, exceedingly intelligent and very gifted musically. By age 3 he had already learned songs in English, German, French and Hungarian. At that age he developed severe pneumonia with meningitis. In his delirium he sang songs incessantly and emerged from that delirium with marked slowing and retardation, which finally, because of accompanying temper outbursts and behavior, required his admission to Letchworth Village. His I.Q. was measured at 46 (age 7 years 5 months). He became a loner, given to severe temper outbursts and egocentric, very excitable behavior.

At Letchworth X. took great pride in his musical accomplishments. He played by ear and by sight, both classics and jazz. In one testing before an accomplished musician he played the "Anvil Chorus" from *Il Trovatore, Lohengrin, Tannhäuser* "March," "Tarantella" from *Carmen,* Mendelssohn's "Funeral March" and many other classics. He read, on sight, "Marche Grotesque," by Sinding, Chaminade's "The Flatterer" and Heart's "Melody by Engelmann." He could accompany the phonograph or a vocalist with no difficulty. He had perfect pitch.

Minogue comments that the most important single factor in this boy's talent was his phenomenal memory for time, places, events and any composition he ever learned. He had a remarkable ability to imitate as well.

The family background showed both musical and intellectual giftedness. Both his parents were highly intelligent, his father's mother and cousin were gifted pianists and a sister was a skilled violinist. Apparently X. was born intelligent and savantism did not occur until acquired mental deficiency, following illness, affected intellectual functioning but spared musical skills. Minogue aptly labeled this circumstance as "secondary mental deficiency with musical talent." Because X. was robbed of intelligence (except for exceptional memory) but not of the special talent of music, and because there was an absence of any creativity or ability to produce any original composition, Minogue concludes that this case shows that musical ability is a function apart from general intelligence. "This fortunate combination of memory, sense of rhythm, pitch discrimination makes a striking talent. Were any of these lacking, or destroyed, the whole gift would go with it."

HARRIET

Dr. David Viscott, in 1969, took an entirely different tack in his attempt to understand another musical savant.[18] After four years of psychotherapy with Harriet, he describes her case with unusual attention to the psychodynamic interaction between her personality traits and her special musical skills.

Harriet was the sixth of seven children. When she was an infant her crib was placed directly against the grand piano of the studio where her mother, trained in an Italian conservatory, taught piano and singing. Music was Harriet's continuous companion. Except during periods between lessons the baby was largely ignored, was isolated from other children and, except for her exposure to the music, was sensorily deprived. According to Viscott, one evening when Harriet was 7 months old, "her father heard a familiar musical noise coming from her room off the studio. She was lying on her back in her crib and humming in perfect pitch, tempo, and phrasing the 'Cara Nome' from Rigoletto, a popular aria of the mother's students. She also sang their vocalises, their exercises, in all keys major and minor, and with the proper accents, phrasing and pitch."

Harriet developed head-banging and rocking. She did not cry or smile or even make sounds. She was kept in her crib both day and night until age 2. Then, because her mother became ill, Harriet for the first time had contact with other children, but she was impossible to control. She seemed bent on destruction, walking around the house at age 3 with a stick, keeping tempo. Her production of any kind of sound was an obsession, and it was her attempt to produce sounds, rather than to destroy, that led to her pounding and attacking everything in sight. She did not talk.

At age 4 she played the piano as well as violin, trumpet, clarinet and French horn—all of the instruments in the house that her siblings could play. It was not until age 9 that she developed speech and that toilet training was established.

Harriet's perfect pitch was not only highly developed but had an almost driven quality to it. Viscott gives this account:

On one occasion when she was 4, one of the mother's students was having great difficulty singing a high note from the "Bell Song" in Delibes' Lakme. After the third excruciating attempt, Harriet appeared at a gallop with her head bent and began to butt the pupil out of the house, injuring the student's back in the process. On other occasions at this age her siblings would tease her by hitting a poorly tuned note on their practice piano; when she came after them, squealing with pain, they would block her from the keyboard and watch her grow more and more desperate as they banged away at the note. One day they forgot to lock the keyboard and returned to find the key—and the hammer as well—ripped out of the piano.

Harriet could read music, despite the fact she had never been taught to. She had a prodigious memory. She could give the date and weather for every day she had heard it announced on the radio. She memorized pages of the Boston phone book and remembered every telephone number ever given to her. Harriet had calendar calculating skills over a 50-year time span. She had extremely vivid recall of any event in her past, but her recall seemed almost devoid of any feeling or emotion.

She attended school until age 16 but was a poor student. At age 18 she got a job working in the kitchen of a state hospital, the same hospital to which she would be committed at age 40, deluded, confused and suicidal after her carefully and obsessively structured life was interrupted by an injury that required her to miss work. She was admitted to the hospital manifestly psychotic, hallucinating, depressed and deluded.

Her I.Q. was measured at 73. Her memory quotient was 104, which was normal for her age. Her short-term memory, as measured by her ability to repeat back short series of numbers spoken to her (digit span), was normal and her ability to remember other new material was excellent as well. However, her capacity for abstract reasoning, as compared to the concrete or rote memory function she excelled at, was extremely impaired. She could not define simple words, and her arithmetic was very poor.

Of course, music was her striking ability. Viscott describes it thus:

Her knowledge in music is breathtaking. She can identify almost any major work in the entire symphonic repertoire, and give the key, opus number, date and place of first performance, and the vital statistics of the composer. Her knowledge of operatic works is even greater than her knowledge of instrumental works. What is most striking is that she knows the works of the lesser composers as well, and is familiar with literally thousands of compositions, ranging in scope from Monteverdi to Stockhausen! Once she begins to describe a work, she begins to remember details about each performance she has heard, who conducted, and so forth. She has attended every concert of the Boston Symphony Saturday evening series for well over two decades. She knows the name, age, address, family structure, indiscretions, marital problems, and personal musical history of every member of the entire orchestra. She rhapsodizes over conductors and can trace their musical genealogy back a hundred years. . . .

In addition to playing the piano Harriet could also play the violin. On the piano she could harmonize a melody or improvise a counterpoint or variation on a theme with ease. She has perfect pitch. Technically she could change the key of a piece she is playing on command, moving to a relative minor or major instantaneously. Once asked to play Happy Birthday on the piano, she was asked to play it as Mozart would have done it, and immediately played the bass line to Mozart's first piano sonata and altered the harmony to fit the theme of Happy Birthday. Adding figures and trills characteristic of Mozart, she later did that in the style of Beethoven, Schubert, Debussy, Prokofiev, Verdi, and others. She was able to improvise the right hand in the style of one composer and the left hand part in the style of another composer!

Viscott concludes his description of this remarkable woman with a very detailed psychoanalytic and psychodynamic analysis of the meaning of music in her life: "Music became a special language and it remained the language of an endless infancy."

THE CASE OF "S."

S. was a normal, full-term infant born into a family with no history of mental illness. Both parents were college graduates who had no special proficiency in music. While in the hospital after his birth, S. contracted epidemic encephalitis leading to permanent brain damage. He had no language until age 5 but was able to hum songs he heard on the radio or phonograph from an early age.

When S. was 38, Raymond Levee became his tutor, and a very detailed account of S. was presented by Anne Anastasi and Levee in a 1960 article.[19] They describe S. as extremely compulsive, lethargic and lazy. S. had a deep-seated abhorrence to change in schedule and unrelenting rigidity in other areas as well. Once when Levee arrived 15 minutes early for a session, S. would not allow him to enter the room until exactly the appointed time. The music room was his personal domain, which he often asked people to leave. He had many child-like mannerisms, including making faces, talking to mirrors, balancing objects on his head, kissing inanimate objects in the room and pacing. He could be excessively boorish, pushing people out of his way, licking his plate and utensils after a meal and belching loudly. His speech was sing-song in nature with pronounced echolalia.

S. displayed two outstanding talents—music and memory. He could reproduce, verbatim, printed materials more than two pages in length after only a single exposure. He remembered, flawlessly, family events and their times and places. There was a peculiarity here, however, in that right after an event—say a week or two afterward—he seemed unable to recall it, but after several months, and ever after, he would recall it in tremendously fine detail. He had a very large store of historical names, events and dates about American heroes of all types. About classical European composers he knew similar facts: their birthplaces and birth dates, titles and dates of their compositions, places and dates of the first playings of those compositions and the dates and places of the composers' deaths.

His instrument was the piano. He was a sight reader, although he could play by ear on occasion if he wished to do so. Those musicians who came in contact with him, including some of considerable renown, found S.'s musical ability to be outstanding. S. played piano for leading chamber orchestras and played with a number of ensembles.

Although S. seemed to develop some understanding of music theory, he was unable to explain that knowledge. Like so many savants, S. somehow unconsciously incorporated the laws of music with no real ability to use or explain them, cognitively or consciously. He never used that theoretical knowledge for either improvisation or composition.

S. liked only classical music performed by experts and had no interest in the music of contemporary composers. His perfect pitch made it difficult for him to tolerate the discordant notes of some modern music. In his own performances he was a perfectionist and never seemed to play just for enjoyment. His playing was extremely important to him, and he often practiced nine hours a day. When playing piano he showed intense interest, concentration and strength and considerable emotion. Even subtle nuances of expression appeared in him when he was at the piano, but not when he was involved in other activities. In all other matters he seemed indifferent, distracted and distant.

Testing showed that S. had an I.Q. of 67, a mental age of 10. He did show high digit span ability, six numbers reversed. He performed well on tests of rote memory and concrete verbal skills but did poorly with language and tests of abstract ability, concepts or symbols. He was able to repeat—orally and in writing—whole paragraphs verbatim but could not then interpret or relay the contents of what he had just read. His reading was at about a fifth-grade level. He failed all the tests of abstraction and, in general, presented a picture of a brain-damaged individual.

The authors conclude that in the case of S. several factors were interacting. There was, first of all, brain damage with preservation of some concrete abilities and, of course, musical ability. Second was "superior auditory sensitivity," which was linked to the musical ability. And third, a very supportive emotional climate and a stimulating musical atmosphere in the home allowed the musical ability to grow and provided S. rewards and reinforcement. After studying S. in detail, and after reviewing the literature on musical savants up to that time, Anastasi and Levee concluded that no one theory put forth so far could explain the savant and that surely there was no single factor that could explain S. They welcomed further inquiry.

THE CASE OF "L."

L. is a 23-year-old female reported on in 1941 by William A. Owens and Walter Grimm from an institution for developmentally disabled persons in Faribault, Minnesota.[20] She had a measured I.Q. of 23, much lower than that of many other savants. Her speech was extremely limited. The daughter of a miner, she had four normal sisters, two of whom played piano by ear. L. was exposed to the piano at home at age 5 or 6. There was no family history of either retardation or exceptional musical ability. She entered the institution at age 14.

Her special ability was in being able to play on the piano any piece sung or hummed to her. This ability was in striking contrast to her overall handicaps. She immensely enjoyed playing the piano for others on the ward, but left to herself, she would play tunes as soon as she heard them over the radio. She had no ability to play a tune referred to by its name—she always required a stimulus in order to begin playing. She had perfect pitch and would play in the exact key hummed or sung, but her technique was far from perfect. She showed more ability with her right hand than with her left, and the left hand often did not provide true harmony.

Owens and Grimm point out that the noteworthy element of this case is not just that the ability exists, but that it exists in a person with such a very low I.Q.: "While the kind of ability she manifests is not unknown in those of low intelligence, the degree is so far above anything we have even observed in defectives of, perhaps, three times her mental age that it constitutes, in our thought, a noteworthy discrepancy."

THE CASE OF ANOTHER "L."

One of the most thorough analyses of a single savant is contained in a five-year study, reported in 1941, by Dr. Martin Scheerer, Eva Rothmann and Dr. Kurt Goldstein[21] of an 11-year-old boy whom they referred to as L. He was an erratic, hyperactive and socially aloof child, who alternated between being impulsively driven or entirely self-absorbed. He particularly delighted in using his calendar calculating skills and could name the day of the week for any date between the years of 1880 and 1950. He was also a lightning calculator. His digit span was 7 forward and 6 backward. He also was a spelling memory bank and could spell any of his words backwards or forwards without error.

L. showed remarkable musical ability but there were equally remarkable gaps in that ability. He had perfect pitch and would play the piano for hours on end. At age 12 a well-known musician played an original composition for him and L. repeated it perfectly on a single hearing. Although he had been trained to read music, he refused to learn pieces that way, always preferring to play by ear. He would not play any piece upon request and always followed his own repertoire sequence, usually after being stimulated by hearing a piece of his choosing on the phonograph. He preferred operas by Verdi and the works of Beethoven, Schubert and Tchaikovsky; he especially loved the opera *Othello* and could sing the "Credo," "Si ciel" and the "Adagio Pathetique" from beginning to end in Italian. Occasionally he would sit at the piano and play what seemed to be short compositions of his own, but he never repeated them, and therefore, they could never be recorded or identified separately. He could retain words and names related to music almost indefinitely.

His I.Q. was measured at 50 on the Stanford-Binet when tested at the chronological age of 11. An EEG and a pneumoencephalogram were normal, indicating no clear evidence of structural brain damage. There was no family history of mental illness or developmental disability. Some relatives were reported to have had musical ability but no special talents were evident. L. was an only child, the product of a normal birth and delivery in December 1926.

At age 3 he showed an unusual interest in music, rhythm and counting, in contrast to his slow development in other areas. He could identify numerous recordings by name if only a part of the melody was played. By age 5 he could identify with absolute accuracy what recordings were on the other side of a record being played. At this age his perfect pitch was discovered. As Scheerer, Rothmann and Goldstein note, "He is tone sure. First, he calls the notes on the piano by numbers, counting them according to the position on the keys while he is playing. Hearing his mother play, he will say 'You are playing the 25th note.' Later he is told the names for the keys and retains them at once. He connects the names with the keys and their sound, and soon can tell what note is being played without seeing it." At age 9 L. became obsessed with a phonograph record of *Othello* and would listen to, and play, little else.

The remainder of the very detailed account of L. addresses the issues of causation and attempts to explain not only this case but the idiot savant as a whole—the thoughtful theoretical structure put forth by the authors will be summarized later in Chapter 11.

The most recent and complete look at the musical savant is an extraordinary research study of a person called N.P., conducted by John Sloboda, Beate Hermelin and Neil O'Connor of London.[22] The study compared the savant to nonsavant musical prodigies, in support of the view that general intelligence is not a prerequisite for certain kinds of skills.

Although it was known that Mozart reportedly wrote out an entire score of Allegri's *Miserere* after only one hearing, the only comprehensive study or documentation of prodigious musical ability prior to this research was done by Dr. Geza Revesz, who in 1925 did a careful analysis of a young Hungarian musical genius called E.N.[23] At age 7, E.N. had an international reputation for precocity of piano performance, composition and improvisation. He also demonstrated a remarkable musical memory both in terms of repertoire and retention, but that memory was not uniform over the entire musical spectrum. His memory for "melodious pieces harmonized in a simple manner" was far superior to his memory for "musical pieces of a strange character, such as melodies with complicated accompaniment and peculiar harmonies." Revesz also noted that E.N. was better at memorizing when he could see the score and play the notes than he was when a piece was played to him. Sloboda concludes, based on Revesz's detailed description, that "E.N. possessed memory capacities that were truly outstanding, by any standards."

The discovery of N.P., a 23-year-old male, autistic musical savant who had "an alleged memory capacity equal to anything reported in the literature on prodigies," motivated Sloboda et al. to study him in detail to determine whether the musical genius he had in common with a child prodigy such as E.N. was similar or different in some way.

N.P., an only child, had entered a residential home for long-term placement at age 17. A WAIS test showed a verbal I.Q. of 62 and a performance I.Q. of 60. He had almost no spontaneous speech, made little eye contact and displayed the obsessive and bizarre behavior patterns characteristic of autism. Like many autistic youngsters, N.P. listened obsessively to music from an early age and mimicked speech and music in an echolalic manner. By age 21 he had developed a substantial repertoire of classical piano pieces and was able to learn a new sonata-length piece in three or four hearings. He also played guitar and recorder. He gave local concerts of popular music, hymns and his favorite, classical pieces.

The study had two objectives: first, to document systematically and to analyze in detail the exact memorization process in the savant and second, to see if the memorizing process of the savant, N.P., was identical to that of the normal I.Q. prodigy, E.N., which had been reasonably well documented by Revesz. With these findings the researchers sought to validate their hypothesis that human intellect is but a group of partially independent intelligences and that these independent intelligences can develop to some extent separately from one another. The researchers also hypothesized that the musical memory of the savant was not merely an eidetic, literal one, but instead depended on certain more elaborate codings and techniques just as did the memory of the musical prodigy of normal or high intelligence.

The memorization expertise in E.N., and presumably other prodigies like him, depended on the detection of familiar structure in the material to be remembered. Notes linked by familiar harmonies or rhythms, for example, were more easily recalled than more random notes without such links. Likewise, pieces using the more typical diatonic scale (do-re-me-fa-so-la-ti-do) were more easily and correctly recalled than those using the more complex and dissonant chromatic scale (all 12 tones of the octave). Sloboda uses the term "structure preserving" to differentiate memory that depends on familiar codings and sequences from eidetic or literal memory, which does not depend on such sequences and should do as well with random notes as with those linked by any particular harmonies, melodies or rhythms.

All of us do better in remembering musical notes if they are linked into a melody than if they simply occur in some random sequence. I could recall more easily the 27 notes in "Row, Row Row Your Boat" than I could 27 notes that were presented randomly. If my memory were simply eidetic, then the presence or absence of links should not matter. There are other musical structures on which musicians characteristically depend in recalling music; these include harmonies, particularly those of the more familiar diatonic scale. E.N., for example, as pointed out above, remembered pieces with melodies and simple harmony much better than pieces with complicated harmonies or accompaniments.

If the savant uses such structure preserving techniques there should be better retention of structure-based knowledge than of nonstructure-based knowledge. If structure preservation is important, as it is in nonsavant prodigies, then savants should perform the same as nonsavants on structure preserving tests of memory, as compared to tests where structure preservation is nonexistent.

Sloboda and his colleagues began their study of N.P. by recording exactly, measure by measure, the recall of this savant and comparing it to that of the only musical prodigy well-documented at that time, nonsavant E.N. The researchers then had N.P. listen to performances of two pieces, Opus 47, No. 3 ("Melodie") from Grieg's *Lyric Pieces* and "Whole-Tone Scale" from Book V of Bartok's *Mikrokosmos*. The Grieg piece represented conventional diatonic harmony with a simple two-bar motif repeated at various pitches and with various elaborations throughout the piece. The Bartok piece was mildly atonal with never more than two notes sounding simultaneously. Those same two recordings were played for a professional musician of average intelligence, about the same chronological age as N.P. and with about the same number of years of experience with the piano.

N.P. was able to memorize the Grieg piece to an almost note-perfect level after 12 minutes, having heard no section of the piece more than four times. The professional musician did well only on the first eight bars and then did very poorly compared to N.P. The error rate for the musician was ten times that of N.P.

On the Bartok piece the professional musician did better than the savant. N.P. learned this piece poorly, with four times the error rate of the musician. The authors indicate that if N.P.'s memory were simply eidetic or mimetic, there should have been no difference in his error rates on the two pieces.

Their research confirms, in their view, that savant ability is structurally based, like that of high I.Q. prodigies. They admit that they are still baffled as to why N.P. knows how to play the piano at all and to why this obsession with music began and continues in this otherwise severely disabled man. They are also unable to explain the moderate improvisatory skill they saw. They conclude, however, thus:

> Our study lends support to the notion that general intelligence, as manifested through high I.Q. scores or a wide range of intellectual accomplishments, is not necessary for the development of high levels of musical memorization skill. Although the idiot savant is unusual in the lopsidedness of his intellectual profile, we would suggest that the cognitive architecture of his skill resembles that of a high I.Q. expert in essential respects. When we look at the memory capacity of N.P., E.N., and possibly Mozart, we are looking at essentially the same phenomenon.

One additional observation about N.P. is worthy of mention because it is characteristic of most of the savants described thus far, beginning with Blind Tom. The music of the savant, while impressive in structure and accuracy, is almost always devoid of expression and innuendo. Sloboda sums up this feature of musical savants nicely when, speaking of N.P., he describes that savant's playing as "wooden and metronomic in the extreme. It seems as though N.P. generally retains the structural 'husk' but discards all the expressive 'flesh.'" This same colorless,

stereotyped, mechanical, "husk without flesh" quality that characterizes the performance of the musical savant also permeates, as will be
seen, his or her performance in other areas of special skill.

THE SAVANT AS A COMPOSER

Reproducing music one hears and composing new music are two quite
different skills. Likewise, the addition of improvisations to an existing
piece and the creating of an entirely new score are also different. We
have seen that Blind Tom, Harriet and L.N. could improvise. But, can
the savant compose or is his creative music skill limited to improvisation? Beate Hermelin, Neil O'Connor and Sara Lee studied this question in a 1986 study done at the University of London Institute of
Education.[24]

They began the study with five musical savants. All were males, ages
18 to 58. The average I.Q. was 59 with a range of 50 to 69. Three of the
patients were blind and two were diagnosed as autistic. Two of the
three blind subjects had congenital blindness and one had retrolental
fibroplasia associated with premature birth. One subject's musical ability was noted at age 8 when he spontaneously took the teacher's place
at the piano and played everything he had just heard. Another invented
a wide variety of his own songs with lyrics. The third subject improvised
on the dulcimer or the recorder. The fourth had a keen musical memory; he obsessively adhered to music as he remembered it and would
become very upset when a piece was played in any key or form other
than the one in which he had first heard it. The final subject could play
any song he heard immediately on the piano with proper chording and
harmony.

A control group of six children between the ages of 9 and 17, all of
whom were proficient on the piano and, in some cases, on another
instrument as well, was formed. These children were compared to the
savants on a number of tests. Eight separate tasks were used, five to test
musical inventiveness and three to test overall musical competence.
Musical inventiveness was defined as (1) the ability to continue appropriately a theretofore unknown tune when it was begun and then
stopped; (2) the ability to play or sing a song of new invention; (3) the
ability to produce an accompaniment to a new tune played by the
examiner; (4) the ability to produce simultaneously both a new melody
and the accompaniment; and (5) the ability to improvise over a twelve-
bar blues sequence played to the subject. Musical competence was
measured on the quality of timing and rhythm, the degree of complex-

ity of the inventions and the ability to modulate and produce a regular phrase length.

On all eight tests the savants were clearly superior to the control group. The researchers conclude that, by accessing a system of relevant rules and structure, the savant can invent as well as reproduce music that conforms to those familiar structural patterns. This ability is independent of general intelligence or cognition as such and is derived from culturally familiar musical rules. In that sense musical savants and musicians of normal or superior intelligence share the same musical memory as part of their respective talents.

The savant can compose, they conclude, not just improvise. That ability depends on an unconscious sense of the rules of music more than on general intelligence. Like the calendar calculator, who has tremendous ability with no cognitive sense of method, the savant plays brilliantly without understanding how.

Some describe music, simply, as unconscious counting because stable sets of rules, regularities and relationships—predictable structural patterns—exist in both music and math. It is an unconscious access to these rule-governed structural relationships that allows many savants their special, spectacular skills in the particular areas of math and music. That these two skills appear with such regularity, considering all the skills in the human repertoire that might otherwise also be represented, is more than coincidental. It points to the similarity between math and music. This same type of unconscious access will be explored later when we look at the calendar and the lightning calculators.

SOME FINAL CASES

Dr. Bernard Rimland has the largest case registry of autistic children around the world. In 1978 Rimland looked at the incidence of savant skills in 5,400 such children as those skills were reported to him in detailed questionnaires filled out by the parents of these children. As part of the questionnaire, the parents were asked to list any "special abilities" the child might have.[4] Five hundred thirty-one of the children, or 9.8 percent, were reported to have some such special skill. The sex ratio in this population was 3.54:1, males to females, which was almost exactly the same as the sex ratio in the disorder overall. Savant skills were much more common in the subgroup of children with Early Infantile Autism than in subgroups displaying more loosely defined autistic symptoms.

Rimland did a more thorough analysis and follow-up on 119 autistic patients with special skills (some of whom had Early Infantile Autism).

Of those 119 patients, 63 (31.7 percent), had musical skill, which was the most commonly reported special ability and was usually linked with phenomenal memory. The musical skill was most often, but not always, auditory, as can be seen from some of the examples that Rimland provides:

> . . . can play anything he hears once on a piano or any instrument with keys, has perfect pitch.

> She can sing any note you tell her to and can tell what note (and key) is being played. Ilene woke up singing as an infant and never let up. Ilene knows practically every song ever written—who wrote it, what show it is from (or film), who first recorded it, in what year it was popular, etc. She also has a large command of the classical repertoire. She composes at the piano and has taught herself to play the guitar as one would play a zither—on her lap—sliding her finger up and down all the strings at once.

> First noted musical and photographic ability at age 2. With "tape recorder" accuracy, she would explode from her silence with a total song with words—long verses—pages read, etc.

> Interest and talent in music from very early age. At 19 months sang many songs using perfect pitch. At 2 years, knew 20 songs, many quite long and tricky, like "Arkansas Traveler," using marvelous pitch and perfect rhythm. At 35 months, could play all these on the piano, using one finger, but the effect was perfect (never a missed note, except first or second trial). Able to play any song in any key on piano. At 4 years old, played melodies from sonatas that she heard me practicing and once did a very spectacular thing—played through a whole book of "vocalices" one after another, each in a different key (as written) without mistake, showing a wonderful musical and pitch memory. At 6, she "found" triads to accompany single melody notes, changing the harmony exactly as needed without much trial and error. Since she couldn't be taught "fingering" this made her agility at keeping in rhythm quite surprising! Her special school used her as "musical accompanist," age 4 to 6, for "nursery class." A visitor to the school even supplied her and a teacher with tickets to the San Francisco Symphony, which our daughter enjoyed very much. At 3, she sat through a three-hour performance of *Peter Grimes* (opera) on TV, although she didn't have enough patience for *Sesame Street*, and she remembered a couple of arias the next day.

The association between Early Infantile Autism and savant skills will be explored in depth later. Suffice it to say here that savant skills are very frequent in this group of patients and musical skills are the most frequent overall. The link between mental handicap and music becomes evident when studying this population.

Two other cases merit mention, both studied by H.J. Rothstein in

1942.[25] The first is a case of acquired savantism in a 42-year-old male who was not mentally handicapped until contracting spinal meningitis at age 3. Following that, a special musical ability emerged amidst considerable other disability. At age 7 he began playing piano with an excellent sense of rhythm, pitch discrimination and tonal memory. His playing, like that of so many savants, was characterized by being "mechanical without emotional expression, style, deftness or technique." Special note is made of the fact that this particular savant did not improvise, interpret or compose. Music had become the sole object of his existence, yet peculiarly, he was unable to play songs on request and could only play what came to his mind at random. Rothstein's second case is that of a 36-year-old male with a mental age of 4 who could play harmonica and drums. He would constantly drum with his fingers in a pronounced rhythmical fashion. His musical ability, however, was limited to a primitive level of reproducing tunes in which rhythm predominates. He was chiefly fond of swing music, favoring ten or twelve of the then popular bands.

What conclusions can be drawn, then, regarding the savant and musical genius? Well, first of all, certainly the association is a frequent one, with musical skill being the most frequent of all the skills seen in this unusual condition. Secondly, the close association of blindness, mental deficiency and musical genius is even more striking, much beyond what one would expect from chance alone. Some specific brain pathways must be uniquely linked, or activated, by this unusual but recurrent association of deficiencies, producing a spectacular superiority within this narrow area of skill. This association occurs most often with premature birth and retrolental fibroplasia, and raises some most interesting research questions that will be addressed later. Third, the types of musical skills and traits seem very constant from savant to savant—insistence on sameness, perfect pitch and prodigious memory with ability to repeat exactly, mistakes and all, pieces of extraordinary length and complexity. Fourth, as remarkable as the musical skills are, they are mechanical, stereotyped and devoid of emotion or passion. Fifth, the musical skill is almost always with the piano. And finally, creativity is most often limited to improvisation and producing variations on a theme rather than producing new themes and new pieces, although some instances of new music inventiveness have been described.

Every one of those conclusions, however, raises new questions. Why does this close association between music superiority and mental deficiency exist? Could the same pathologic process that produces a certain type of blindness produce similar damage elsewhere in the brain, creating this unique musical outcome? How can the savant know and operate within the complex rules of music yet know so little else? Is music, after all, only "unconscious counting" that depends very little on intellect, comprehension and understanding? Does emotion, training and nurture have anything to do with the emergence of these spectacular abilities or is it all attributable to nature, genes and brain circuitry?

Some of these same questions are also raised by the other savant skills, so let us look at those other skills before trying to answer these questions.

3

If This Is June 6, It Must Be Friday: The Calendar Calculators

On what day of the week was your tenth birthday? In what years did your birthday fall on a Tuesday? In the year 2000, how many days are there between your birthday and Easter? What was the weather like the day you turned 21? The year is 91360; on what day of the week will June 6th fall that year? If you were still living in that year, how old would you be?

Don't know? George does.

George and his identical twin brother, Charles, are simply astounding. They are calendar calculators. Give them a date and they can give you the day of the week over a span of 80,000 years, 40,000 backward or 40,000 forward. Ask them to name in which years in the next 200 (or any 200) Easter will fall on March 23 and they will name those years with lightning rapidity, faster than a computer and just as accurately. They can tell you what the weather was like on any day of their adult life, but they will have forgotten your name by the end of a brief visit. They cannot count to 30 but they swap 20-digit prime numbers for amusement. They cannot figure out the change from a ten-dollar bill for a six-dollar purchase, but they can factor with ease the number 111, or almost any other number you name. They can remember 30 digits but cannot add.

While there have been other known calendar calculators, there have been none quite like George and Charles.

In May 1964 William A. Horwitz and his co-workers Clarice Kestenbaum, Ethel Person and Lissy Jarvik, all psychiatrists, presented the remarkable case of George and Charles to their colleagues at the annual meeting of the American Psychiatric Association in Los Angeles.[26] Horwitz's presentation of the case details of these two incredible savants was not to be soon forgotten.

George and Charles were born three months prematurely. It was their mother's fourth pregnancy. They were delivered by Caesarean section as two of a set of triplets, two boys and a girl. The girl died within twelve hours. The boys were kept in incubators for two months. Both had convulsions when they were removed from the incubator but neither had any convulsions at any other time in his life.

George held up his head at 6 months and sat at 9 months, but did not walk or talk until he was 2½ years of age. Charles lagged behind George. Both displayed head banging, hand biting and destructiveness. Institutionalization was advised by their pediatrician when they were 3 but both remained at home.

At age 6 George was already a calendar calculator. He spent hours looking at an almanac with a perpetual calendar and later played endlessly with a silver perpetual calendar his father brought him to replace the printed one. A paternal aunt who was a legal secretary would call George to check dates on documents with him. Charles, meanwhile, showed no interest in dates and did not read the almanac.

The twins were not especially close until age 9, when they were admitted to Letchworth Village in New York State where they stayed for 15 years. There they became inseparable and Charles became interested in dates as his brother was. The fighting, biting and destructiveness continued there. In 1963 they were transferred to a different facility, where their behavior improved. Both twins were severely myopic but, according to Horwitz, neither had retrolental fibroplasia, even though they had spent two months in incubators. Both boys had an exquisite sense of smell and frequently approached people and sniffed them. They could pick out their own slippers or clothes by smelling them. Both boys showed almost constant rocking and swaying movements.

The father of these twin boys was a successful businessman and the mother was a homemaker; their marriage was tempestuous. Their first child died at 13 months following convulsions. The next two children were girls, both of whom ultimately became nurses. The mother was 40 when the triplets were born.

The results of various studies on the twins suggested monozygosity (development from a single fertilized egg), which would identify the boys as identical twins. The results of a number of other laboratory studies testing for a variety of genetic and metabolic conditions were all normal. EEGs were also normal. At age 24, when tested by Horwitz, the twins' I.Q.s were between 60 and 70, although earlier tests at Letchworth Village had placed their I.Q.s in the 40 to 50 range.

The 1964 report gives further details pertaining to their calendar calculating and mathematical skills:

> When asked in what years April 21st will fall on a Sunday, each will answer correctly 1968, 1957, 1963, 1946, etc. When encouraged, George can continue as far back as 1700. When asked in what month of the year 2002 does the 1st fall on a Friday, George gave March, February, and November—correct answers. They can also tell you correctly that the 4th Monday in February, 1993 is the 22nd or that the 3rd Monday in May, 1936 was the 18th. This is even more impressive when we note that like many other calendar calculators reported, George and Charles cannot add, subtract, multiply or divide simple single-digit numbers. For example, the product of 3 × 6 might be given as 8. Although they cannot add up to 30, when given your birth date, they can accurately tell you it is 30 weeks until your next birthday or 13 weeks since you last had a birthday. George can tell you the year a particular famous man in history—for example, George Washington—was born and how old he would be if he were alive today.

Dr. Arthur P. Holstein provided a very interesting discussion of that paper at the 1964 meeting. He pointed out that chromosome studies were normal in the case of the twins and that the type of mental retardation they showed was one associated with the particular visual defect present—chorioretinitis. Transmitted as a Mendelian recessive gene, this form of hereditary mental retardation explained the low I.Q.s and argued against these being cases of infantile autism now grown up. He pointed out the twins' inability to think abstractly, as was demonstrated by their ability to subtract apples, but not dollars. He commented as well that the twins' remarkable memory seemed to have developed separately from general intellectual ability and that, therefore, I.Q. and certain mental capacities need not, as is commonly believed, be necessarily linked.

Four years after having discovered and described the twins, Horwitz put forth some ideas to try to explain them.[27] He had carried out a number of tests, including one in which he had called out some 300 random dates. The twins then gave the days of the week on which these dates would fall. George's range was seemingly unlimited: already then he was able to give a correct day for a date in the year 32011. Charles had a more limited range. Both boys answered in a flash and George's error rate was extremely low, 10 errors in 292 trials. Horwitz concludes that both used rote memory to master a 400-year time span which then repeats itself in 400-year constant cycles. Neither boy knew the difference between the Gregorian and Julian calendars (the changeover occurred in 1582) so that when testing went backwards in time there always needed to be allowance for the 10-day difference in the calendars. Horwitz surmises that the calculations were done by subtracting rapidly in multiples of 400, leaving the remainder in the present 400-year cycle as the correct answer.

Dora Jane Hamblin also described the twins in some detail when they were 26 years old and patients at the New York State Psychiatric Institute under Horwitz's care.[28] George and Charles both said that they did "see" numbers in their heads, but they indicated that they did not see whole pages of a calendar. "It's in my head and I do it," explained George—this was his only insight into his ability. "When was George Washington born?" they were asked. "February 22, 1732" was the instant answer. "If he were still alive in the year 2000, how old would he be on his birthday that year?" The reply, "268 years," came in 8 seconds.

Hamblin points out why calculating Easter was a particular problem for the twins (or for anyone for that matter):

> Easter Sunday's date was determined with fine calendar illogicality in the year 325 A.D. by august delegates to the First Council of Nicaea, the precursor of the Ecumenical Council which recently closed in Rome. In 325 the church fathers decreed that Easter would fall on the first Sunday following the 14th day of the Paschal, or Easter, moon and that Paschal moon should be the first moon whose 14th day came on or after March 21. Since the moon's month is 29.53059 days long—the time it takes the moon to go through its phases—and since the earth's month is 30 or 31 days, with 28 or 29 for February, the moon calendar and earth calendar are rarely in phase. Easter can turn up as early as March 22 or as late as April 25.

No wonder the twins had problems with that date. Yet, they did master it—through memorization, Hamblin postulates.

From the beginning of adult life onward the twins became adept at remembering the weather and a variety of other minor details of *each* day of their life. "Given a reminder of a specific day, they can fill in such details as which assistant or nurse had a cough, or the name of the patient who had picked on them," Hamblin notes. Nothing was more striking than their memory for the weather. George remembered the weather on November 22, 1963 as being cloudy in the morning and sunny in the afternoon, with the sun coming out about 1:00 P.M. What was the weather like on May 24, 1962? "It was cloudy in the morning, got sun in the afternoon." What was the weather like on December 3, 1952? "It was cloudy in the morning, cold. Little raindrops came down that day."

The twins could read if the print was large and words were simple. Their memories did not extend to topics other than calendar calculating or events and weather of their lives. They were unable, for example, to memorize and retain a list of the U.S. Presidents.

Oliver Sacks, in a superbly insightful and capturing description of the twins, tells of them and their talents 18 years after the Horwitz article:[29]

> They are, indeed, unprepossessing at first encounter—a sort of grotesque Tweedle dee and Tweedle dum indistinguishable, mirror images, identical in face, in body movements, in personality, in mind, identical too in their stigmata of brain and tissue damage. They are undersized, with disturbing disproportions in head and hands, high-arched palates, high-arched feet, monotonous squeaky voices, a variety of peculiar tics and mannerisms, and a very high degenerative myopia, requiring glasses so thick that their eyes seem distorted, giving them an appearance of absurd little professors, peering and pointing, with a misplaced, obsessed, and absurd concentration. And this impression is fortified as soon as one quizzes them, or allows them, as they are apt to do, like pantomime puppets, to start spontaneously on one of their "routines."

Sacks points out that their memory for digits is exhaustive and possibly unlimited; they can repeat 3 digits, 30 digits or 300 digits with equal ease. He describes the twins playing a number game, exchanging 20-digit prime numbers (a prime number is one that can be equally divided by no whole number other than itself or one). He describes another startling ability of the twins, which he observed when a box of matches fell from a table and scattered on the floor. Both twins cried "111" simultaneously. When Sacks counted the matches, he found there to be exactly 111. The twins not only "saw" the matches as they fell but then said in unison "37, 37, 37" followed by "111." They had not only seen the matches but had factored their number of 111 without any concept of what factoring was and without being able to understand multiplication, division or any other rules of arithmetic.

The twins' ability with the calendar extends far beyond naming the day of the week on which a given date fell or will fall. For example, if asked in what months Wednesday will be the third day of the month, beginning in the year 2000, they will answer immediately. Other such questions might be: "In what months of the year 2002 does the first of the month fall on a Friday?" and "In what years in the 20th century does April 21 fall on a Sunday?" The twins can do the complicated corrections that must be made for leap years, and they do them accurately. They know that leap year comes every four years and they adjust for it. However, when the number 4 is presented to them in simple arithmetic they cannot accurately add it to, or subtract it from, other numbers.

George is boastful about his abilities. He also enjoys challenging visitors by asking them when their birthday was and then asking them in what years their birthday was on a Thursday. When the visitor cannot answer quickly, he recites the answer in a somewhat condescending, bragging manner, and inquires why the visitor, whose birthday it is, cannot tell those dates when he, whose birthday it is not, is able to. When asked how he does it he says, "It's fantastic that I can do that."

Horwitz concludes that the twins' skill is a peculiar and unique kind of rote memory. Sacks concludes that it is an "immense mnemonic tapestry" in which the twins literally see a whole landscape of numbers they have encountered in their life, among which they browse, with which they play and from which they choose or read when giving an answer. Hamblin states simply that she cannot explain the twins' skill. Perhaps for now George's explanation will have to suffice: "It's in my head and I can do it . . . It's fantastic I can do that."

And it truly is.

Sacks provides an update, and a commentary, on the twins in his brilliant article about them. It is a bittersweet look at the two brothers as their lives have proceeded and compels us to reach our own definitions regarding what is progress with the savant. Do we leave them alone in their strangeness and uniqueness, often so narrow as not to be "practical"? Or, do we teach them to broaden out, like the rest of us, with the hope that they can do so without trade-offs and losses, with the hope that they can have it both ways. Sacks' commentary points up that dilemma best:

> This serenity was, in fact, interrupted and broken up ten years later, when it was felt the twins should be separated—"for their own good," to prevent their "unhealthy communication together," and in order that they could "come out and face the world . . . in an appropriate, socially acceptable way" (as the medical and sociological jargon had it). They were separated, then, in 1977, with results that might be considered as either gratifying or dire. Both have been moved now into "halfway houses," and do menial jobs, for pocket money, under close supervision. They are able to take buses, if carefully directed and given a token, and to keep themselves moderately presentable and clean, though their moronic and psychotic character is still recognizable at a glance.
>
> This is the positive side—but there is a negative side too (not mentioned in their charts, because it was never recognized in the first place). Deprived of their numerical "communion" with each other, and of time and opportunity for any "contemplation" or "communion"

at all—they are always being hurried and jostled from one job to another—they seem to have lost their strange numerical power, and with this the chief joy and sense of their lives. But this is considered a small price to pay, no doubt, for their having become quasi independent and "socially acceptable."

FROM ONE EXTREME TO THE OTHER

Charles's and George's handicaps are evident but are overshadowed by their tremendous ability with dates and their prodigious memory. They have speech, they did learn to communicate with each other—albeit in a rather strange fashion, often using numbers as we might use words—and they did function fairly well within their narrow ranges. It is puzzling as to how they can be calendar calculators when, outside of that, they can calculate nothing, but it is not incomprehensible. Their facility with some types of numerical functions makes this one outstanding ability at least believable.

But imagine a case where there is no language at all, but instead a mutism caused by a severe paralysis that allows no more than a movement of the upper lip for a "yes" and a smile for a "no"; a case where the entire vocabulary is the word "buh" for bottle and where the measured I.Q. is 8! How could such a person have any facility with numbers at all, let alone ever learn to calendar calculate? It seems impossible.

But A. Dudley Roberts described just such a case in a 1945 article in the *Journal of Genetic Psychology:* "The patient was able to name the day of the week for any date from 1915 to the present time. Since he was classified as a helpless idiot, this seemed to be an ability which merited investigation. The patient, in fact, has no language responses at all, and so far as the writer can learn, never did have. He gave his answers to the questions regarding the day of the week by nodding or shaking his head when the questioner asked 'Is it Monday, Tuesday,' etc."[30]

The patient, who had been born in 1916 and was 27 years old when tested by Roberts, had three brothers of normal intelligence. His birth had been uneventful, but at 6 months of age he had had what was believed to have been encephalitis, which left him totally paralyzed except for some very limited head and face movement and restricted, slow spastic movements of his hands and toes. In 1933 X-ray studies of the brain were carried out by pneumoencephalography, a then-useful procedure (now replaced by the CAT scan and other newer imaging techniques) wherein air was introduced into the central nervous system by lumbar puncture, producing sufficient contrast in brain structures so that abnormalities could be detected using skull films. That study had shown clear and serious central nervous system damage, including "an entire absence of the cortical markings over his fronto-parietal region— the appearance like that found in adhesive arachnoiditis. There are fewer convolutional markings over the occipital lobes and the fissures are abnormally deep. The posterior horn length is increased, which is a usual finding in this type of idiot. There is a patchy distribution of air over frontal lobes showing pathology also. There is some asymmetry of the ventricles." In short, there was considerable evidence of scarring and atrophy from the earlier encephalitis, especially in the anterior or frontal areas of the brain, although damage was evident in the more posterior portions of the brain as well. This simply documented a widespread organic basis for what was a very pervasive paralysis and mental disability.

Roberts describes the patient thus:

> The patient spends his time in the bed, in a wheel-chair, or on the floor when he gets tired of the other two. He must be moved from one place to the other by other people although he is able to manipulate the wheels of his chair in a forward direction by use of the toes and in a backward direction by use of his hands. These movements are very difficult and slow. He weighs 100 pounds, has dark skin, black eyes, and black hair. His face has a pleasant expression when not distorted by spastic grimaces. He communicates his desires by grunts and gestures, many of which are rather wild and uncontrollable because of his spasticity. The nearest approach to speech which the writer has heard was the sound "Buh" for bottle. The chief constituent of his food is milk. Attendants who are accustomed to him can interpret his signs readily. He easily makes known when he wants a drink or has other bodily needs. If he wants his radio off or on he points toward it and grunts. He is able to tell time.

> He listens to the radio a great deal, particularly to the Detroit Tigers' ball games. He likes to bet on the games with attendants and other employees of the institution. He signifies his desire for a bet with a broad grin and holding out his hand for acceptance of the bet. These bets are usually a bar of candy and it is not on record that he has ever paid off when he lost. He was the only person in the hospital who picked the last World Series winner.

> Intercourse is maintained by asking questions which must be phrased so that they can be answered by "yes" or "no." The "no" responses become vestigial—a movement of the right side of his upper lip. However, there is no mistaking the smile which accompanies the "yes" response—a smile which says one has finally asked the right question. He knows his own age and date of birth and is correctly oriented to time and place.

When, in 1933, the patient was formally tested to determine his I.Q. level his chronological age was 17 years and 7 months, but he had a mental age of 1 year and 6 months, or an I.Q. of 8. Obviously his severe handicaps, including the absence of language, precluded precise testing, but by using a multiple choice format in tailored testing it was determined that the patient had arithmetic skills of 1 digit, adding and subtracting, without being able to multiply or divide. He had a word comprehension of 7 words and a digit span of 5 forward and 4 backward.

Roberts then proceeded to test this subject to try to discover his "trade secret." Noting that the patient always stared at the ceiling when calculating, Roberts concluded that he was using eidetic imagery to process the dates and reach his answer. He did some tests for eidetic imagery, using as control subjects two psychology department assistants and two children of superior intelligence with I.Q.s of 141 and 139. A series of pictures in a children's workbook was used, and 57 questions were asked following a 30-second exposure to each picture. The patient answered correctly 68 percent of the time; the psychologists, 47 and 43 percent; and the children, 55 and 60 percent. Six months later the patient correctly answered 5 of 6 questions asked about one particular picture during a recall test. The assistants and the children were unable to recall any of the details of the picture. After conducting several other tests Roberts concluded that eidetic imagery was an important factor in this calendar calculator and was probably the whole explanation for the phenomenon in this particular patient.

This case is so striking because of the severe limitations of the patient overall, but, despite those limitations, the calendar calculating ability still was able to surface, mysteriously, as if it were some kind of primitive, innate ability. In George and Charles that ability seems unlikely. In this case it seems impossible.

AN INVESTIGATION OF CALENDAR CALCULATING IN A SINGLE SUBJECT

Dr. A. Lewis Hill was bothered by Horwitz's conclusions about George and Charles and the explanation for their unusual abilities.[31] Hill was also dissatisfied with the three theories usually advanced to explain calendar calculating in the savant. In his 1965 article, Horwitz had summarized these: (1) eidetic imagery, (2) rapid calculating ability and (3) use of memorization as a compensatory mechanism to substitute for normal learning. Hill set out to test the hypotheses using a calendar calculator who had developed that ability as a youngster.

Hill's patient had been institutionalized at age 6½, at which time his I.Q. measured 54. His diagnosis was congenital syphilis. He had some savant skills, including the ability to play 11 musical instruments, to draw elaborate pictures of houses and to remember important dates. But clearly his outstanding ability was in calendar calculating. Hill began some systematic tests. The patient's digit span was 5 forward and 5 backward, hardly remarkable. Tests for eidetic imagery showed none to be present. The ability to calculate, as such, was also absent and there was no evidence of use of a mathematical formula. A formal test was constructed to test for a system that used key dates and counting; no such system could be verified.

Hill concludes that his subject did not use eidetic imagery, did not calculate based on any mathematical principles and did not seem to be using his skill as a compensation for normal learning. Rather, the patient's skill was due either to an unusual ability to concentrate and thus to memorize over a remarkable span of information, or else was based on simple rote memory like "adolescents who learn the statistical information pertaining to their favorite sports." The special ability of the savant, he concludes, is the ability to concentrate over an extended period of time.

SOME OTHER EARLY CALENDAR CALCULATORS

Dr. J. Langdon Down tells of a case where the patient's "specialty is the calendar, and if given any date during the last five years he will state the day of the week correctly without any hesitation."[1] Dr. A. Witzmann presented a case at the 1908 meeting of the Society for Psychiatry and Neurology in Vienna of a 20-year-old man who had calendar calculating ability over a 1,000-year span. He correctly answered the following questions: What was the day of the week on October 3, 1907? Answer: Thursday. What was the day of the week on June 14, 1808? Answer: 1808 was a leap year; June 14 was a Tuesday.[11] The patient could read and write poorly and "was backward in arithmetic." Witzmann hypothesized that the man had memorized the date of Easter for each of the 1,000 years in his calculating span and that this, together with "some kind of simple code of his own devising, enabled him to give the correct answers almost immediately."

Dr. Macdonald Critchley used the term "brain athletes" to describe his patients whose special abilities stood out conspicuously against a general background of serious limitations.[32] He outlined a case of a "megalencephalic idiot, tetraplegic, with periodic epileptic fits. His speech was lalling and he frequently laughed in a vacuous fashion." The patient, however, could recall when attendants had first come to the ward and when they had been transferred, as well as every day on which a fellow patient had died. He could correctly name the day of the week for any date. The days for given dates in a 15-year time span came very quickly, but the days for given dates in the remote past or the distant future took longer to compute and were sometimes inaccurate. "It seemed likely that some process of mental calculation was entailed, and not pure hypermnesia [increased retentiveness of memory]," Critchley concludes.

Critchley's explanation of the calendar calculator? "Even in the case of the calendar artist, memory is more important than reckoning. The subject has probably committed to heart some key date like Christmas Day or the following first of January. These dates fall on the same weekday, which in turn corresponds with February 5th, March 5th, April 2nd, May 7th, June 4th, July 2nd, and so on, except in a Leap Year."

A. Fauville cites a case of a 12-year-old boy with a mental age of 5.4 on the Binet scale who was a calendar calculator.[33] His explanation for this ability was "that the boy was formerly completely absorbed in the activities in which he showed special aptitude, with a consequent neglect of other types of behavior, thus explaining his inferiority in social activities and verbal intelligence."

Hiram Byrd's description of one of his cases is best given in his own words:

> Eugene Hoskins is his name. He lives at Oxford, Mississippi, a University place of about three thousand people. He is well known about town for his eccentricities, but more especially for his uncanny knowledge of dates. A bystander said to him: "I was married on the 8th of June, 1901." Without a moment's hesitation Eugene said: "Dat was Satu'day." Given the month, day and year, he will give the day of the week. He never fails, never hesitates. Vary it if you will by giving the year and month and asking what day of the month was the second Tuesday, or the fourth Friday—he answers just the same. It is one of the diversities among the university students to get old calendars and try him out. He is a never ending source of entertainment for them.
>
> I have said he never fails. That is, so long as you stay within his limits, for he has limits. Go beyond that and he is at sea. He can't go back beyond 1901, and can't go forward beyond 1924. But during these 24 years success is 100 percent. It should be noted, however, that his limits have not always been so advanced. Mr. Harvey remembers when he could not go beyond 1920, and Eugene himself admitted to me that he is advancing his limits and hopes to reach 1925 by next year. Asked how he does it, Eugene says he can't tell you—that he doesn't know

himself. So the impression has gone forth that it is a sort of supernatural gift.[34]

Byrd came across a notebook belonging to this patient, who had a mental age of 9. The patient had memorized the contents of this notebook and could recite pages as if he were recalling them as one recalls pages from a stored computer disk. Yet, Byrd admits that some dates were not written down and were therefore not committed to memory from the notebook. Nonetheless, Byrd claims that the patient's phenomenal ability to memorize "accounted for his remarkable ability to name dates."

AN INVESTIGATION OF CALENDAR CALCULATING IN MULTIPLE SUBJECTS

In 1981 Arnold M. Rosen studied two calendar calculators in his adult out-patient clinic.[35] The first was a 25-year-old man with an I.Q. of 79. The patient stated that he had learned the skill at age 6 from a telephone book that contained a perpetual calendar. The second was a 36-year-old man with an I.Q. of 97. He too had developed this skill at about age 6. The primary psychiatric diagnosis for both was "autistic."

Rosen constructed and applied a variety of tests to determine the method of calendar calculating used here and subjected the results to rigorous statistical analysis. Using some of the same procedures and test dates used by Hill on a single subject, Rosen presented 192 dates both orally and visually. Rosen assessed reaction times and errors, reaction times to various dates and reaction times to various calendar variables; he concluded at the end of his complex analysis that both subjects had an extensive knowledge of the systematic calendar changes and actually calculated future dates by extrapolating from past dates. The month of December seemed especially crucial as a keying point. Yet both subjects, like the others who have been discussed, were unable to describe whatever system they were using. Like George and Charles, they explained it away by saying simply that they "knew it." Yet Rosen concluded that the date of December 1 seemed pivotal in the system of "keying off" used by both subjects. In Rosen's view, this was actually a method for simplifying calendar operations and not a true system.

Along with calendar calculating ability, both subjects had prodigious long-term memories within narrow areas of their interests.

In 1971 Edward Hoffman reviewed the theories to date concerning the idiot savant, noting that they differed widely.[36] None seemed to satisfy him or to explain a particular patient of his with calendar calculating ability. His subject was age 13, had an I.Q. of 61 and had secondary brain damage, epilepsy and mild spastic quadriplegia. The patient could perform simple arithmetic and read at a third-grade level. His favorite activity was calendar calculating.

The patient stated that, at age 8, he had learned a calendar calculating method in which he used a memorized series of key dates and then counted forward or backward, using the days in each month to reach the desired date. His span of calendar calculating was only about eight years, however, and when tested by Hoffman, he responded accurately only within that time span.

To explain this phenomenon, Hoffman argues that "special abilities" such as prodigious memory or rapid calculation are not confined to the savant but occur in persons representing the whole spectrum of intelligence. These special abilities can, then, occur alongside normal intelligence or limited intelligence and are not peculiar to the savant. Also, he argues, certain persons—those, for example, in solitary confinement or those deprived in some manner of normal social outlets—often resort to learning or memorization such as seen in the savant as a compensatory device to preserve normal cognitive thinking. Since the retardate often is in a form of social isolation as is common in many institutional settings, it is not surprising, according to Hoffman, that these same mechanisms come into use. Beyond such social isolation, however, Hoffman notes that autistic patients and many retardates show diminished sensitivity to outer stimuli due to some intrinsic characteristics of their disabilities; both are therefore already in a state of relative sensory deprivation and are particularly receptive then to the development of some "special abilities." Finally, Hoffman proposes that the other major contributing factor in the production of these special abilities is intense motivation as a form of stimuli-seeking, coupled with the reinforcement of that motivation that comes from the success and special attention the patient gets from displaying his skill.

He sums up his final conclusion thus:

The idiot savant may now be viewed as essentially a "normal" retardate, who through intense motivation due to social and sensory isolation, coupled with the relative absence of outer, interfering stimuli, gradually learns to perform what have previously been considered to be unique, "special" abilities. He [the savant] constructs a triad of "normal" nonabstract thinking that happens to exist in the savant in the absence of "normal" abstract thinking, coupled with sensory isolation and deprivation, along with tremendous motivation and the reinforcement that naturally follows. The savant is not thus special in his or her abilities uniquely, but rather the specialness and uniqueness lie in this combination existing together.

BLINDNESS, MULTIPLE HANDICAPS AND CALENDAR CALCULATING

R., a 16-year-old girl born January 24, 1948, was reported on by Edmund J. Rubin and Sheila Monaghan in the *American Journal of Mental Deficiency* in November, 1965.[37] The case was particularly interesting because R. was female and was completely blind, the latter fact ruling out the theory that eidetic imagery is an explanation in every case.

R. was one of twins born 2½ months prematurely. Each twin weighed 2 pounds, 9 ounces at birth. R. was totally blind while her twin had partial vision. Retrolental fibroplasia was diagnosed in both. R. also had a slight left-sided paralysis of both limbs (hemiparesis). The parents were devastated by the handicapped twins, and for the first three years of their lives the twins were virtual crib babies. When the twins were 4 years old a skilled homemaker began working with the family and the two girls. Rather striking progress was made by R.'s twin sister, who thus became the pride and joy of the parents, leaving R. even more alone, restricted and rejected. Undoubtedly, the other twin's partial vision gave her a decided advantage and considerably more attention.

At age 5 the twins were sent to separate part-time nursery schools. During this year R. had several convulsive seizures. She was placed in private special classes and schools. At age 15 she could write braille at a first-grade level. At age 16 she was functioning overall at a first-grade level. I.Q. was measured at 51. Digit span was 7 forward but 0 backward.

The calendar calculating ability of R. was noticed at about age 10 or 11. The twin sister had some of the same ability but a wide variety of other interests kept that skill quite unused. With some encouragement from a teacher who noticed and valued that skill, R. began to use it with considerable satisfaction. "I'm a calendar girl," she would say proudly. Her calendar span was fairly narrow, covering 8 years. Tested with 40 dates occurring within those 8 years R. had an accuracy rate of 83 percent, which was raised to 93 percent when she corrected for an error she had consistently made by not taking into account leap year for one of the years. Rubin and Monaghan appropriately point out, "Even though the span of years covered by R.'s calculating ability is somewhat small when compared with other calendar calculators cited in the literature, it should be pointed out that in this case the subject has been totally blind since infancy."

The researcher compared R.'s responses to those of five retarded, age-matched, nonblind girls and five nonblind girls of normal intelligence. The ability of R. was far superior to that in any of those individuals. Her response time was particularly quick, often under five seconds. R. admitted that her method involved practicing dates whenever she could. No calendar in braille was available to her so she relied entirely on memory. Her memory for dates was coupled with a striking ability to remember information about a whole variety of minor incidents, such as what she had eaten on the day she first met a particular teacher, who had a toothache on which date or which visitors came to visit on which date. There was, then, a strong association between particular dates and particular events in her life.

A number of things about this case are especially interesting. First, there is the association again here of prematurity, retrolental fibroplasia and savant ability—in this case, calendar calculating. Test scores of this savant show the usual poor abstract ability, which suggests that brain damage, along with compensatory coping skills, were important contributing factors to the special skill. But in this case there must have been other such factors because the patient was totally blind, had very limited braille skills and had no braille calendars available to her. Those facts would rule out visual eidetic imagery as the mechanism here; some other method not dependent on vision or tactile input must have been operating. The blindness here is especially intriguing and raises new avenues of inquiry about calendar calculating methods in all savants with that special skill. Rubin and Monaghan conclude, correctly it seems to me, that "R's case serves to bring out that the etiology of any one case of idiot savantism involves the interaction of a multiplicity of factors."

CALENDAR CALCULATING: MATH OR MEMORY?

The most recent accounts of calendar calculators, and the most recent studies of this unique talent, are in work being done by Drs. B. Hermelin and N. O. O'Connor of the Institute of Education in London. In a 1984 experiment, Hermelin and O'Connor analyzed speed and error rates for eight idiot savant calendar calculators for past and future dates.[38] Error rates and response rates were greater for more distant dates in either direction, but the savants were much more error-prone with future dates. Hermelin and O'Connor concluded that memory alone could not explain the skill. They postulated that, in addition to using some arithmetic calculating skills, the savant also used the rules that govern the Gregorian calendar. In fact, one of the eight subjects stated that he was aware of, and used, the fact that the Gregorian calendar repeated itself every 28 years.

Of the eight savants, six were male and two were female. The ages ranged from 17 to 36. The average I.Q. measures among them were 61 verbal and 65 performance, with full-scale I.Q.s ranging from 38 to 88. Diagnoses ranged from schizophrenia and autism to brain injuries.

In 1986 the researchers tested in greater depth to see whether these savants used any of these three rule-based strategies: (1) in any non-leap year, any given date in November will fall on the same day of the week as it does in March, and this same relationship holds for April and July, February and March, September and December, and October and January; (2) the Gregorian calendar is structured in such a way that identical years recur, with certain restrictions, every 28 years; (3) where leap years are not involved, the first day of the succeeding year moves one day forward and the first day of the preceding year moves one day backward.[39] The hypothesis was that the calendar calculators correctly respond more quickly to questions that allow them to take advantage of those rules than to questions that are less related to the rules.

They devised a number of carefully constructed experiments, using dates that were easily related to these rules and dates that were more remotely connected (for instance, dates in a leap year). They also devised an ingenious experiment with colored dots that allowed transposition of the rule-based calendar strategies to colored-dot sequences.

The researchers concluded several things after a detailed analysis of the many responses. First, all the calendar calculators used both memory and arithmetic skills for past years and for less-remote years, whether in the past or the future. All also did use rule-based strategies; however, they did so for more difficult dates when their easier-to-use memory and arithmetic skills were not sufficient.

Second, some of the subjects were actually able to articulate these rules and this seemed to be a function of higher I.Q. Analogous to this would be the fact that many persons use language without being able to verbalize rules of grammar and sentence construction. They may not know how they use language, but they can use it nonetheless. All of us learned language that way initially and only later, when we took our English classes, did we learn about the "rules" by which we were already operating.

Third, those of the eight calendar calculators with the higher I.Q.s, relatively speaking, were able—albeit with some considerable difficulty—to transfer the calendar rules to the colored-dot sequences.

Thus, while rule-based strategies were employed by all the subjects, an understanding of those strategies and the ability to transfer them were functions of higher or lower cognitive ability.

Hermelin and O'Connor point to the analogous findings reported by Frank D. Mitchell in 1907 regarding great calculators.[40] Some persons never progressed beyond literal counting. A second group used knowledge of arithmetic procedures rather than mere counting. A third group went even further and used algebraic methods to short-cut the arithmetic procedures. Thus the calendar calculators, like the lightning calculators, have differing levels of sophistication among them and use simpler methods for simpler problems, reserving more complex methods for more complex computations.

Is it math or is it memory? Hermelin and O'Connor conclude that it is both, and that it just depends on what date is given and how complex the problem is. It is memory and it is math.

AND THEN THERE IS BENJ LANGDON

Dr. Bernard Rimland reported a most interesting circumstance in his article on autistic savants in *Psychology Today* in August, 1978.[41] The Psychiatry Department of the University of Oklahoma had gone to the New York hospital where George and his brother Charles lived to do a film on these remarkable twins. Two researchers, Barnett Addis and Oscar Parsons, sought to have a graduate student, Benj Langdon, see if he could learn to calendar calculate with any of the skill that the two brothers demonstrated. Rimland notes:

> Langdon practiced night and day, trying to develop a high degree of proficiency at some rather complex calculations that involved memorizing a one-page table. Langdon became quite good at the calculating. But despite an enormous amount of practice, he could not match the speed of the twins for quite a long time. Then suddenly, he discovered he could match their speed. Quite to Langdon's surprise, his brain had somehow automated the complex calculations; it had absorbed the table to be memorized so efficiently that now calendar calculating was second nature to him; he no longer had to consciously go through the various operations.

Rimland concludes that this quantum leap in ability took place as Langdon's capacity migrated from the left brain to the right brain. Whether or not that is what actually occurred, the ability to carry out activity automatically as a result of continual practice—whether or not one consciously works at that activity or cognitively understands *how* one does it—is the ability that enables savants, and the rest of us, to do much of what we do. We all know the "I've got it" experience, which represents the point where an activity becomes automatic. Remember, for example, when you mastered riding a bicycle—that point when everything suddenly became clear. From then on, riding just came naturally and you rode without all the thought and motion that you had expended while learning to ride. Now try to put the experience of natural, "automatic" riding into words when someone asks you the simple question, "How do you ride a bike?" The experience is difficult to express.

Langdon's experience is, in reverse, like that of a woman who suddenly "unlearned" her musical skills when she began to study music more systematically. After the *60 Minutes* program on Savant Syndrome, a woman wrote to me about her relative and the mysterious "migration" of musical ability that occurred when this woman began the formal study of music. She had been a professional. For years she had had the ability to play by ear and could play back a song after a single hearing. In her fifties she tired of being a professional and decided to pursue a career as a pianist. She closed her practice and entered a conservatory to study that which had always come to her so naturally. As she studied music, her "gift" left her; she found herself playing at a beginner level. Her skill seemed to have "migrated," to use Rimland's term, to elsewhere in her brain. Her natural ability has never returned.

BEYOND MEMORY, BEYOND MATH

So what does all of this mean? After a century of study, from Down's careful observations to Hermelin and O'Connor's systematic study 100 years later, what can be said about calendar calculators? Well, for some calendar calculators, the mechanism is memory and memory alone. For them calendar span is limited to the span of their memory, and they usually do better with future dates. While some might attribute the calendar calculator's skill to eidetic memory, formal studies have shown that not to be the case, and certainly Rubin and Monaghan's case of a totally blind calendar calculator would preclude visual eidetic imagery from being a universal mechanism.

Other calendar calculators use some arithmetic or counting methods to arrive at results. With constant practice they can carry out these functions very quickly—in these cases, it is the speed of the calculation, not the complexity—that astounds. This method is based on *conscious* learning, which begins with some specific system or rules that, with constant repetition, soon become unconscious—just as one's initial, conscious and deliberate efforts at touch typing soon become, with practice and repetition, unconscious and automatic. It is this conscious to unconscious transition that occurred when nonsavant Langdon, described earlier, found that after much practice he could calendar calculate without always consciously thinking of the formula, rules and methodology.

But the underlying method for most savant calendar calculators—especially someone as severely limited and handicapped as the startling case reported by Roberts, where I.Q. was exceedingly low and language absent except for "yes" and "no" replies—is the ability of the human brain to form unconscious algorithms on the basis of examples. An algorithm is an explicit procedure or formula for calculating something. In this type of *unconscious* learning, prolonged and repetitious examination and study of specimens or examples of some subject (in the case of the twins, the perpetual calendar) allows one to inculcate and incorporate complicated equations or formulas, which can then be applied with no conscious or cognitive understanding by the person using them. By simply using the perpetual calendar over and over the twins ultimately incorporated the algorithm, or formula, of the calendar with no conscious idea of what that specific formula might be, nor even any idea that such a thing as a formula exists. They could not have begun learning to calendar calculate by consciously calculating dates, for they were able to consciously calculate nothing. They could not even add or subtract.

This unconscious learning, this "memory without reckoning," is, in the savant, I believe, the result of unique circuitry that bypasses—in a way we will see later—the usual pathways and way stations that the rest of us use in our day-to-day thinking and memory. It is not just, I believe, an enhanced concentration or compensation for impaired learning; it is a unique ability—based on unique circuitry—at the core of Savant Syndrome that cuts across the otherwise seemingly disconnected abilities in this mysterious condition. Memory—of a peculiar and special type—is central to the condition and gives the calendar calculator, like the other savants, his or her awesome, mystifying ability.

4

The Brilliant and
the Backward:
The Lightning
Calculators

Steven B. Smith, in his excellent book *The Great Mental Calculators*, reviews the psychology, methods and lives of many well-known and not so well-known calculating prodigies.[42] The majority of his examples are geniuses and prodigies, but several are persons of very low intellect who qualify as savants. Smith notes that this particular skill occurs more frequently among the brilliant and the backward than among those of more average intelligence, and he attributes this to a property he notes at either end of the intelligence spectrum—an uncommon tolerance for what most people would find intolerably dull. (Exceptional musical and artistic skill, on the other hand, are found more evenly distributed along the intelligence spectrum—possibly because the average person is not as quickly bored by these as by math.) All the great calculators, Smith notes, whether gifted or handicapped, have "made numbers their friends" and particularly in the case of the handicapped, have memorized great quantities of data and then, in some mysterious fashion, have unconsciously incorporated the complex formulas and algorithms involved. Smith focuses mainly on the brilliant; we will look at the backward.

THOMAS FULLER

Dr. Benjamin Rush was a psychiatrist who is often referred to as the father of American psychiatry. A prominent patriot, he was a signer of the Declaration of Independence. He was intrigued with the case of Thomas Fuller and read a lengthy letter about Fuller before the Pennsylvania Society for the Abolition of Slavery in 1789.[43] Fuller was a lightning calculator "of such limited intelligence who could comprehend scarcely anything, either theoretical or practical, more complex than counting."

Fuller was born in Africa in 1710 and at age 14 was brought to Virginia as a slave. No I.Q. tests or other clinical descriptions are available to precisely establish his intellectual level, but the information available certainly points toward serious mental handicap. Of course he had no schooling.

Fuller's fascination and preoccupation with calculating began in childhood when, after learning to count to 100, he counted the hairs in a cow's tail (2,872). Following that he counted the grains in a bushel of wheat and the grains in a bushel of flax seed. From that point forward he could calculate with perfect accuracy a whole variety of equations, most of which were related to the simple work he did in the field and on the farm where he worked all his life. He could easily do 9-digit multiplication and a variety of other computations.

In 1788 Fuller was presented with three questions. The first was "How many seconds are there in 1½ years?" Fuller required two minutes before giving the correct answer of 47,304,000. The second question was "How many seconds has a man lived who is 70 years, 17 days and 12 hours old?" After only 90 seconds Fuller answered 2,210,500,-800. One of the two interviewers told Fuller he was wrong, upon which, according to Rush's account, Fuller replied, "Masa, you forgot d' leap year." The interviewer, correcting himself and adding the seconds of the leap year to the others, came to Fuller's correct calculation.

The final question was "Suppose a farmer has 6 sows and each sow has 6 female pigs the first year, and they all increase in the same proportion to the end of 8 years, how many sows would the farmer then have?" After 10 minutes the correct answer was given: 34,588,806.

Fuller's obituary, quoted by Rush as it appeared in the *Columbian Centinal* in 1790, is particularly insightful:

> The power of recollection and the strength of memory were so complete in him that he could multiply 7 into itself, that product by 7, and the product so produced by 7, for 7 times. He could give the number of months, days, weeks, hours, minutes, and seconds in any period of time that any person chose to mention, allowing in his calculation for all the leap years that happen in the time; and would give the number of poles, yards, feet, inches, and barley corns in any given distance, say the diameter of the earth's orbit; and in every calculation he would produce the true answer, in less time than 99 men in 100 would take with their pens.

Fuller died in 1790 at age 80, never having learned to read or write in spite of his extraordinary power of calculation.

JEDEDIAH BUXTON

Jedediah Buxton also lived in the 1700s. Like Thomas Fuller, Buxton was a lightning calculator who was very limited intellectually. He had had no formal education and was unable to write his name. According to an article that appeared in *Gentlemen's Magazine* in 1754, "his perpetual application to figures has prevented the smallest acquisition of any other knowledge, and his mind seems to have retained fewer ideas than that of a boy 10 years old, in the same class of life."[42]

Buxton was also a character. He kept track of the free beer and ale given him during his life, and of everyone who gave it to him (5,116 pints from 57 different persons). On his list of those freebies was 72 pints for a "gathering for his dead cow." Smith points out that Buxton gave new meaning to the phrase that Buxton often used—"drunk with reckoning."

Buxton liked to count. E. W. Scripture describes his obsession as follows:

On his return from a sermon he never brought away one sentence, having been busied in dividing some time or some space into the smallest known parts. He visited London in 1754, and was tested by the Royal Society. On this visit he was taken to see King Richard III, performed at Drury Lane Playhouse, but his mind was employed as at church. During the dance he fixed his attention upon the number of steps; he attended to Mr. Garrick only to count the words that he uttered. At the conclusion of the play they asked him how he liked it. He replied such an actor went in and out so many times and spoke so many words; another so many, etc.[43]

Buxton's ability and tremendous capacity to remember numbers in gigantic strings and his ability to carry out calculations with great speed can be judged by his responses to questions he was asked. For instance, he was once asked, "In a body whose three sides are 23,145,789 yards, 5,642,732 yards and 54,965 yards, how many cubicle ⅛ths of an inch exist?" Five hours later he gave the correct 28-digit answer—and he could give that answer *backward or forward*. Asked the number of barley corns required to reach 8 miles, he assumed 3 barley corns to the inch and gave the answer of 1,520,640. When asked the number of times a coach wheel 6 yards in circumference would revolve when traveling the 204 miles from York to London, Buxton correctly gave the answer: 59,840 times. It took him 13 minutes to compute that response.

Buxton put some of his calculating skills to good use—he could pace off land as accurately as it could be measured.

Buxton was once asked to determine the cost of shoeing a horse with 140 nails if the price was one farthing for the first nail and the price doubled for each of the remaining 139 nails (2^{139} farthings). Buxton's answer was 725,958,238,096,074,907,868,531,656,993,638,851,106 pounds, 2 shillings and 8 pence. A modern-day computer shows the answer to be slightly wrong, although the first four digits and the last eight digits are correct, as are the odd shillings and pence. Buxton attempted to square that number (2^{139} squared), and it took him 2½ months to do so. The answer, in his unique terminology, was 78-digits long, incorrect by modern calculation in only one digit.

It took Buxton 15 minutes to answer the question, "Suppose sound moves 1,142 feet in one second of time, how long then, after the firing of one of the cannons at Retford, may the same be heard at Haughton Park, taking the distance of five miles?" His answer: "23 seconds, 7 thirds and 46 remaining."

Scripture was intrigued with the memory of both Fuller and Buxton. Both could leave long computations half done and, at the end of several months, resume the problem-solving exactly where they left off. Scripture, in fact, ranked memory above rapidity in setting the lightning calculators apart from the rest of us. The accuracy of memory in Fuller and Buxton was astounding. In his judgment Buxton had the most accurate memory of all the lightning calculators: "Although an accurate memory for a long time may not be possessed by every rapid calculator, he must be able to retain before the mind with absolute accuracy the results of the various processes performed till he has finished the problem. This we can presuppose in the case of every one of the arithmetical prodigies, and indeed it seems to have been the one thing in which Buxton was superior to ordinary mortals."

OTHER EARLY LIGHTNING CALCULATORS

Dr. J. Langdon Down mentions several of his cases "where the power of mental arithmetic existed to an astonishing extent."[1] He describes a 12-year-old lad who could multiply any 3 figures by 3 figures with perfect accuracy as quickly as Down could write the 6 figures on paper. Down commented that the boy was so limited otherwise that he could not recall Down's name after 2½ years of seeing him and talking to him daily. Another boy could multiply 2 figures by 2 figures, while still another could multiply 2 figures by 2 figures in a short time and later could multiply 3 figures by 3 figures. "None of them can explain how they do it, I mean, by what mental process," Down notes.

Dr. Alfred F. Tredgold also comments on the "extraordinary capacity for arithmetic and calculation" in some savants.[12] He reports one subject who, if told the age of someone, could calculate, within a short time, the number of minutes that the person had lived. Tredgold recalls a patient of Dr. D. Adam Wizel's who could divide 576,560,336 by 16 with "astonishing quickness." She also carried out multiplication functions such as 23×23, 45×18 and 78×78 almost instantly, using some "peculiar method of her own," yet she could not add or subtract. He refers to several other instances where mentally handicapped patients "possess the same gift, although markedly lacking in other scholastic requirements."

The tenth edition of Tredgold's *Textbook on Mental Deficiency* (by Drs. Roger F. Tredgold and Kenneth Soddy) refers to another lightning calculator—a blind male with a "faculty of calculating to a degree little short of marvelous." He could give the square root of any 4-digit number in an average of 4 seconds and the cube root of any 6-digit number in about 6 seconds. His ability is further described:

> When he was asked how many grains of corn there would be in any one of 64 boxes, with 1 in the first, 2 in the second, 4 in the third, 8 in the fourth, and so on, he gave answers for the fourteenth (8,192), for the eighteenth (131,072), and the twenty-fourth (8,388,608) instantaneously, and he gave the figures for the forty-eighth box (140,737,488,-355,328) in six seconds. He also gave the total in all 64 boxes correctly (18,446,734,073,709,551,615) in forty-five seconds.[44]

Arthur Phillips, in his paper "Talented Imbeciles," reports the case of Obadiah, a patient diagnosed as a "high-grade imbecile" with a "numerical obsession."[45] Obadiah counted continually and translated everything into numbers. He had a gift for rapid computation although he had never had a single lesson in arithmetic. Phillips describes him this way: "Sometimes with the swift weaving of his nervous fingers, sometimes in silence, his body quiet, his face alone showing nervous tension, this 6-year-old prodigy solved problems in multiplication, division, and fractions to an extent that was nothing short of phenomenal. No boy with such an endowment could be classified as an imbecile on the intellectual scale. His intellectual deficiency grew out of an excess of intellectual quality and achievement in one direction."

Sabine was 22 when Dr. Wizel first encountered her.[46] She came from a musical family; her father was a professional musician and a brother was a violinist with a prodigious memory and a perfect ear for music, according to Dr. Abraham A. Brill, who recounts this case in detail in his 1940 treatise on lightning calculators.[47] Sabine was a normal, bright, active child who began school at age 6. She was a good student and progressed rapidly. As a child she suffered a severe typhoid infection with convulsions and a long period of unconsciousness. When she regained consciousness she was blind, mute and completely changed mentally. Whereas before she had been pleasant and docile, she was now "unclean, destructive, and entirely disoriented and took no notice of anything about her." She did regain her sight, and while her speech returned to some degree, she never regained her normal intellectual functioning. At age 11 she was "very childish and subject to infrequent convulsive attacks."

At age 13 she became interested in coins, and she soon was able to count them and recognize their value in larger denominations. She also played with buttons and often divided her coins and buttons into groups of 16. When asked how many coins she had she might say, for example, "$6 \times 16 + 8$ more." She could add, multiply and divide quickly and accurately. She could quickly square numbers from 11 to 99. It took her 10 seconds to square 97. Division was more difficult, but she did that also with puzzling rapidity.

Sabine showed another "astonishing talent." When asked to multiply 23×23 she immediately answered 529, but then she added voluntarily that 529 was the same as $33 \times 16 + 1$. When asked to multiply 14×14 she answered 196—which, she added, was the same as $12 \times 16 + 4$. She also had a talent for rhyming and often answered questions in rhymes—answering correctly sometimes and senselessly other times.

Wizel classifies Sabine as an "imbecile" with wildly fluctuating moods. There are no I.Q. scores for reference points, but she certainly was a very limited girl. Sabine is of special interest because she was female, so rare among the lightning calculators and savants in general, and because hers is a case of acquired Savant Syndrome following, in this case, severe illness with central nervous system involvement.

S. JUNGREIS

In the same 1940 article, Brill describes a lightning calculator who, though not mentally deficient and therefore not a savant, is of sufficient interest to be recalled here. His case demonstrates that savant-like skills can appear and disappear just as suddenly in normal persons as they sometimes do in the savant.[47]

S. Jungreis was first seen by Brill at age 6. He was already a wizard at mathematics. According to an account from a 1917 issue of the New York *Evening Journal* he was able to add formidable columns of figures without being able to distinguish one Arabic numeral from another. He knew only the written number 3. The article described the boy as carrying around in his bulging forehead an automatic adding machine that ground out mathematical problems that he did not even pretend to understand. In an instant the answer would pop out of him with almost parrot-like glibness. He added 6-digit numbers more easily than ordinary persons could add single-digit numbers. He was invariably correct.

Like that of other lightning calculators, the boy's memory was astonishing. Brill notes, "the force of his memory was such that he could repeat by heart the numbers I gave him from 5 to 45 minutes later." As with many savants, his special talent was discovered quite by accident. One day he was with his older brothers while they were doing arithmetic and sharing answers out loud. What they thought were just random numbers being called out by their younger brother turned out, to their astonishment, to be the correct answers even though, at that time, he could neither read nor write. His I.Q. was measured at about average when this special skill was added into the scores, but the child had developed very slowly, spoke in a peculiar sing-song fashion and exhibited other autistic-like symptoms and behavior.

The most interesting aspect of this case surfaced when Brill met the patient years later at age 27. The gift of lightning calculating had left him, at age 9, as suddenly as it had appeared. In fact, at age 27 S. Jungreis had no more mathematical skills than the average person. That this skill had disappeared within weeks of his father's death was of special interest and speculation to Brill.

Brill spends a great deal of time exploring the nature of savant skills, which he considers to be "some peculiar manifestations of memory," and we will look at some of his speculations in more detail later. He concludes that in all the lightning calculators, remarkable memory was a prerequisite to the savant abilities. The memory was of a special type, something he calls "memory without consciousness," which he likens to the kind of process we experience when we solve problems or come to some insight while we sleep, when the mind is at work drawing on memory in an unconscious manner. He takes something of a quantum leap forward from that, however, and postulates that since the kind of skills seen in the lightning calculator can appear as early as age 4 or 5, before the child has a conscious fund of knowledge on which to draw, the abilities and skills must be transmitted in some hereditary or instinct form—that they must be memories from a sort of collective unconscious transmitted through generations. He characterizes this as "an unconscious recollection of our ancestors."

Brill states:

> Without further speculation we may conclude that like the neurotic who is seriously handicapped in his adjustment to life because he has to cope with a fragment of his infantile sexuality in adult life, the infant prodigy is even more afflicted because for some as yet unknown reasons he has to cope with a fragment from his phylogenetic [hereditary] existence. His talent, which strikes us as uncanny, is therefore not so strange when considered in the light of phylogeny. But, as our present mode of living is so far removed from that of prehistory, none of these prodigies could maintain themselves long in our society without special care. Left to themselves, they soon would perish. Maybe Shelley was not so crazy after all when he said to a woman with a baby in the street, "Will your baby tell us anything about preexistence, Madame?"

MORE ON INHERITED SPECIAL ABILITIES

David C. Rife and Laurence H. Snyder, from the department of zoology at Ohio State University, had their ideas on the role of heredity in understanding the idiot savant and presented their observations in a 1931 article on that topic.[16] In it they sum up their viewpoint on the matter thus: "It would seem therefore that in the case of the feebleminded individual showing marked special abilities, they had received purely coincidentally two sets of hereditary factors, those for feeblemindedness and those for special ability." They allow also, however, that environment—specific opportunity and special training—can help shape and mold savant skills but that this factor is secondary to inheritance. In their studies they looked at reports on 33 savants in a variety of settings in the United States but observed personally 9 individual cases, on which they placed special emphasis because these cases showed strong family histories supporting the talents. Of the 33 savants, 8 had mathematical ability.

Rife and Snyder gave emphasis to one case of lightning calculating— that of a 27-year-old male with a mental age of 3. His special mathematical ability appeared when he was a small child. He would scribble figures on the bathroom tiles or anywhere else if given the opportunity. He never learned to talk and could not point to his eyes or ears when asked to. He was institutionalized at age 16.

While the patient was incapable of conversing at all, or of understanding verbal requests, if one were to write figures such as 2, 4, 8 in a vertical column, he would immediately continue the series: 16, 32, 64, etc. According to the report: "When the series 2, 4, 16 was started, he immediately continued this one, the sixth number being 4,294,967,296. Then 9 – 3 was written in the attempt to indicate square root. Under this several numbers such as 625, 729, and 900 were written. The square root of each was immediately and correctly written."

The patient showed additional abilities in multiplication, in which he computed in his head his computations for problems that required several digits to be multiplied by several digits, only writing down the answer. Addition and subtraction skills were very limited, however; he gave incorrect answers to the simplest of problems. There was no outstanding mathematical ability in the family although, according to the researchers, "the mother was fond of and good at mental arithmetic." There was no history of developmental disability in the family except for a first cousin on the father's side.

GEORGE

George was a 9-year-old boy studied in depth and reported on in detail by Barry Nurcombe and Neville Parker in a 1964 overview article on the idiot savant.[48] George was the fifth of eight children, all of whom were of normal intelligence, as were their parents. George was a frail and weak child with a congenital heart condition that caused frequent "gasping turns," during which he would turn blue and nearly lose consciousness; these episodes occurred several times each week. He was slow in reaching developmental milestones: he was 2 before he began to walk and he was essentially without speech until age 6.

He was an aloof youngster who spent most of his time reading or drawing. He had an intense obsession with sameness. His favorite pastime was watching trains go by; he would carefully count the cars as they passed. At age 10 he was unable to dress himself, and even at 16 he still had difficulty accomplishing this alone.

His behavior was extremely disruptive; he continually made odd noises no matter what he was doing. At home he spent most of his time sitting alone with dictionaries and encyclopedias and would repeat over and over what he had read in them. The rest of the time he would go around the home arranging and rearranging furniture in an orderly fashion, exhibiting his intense compulsivity.

George had a large vocabulary but his verbalizations were often random and his ability to use language meaningfully was limited.

His mathematical and memory abilities, however, are described thus:

> His ability in addition of numbers was truly remarkable; for example, he answered to the following sum, 32560 + 8247 + 3819 + 4158, in a few seconds after the figures were quickly written down. His formal rote historical knowledge was staggering. He had been demonstrated at three clinical meetings, and members of the audience had been given correct answers to the questions of dates and formal information they asked him. He gave the date and place of birth of Freud, Jung, Charcot, and Hughlings Jackson on one occasion. He appeared to have an unending supply of unconnected information.

Like all the other savants, "he was unable, or unprepared, to describe how he accomplished these feats of memory."

Formal testing was done with a great deal of difficulty. On one occasion George insisted and persisted in counting the seconds as they went by in the test session. Test results showed him to be a "borderline mental defective" with I.Q. scores of 48 performance, 97 verbal and 72 full-scale. All the psychologists doing the testing concluded that the diagnosis here was more one of autism or schizophrenia than mental deficiency as such. Overall it was felt that he was an autistic child who had undergone partial recovery as he had grown up.

FLEURY

Fleury, a lightning calculator who lived early this century, was first described in Macdonald Critchley's colorfully entitled book *The Divine Banquet of the Brain* as "a blind, intractable, destructive imbecile" who Critchley considered "more remarkable still."[32] Smith gives more details on this most interesting case in his 1983 book *The Great Mental Calculators.*[42]

Fleury was born blind and, even at age 10, had difficulty walking, bathing himself and feeding himself. He was restless and destructive and made tic-like movements. Schooling was attempted and, interestingly, he found arithmetic particularly difficult. When he was 15 it was decided that he was not educable and he was institutionalized.

According to Smith's account, Fleury became very frightened when a patient sitting next to him had an epileptic seizure, and to blot that memory from his mind he decided to concentrate on the subject most difficult for him—arithmetic. To his surprise calculation suddenly came easily and he excelled at it. His special ability became apparent in the hospital setting, and after leaving the hospital, he gave public demonstrations of his lightning calculating throughout France, England and the United States.

In 1927 in France he underwent tests of his abilities given by Dr. Osty at the International Psychical Institute. Problems included multiplication, division, squaring, square roots and algebra. For example, according to Smith's account:

> $2^{30} = 1,073,741,824$ was given as an answer in 40 seconds. Fleury was asked for the values of x and y in $x + y = 707,353,209$, where x and y are integers and y had four digits. In 28 seconds he found $891^3 + 5,238$. In a second such problem he was given $211,717,440$ and came up with $596^3 + 8,704$ in 25 seconds. He was asked to express $6,137$ as the sum of four squares. The first answer, given in 2 minutes 10 seconds, was $74^2 + 20^2 + 15^2 + 6^2$. The second answer was given 10 seconds later: $78^2 + 6^2 + 4^2 + 1^2$. A third answer was obtained after a minute and 20 seconds: $76^2 + 15^2 + 10^2 + 6^2$.

Critchley reports that Fleury determined the cube root of $465,484,375$ (which is 775) in 13 seconds. Multiplying 287×341 took him 10 seconds. Fleury also was a calendar calculator proficient with both the Julian and Gregorian calendars. One unique and remarkable feature of Fleury's skill was the fact that he was a tactile calculator; as he calculated, his fingers would move with extreme rapidity, using his jacket lapel as some sort of arithmetical braille. Critchley remarks that Fleury "could solve algebraic problems with great rapidity. He was incapable however of grasping even the rudiments of geometry."

A FINAL CASE

In 1973 Dr. Walter Steinkopff described the case of an "epileptic imbecile" who was born in 1912 and who died at age 55 during an epileptic seizure.[49] He was the third of ten children, and there was no history of mental retardation or epilepsy in the family. During the second grade, F. Sch., as the patient was referred to by Steinkopff, began to do arithmetic, and by the end of the year his arithmetic skills surpassed those of the teacher. At age 7 he taught himself to play the accordion by ear, and also began to play the zither and the harmonica. His behavior was infantile and exceedingly disruptive at school. He failed there and then began living a simple life at home. He enjoyed going to the grocery store where he would follow customers around, tallying their total bills before they reached the checkout counters. Steinkopff notes that the patient was sometimes able to put his skills to practical use; he would occasionally help store personnel take inventory, and once, when the adding machine at the Health Department broke down, he was called in to do the department's quarterly calculations.

He had calendar calculating skills within a span of 97 years. He could do addition and multiplication, including the squaring of two- and three-digit numbers. He did his calculating with amazing speed, which increased if the number 27 was in the problem. He never wrote down his calculations and seemed to be talking to himself as he proceeded.

Peculiarly, he refused to do subtraction, although he said he was quite able to do so. He disliked fractions, and any division problem that did not divide out evenly seemed to upset him and his compulsive sense of order. He would do problems that were presented as figures but refused to answer questions presented in story or statement form.

No formal I.Q. level is given but his severe epilepsy and other limitations point to considerable central nervous system dysfunction and handicap. He required hospitalization ultimately because of his constant and severe seizures.

BACK TO THE BEGINNING

"The arithmetical prodigies might be divided into two classes, the one-sided and the many-sided," Scripture notes in his 1891 treatise.[43] We have looked at the one-sided here, at those who can do fantastic calculating feats, but little else. Smith, in his 1983 book on arithmetical prodigies, notes this dichotomy between the very bright and the very limited, who seem such unlikely co-owners of this extraordinary gift.[42] These co-owners, in fact, share another gift as well—the gift of prodigious memory. If one were to rank them on a scale of memory quotient rather than intelligence quotient they would be equals—and certainly superior to most of the rest of us. Scripture referred to the "one-sided" as mere "reckoning machines." I would call them mere memory machines, with one added quality—the ability to unconsciously incorporate sequences, whether of notes in music, of dates in calendar calculating or of numbers in lightning calculating, with no conscious knowledge of the rules of music, calendars or mathematics. This is the same phenomenon that occurs when we unconsciously incorporate language before we know anything of verbs, pronouns or adjectives as such. In the savant this unconscious incorporation, or "reckoning," is only in certain limited areas, for their skills, however many they have, do not include the acquisition of language.

Memories of savants and prodigies are extraordinarily accurate, deep and rapid. Visual imagery is the type of memory most often used. In some savants, however, either auditory or tactile imagery may be used as an alternative to visualization. Whatever the type, the imagery of savants and prodigies sometimes has an especially striking width and vividness in addition to the depth and quickness described by Scripture, and by Oliver Sacks in his observations of George and Charles 95 years later.[29,43] Scripture describes the depth and quickness thus:

> All the arithmetical prodigies possessed a remarkable impressibility; they were able to grasp large numbers of figures on only once seeing or hearing them. Dase, moreover, has given special proofs of this power by his experiments in rapid counting. "When you throw a handful of peas on the table a casual glance is sufficient to enable him to tell you their number. He did the same . . . with the points of dominoes at which he gave only a momentary glance in order to tell you their sum. He counted the letters in a line on an octavo and quarto page after a hasty glance. Twelve figures being written down . . . he would just dip his eye upon them, not resting on them more than half a second. He would then repeat them backwards and forwards and name any one at command, as the ninth or the fourth."

Charles and George showed that same trait and ability when they counted the 111 spilled matches even before the matches reached the floor.

Smith concludes that, to the savant and to the genius, numbers are toys, playthings and friends to be courted and played with for enjoyment and pleasure. Alfred Binet, after studying his two calculating prodigies, invokes use of the unconscious which "is perhaps capable of foreseeing the solution to a problem or long arithmetic operation without carrying out the details of the calculations."[9] Oliver Sacks is impressed with the idea of a vast "mnemonic tapestry," in which a whole landscape of numbers appears and from which the lightning calculator simply chooses correct answers, as if he were looking at some gigantic list.[29] Scripture focuses on the depth, accuracy and rapidity of memory to describe the complexity and velocity of the lightning calculator.[43]

Perhaps they are all correct, at least in part. Like the blind men describing an elephant based only on study of one small part of the whole creature, each of these investigators draws conclusions about savant memory and ability as a whole based on what may be constricted or narrowed focus on only one part of a more complex mechanism in the savant. A final synthesis and conclusion may need to include more information. We need, therefore, to venture on.

5

"An Exaltation of Memory": The Mnemonists

"The feeble-minded tend to show a high development of memory," Howard Ellis Jones notes in an article entitled "Phenomenal Memorizing as a Special Ability," which appeared in the *Journal of Applied Psychology* in 1926.[50] Dr. Alfred F. Tredgold notes that "in a considerable proportion of idiot savants the gift is one of memory in some form or other."[12] Dr. William W. Ireland refers to "imbeciles with unusually tenacious memories."[10] Dr. A. Witzmann notes that "idiots have been found to possess a special faculty of storing in brains and reproducing at will masses of figures, like railway timetables, budget statistics and entries in bankbooks."[11]

David, who greeted me at Winnebago my first day on the unit, had memorized the entire bus system of the city of Milwaukee. Leslie, with his repertoire of thousands of songs, has a tremendous memory. George remembers what the weather was on *every day of his adult life*. Prodigious memory seems to be characteristic of every savant, but for some, hypermnesis itself is their special ability. Dr. Macdonald Critchley uses a delightful phrase to describe the condition of these savants—"an exaltation of memory."[32]

The gift of words is not the same as the gift of language. The savants all demonstrate the vital difference between being able to remember words and being able to comprehend them, connect them and use them in useful language. Dr. J. Langdon Down uses the interesting phrase "verbal adhesion" to describe the ability of the savant to remember huge quantities of words, well beyond the range of most of us, while being virtually unable to comprehend them.[1] Sarah Warkfield Parker, in her description of her student Gordon, says it even more colorfully when she points out that owning a kiln of bricks does not make one a mason.[51] Indeed, it does not.

GORDON

Gordon was a student of Parker's. Parker, in turn, was a student in special education of Dr. Lightner Witmer's. In 1917 she gave Witmer a delightfully readable report about Gordon entitled "A Pseudotalent for Words—The Teacher's Report to Dr. Witmer." Also, Arthur Phillips provides his view of Gordon in his 1930 article "Talented Imbeciles."[45] Gordon is a study in contrasts. Parker reports that Gordon at first recited poetry and then came forward "with a courtly bow and cordially proffered hand that would do credit to the most punctilious of the old time southern gentlemen. 'Have you ever been to Savannah?' he asked, bending toward me graciously." He then sang "The Toreador" and solos from *Carmen*. But, in stark contrast, she further reports:

> . . . this finished young gentleman of ten with the society manner and excellent memory stood very near the zero point in the scale of social efficiency, and as sixteen months of subsequent observation proved, he is incapable of being trained to even a passable level of such efficiency. Underneath his excessive excitability to a certain few stimuli which interest him lies an organism of low vitality and sluggish response to material environment. With the exception of a few charged areas energized for immediate and violent response, his mind is in a state of unperceiving, irresponsive detachment from surroundings.

Gordon could learn nonsense jingles, college yells and rhymes on a single hearing. He was able to repeat, verbatim, a story of 1,500 words after six or seven readings. He had an impressive recall of words and sounds from his environment and a remarkable ability to retain those auditory images. Poetry learned on a single reading was retained, verbatim, for 12 months with ease. Just hearing these melodious words or the sound of music gave him delight, as if he were savoring a fine wine or looking at a pretty painting. He would often ask to have something repeated, as if he just wanted to hear the sounds of the words: "Gordon loves the sounds and says them over and over to himself for sheer pleasure in words." He seemed exquisitely sensitive to sounds, almost painfully so if the sounds were loud; loud noises seemed to make him tremble and cower.

Of Gordon's ability to store words, Parker states:

> It would be impossible to keep a record of even a hundredth part of the verbal images conspicuous in a single day's observations. It is signif-

icant, however, that in a great mass of material collected in sixteen months' study of Gordon, including diaries, letters, records of conversations, recollections, oral and written reproductions of stories, etc., I have, exclusive of twenty-six stories reproduced verbatim almost in toto, a record of one thousand forty-four distinct verbal images and fifty-four repeated fragments of conversation. It can, therefore, be strongly substantiated on inference from behavior, that Gordon's mechanism for the reception and retention of verbal impressions is particularly active, in fact, that he has a definite gift of words.

But, after a rather detailed analysis of Gordon's comprehension, or lack of it, regarding those words, Parker concludes that the gift of words is not the gift of language—Gordon understands little of what he is able to store and recall.

Gordon is described by both Parker and Phillips as scoring zero on the scale of "social efficiency" and as a "low grade imbecile" on the mental scale. He was a "mongoloid type" with the usual signs of that disorder. His memory span was 5 digits and 10 syllables. The Binet showed him to have a mental age of 8. He ate "wretchedly at the table stuffing his mouth in an apparent inability to swallow." He could not dress himself. He had an impulse to twist and tear things and often acted on that impulse, destroying eyeglasses and watches with some regularity. Like many savants, he was quite boastful.

Parker defines Gordon's situation as "the peculiar union of conspicuous and permanent deficiencies with equally conspicuous gifts." She gives, however, a plan of remedy, her lesson plan if you will, for approaching defects such as Gordon's:

> Such a case, though tantalizing in its specious doubtfulness, is not hard to deal with when its limitations are once understood and accepted. The obstinate deficiencies cannot be remedied. The few capacities are energetic enough, if wisely directed, to develop themselves. For Gordon the program is simple; first, the physical building up of his weak and degenerate organism; secondly, tactful management to eliminate in so far as possible, the nervous elements of fear and self-consciousness; thirdly, a careful use of his suggestibility to fix, if possible, the suggestion of certain useful types of behavior; fourthly, the development of his appreciation of literature and his gift of expression as a resource for his necessarily lonely, protected and inactive life.

SOME OTHER EARLY MNEMONISTS

Dr. Edward Sequin, in 1866, gave this description of A.:

> A., real simpleton, utterly without judgment; he has a memory which is prodigious, and a singular tendency to make puns. If desired to give

an account of almost any prominent event in ancient or modern story, he will repeat whole pages of what he has read, and there is no stopping him. How impossible is it in the present state of our knowledge, to account for such a human being, with a memory of incredible power, with a capability of exercising a certain handicraft, and yet without any faculty that could guide him in the commonest path of daily life.[8]

When asked for an account of the Peloponnesian War, A. gave extensive details: the duration, date and cause; the resources of the combatants; the gains and losses on either side; the temporary peace; the renewal of the war after the Spartan success; and the final defeat of the Athenians by Lysander.

Down notes that "extraordinary memory was often associated with very great defect of reasoning power. A boy came under my observation who, having once read a book, could ever more remember it. He would recite all the answers in 'Magnall's Questions' without an error, giving in detail the numbers in the astronomical division with the greatest accuracy."[1] Down used the interesting term "verbal adhesion" to describe what he felt was a process of simply reciting, without any real comprehension. Down gave the same boy Gibbon's *Rise and Fall of the Roman Empire* to read. On reading the third page the lad skipped a line but found his error and retraced his steps. "Ever after, when reciting from memory the stately periods of Gibbon, he would, on coming to the third page, skip the line and go back and correct the error with as much regularity as if it had been part of the regular text," Down notes. This patient, as he grew older, had a memory "less tenacious" but was always able to recall those works he had committed to memory earlier in his life.

Another patient of Down's could tell the tune, words and number of nearly every hymn in a particular hymnal. Several of Down's child patients had extraordinary memory for dates and past events. One boy could tell without fail the address of every confectioner's shop he had visited in London, as well as the date of each visit. Another could tell the time of arrival of each of the other children at the hospital; still another knew the home address of every resident and "they are by no means few," reports Down.

In 1897 Dr. Martin W. Barr read, before the Philadelphia Neurological Society, a paper entitled "Echolalia With the Report of an Extraordinary Case."[52] In the paper Barr, the Chief Physician of the Pennsylvania Training School for Feeble-Minded Children in Elwyn, Pennsylvania, describes the case of a 22-year-old epileptic man "with the intelligence of a child of five." Birth and early development were normal, but at age 16 months he had petit mal seizures and at age 4 he developed more fulminating epilepsy. While his speech as a child was at first normal, he developed a habit of "peculiar repetition" which, along with his precocious memory, "first attracted the attention of those about him as evidencing something wrong."

Barr then describes the extreme echolalia in this patient: "When addressed he rarely fails in repetition before reply. Thus one may ask: 'How old are you, Kirtie?,' and he will immediately repeat, taking words and tones, 'How old are you, Kirtie?' " Barr also describes the memory of this patient as being phenomenal and reports that he could recall, for years afterward, the visits of his parents, many other incidents and the names of boys and attendants who he had encountered but then had not seen or heard of again. He would catch the tunes of all the then-popular songs on a single hearing and repeat the words verbatim.

Barr describes one of his tests of this young man:

One of the most interesting experiments with him appears all the more wonderful when we consider his low mentality. As before stated, he not only repeats words, but also imitates voice and tone of the speaker and frequently follows accurately in pantomime of every movement. One afternoon I gave him, in rapid succession, words and sentences in nine different languages: English, French, German, Spanish, Italian, Japanese, Latin, Greek and Norwegian, and each time I found that, although the words were unfamiliar and would have been difficult for an ordinary person, certainly for a normal child, Kirtie took the pronunciation with facility, his voice keeping pace with mine as I repeated:

"I am here with thee and thy goats, as the most capricious poet, honest Ovid, was among the Goths."

"Liberty! Freedom! Tyranny is dead! Run hence, proclaim it—cry about the streets, liberty, freedom and enfranchisement!"

"Pas à pas on va bien loin."

"Wir seufzen im nächtlichen Winde. Vom Zweige ein Wink so fern."

"Superabundantissimente."

"Vedi! le fosche notturne spoglie, de'cieli sveste l'immensa volta."

"Namu miò hô ren gé Riô."

"Potentissimus est qui se habet in potestate."

"Zöe mou sas agapo."

"Min norske vinter er sa vakker, med hoida snebedakte bakker og grónne gran med pudret haar."

Tredgold mentions Barr's case when discussing motor skills in the savant, noting that those cases in which an imbecile reels off cantos of poetry verbatim probably also belong in this category. He recounts several cases of his own, as well, including one of a 65-year-old gentleman whose penchant was biographical history.[12] "It is only necessary to mention to him the name of any prominent personage in early or ancient history, and out there flows in a steady, unhesitating stream a full account of his birth, life and death." Tredgold's other case was a 56-year-old man whose memory was exceptional for events in his own life and in the life of the institution in which he lived: "He is a most valuable referee on matters connected with the previous life of the institution, and can repeat the year, month, and day of coming and going, of all the medical officers during his period of residence."

Tredgold tells of a patient of his colleague Dr. Forbes Winslow: "[He could remember] the day when every person had been buried in the parish for thirty-five years, and could repeat with unvarying accuracy the name and age of the deceased, and the mourners at the funeral. But he was a complete fool. Out of the line of burials he had not one idea, could not give an intelligible reply to a single question, not be trusted even to feed himself." Tredgold also mentions two cases of Dr. Henry Maudsley's: "an imbecile who could repeat verbatim a newspaper he had just read, as well as another more remarkable patient who could repeat backwards what he had just read."

THE PHENOMENAL MEMORIZING ABILITY OF K.

Harold Ellis Jones of Columbia University provides a look at phenomenal memorizing as a special ability in the case of K., whom he studied extensively in 1926.[50] At age 38 K. had a mental age of 11 years and 10 months. His entire vocabulary consisted of 58 words. His social maturation was slow, and he had a speech impediment and a markedly effeminate manner. As a child he developed a passion for measuring and counting. The patient, himself, recalled, "One month I counted the number of bites of food I took, and it was 9,510 bites. I counted the number of steps doing chores around the house and the number of steps from our doorstep to the Post Office four miles away." K. left school at age 17. He began his career as a "memory artist" when he was promised a job if he could memorize a 1910 census for towns over 2,000 in population. He accomplished that feat in three weeks by working six to eight hours each day. He then expanded his memorization to other kinds of information, including the following assortment of facts:

1. The population, by the 1920 census, of every town and city in the United States over 5,000.

2. The names, the number of rooms and the location of about 2,000 leading hotels in the United States.
3. The county seats of all counties in the United States.
4. The populations of 1,800 foreign cities.
5. The distances of all cities in this country from New York and from Chicago, and also the distance from each city or town to the largest city in its state.
6. Statistics concerning 3,000 mountains and rivers.
7. The dates and essential facts connected with over 2,000 important inventions and discoveries.

When tested on these facts, his accuracy rate in giving the populations of 50 randomly selected cities with 5,000 to 200,000 inhabitants was 95 percent. His reaction time in linking city to population was 1.4 seconds for larger cities and 2.9 seconds for cities and towns with a population under 20,000. He could give the population of a city when presented with the city's name or could provide the name of the city when given a population number. His facts were impeccably organized. His associations became so prodigious that it was difficult to find a number that he could not break into familiar sequences. When given the number 4836179621 he studied it for 35 seconds and, after a four-hour interval, recalled it without error. He described his method as follows: "When I saw this number I read it as 4,836,179,621. I remembered 4 because of the 4th of July. 836 I just had to memorize without any help but if I were doing it again it probably would occur to me that 836 was the Chinese population in the State of Texas in 1910, and then I couldn't forget it. 179 is easy to remember because that is the number of miles from New York to Harrisburg, and 621 is the number of a house I know in Denver, Colorado."

He broke up the number 30249385274 and assigned the following associations: "30 is the number of days in a month. 249, if that were 149 it would be the distance from Chicago to Peoria, Illinois. 385, I once paid $3.85 railroad fare going from Cheyenne to Wheatlands, Wyoming. 274, I can remember that by putting a 6 in front of it for the time being, for 6274 is the seating capacity of Hippodrome."

He gave some insight into his method by stating: "I can memorize things best when I see them on paper, and best of all when I write them down. Anything new I usually like to write three or four times so as to be sure not to forget it. About once a year I try to brush up on everything I know, and go over all the facts in my notebooks."

K. had little or no abstract ability and was unable to grasp verbal material, except in very small units. His responses to certain sentences presented during testing were of a type that could be associated with a 12-year-old. Specific tests showed a digit span of 6. On other subtests it was evident that K.'s ability for verbal learning was very limited. Jones sums up this case by stating, "It appears from this evidence that K.'s capacity for verbal learning (as measured by immediate recall for memorizing confined to a standard period) is inferior to the adult norms, and is in fact close to the level achieved in his test of general intelligence. We are not then confronted with the task of explaining a high memory ability coupled with a dull intelligence, but rather with the analysis of the *drive* which has led a person with inferior general capacities (as inferior in his special field of memorizing as in other functions) to devote his life to pseudointellectual activity."

SPECIAL ABILITY WITH BELOW AVERAGE INTELLIGENCE

June E. Downey of the University of Wyoming describes the case of a man who called himself the "World's Champion on Memory."[53] While he was not an idiot savant, his I.Q. was below average, and Downey was struck by "the subject's special ability which stood out in a startling fashion against a background of the most mediocre comprehension."

Nothing is recorded about the background of this man, but he had a talent for repeating from memory numbers seen on cash registers, automobiles, freight trains and the like. Downey heard him repeat from memory numbers on freight trains in the order in which the train's boxcars passed him while he worked as a brakeman. The conductor had kept a written record of these numbers in a notebook and the record covered several pages, none of which the "World's Champion on Memory" had any problem recalling and reciting.

Formal testing found this man to have a visual memory span of 27 digits with only three errors. In a second testing, he studied 27 new numbers for about 70 seconds and then recited them in 28 seconds. Asked to reproduce the two sets he had memorized—54 digits in all—Downey's subject was able to recall 35 in their proper order. She considered that an extraordinary feat in view of his I.Q., which was measured at year 14 on a Terman Adult Test. While that test showed an I.Q. of 92.6, she notes that, had she used a year 12 test, it would have been lowered from that level.

Of considerable interest was the fact that his auditory memory was very poor, with a capacity of only 6 digits backward and only 8 forward, in contrast to his exceptional visual memory. He showed almost no skill in solving problems that required any reasoning ability and showed very poor facility for interpreting proverbs. His vocabulary tests showed serious limitations in comprehension and definition, with an "inclination to resort to wild guessing and his tendency to grandiloquent verbiage." Downey concludes that the secret of achievement here was an interest in numbers and the constant playing with them, which together led to an ability to handle numbers by grouping them in certain ways and then by grouping the groups into units. Numbers had become his friends.

SOME FINAL CASES

Critchley describes two cases.[32] The first is that of "a diminutive, docile, microcephalic imbecile of 72 years who had been an inmate since he was 16, was able to correlate a number of a hymn with its first line and usually with the complete text. Moreover he was able to give the dates of arrival and departure of the hospital staff who had come and gone over his 57 years' experience." The subject in the second case was able to memorize a large number of telephone numbers and recall long lists of automobile dealers and their addresses, as well as voluminous business information:

> His special abilities began to show themselves in his intense preoccupation with the New York Stock Exchange. He continued to collect thousands of magazines which he perused chiefly for their financial news. The boy was able to reel off the top 500 North American Industrials in their appropriate order; he could recite from memory their assets, turnover, dividends, share prices, the chief periodic fluctuations, the President of each company, and the main as well as the subsidiary company so often concealed beneath a proprietary name or set of initials.

Hiram Byrd describes a patient of his who was a calendar calculator but whose ability extended well beyond memorizing dates.[34] The patient was fond of music and played guitar. He met all the trains that passed through his little town of Oxford, Mississippi, and his notebook was full of locomotive engine numbers. Given the first few numbers on a page of the notebook, he would repeat all the rest of the numbers on the page without effort. Testing showed a mental age of 4. His digit span, however, was less than 5 in spite of his ability to remember numerous dates. He had committed to memory a large number of places, and as with the train numbers, he would repeat all the places he had written on a page of the notebook if he were given the first three or four places appearing on the page. Byrd's phenomenal memorizer was able to repeat a large number of county seats accurately and name capitals of a large number of states in spite of his extremely limited intelligence.

David C. Ryfe and Laurence H. Snyder list several cases as well:

In an Ohio town near us there lives a feeble-minded boy, probably of imbecile mentality, who has memorized the telephone directory, and also has a passion for learning the numbers on automobile license tags. He often performs before audiences, giving the telephone number or license tag number of local persons, when asked to do so. There lived in Indiana several years ago a boy who had an amazing capacity for remembering numbers. No data have been found in regard to his exact mental age, but judging from the records, he was probably a high grade moron. He would go to a railroad crossing, and if a freight train passed by, would be able to repeat from memory the numbers of all the cars, after it had passed. As these numbers often run up into the tens and hundreds of thousands, this was an astonishing feat, to say the least.[16]

Albert C. Cain studied the special "isolated" abilities of severely psychotic children and described many of the skills, seen here as the "islands of intelligence," so frequent in youngsters with Early Infantile Autism and other forms of severe mental disturbance.[54] He describes one such isolated ability in a patient by the name of Millie:

But Millie has a phenomenal memory. She repeats verbatim (typically not upon request) lengthy conversations or radio or TV material, often heard years before. She accurately reads and reproduces (including the spelling) virtually any word she has seen even once, including words many years beyond her age level, and quickly corrects others' misspellings of such words. She writes backward almost as readily as she writes forward. These activities rarely occur in direct correspondence with school, ward, or activity group learning situations, demands, or expectations; rather they occur when Millie is drifting about in isolated fashion, or fleetingly jamming herself into oblique object-contact, or is off on her own absorbed tangent amidst group situations.

Finally, Louise LaFontaine tells of a boy named Carl, who had the ability to remember an unusually large number of dates, as well as a variety of other information:

Carl had gained a reputation, during the twenty years he had been at the state school, for his unusual ability to remember dates, descriptive details about cars and license plate numbers. He was able to tell the examiner on two different occasions the birthdays of several (over 20)[2] people in the institution, the type of car they owned, and, in many instances, the license plate number. He also recited the birthdays of numerous TV and movie personalities, Presidents of the United States, and some prominent people in the sports world. Since a second interview with Carl was planned, he was told the birthdays of several people in the examiner's family at the end of the first interview. When asked if he recalled these dates at the time of the second interview (about three months later), he was able to answer correctly with the exception of some confusion about the individual names. He was also given a similar series of dates at the beginning of the second interview without associating the dates with any individual. When asked to repeat these dates some thirty minutes later, he was unable to give any correct answers.

Carl indicated that he practiced remembering dates, but he did not seem to know how much time he spent doing this. He did not appear to be extremely enthusiastic about his ability, and he did not actually seem to consider it an unusual thing. He was, however, quite willing to respond to all questions related to this ability, but this was in keeping with generally responsive, cooperative behavior.[55]

In a 1974 interview, this same patient was able to remember the birthdays and birthplaces of numerous movie stars and politicians.[56] He also remembered the paper route he had once had, the names of all the customers on the route, the streets of the route and the number of papers he had sold. This patient was institutionalized at age 19. His I.Q. was measured at 51 in 1968 and at 64 in a subsequent testing in 1974. In addition to his mental handicap he had a spastic paralysis of the right leg. He spent the last part of his life in a nursing home where his tremendous memory was not only a source of satisfaction and reinforcement for him, but also a source of great amazement and entertainment for the other residents.

This chapter has focused on savant cases where memory *is* the special skill and has recounted some tremendous feats of memorization. But the phenomenal memorizing ability of *all* savants is one special ability they all hold in common. Whatever sets one savant apart from another, it is the prodigious memory that welds the condition together. We will take a much closer look at memory function itself, not just the feats of memory, in a later chapter.

6

The Cats' Raphael
and Other
"Rara Avis"

Musical interest in children, whether they are of normal intelligence or are mentally handicapped, is universal. Musical ability is common. Musical genius is frequent. Not so with artistic talent. In a search for talented child artists, Florence Goodenough discovered that while child musicians were not uncommon, the child artist was a "rara avis." In her 1926 studies, which established drawing ability as one method of assessing intelligence, she noted, "In spite of careful research the writer has been unable to locate a single child under the age of 12 years whose drawings appeared to possess artistic merit of a degree at all comparable to the musical genius occasionally shown by children of this age."[57]

It is not surprising then that among savants musical genius as the special ability is quite common, but phenomenal art ability is rare. That makes the case of Nadia all the more spectacular.

Nadia appeared in the office of Elizabeth Newson at the University of Nottingham Child Development Research Unit on a January afternoon in 1973. She was 6 years old. Her mother brought along a bundle of Nadia's ball-point drawings. Newson summarized her reaction to viewing these drawings that first day: "My first reaction to the drawings was to marvel; my second, I am ashamed to say, to doubt." The case was assigned to a psychologist on duty that day, Lorna Selfe, who fortunately saw the spectacularly rare but phenomenal art ability of this very talented, but very handicapped, girl, and ultimately wrote a remarkable book about Nadia.[58]

Nadia was a child with all the signs and symptoms of Early Infantile Autism—early onset, obsessive need for sameness, ritualistic behavior, impaired socialization, echolalia and extremely limited language function. At age 6 she could not even combine two words, except in very simple phrases. She often used unintelligible jargon, had uncontrollable episodes of screaming and was destructive. That behavior alternated with mutism, excessive slowness and withdrawal. She would stare into space for long intervals or wander aimlessly around the room. She avoided eye contact and any physical contact whatsoever.

A complete medical and psychological examination in London at age 5 provided a diagnosis of "autistic behavior and possible considerable psychiatric disturbance." X-rays showed a "brachycephalic" (shorter than normal) skull. An EEG was minimally abnormal. Further testing at age 6 gave more evidence of both her handicaps and her genius. Her obsessiveness, temper, withdrawal and rituals were all mentioned and described in detail once again. Musical interest was present to some degree but there was no special musical ability. She was left-handed. One particular ritual and obsession was noted—that of cutting strips of paper into incredibly thin strips with an astounding regularity and precision. Like other autistic children she had little sense of ordinary dangers and risks and could not be trusted to keep from running into traffic or subjecting herself to other hazards.

Her drawings, at age 3, were phenomenal, not just in relation to her handicap, but in relation to any other child of any age or intelligence. Newson and Selfe, who had analyzed, categorized and rated 24,000 "pictures of mummy" that had been drawn by children throughout England for a competition and had ultimately been the basis of an exhibit on that topic presented by the British Association for the Advancement of Science, agreed that her drawing ability was extraordinary.

Nadia's drawings were inspired by pictures usually seen only once; rarely did she return to the original picture for reference. Her motor coordination was incredibly refined, and she drew rapidly, with uncanny precision, often drawing interrupted lines that she would later connect. When she drew she would place her face very close to the paper. She demonstrated an extraordinary amount of manual dexterity, particularly considering her clumsiness in many areas other than drawing. Her favorite subjects were horses, but she drew many other animals as well and some human figures. Her astonishing drawing ability revealed an accomplished sense of perspective, proportion and movement. She developed, really, a style all her own. Nadia's drawings were known for their inventiveness, for their use of shading and shadow and for the artist's ability to represent three-dimensional objects in two dimensions.

Nadia's gift was her drawing; language, or the lack of it, was her deficit. It is the absence of language in Nadia that formed Lorna Selfe's basic hypothesis about her and her extraordinary drawing ability. Selfe postulates that visual imagery is used as the initial "language" by all of us when we are children. As we mature, language becomes a "shorthand" for this visual reality, and in the developing child, mental imagery is supplanted by language and decays through lack of use. Selfe proposes that since language failed to develop in Nadia, visual imagery did not fade, but indeed developed even more fully, in her drawing, in a compensatory manner to offset her language deficit. Language was the trade-off, the price to be paid, for the spectacular drawing ability.

What would happen then if Nadia were to develop language? According to Selfe's hypothesis, the drawing skill would disappear. And that's exactly what happened with Nadia. She entered a school for autistic children at age 7 and her language, through specific strategy and effort, improved. Her special drawing ability, regretfully, vanished, as if there were indeed a trade-off. As her language increased, her drawing ability disappeared. She would seldom draw spontaneously, and when she did draw, it was without the flare, poise and skill that her earlier drawings displayed. Whether the skills "migrated" from one part of the brain to another, or whether they in fact disappeared, seemed moot—they were unavailable and absent in either event: "Sadly, Nadia seldom draws spontaneously now, although from time to time one of her horses appears on a steamed-up window!"

The postscript by Newson is poignant and to the point. "Is this a tragedy? For us who love to be astonished, maybe. For Nadia, perhaps it is enough to have been a marvelous child. If the partial loss of her gift is the price that must be paid for language—even just enough language to bring her into some kind of community of discourse with her small protected world—we must, I think, be prepared to pay that price on Nadia's behalf."

Nigel Dennis, however, in a 1978 review of the book on Nadia, asks an equally pointed question as he views this substitution of talking for drawing:

> We are left with a genius who has had her genius removed, leaving nothing but a general defectiveness. What are we supposed to think about such a curious cure? . . . How can any psychologist believe that when you are feeble-minded, it will buck you up to think that you were a world-beater at age 5? "Some kind of community of discourse with her small protected world"—what do these soapy euphemisms mean but a life confined to a mental home? As for us who "love to be astonished," it is surely our business to take a more intelligent view of what genius has to give us, and to see tragedy in its careless destruction.[59]

Whether such an actual trade-off occurred in Nadia when deliberate efforts were made to "educate" her is, of course, a crucial question in dealing with all savants. I described earlier the nonsavant attorney turned musician who lost all her musical genius when she began to study music rather than simply use the gift and talent that she had had up to that point in her life. The implications of there being such a trade-off potential in savants are rather treacherous and ominous. In the case of Nadia, could there have been an alternative explanation for the loss of her drawing ability?

It is quite clear that brain damage did exist. Selfe concludes that "it seems likely then that in Nadia's case, on the basis of her EEG report and shape of her skull, damage occurred to the temporal lobe area and specifically to the language areas located there." The EEGs that Selfe refers to showed minimal, but definite, intermediate slow activity, slightly more obvious over the right sylvian region, with some sharp elements in those areas as well. These are the speech centers of the brain. Since Nadia was left-handed the right hemisphere was likely dominant and lesions there could clearly interfere with language acquisition.

But other savants have brain damage as well and those trade-offs do not occur. Blind Tom lost his musical skills after the death of his master, and a number of other cases demonstrate an association between the death of an important person in the savant's life and the loss of savant skills. Nadia's mother died about the same time as the efforts to teach Nadia useful language began. Could the loss of her mother have been the dynamic here?

Finally, it could be that both the education venture and the mother's death were linked only coincidentally, time-wise, with the loss of these savant skills and that there exists no cause-effect relationship whatsoever. Later, we will further explore this question with respect to Nadia and the other savants since it is such an important and crucial question when determining how to approach the savant in light of such potential risks.

KIYOSHI YAMASHITA

Kiyoshi Yamashita was born in 1922 and endured a most chaotic early life that included his mother's several marriages, a disastrous earthquake and final abandonment by his mother. Yamashita was placed in a home for retarded children and it was there that his special talent became evident. He produced phenomenal paper montages. His I.Q. was measured at 68.

Yamashita was tutored intensively within the area of his skill by two well-known artists. At age 35 a booklet describing and depicting his work was published by Dr. Ryuizaburo Shikiba.[60] The skills of this savant were considered to be spectacular in their own right, not just in relation to his handicap, and critics throughout Japan considered his works to be exceptional by any standards. The press referred to him as the "van Gogh of Japan." In contrast his other behaviors were primitive and led to another press description of him—"wandering genius." He did wander about the country begging for food and sleeping wherever he could.

Ogden Lindsley explores this case in considerable depth in his article "Can Deficiency Produce Specific Superiority—The Challenge of the Idiot Savant."[61] He argues forcefully that many savants, including this one, do have superior skills that are remarkable by any standards, not just against the backdrop of mental handicap. He also rejects the "mystery" of the savant, feeling, as I do, that the savant is no more a mystery than any other unstudied phenomenon—"to call specific behavioral superiority a 'mystery' is merely to sugarcoat scientific neglect." To document this neglect Lindsley points out that, of the 1,246 listings under mental deficiency or mental retardation in *Psychological Abstracts* from 1947 through 1963, there were only two references to the idiot savant, and in a similar listing of 16,096 references in another major psychological reference work, there were only five notations on the idiot savant over a 23-year span. Regarding this scientific neglect, as well as the value of single case studies, Lindsley notes: "This ratio is more representative of the population density of idiot savants than of their scientific and social potential. . . . nature does not always yield her secrets to democratic research designs."

Lindsley holds that the superior skills of the savant are not merely compensatory nor are they the product of intense reinforcement. Rather, they are *integral* to the handicap, not a compensatory result of it. This is the result of a number of factors in the savant, including less reflex competition from other behaviors, increased reinforcing power, hypersensitivity to stimuli in the area of skill, easier behavioral choices because of lessened repertoire and fewer competing behaviors to extinguish. Lindsley argues that, rather than spare teaching the savant techniques and greater skills within his area of expertise, lest the gift be spoiled and vanish, we need to activate, encourage and actively teach the savant whatever we can to fully actualize the special talent and skill to its highest potential. Only then will the deficiency allow the superiority to be fully produced.

This is an encouraging view.

Yoshihiko Yamamoto is a renowned Japanese artist born near Nagoya City three years after World War II. [62-64] At age 6 months it became apparent that this child was hydrocephalic (having an abnormal accumulation of fluid in the brain, producing a markedly enlarged head) and seriously mentally handicapped. At age 6 he was not toilet-trained and could not talk. Because of a moderate hearing loss he was put into a school for the deaf. At age 12 his mental age was 3 and his I.Q. was measured at 23. He entered special education classes and his teacher, Takashi Kawasaki, used Yamamoto's drawing skills, then evident, as a way of trying to communicate with him. An extremely accurate sketch Yamamoto drew of Nagoya Castle was transferred to a wood block for print making. That was Yamamoto's medium! His skills accelerated rapidly. His works began to sell and his reputation spread.

As with so many other savants, Yamamoto's compulsivity and obsessive behavior were prominent. His daily schedule was absolutely rigid and precise. At age 26 his I.Q. was measured at 47, with visual perception and memory scoring above normal. Yamamoto's teacher, Kawasaki, addresses the question of why this savant draws. Is it for praise? Is it just to use his skills? Is it for enjoyment? Whatever the reason, according to Kawasaki, "it is his life. It is his spirit."[62]

Drs. Akira Morishima and Louis Brown believed that since Yamamoto's classmates, exposed to the same kind of teaching, did not progress to his level of skill, there must be something unique about Yamamoto himself that explained his talent. They found that there was in this savant above average visual perception while other cognitive functions were retarded. This single isolated cognitive ability allowed extensive development of a skill in this one area, utilizing a "narrowing of stimuli" process made possible by this particular brain pathway. Morishima and Brown felt that there was evidence of left hemisphere damage.

Yamamoto's favorite subjects were castles and ships. His very narrow attention span and the long periods he spent working on his print works, together with his constant, disciplined practice, helped produce his great works. Gradually his art skills expanded from print works to watercolors to oils and, later, to the oriental brushing used in bamboo paintings. His works gained international renown and were exhibited in the United States as well as in Japan.

SHYOICHIRO YAMAMURA—THE INSECT ARTIST

Morishima and Brown report another case of an artist savant with an atypical talent for drawing animal and insect pictures.[65] Shyoichiro Yamamura had suffered a series of very serious childhood illnesses that resulted in extremely delayed speech and language development. He did not use even single words like "mother" until he was 14. Yamamura had two interests while attending school—observing and catching insects and then drawing them. Except in this one area, his memory and attention span were extremely poor. His I.Q. was 48–53. He would often leave the classroom to chase a butterfly that flew by the window. At age 11 he was put into a special school after failing in regular classes. There his teacher was quick to identify and encourage his highly developed talent.

Yamamura remained an isolated and withdrawn child who rarely interacted with the other students. He spent hour after hour observing his insects, which he was allowed to keep in large numbers in the classroom in a specially constructed cage. At age 19 Yamamura was still unable to make his own bed or carry out other activities of daily living. A deliberate effort was made to involve him in the active and productive work of farming, rather than allow drawing to be his sole activity, so that he might support himself or contribute to his support. Interestingly, with this broadening of education, his drawing skills improved as well. He began to use new methods, including finger painting, at which he became particularly proficient. He would use his fingernails to paint minute portions of his creatures. He would replicate the insects in finest detail without patterns and without referring back to the insect itself. His motor skills improved also; he often would cut out elaborate insects less than 1 cm in size, as if to produce some of them life-size. Just as impressive as his prodigious memory for insects was his seemingly inexhaustible attention span for this one special subject, beyond which his interests were narrow to nonexistent.

Morishima and Brown use this case to inspire special education teachers to identify, nourish, encourage and enrich whatever skills exist in handicapped persons in the hopes that, as with Lindsley's patient, superiority will come from deficiency, even if in just a single area of endeavor. They do not fear a trade-off of greater general skills for lesser special talent, for in this case quite the opposite occurred—the special skill proliferated together with overall function. It is an encouraging case.

There are fewer early savant artists in the historical literature than there are other types of savants, reflecting the fact that artistic genius, unlike musical genius, is very rare. Dr. Alfred F. Tredgold does mention the drawing abilities of Pullen, the Genius of Earlswood Asylum, and of Pullen's mentally deficient brother.[12] Crayon pictures drawn by these talented savants adorned the walls of the hospital where they were residents.

But it is Gottfried Mind who is probably the most well-known and renowned artist among the savants.[12,66] Tredgold's description of Mind can hardly be improved upon, so I quote it here in its entirety:

> Occasionally the talent for drawing passes beyond mere picture-copying, and shows the presence of a real artistic capacity of no mean order. This was the case with the celebrated Gottfried Mind, who had such a marvelous faculty for drawing pictures of cats that he was known as "The Cats' Raphael." Gottfried Mind was a cretin imbecile who was born at Berne in 1768, and died in the same city at the age of forty-six years. At an early age he showed considerable talent for drawing, and as it was obvious that he would never be able to earn his living in any ordinary occupation, his father's employer interested himself in providing young Gottfried with some training. He could neither read nor write, he had no idea of the value of money, his hands were remarkable for their large size and roughness, and his general appearance was so obviously indicative of mental defect that his walks through the city were usually to the accompaniment of a crowd of jeering children. In spite of all this his drawings and water-colour sketches of not only cats, but of deer, rabbits, bears, and groups of children, were so marvelously lifelike and so skillfully executed that he acquired a European fame. One of his pictures, indeed, of a cat and kittens, was purchased by King George IV.

Several of Mind's works are presently in museums in Berlin, Zurich and Berne. In 1971 one of his works sold for 1,000 pounds Sterling, and in 1974 another sold for 550 guineas.

A MODERN-DAY STUDY

Drs. B. Hermelin and N. O. O'Connor, whose work with musical and calendar calculating savants was summarized earlier, also examined artistic savants to see whether their abilities were simply exceptional graphic and drawing skills combined with unusual rote memory, or whether these abilities also represented knowledge of and access to a "picture lexicon" comparable to that seen in skilled artists of normal or high intelligence.[67] If the artistic savant had the same "artistic intelligence" in that one narrow area as do artists of normal or high intelligence, in spite of severe defects in other areas, that would serve as some proof of the existence of separate systems of intelligence rather than intelligence that functions as, and can be measured as, a single system.

The term "picture lexicon" is used to describe the whole memory store of shapes, imagery, proportion, dimensions and spatial representations to which highly skilled artists of normal or high intelligence have been shown to have access. This unconscious store of what might be called the "rules of art" is comparable to the store of mathematics rules or music rules that is automatically accessed, in some unexplained fashion, by savants with those abilities described earlier. There are specific tests that can be used to confirm the presence or absence of this art lexicon, this store of rules of art.

Some famous nonsavant artists, including Michelangelo, Millais and Toulouse-Lautrec, showed precocious early performance linked, as in the savant, to unusually vivid visual memory. These same traits were seen in artistically gifted, mentally retarded autistic children studied by Selfe after her monumental work with Nadia. In comparing artistic ability in these children with that in normal youngsters, she found that the children in the autistic and retarded group were superior in the use of photographically realistic proportion, the representation of three-dimensional space, the depiction of size with distance and the correct drawing of occlusion and overlap of objects.[154] Further, earlier work by Hermelin and O'Connor had demonstrated that a group of artistically gifted normal children had possessed a superior visual memory and better access to a "picture lexicon" than had an I.Q.-matched but nonartistic group.[155]

To search for an artistic intelligence operating independently of I.Q. measured overall, the researchers compared five savants whose artistic output was judged to be at art school entrance level to a control group of mentally handicapped subjects who resided in similar schools or centers and were matched for mental age and diagnosis, but who showed no special art ability. The average chronological age in the savant group was 19 years and 3 months; it was 22 years and 6 months in the control group. The average I.Q.s as measured by the Columbia Mental Maturity Test were 47.4 for the artistic group and 46.2 for the control group. Matching was done on the basis of the Columbia I.Q. score and, as closely as possible, on diagnosis. Five separate tests were administered to both groups; included were a standardized draw-a-man test; a test of ability to draw abstract shapes from memory; a short-term visual memory test; a test of ability to reproduce concrete, representational (house, chair, car, tree, rural scene) drawings as compared to abstract, nonrepresentational ones; and a test for ability to identify a complete picture based on brief exposure to only portions of the total drawing. In this latter test five drawings (shoe, boat, cot, bird, goat) were presented and the subjects' task was to identify each in the least number of exposures.

In all tests the savant group was superior to the I.Q.-matched control group with no special artistic talent. Both groups did better with concrete drawings than with abstract drawings, but on those tests that did not rely simply on ability to copy, but required the use of either short-term memory or a stored "picture lexicon," the savant artists performed significantly better than did the members of the control group. Since these same two abilities are found in all artists, whether of subnormal, normal or high intelligence, they must be I.Q.-independent. In the minds of the researchers, this points toward separate systems of intelligence rather than a single system. It also, as in the case of the musical savants and calendar calculating savants, confirms the presence of and access to a complex and highly integrated body of knowledge, or "lexicon," within the narrow range of the special skill, even though such knowledge and stores of information in some or all other areas is severely limited.

The concept of a lexicon—whether musical, mathematical or artistic—is an important one because it goes well beyond the term "talent" defined only in terms of special motor or mere reproductive skills. In the case of the savant artist, the "talent" goes, for example, beyond simply having a gift of unusually facile small-muscle control in the hands and fingers, coupled with exceptional coordination. There is much more, including particularly the storage of and access to a whole complex system of information and relationships intrinsic to the structure and performance of art, a storage and access shared by equally skilled artists not impaired in general intelligence overall.

RICHARD WAWRO—WITH EYES WIDE OPEN

Finally there is Richard Wawro, a modern-day Gottfried Mind.[68,69] At the time of this writing Wawro is 33 years old, legally blind and diabetic. When Richard was 3 years old, his parents were told that he was moderately to severely retarded, with an I.Q. estimated at about 30. He also showed considerable autistic behavior, with the characteristic obsession for sameness, withdrawal and bizarre mannerisms. As a child his behavior showed constant hyperactivity with yelling, screaming and violent temper tantrums, alternating with mutism. He did not have useful language until age 11. He required a number of surgeries for cataracts on both eyes during his childhood. Ritualistic behavior included, according to his father, twirling while walking, a preoccupation with crawling to the piano and striking one key for hours at a time and spinning objects endlessly.

Richard began drawing at age 3 when he was given chalk and a slate in a neighbor's kitchen. He immediately covered the tiny chalkboard with numerous images. At age 6 he entered a center for emotionally disturbed children near his home in Edinburgh, Scotland. There he was introduced to drawing with crayons, and his talent became immediately apparent. When Richard was 12 years old, Marian Bohusz-Szyszko of the Polish School of Art in London viewed Wawro's drawings and was "thunderstruck"; she described the works as an "incredible phenomenon rendered with the precision of a mechanic and the vision of a poet."

Richard's sole medium is oil-bound crayon. He uses literally boxes and boxes of Swiss oil crayons to create his pictures, which, remarkable in their depth and color, may be drawn on cards as small as $5'' \times 7''$ or may be landscapes as large as $17'' \times 24''$. He does not sharpen his crayons but achieves remarkable detail and precision by using the edge of a crayon as it naturally develops. He uses layer after layer of crayon in some scenes to achieve the rich color, deep texture and delicate shadings he seeks. The final touch is a buffing motion with a white cloth to obtain the sheen his pictures all have, as if they have been sprayed with lacquer. Because he is so severely nearsighted he draws with his face only inches away from the paper. His drawings can take a few moments to several days to complete, depending on their size and complexity.

At the completion of each drawing, Richard takes it to his father for approval and then receives appropriate and deserved compliments, followed by a mini-celebration, in which he and his father raise joined hands in a sort of present-day high-five, as if he had just become world boxing champion. They hug and dance around the room together. As often as that has been done—1,600 of Richard's drawings have now been cataloged and exhibited worldwide—it is as real, warm and spontaneous as if each time were the first. He and his father share an unmistakable enthusiasm and appreciation for each other. Richard's mother, who loved and appreciated him unconditionally, died in 1979. In spite of their closeness, Richard did not stop his work upon her death.

Like other savants, Richard has a phenomenal memory. He remembers where he drew each of his pictures and has each of them precisely dated in his mind. He uses no models for his drawings, but draws from his memory of images seen only once, on television or in a book at one of the bookstores he loves to visit. Or, perhaps he will draw from memory a landscape scene he has viewed through the binoculars he uses to hone his vision. While he has perfect recall, as demonstrated in many of his pictures, he often adds his own touches, interpretations or improvisations to the images. He seems especially fascinated with light—its source and its dispersion—and the tones he uses to capture lights and shadows are masterful.

For Richard, art is his life and his love. He works intensely and obsessively. He takes pride in his talent and loves to share it.

Richard had his first exhibition at the Demarco Gallery in Edinburgh when he was 17 years old. He is now known worldwide; he has sold over 1,000 pictures and has had works in more than 100 exhibitions. One of his exhibitions in London was opened by Margaret Thatcher when she was Minister of Education. She owns several of Richard's works and ranks him as one of her favorite artists. Pope John Paul II likewise owns several of Richard's drawings. Richard's first U.S. showing was in November 1977 during a conference on creativity in gifted and talented children held in New York City. Prices of his works range from $100 to $2,000.

A most impressive and moving documentary film entitled *With Eyes Wide Open*, produced by Dr. Laurence Becker of Austin, Texas, had its world premiere in Austin on May 15, 1983. It has since won numerous awards worldwide. The film grew out of Becker's special interest in the gifted and talented. In the film some of Richard's autistic and ritualistic behavior is still evident, as are his serious language difficulties, but those limitations are dwarfed by the genius so prominent in Richard Wawro. Any hesitations that one might experience, after the case of Nadia, to encourage the savant to excel, to acquire language and to practice and perfect his or her talent have been dispersed by Richard Wawro. As his art has developed, so have his language and socialization. There has been no trade-off. He is more effective in both now than he was seven or eight years ago. He recently has learned to sign his name, something that, given his art talent, one would have thought would have come easily. It did not come easily, but it did come. He is proud to be able to do that; his progress is refreshing and inspiring. Yet his pictures really need no signature; they are so distinctive and individual that they are like a signature—the fingerprints of a genius.

Significant, I believe, to Richard's growth as a person and an artist, is the unconditional acceptance he received, beginning with that of his parents, who like many parents of savants looked beyond the grim prognosis and continued to tend to that which was right with Richard instead of despairing over that which was wrong. Becker's description of Richard's parents, and his summary, says it best:

Richard's Polish father is a great storyteller and a gentle tease. His Scottish mother in manner and tone and twinkle of eye reflects the quiet, sensitive, and sensible charm of this warm people. Richard's parents have provided an atmosphere rich in caring, in enduring, in continuing to do what is necessary, ever holding the wonder and beauty and mystery of his incredible life very carefully, almost reverently, if not a bit fearfully, in their hands. His spirit which for so long was buried deep within has been carefully nurtured by a quiet strength which trusted its own instincts, by a patient strength which endured without always knowing why, and by a gentle strength which continued to love without a single guarantee that even one flower (let alone over 1,600) would ever come into being.

To walk into a room at an exhibition and to be surrounded by Richard's pictures is to share in his search for the light. To join, even briefly, with him and to look at a new kind of world through the eyes of one who receives his gift of sight, severely limited though it may be, with eyes wide open is to rejoice and be glad that his eyes have enabled us to see so much more clearly than we ever imagined before the beauty and wonder in the ordinary world which daily surrounds us.

7

From Mr. A to Mr. Z: Other Savant Skills

The vast majority of savant skills fall into the categories described in the preceding chapters. There are, however, some assorted, less common skills that deserve mention and description.

MECHANICAL ABILITY: EARL

James Henry Pullen, the Genius of Earlswood Asylum (described in Chapter 1), might be considered "the dean of mechanical savants." But there were others. Earl, described by Arthur Phillips in 1930 as one of his "talented imbeciles," had an I.Q. of 65.[45] At age 11 he was learning at a second-grade level. Phillips describes Earl as having a "sugar-loaf head," small and coming to a rounded peak at the top. His walk was impaired, he had a stooped posture and, in the clinic, he was "the picture of apathy." He was, however, well-behaved and easily managed and seemed quite content. Earl had mechanical talent out of proportion to his intellectual and speech limitations. At one point, without suggestion or help from anyone, he took a clock apart and rigged it up as a windmill, which ran very well. His performance on all subtests for language and comprehension placed him inferior to 99 percent of 10-year-old boys. However, on tests of mechanical ability, dexterity and mechanical comprehension, he did unexpectedly well—in one of those subtests, which often gave college students difficulty, he placed in the upper 99 percent of persons his age. In tests of concrete material (pictures of specific objects) and discrimination of form, Earl displayed intelligence, efficiency and superior ability.

Earl was able to make a model ferry boat out of wood after seeing a picture in a newspaper. He could draw blueprints of airplanes and boats with excellent coordination and detail, and he had an uncommon amount of knowledge about the parts and the operation of such vehicles. "His interest in mechanical matters is in striking contrast to his lack of interest in the things which ordinarily absorb the attention of a boy 10 or 11," notes Phillips, who suggests vocational training as an approach here rather than traditional efforts to teach language, reading and arithmetic. Specifically, he deplores methods of teaching that attempt "to eliminate the defects rather than training the talent," noting that some teachers prefer to make a deliberate effort to keep the child from doing what he likes to do and to require him to do what he does not like to do.

In concluding his comments on this case Phillips holds out a note of optimism and practicality regarding the mechanical savant. Contrasting Earl with his two other cases of "intellectual talent," Phillips notes that mechanical ability, even though coupled with severe intellectual deficit, "may fill a place in life while one who is a mental imbecile with a prodigious intellectual talent may fail to do so." Phillips then provides a prognosis: "Earl's mechanical talent combined with his social conformity gives him a place to stand and a niche to fill in human society."

MECHANICAL ABILITY: THE CASE OF MR. A.

Dr. Edward Hoffman and Russell Reeves, in 1979, described a patient they named Mr. A. as a case of unusual mechanical ability in a moderately retarded, institutionalized man.[70] The oldest of several children, Mr. A. had a normal birth and delivery. Developmental milestones were somewhat slowed in that he was weaned at 18 months, was toilet-trained at 30 months and began to dress himself at 40 months. He did not speak until age 10. Although he did attend school he did not learn to read or write and was unable to sign his own name. At 18 he had an infection that permanently damaged hearing in both ears. At that time he was placed in a state institution. His I.Q. was measured at 40, with a mental age of 6 years 5 months. His diagnosis was "cerebral defect, congenital."

During the 27 years that he was institutionalized, between 1950 and 1977, intelligence tests typically placed his I.Q. at 50 to 65 with much better performance scores than verbal scores. He was able to meet his self-care needs, tell time and make change, but although he did eventually learn to write his name, he was still unable to read or write anything else. In the institution Mr. A. repaired clocks, appliances and bicycles for other residents. He was able to disassemble and clean various types of equipment, run the film projector and build furniture and lamps. Almost all his time was spent in his mechanical pursuit. He received much praise and attention from other residents and staff members and was proud of his talents. Except with respect to his mechanical ability, his behavior was quite typical of persons of his limited mental capacity.

In 1978 Hoffman and Reeves set up some specific tests to assess his mechanical abilities. In one he was given a broken electric alarm clock to repair, and in another he was given a ten-speed bicycle that was broken in several places; he repaired both, easily and quickly. Hoffman and Reeves concluded that the tremendous reinforcement that the patient received as a result of his skill served to continually strengthen his mechanical abilities, which he perfected and honed through constant practice and performance. The researchers felt that external factors here, particularly the reinforcement, were crucial in this and other cases of Savant Syndrome. They concluded that the requisite conditions for Savant Syndrome were: (a) a minimal cognitive level of functioning; (b) intense practice and motivation; (c) strong reinforcement to develop and maintain the unusual ability; and (d) an idiosyncratic pattern of intellectual performance, as shown in this case, with superior aptitude and preference for mechanical tasks.

MECHANICAL ABILITY: MR. Z.

As a challenge to the Hoffman and Reeves explanation, psychologist T. L. Brink presented the case of Mr. Z. to demonstrate that the key to Savant Syndrome lay outside environmental factors, involving rather an organic etiology, specifically right brain/left brain dichotomy.[71] This particular theory will be discussed in more detail later. The case of Mr. Z. is interesting not only from this theoretical standpoint but because it is a case of acquired savantism with specific etiology and a localized brain lesion.

Mr. Z. was a middle child with eight brothers and sisters. His birth and childhood were normal and he seemed to be of average intelligence. He began school at age 7 and progressed rapidly. His father had a good deal of mechanical ability and was well-known for his ingenious design of the family home and his ability to repair almost any kind of device. When Mr. Z. was 9 years old his father was murdered and during the gunfire the boy suffered a wound from a small caliber pistol. The bullet entered the left temple at the hairline and exited through the back of the head. For two years Mr. Z. was mute, deaf and paralyzed on the right side. He gradually regained his hearing and the use of his limbs. Speech returned more slowly.

When Mr. Z. did regain speech he had completely shed the dialect of the region of his birth. He also had forgotten how to read, write and do arithmetic. He did manage to relearn the alphabet and learned how to write letters with his left hand. He was able to copy pages of written material but was unable to complete words or sign his name without a model to follow. He responded to questions in a very slow manner, taking long pauses as he looked for the next word, and seemed to be incapable of abstract thinking.

Mr. Z. found full-time employment alternately as a ranch hand, a gardener and a factory worker. His right side had less muscular development, poorer coordination and less sensation than his left side. Nevertheless, he learned to ride a bicycle. When he and his family moved to a strange community he never got lost, although he could not remember street names. According to Brink, Mr. Z.'s gardening, carpentry and mechanical talents were "outstanding." He could dismantle, reassemble and modify multi-gear bicycles. He designed a punching bag that would simulate the bobbing and weaving action of a live opponent. He was able to accurately copy pictures. He developed a repertoire of tricks with strings and small objects, which he demonstrated to others. Although the tricks seemed simple, no one else was able to do them.

Brink notes that Mr. Z. was a man of high motivation and intense practice. Like Mr. A., he received much reinforcement from family and teachers. Brink concludes that Mr. Z.'s unusual mechanical abilities "can perhaps be traced to heredity, an undamaged right hemisphere, and, of course, sufficient motivation, practice, and reinforcement. Whether such abilities were inherited or whether they were due to some form of overcompensation (an injury to the left hemisphere stimulated the increased development of the right hemisphere) cannot be inferred from this case." Brink further concludes that the case of Mr. Z., while closely paralleling that of Mr. A., more clearly supports *organic* factors rather than the purely environmental factors suggested by Hoffman and Reeves in their study. The fact that the savantism was acquired, and that a discrete lesion limited to one hemisphere was present, has many etiologic implications, which will be discussed later.

UNUSUAL SENSORY DISCRIMINATION

In some savants the special talent consists of an extraordinary sensitivity or sensory perception. Dr. Alfred F. Tredgold refers to Jules Voisin's case of a patient with a "wonderful delicacy of smell."[12] Tredgold also cites one of Dr. J. Langdon Down's cases—a "boy at Normansfield whose sense of touch was so delicate and fingers so deft that he could take a page of the Graphic and gradually split it into two perfect sheets, as one would peel a postage stamp off an envelope."[1]

Drs. Paul Bergman and Sibylle Escalona of the Menninger Foundation described unusual sensitivities—visual, auditory, tactile, olfactory—in very young children who, they learned in later follow-ups, developed psychosis.[72] In their report exploring the relationship between unusual early sensitivities and psychosis they gave several interesting examples. Some of the children they described were clearly autistic with savant skills. One had an unusual ritual of smelling everything and seemed intensely aware of all odors. He would smell his own clothing and he loved perfumes and powders. He was aware of his mother's smell when she came from the kitchen or other places. Another had a very acute sense of smell and was unusually discriminating with respect to the taste of foods. Still others showed unusual sensitivity to sound, light and/or touch, but the presence in all the cases of unusual olfactory discrimination is of particular interest.

Dr. William A. Horwitz, in his study of the savant twins Charles and George, comments on their unusually sensitive sense of smell: "Clinically both seem hyperosmic; frequently both go up to people sniffing and smelling. Although each can pick out his own shoes and bedroom slippers by smell, on quantitative smell tests neither performed better than average."[27]

EXTRASENSORY PERCEPTION

Dr. Bernard Rimland describes several instances of extrasensory perception in his autistic savants.[4] In his sample of approximately 5,400 autistic children, 561 cases, or approximately 10 percent, were reported to have special abilities. Four of the 561 cases were based on reports from parents who claimed that their child had consistently exhibited signs of extrasensory perception. In one case, the parent reported that "teachers have also noticed that George probably has ESP. He seems to be very psychic. We would decide to pick up George from school suddenly, if we were in the area (he usually rode the bus). He would tell the teacher we were coming, and he would come to open the door when we arrived. So he has many special abilities, but cannot write his name or write a sentence." Two other reports made by parents describe children with, in one case, "an extraordinary ability to hear conversations out of range of hearing, and to pick up thoughts not spoken" and, in another case, "verified ESP . . . first observed around age 4." The child in the latter case "accurately related an accidental occurrence known only to her father. His watch crystal fell out in the bathroom and was immediately replaced. Michelle accurately related the entire incident back to her father a short time thereafter. Several dozens of similar 'clairvoyant' instances have occurred since this first incident. Statistical probability of coincidental knowledge nil."

The parents of Ellen, a blind musical savant who is described in detail later, report three instances of unusual perception on her part. One perhaps could be explained by heightened auditory discrimination: In that instance the driver of the special bus that picks her up each day to take her to her classes gave the usual very brief horn beep when picking her up one morning. Instantly Ellen said, "New bus." On checking, it was determined that indeed a different—and new—bus was waiting. The difference in the sounds of the horns was imperceptible to her parents. The other instances are more difficult to explain. One week before Christmas she announced what would be in her gift packages, although she really had no way of knowing and had not been given any clues as to what those gifts might be. Another instance had to do with a telephone call. Ellen's sister, for a variety of reasons, always calls her parents' home during the day and, only under special circumstances, does she call in the evening. At supper time one evening Ellen told her parents that her sister would be calling. Her mother assured her, for the above reasons, that there would be no such call. Shortly thereafter the telephone rang and Ellen answered it, knowing it would be her sister, who it was. The sister had been called out of town unexpectedly and wanted her parents to know that. Ellen somehow knew that the call was coming.

A PRECISE SENSE OF TIME

Ellen also possesses an uncanny sense of time. She is able to tell exactly what time it is without ever having been exposed to a clock with braille hands. She also will bolt down the stairs at certain intervals, exact intervals, to listen to radio or television commercials at the precise moment they are aired. As described in more detail later, the sudden acquisition of that skill is even more puzzling. It occurred at age 8 when Ellen's mother tried to help Ellen overcome her strong fear of the telephone. Her mother coaxed her to listen to the "Time Lady." After listening for less than ten minutes Ellen returned to her room where she mimicked what she had just heard. She correctly continued on, after the last minute-and-seconds reading of the hour, to the next hour: when she came to "one fifty-nine and fifty-nine seconds," Ellen correctly stated, "The time is . . . two o'clock." During the time Ellen had listened to the taped message there had been no change from one hour to the next so no explanation exists as to how she was able to sense and then carry out that time transition.

Down, in his original description of the idiot savant, describes a similar case:

> This was the case of a boy who had a very unusual faculty of which I have never met another example, Viz. the perfect appreciation of past or passing time. He was 17 years of age, and although not understanding, so far as I could gather, the use of a clock-face, could tell the time to a minute at any part of the day, and in any situation. I tried him on numbers plus occasions, and he always answered with a great amount of precision truly remarkable. Gradually his response became less ready and he would not or could not reply unless he was a little excited. He had to be shaken like an old watch, and then the time would be truly given. Gradually his health became enfeebled and the faculty departed. At an autopsy I found that there was no difference in his cerebrum from an ordinary brain, except that he had two well-marked distinct soft commissures. My explanation of the phenomenon was that every movement in the house was punctual and he had data from which he could estimate the time by accurate appreciation of its flux.[1]

SENSE OF DIRECTION

Numerous investigators have described, if only incidentally, the precise sense of direction that many savants have, manifested in a rather astonishing ability to get from one place to another through complicated routes. The routes are usually remembered with exact precision many years later even if they have not been traveled for a long period of time. When musical savant Leslie Lemke and I appeared on the *AM Chicago* show in 1985 we were joined by a savant who was a map memorizer. He was 18, and although he was clearly autistic, he had memorized the highway atlas of the entire United States. He could recite, with the detail and precision of a premapped route from a travel club, the route from any one point in America to any other point. On this particular show, host Oprah Winfrey asked him how she might get from Chicago to Charlotte, North Carolina. He described in rapid-fire, staccato fashion a route that began at the Loop in downtown Chicago and then followed various interstates. He included instructions on when to make left and right turns as he gave directions—I-90 to Gary, Indiana, then a right down I-65 to Louisville, a left on I-64, etc.—until the directions ended on I-75 in Charlotte, N.C. The entire recitation took less than 30 seconds.

A letter I received from a woman about her 70-year-old relative, who was living in a home for the mildly retarded, pointed out that same skill. She indicated that his outstanding ability was his memory, which enabled him, among other things, to calendar calculate. With respect to a sense of direction, however, she stated, "When a teenager he would go for long walks, be gone all day, and when he got back home he would recite exactly where he went, block for block, in a zigzag route all over the city where they lived. He always came back the same way he went. . . . [When he was] a very small child this particular trait showed up when, on our family excursions to our favorite park, he insisted we go home the way we went, and if we diverted he would lie down on the sidewalk and refuse to budge."

Rimland remarks on that ability in some of his autistic savants by giving a case example: "If we travel in summer to the country, and we have made the trip before, Herbert can lead you to the Lodge; i.e., when you leave the highway and must find the way here and there down dirt roads, etc., he can name every curve, every street you will pass, every landmark, and do this without error."[4]

GENIUS AMONG US

It is remarkable that, with all the skills in the human repertoire, savant skills fall into the few narrow areas we have looked at. Surely there must be some thread of commonality that links these seemingly disparate talents. It seems fitting that the particular skills in this chapter occurred in savants from Mr. A. to Mr. Z. because the first portion of this book was intended to survey a whole century of savants, from A to Z. By bringing all these savant cases together, finally, all in one place, we have been able to better view them, collectively. Common characteristics and striking similarities have become apparent, and some threads of etiology have begun to emerge.

The savants are geniuses among us. They have brightened our world with their skills—through their drawings, their music and their sculptures. But they have taught us something else as well—that great gifts and talent can coexist with disease and defect; that focusing on strengths is more important than resigning to weaknesses; that labels confine but belief propels; and that unconditional love may be a strong remedy for untoward circumstance.

They can teach us more, I am convinced. If we can understand them better, we can understand ourselves better. In the second part of this book we will explore that possibility. But, before we do that, I would like to share with you portraits of three remarkable living savants, in more depth than has been possible in the chapters thus far. These portraits—of Leslie, Ellen and Alonzo—will reveal more clearly the human side, rather than just the scientific or historic significance, of these extraordinary people.

TWO

PORTRAITS

8

Leslie

The mailbox had a big red bow tied on it just as Joe told me it would. I had called him the night before and said I would be driving over the next day from Fond du Lac because I wanted to meet his son Leslie. Could he give me directions? He gave directions and said I couldn't miss the place because he would tie a big red bow on the mailbox. Now, sure enough, there it was. I guess I wouldn't have missed the place anyway because the inexhaustible, unmistakable May Lemke was walking up the sidewalk from the road to the cottage. Leslie was right behind her.

The cottage on Lake Pewaukee was small and modest but eminently cozy; it seemed just right for May, who was equally tiny. Joe was proud of the garden, the view and the lake. Leslie was sitting in a chair in what was now a music room, once a porch. He sat motionless and silent but he looked contented and at ease. He echoed my name, literally, when May told him who I was. Then he sat motionless and mute once again. May could hardly wait for him to play for me. She was so proud. Although he is blind he moved by himself, feeling his way, from the chair to the piano.

Then he played. I don't recall what the song was but I do recall what I felt—astonishment, fascination and inspiration. I still feel those three things now, many years and many tunes later, whenever I see and hear Leslie play. Here was Leslie with his triple handicap—blindness, retardation and cerebral palsy—playing, for this audience of three, a concert worthy of an audience of a thousand. Piece after piece poured forth: hymns, concertos, arias, popular songs and pop, and imitations of singers. Some pieces he sang; some he just played. Some were in English, some in German and some in Greek. To many May danced. The tapes I had seen of Leslie may have faithfully captured the sight and the sound, but they had failed to convey his presence and spirit and the thrill of being there and witnessing, firsthand, this unbelievable dichotomy of handicap and giftedness.

When sitting Leslie was silent, slowed and slouched; when playing he was alert, alive and animated. The spasticity that was so evident when he just sat disappeared as he played. His use of the pedal consisted of putting it down when he began to play and letting it up when he had finished. His singing was just as unmodulated, with little subtlety and innuendo, but with much enthusiasm and gusto. The concert seemed effortless, and while Leslie showed little emotion at other times, now he displayed a sense of real enjoyment. While there seemed to be little expression woven into the songs themselves, the emotion and joy he felt in playing them was evident and obvious. Clearly Leslie loved what he was doing.

May told me this was the third or fourth piano Leslie had worn out. He played hard and he played long, striking rather than touching the keys so that the music roared forth. The pieces ended as abruptly as they began. Between them Leslie was silent again, waiting for a prompting from May as to what to play next. As vast as his repertoire was, he did not move spontaneously from piece to piece. He was a slave to clues from outside himself, and May provided those clues.

When the concert was over Leslie was silent again. So was the house and the lake and the neighborhood, all of which had been audience to this remarkable afternoon concert. There were concerts like this almost every afternoon and evening for a most appreciative audience—May, Joe and Leslie. And sometimes for visitors like myself, or for whole auditoriums full of people. That didn't seem to make any difference to Leslie. He enjoyed each concert equally. Leslie never practiced. He didn't have to because he always got it right the first time. Each time he played, it was a performance—of a most spectacular phenomenon.

Leslie is the most remarkable savant I have ever met, or read about, or studied. He was born prematurely in Milwaukee on January 31, 1952. His mother gave him up for adoption at birth. He spent his first months of life at Milwaukee County Children's Home. There it was noticed that the baby did not open his eyes, which were swollen and hard, with a cloudy cornea. The doctors made a diagnosis of retrolental fibroplasia, a condition often seen in premature babies (Leslie was 5 lb., 3 oz. at birth) in which the retina proliferates wildly and sometimes, as in this case, blocks drainage in the eye, creating childhood glaucoma or a condition called "buphthalmos." At age 4 months the left eye had to be removed. Six weeks later the right eye was surgically removed because of the glaucoma and fear that the eye would burst. That was the source of Leslie's blindness.

Soon thereafter, at age 6 months, this frail and pathetic baby was put into the care of a remarkable woman. May Lemke was then age 52. She had been a nurse/governess and had developed a reputation for the extraordinary skill and love she showed in caring for children, handicapped or well. She was called by the Social Services Department of Milwaukee County, and without a moment's hesitation, May took on the role of foster mother, tutor, therapist, mentor, model, cheerleader and inspiration to this blind, palsied and intellectually handicapped little boy. May Lemke was to Leslie Lemke what Anne Mansfield Sullivan was to Helen Keller. One definition of love is "unconditional positive regard." May, with her Leslie, exemplifies that.

At age 2½ Leslie was sitting up and crawling. A doctor who visited Leslie at that time noted that the child could sing and was speaking clearly but seemed preoccupied and distant. Questions were raised about his being slow; "opinion reserved," the doctor noted cautiously.

At age 3 a neurology consultant noted several interesting things, among them spasticity and difficulty in walking. Certain abnormal reflexes confirmed the diagnosis of a "spastic paraplegia" thought to be due to a birth injury. Also noted was a tendency to repeat phrases, a trait called "echolalia." A year and a half later the doctor noted that Leslie talked freely but, for the most part, repeated conversation. He was able, however, to go to a play refrigerator and name imaginary contents.

Mary Larsen, May's younger daughter, remembers those early years when Leslie came to live with May and Joe Lemke. She remembers Leslie being so tiny, hardly able to cry or move or even swallow. May tended him lovingly with a conviction and belief that never wavered. She believed with all her being—all 4½ feet of it—that God would make Leslie strong and well. By age 5½, Mary remembers, Leslie was walking. While he did not volunteer speech, he could repeat *verbatim* a whole day's conversation, impersonating each individual speaker, using a high-pitched or low-pitched voice, depending on gender. One evening, when Leslie was about the same age, he was found under a bed strumming the bedsprings, as if they were an instrument, in an almost driven, rhythmic way.

A visit to the doctor at that age, 5½, confirmed Leslie's ability to walk. He was also singing songs, could repeat the Pledge of Allegiance and was able to say his prayers. The doctor noted that Leslie's vocabulary was good but that his conversation was repetitious rather than social. While he gave an occasional direct answer, he generally replied by repeating the question. Leslie was constantly active on that visit to the doctor and showed "inexhaustible restlessness." A prognostication was made which, fortunately and miraculously, never came true: "Foster mother has done well, very well, with him but a time will come when institutional placement will be necessary." That time never came. For Leslie that time will never come because of a family that is as dedicated as Leslie is remarkable.

Between ages 7 and 8 Leslie was given a piano. May played and sang for him. She would run his fingers up and down the keyboard so he could identify the notes. Like mother, like son—both played by ear and played very well. By age 8 Leslie played other instruments as well, including bongo drums, ukelele, concertina, xylophone and accordion. The doctor noted on Leslie's annual visit that year that the check-ups were becoming more social visits and less medical consultations as May brought in reports of Leslie's abilities and progress. The doctor's notes of those visits give as much insight into May as into Leslie, recounting, for example, May's theory that the phases of the moon have a clear effect on Leslie's manageability. The doctor's notes from Leslie's checkup at age 8 also indicate that Leslie was quite jumpy, but speculate that this trait might have been acquired from May, who was also quite hyperactive. Although the doctor noted that Leslie was still repeating rather than answering questions, May volunteered that Leslie did better in conversation at home than in the doctor's office. On that same visit, Leslie sang for the doctor and played with the tongue blade, beat time to music and recited some rock and roll song titles. In an indication of how closely May controlled Leslie's day-to-day life, May made it clear that Leslie can have dessert at times, but that was limited to chocolate ice cream as his only delicacy.

By age 9 Leslie had learned to play the chord organ. Medical notes indicate that, at age 10½, Leslie was still not conversant, except for repetition and imitation. He required help in dressing himself. He could not feed himself anything that required the use of utensils.

By the time Leslie was 12 his piano playing and singing were beautiful. Mary recalls Leslie's wonderful soprano voice and regrets that it was never recorded, for such a tape would be a treasure, indeed. He especially loved country and western songs, but "Batman's Theme Song" was clearly his favorite, and he played it like a professional. He loved music and would listen, sitting with his characteristic posture, for hours and hours to records and the radio.

One evening, when Leslie was about 14, he watched a movie on television called *Sincerely Yours,* starring Dorothy Malone and Basil Rathbone. May and Joe watched it too but then retired. At about 3:00 A.M. May awoke, thinking that Joe had left the television on. She went to the living room to check. There sat Leslie. He had crawled over to the piano and was playing Tchaikovsky's Piano Concerto No. 1—the theme song to *Sincerely Yours*—vigorously and flawlessly. Leslie had heard it one time. That was sufficient. He played it through from beginning to end.

To this day, if you ask Leslie to play that piece, you get not only the song, but the whole television introduction, mimicked exactly as he heard it in true echolalic fashion: "Tonight's movie is *Sincerely Yours*, starring Dorothy Malone and Basil Rathbone. As he falls in love with the beautiful black-haired woman.... [you can hear in the background the beautiful strains of Tchaikovsky's Piano Concerto No. 1] And now, the Sunday Night Movie is proud to present. . . ." Usually there is no stopping Leslie once he begins. He's like a juke box: you put in your quarter and you hear the whole song. Until recently the *Sincerely Yours* recitation and lengthy piece were virtually unstoppable. (That was a real hazard during Leslie's live television appearances where time was so very limited.) Leslie can now be persuaded to stop, or at least to bring the piece to an end more quickly, with a gentle tap on the shoulder from Mary.

Leslie has a wide repertoire of classics now but that important one— the one in which his miracle "came into full bloom," as his family says—is still the most impressive and the most moving.

Leslie was 22 years old when, in 1974, he gave his first public concert at the Waukesha County Fair, a few miles from his home. He played and sang his hymns and did his Louie Armstrong and Tiny Tim imitations. He was a smash hit. He was "incredible," the newspaper said. As would occur at all his concerts to follow, the members of the audience at the Waukesha County Fair shook their heads in astonishment and wiped tears from their eyes as he sang his favorite hymns and closed his premiere concert with "Everything is Beautiful!"

It was on Leslie's visit to Fond du Lac in 1980 to present a concert in honor of the foster parents of Fond du Lac County that I first met him. As I mentioned earlier, that concert was also his television debut and national press debut, both of which gave him instant visibility and made him a subject of national interest.

That Christmas season, on December 19, the *CBS Evening News with Walter Cronkite* closed its program on Leslie with these words: "This is a season that celebrates a miracle, and this story belongs to the season. It's the story of a young man, a piano and a miracle." In November 1980 staff from the television show *That's Incredible* had come to Pewaukee and to Fond du Lac to film a segment on Leslie, which aired the following January. Leslie became nationally known and May was deluged with letters, calls and visitors who dropped by the little house on the lake. She loved it; she was so proud.

Staff from the television show *Donahue* saw *That's Incredible*, and in February 1983 Leslie appeared as Donahue's guest. The show that day was as much about May as it was about Leslie. Phil Donahue had a real challenge in keeping May from taking over the show as she wandered about the stage, bubbly and enthusiastic, sharing her "miracle of Leslie" with the audience, her portable microphone trailing behind wherever she went. She gave new meaning to the term "wired for sound." Donahue seemed both astounded and relieved when the hour was over. The audience was similarly astounded and astonished at Leslie's remarkable skills, just as I had been the evening before when, at dinner with Leslie and the Lemkes, we had a Greek waiter who, at May's request, sang some songs in his native language. Leslie had never heard them before. On the way back to the room we came across a piano in the lobby. Leslie not only transposed those songs, in perfect pitch, to the piano, but he sang them back in Greek, exactly as he had heard them.

Leslie's next television appearance was in a *60 Minutes* segment on Savant Syndrome, hosted by Morley Safer. The show, which featured savants George, Alonzo Clemons, and Leslie, aired for the first time on October 23, 1983, and has been rerun many times since then. Safer rates this as one of his ten best pieces. When I went to New York to film my part of that segment, I saw in Safer, the editor and the rest of the crew the same incredulous head shaking and head scratching that I had seen so many times before in people witnessing savant skills for the first time.

Since the *60 Minutes* show, Leslie has been on morning shows in San Diego, Chicago, New York and other cities and on numerous other cable and network shows, sometimes alone and sometimes with other savants. Two of those appearances particularly stick in my mind. One in New York, featuring both Leslie and savant sculptor Alonzo Clemons, was especially touching as Alonzo unveiled his "You Light Up My Life" statue of a colt, which was inspired by hearing Leslie sing that song during one of his earlier television appearances. The other was Leslie's appearance with Oprah Winfrey on *AM Chicago*. The director made the mistake of asking Leslie to play "Rhapsody in Blue"—a very long number—as an opening piece to the program. Leslie doesn't stop for commercial breaks; he plays a whole piece from beginning to end without stopping. I remember seeing the director in a corner of the stage, eyes upward, hands folded, seeming to ask for divine intervention so that there could be a commercial break *sometime* before the program ended.

In 1984 when Leslie gave a command performance for Crown Prince Harold and Crown Princess Sonja in Norway, he met the famed Norwegian pianist Kjell Baekkelund. Baekkelund noted that, to his amazement, Leslie plays with only nine fingers, the little finger on the left hand being relatively useless. He challenged Leslie with Grieg's "To the Spring" composition and put in a deliberate mistake. Leslie played that complex piece back after that single hearing with his usual precision, in this case, mistake and all.

Concert audiences are amazed by Leslie's prodigious memory. After a single hearing of a 45-minute opera tape he can transpose the music to the piano and also sing the score back, in the foreign language in which he heard it. (In addition to recalling music, Leslie delights in reciting any of numerous television commercials, word for word, complete with the announcer's inflection, pauses and emphasis. He has, as well, recall of numerous phone numbers that he has committed to memory, through listening, over the years.)

Leslie's songs are stored indefinitely. I was at a concert he gave for some schoolchildren in 1983. The music teacher who had invited Leslie had him join her in a piano duet called "Canadian Capers." The teacher played Leslie's part for him once and then played her part while Leslie played his newly learned part. They played it together one time. In 1985 Leslie returned to the school, and they played the duet again after a two-year gap during which Leslie had not repeated the piece. In 1986, at a concert Leslie gave at a church camp, the same music teacher asked Leslie to join her in that same duet. He had not had occasion to play that piece in the intervening year, yet when she sat down and played her part, Leslie joined in without hesitation, recalling his part immediately and playing it without error.

At a subsequent concert he demonstrated another remarkable ability. A woman came up during the challenge portion of the concert and sang a solo without accompaniment, a fairly lengthy piece called "Where Is Love?" Leslie, after that single hearing, played it back without error in the same pitch that it had been sung in. The soloist then sang the same number, but this time Leslie accompanied her in perfect pitch, tempo and tune—without flaw.

During the challenge portion of Leslie's concerts, individuals from the audience sing or play something on an instrument and challenge Leslie to reproduce their piece, or they request specific songs. It is essential that the requests be made in written form—if they are shouted out, Leslie programs them in his head in the order received and cannot, or will not, stop playing, whether he is at a concert hall or at home, until he has played every one. When they are written down he can be given one at a time and only as many as can be sung or played in an appropriate amount of time. Before written requests were used, Leslie was often up until 2:00 or 3:00 A.M. playing.

A listing of the program content of one of Leslie's typical performances will give some idea of his repertoire and the breadth of his musical ability and talent. On April 29, 1986, he played and sang the following numbers at the Faith Methodist Church in Neenah, Wisconsin:

PART I—CONCERT

1. "Rhapsody in Blue"
2. "How Great Thou Art"
3. "Amazing Grace"
4. Imitations
   Louie Armstrong
   Jeanette McDonald/Nelson Eddy
5. "The Old Rugged Cross"
6. "Jesus, There's Something About That Name"
7. "I've Never Been So Homesick Before"
8. "The Lord's Prayer"

PART II—CHALLENGE

9. "Doe a Deer" (from *The Sound of Music*)
10. "Mississippi Hotdog" (Suzuki method)
11. "Where is Love?" (vocal)
12. "The Clown" (Kabalevsky)
13. "The Entertainer" (request)
14. "Bridge Over Troubled Waters" (request)
15. "The Rose" (request)
16. "What a Friend We Have in Jesus" (request)
17. "Everybody Loves Somebody Sometime" (request)
18. "The Twenty-Third Psalm" (guitar/vocal)

But Leslie's current skill does not end with mimicking and repetition. He now improvises. Leslie answers challenge after challenge at his concerts by first repeating the challenge tune note for note and then launching into an improvisation—a variation on a theme—for five, eight or even ten minutes. The Suzuki method piece "Mississippi Hotdog," for example, played by a young student at a concert in Neenah, Wisconsin, spawned such an eight-minute improvisation, which ended in a beautiful and gigantic chord swell, the type Leslie loves so much to create. Challenged with the same Bartok and Grieg pieces that John Sloboda and his colleagues used in their study of the musical savant, as described in Chapter 2, Leslie was much better in reproducing the tonal Grieg song than the atonal Bartok number. Presumably the conclusions about Leslie's musical skill would be the same, therefore, as those of the savants in that study.[22]

As Leslie's memory expanded, ironically, May's began to fade. Like others in her family, she began slowly to develop the unmistakable and relentless signs of Alzheimer's Disease. Finally, in 1985, May moved in with her older daughter, Pat Smith, in Winnebago, Wisconsin, and Leslie moved in with Mary Parker Larsen, May's younger daughter, in Arpin, Wisconsin. (Joe Lemke died in the fall of 1987.) Leslie made that transition very smoothly and really without incident. There was some concern that he might stop playing without May by his side—as Blind Tom had lost his gift when Colonel Bethune died—but that did not happen. Mary began providing for him just as tenderly, lovingly and proudly as May had. Leslie remained content and talented.

Since going to live with Mary, Leslie has continued to improve. He looks quite different now than he did when I first met him. He has a styled haircut rather than the rather institutional-style crop he once had and a neatly trimmed beard. Leslie has slimmed down considerably, and he dresses nattily in very handsome suits for his concerts. He now uses quite deftly a fork and spoon to feed himself. His improvisations are impressive, in fact moving, but Mary says he does more than improvise and will have Leslie play and sing a song of his own creation, "Down on the Farm in Arpin," a peppy number in which he sings about the chickens, the ducks and "Mama cleaning the house." In addition to the piano he plays the harmonica, which requires considerable breath control, and the melodeon, which requires considerable finger dexterity. His language is more spontaneous and less echolalic. There has been no trade-off of memory or talent that I can detect with the expansion of Leslie's musical skills. Unlike the case of Nadia, in fact, as musical and social skills have expanded in Leslie, language has expanded also. That feared trade-off of savant skills for language has not taken place either, suggesting other reasons for that exchange in Nadia.

Leslie gives concerts regularly at churches, service clubs, schools, nursing homes and prisons in addition to presenting concerts abroad. Mary feels that Leslie's miracle occurred so that it could be shared, and many of the concerts are given for free. Those that are not usually barely recapture expenses. Any money left after expenses goes to help offset the cost of caring for Leslie and is used to purchase an occasional new suit—and every now and then a piano. Mary has formed the Miracle of Love Ministries to carry out what she sees essentially as mission work to share the gift of Leslie's talent. That ministry is carried out in Arpin, Wisconsin, in a modest way on a modest budget with rather phenomenal results.

Leslie sees May occasionally now, when her health permits. Mary and her sister Pat have vowed to their mother that neither she nor Leslie will ever have to enter a nursing home or an institution, and they fully intend to keep that promise. Whatever else May has forgotten now with the advancement of her illness, she has not forgotten Leslie. His playing and singing still seem to bring recognition. To see them together today, with her infirmity now dwarfing his, is especially touching. Her face still lights up when she says his name and when she hears him play, just as it did that first time I visited them, the day Joe put the red bow on the mailbox. Her pride and love and joy still leap out. Leslie is still May's boy—and what a boy he is!

In August 1986 Leslie had a complete neurological and neuropsychological examination by Drs. Louis J. Ptacek and Robert LaPlant of the Marshfield Clinic and Foundation, Marshfield, Wisconsin. On neurological examination the head was somewhat scaphocephalic in configuration with some flattening and asymmetry of the left frontal, temporal and parietal areas of the skull. There was a slight asymmetry of the face with the left side being somewhat smaller than the right, indicative of scoliosis. There was a slight curvature of the spine. Height was 5'4" and weight was 117 pounds. The left lower leg was approximately 4 cm shorter than the right lower leg, and there was a minimal contracture of the left knee. On muscle testing, the patient had slight, generally relaxed muscle tone, except at the right ankle where there was heel cord tightness and some difficulty moving the right ankle through the full range of motion. There was a definite limp favoring the left leg. On coordination testing, he was somewhat insecure and unsteady. The diagnosis by the neurologist was that of Savant Syndrome; atonic diplegia (cerebral palsy); moderately severe mental retardation; scoliosis; and a shortened left leg probably resulting from subluxation of the left hip.

Formal neuropsychological evaluation was done as well. There he demonstrated echolalia by repeating most of the instructions given to him, but he would carry out simple requests. He had a repertoire of many socially pleasant comments and responses and made some attempts to socially interact with the examiner. There was an effort to carry on a conversation in question and answer format but answers were often contaminated by automatic responses cued to some comment; the word "all," for example, would trigger Leslie's version of the ending of a Bugs Bunny cartoon, "eh, eh, that's all folks." Sometimes comments would include an entire television commercial he had heard previously, which he would repeat, exactly and entirely, along with the more appropriate answer. On the animal list selective reminding test, overall learning was at a level often seen in a 7- or 8-year-old individual. The animal list selective reminding test is administered by naming ten animals to the subject, who is then asked to recall which animals he or she just saw. At first no clues are provided, but then the subject is asked questions such as "Do you remember seeing any dogs on the list?" There was considerable perseveration and repetition of responses, and after repeating many of the animals on the word list, Leslie would go on to name other animals that were not on the list.

On the Wechsler Adult Intelligence Scale—Revised (WAIS–R) intellectual functioning was in the moderately retarded range (Verbal I.Q. was 58). Performance I.Q. was not tested because such testing depends heavily on vision. The verbal portion of the WAIS–R uses 6 subtests—information (29 questions of varying complexity), digit span (9 digits to be repeated backwards and forwards), vocabulary (40 words of varying difficulty ranging, for example, from "bed" to "audacious"), arithmetic (11 problems of varying complexity), comprehension (10 items testing what might be termed "common sense," for example, what one would do if someone were to yell "fire" in a movie house), and similarities (12 pairs of items to detect likeness, for example, how a pear and a banana are alike). Scores are then weighted by using standards that supply a numerical figure, with 10 being average or normal (50 percent of persons scoring between 7 and 13). Scores of percentile groups can range as high as 17 in the highest percentile to 0 at the lowest end. Leslie's scores were: Information, 1; Digit Span, 7; Vocabulary, 1; Arithmetic, 1; Comprehension, 2; and Similarities, 3.

Attempts were made to administer appropriate portions of the new, 4th edition of the Stanford-Binet Intelligence Test. In the verbal reasoning subarea, performance was estimated to be in the moderately to severely retarded range. In the short-term memory subarea, performance was approximately in the normal range.

The Tactual Performance Test gave a good index of Leslie's nonverbal abstract reasoning ability, since subjects are blindfolded for this test and visual difficulties do not interfere with performance. This test consists of a form-board with cutouts to accept 10 wood pieces of various shapes. While blindfolded the subject feels the pieces and the board and, usually without instruction or prompting, begins to fit the pieces into the cutouts. Leslie showed *no* problem solving ability on this test. He echoed instructions when they were finally provided to him and attempted to comply but could not. Even when his hands were put first over the cutout and then over the corresponding piece before him, he could not solve the problem. Left on his own for more than 15 seconds, the response deteriorated into perseverative touching of the blocks used in the test. Abstract ability was essentially absent.

Adaptive abilities were assessed by having the American Association for Mental Deficiency (AAMD) Adaptive Behavior Scale completed by Mary Larsen. For the most part, Leslie functioned in the trainable mentally retarded range with socialization skills being closer to the educable level. Lowest levels of functioning were in the areas of independent functioning, physical development and self-direction.

The neuropsychologist concluded, overall, that Leslie was functioning in the moderately retarded range of intelligence. Except in the area of music and music-related memory, memory functioning in general was in the low normal range. Verbal reasoning skills were in the moderately to severely retarded range. Nonverbal reasoning skills were clearly in the severely retarded range. Except for his tremendous musical performance competence, adaptive abilities were in the trainable mentally retarded range. This correlates with moderate to severe range of psychometric intelligence.

An electroencephalogram (16 channel, awake) was interpreted as being mildly abnormal; some very mild slowing appeared throughout all areas but was particularly prominent in the right temporal region of the brain. Specifically, the background consisted of relatively low amplitude activity with well-formed and symmetric alpha waves (9–9½ Hz) in all areas. There was an excess of even slower activity over the right temporal areas, and even though only intermittent, that change particularly was suggestive of structural abnormality in that area and a CAT scan was suggested.

A CAT scan at the Theta Clark Hospital, Neenah, WI, interpreted by Dr. Timothy T. Flaherty, showed considerable left-side abnormality, especially in the left frontal lobe. On the films there was, of course, evidence of the eyes having been removed. The eye sockets themselves showed an asymmetry with a deformity of the left-eye socket raising the question of an old fracture or some congenital deformity in that area. The entire left frontal bone (forehead area) also showed evidence of that same deformity, with the sinus area contained within that bone very much smaller on the left as compared to the relatively normal sinus area on the right. This deformity resulted in the entire left frontal area being smaller than the right. In addition, there was a relatively large low-density area, compared to the surrounding tissue, in the left frontal area of the brain itself. This defect measured approximately 2 cm wide, 4 cm deep and 4 cm high. This area of abnormality appeared to represent an area of brain atrophy (scarring) consistent with either some previous vascular (blood supply) damage or residual damage from a previous brain abscess (infection). There were associated areas of brain damage and atrophy in the anterior and, to a lesser degree, posterior portions of the left parietal (central) lobes and, to a minor degree, in both the left and right occipital (posterior brain) lobes. This finding of clear left-side brain damage is very significant as will be seen in the discussion of left brain/right brain damage and dysfunction in Chapter 11.

There have been many efforts to share the Leslie Lemke story in books, television programs, magazines and newspapers. A feature-length television movie, *The Woman Who Willed a Miracle,* starring Cloris Leachman as May Lemke and Leif Green as Leslie, won four Emmy awards. The most accurate portrayal of this remarkable story, however, was in a film entitled *An Island of Genius,* produced by the Weyerhaeuser Corporation and released in 1987. It begins with the quote by Jean-Paul Sartre that "every human being has a project." For May the project was not letting a frail and handicapped infant die. For Mary it is to "bring this miracle into its full bloom." For Leslie it is to experience and share his astonishing ability to whatever heights it might take him.

He has not yet reached his limits. Mary and Leslie regularly perform on a rather rigorous concert schedule that takes them around the country and around the world. Leslie recently completed a tour that included 26 cities in Japan. His repertoire now includes thousands of pieces and is continually expanding. He is gradually becoming more polished in his presentations, more spontaneous in his conversations and more sociable in his interaction. He loves what he is doing, is remarkably good at it and enjoys the appreciation and applause of his audiences, whether large or small, prestigious or ordinary, young or old. He has not reached his limits. His "project" continues. We are the fortunate beneficiaries of it.

9

Ellen

Ellen loves the musical *Evita,* so much so that she memorized it within a week of hearing it for the first time. Now each evening she plays the album at *exactly* the same time, accompanying it on the piano and singing the words exactly as they occur. She loves Tchaikovsky's Violin Concerto as played by Itzhak Perlman and the Philadelphia Orchestra, and whenever her mother plays it on the stereo, Ellen drops everything and comes to the living room to listen, sitting motionless and smiling with obvious pleasure until the very last note is played. She knows and sings the major themes of concertos and symphonies, and there seems to be no limit to the music she can remember. She is transfixed by the mathematical construction of music by Bach, as if she understands it by instinct. She plays and sings "Love Me Tender" on the guitar with the same ease with which she plays *Rhapsody in Blue* on the piano. She has a repertoire of hundreds of songs. After just a single hearing the songs are stored permanently and can be recalled flawlessly.

But Ellen is completely blind. At 29 years of age, she improvises, playing rock and roll songs in minuet form, or vice versa. She has an I.Q. of 50. She has a superior spatial sense, a remarkable memory and an astonishing musical talent. Her sense of rhythm is pervasive. She seems driven by time and by schedule, rushing to listen to commercials on any nearby radio at exact times throughout the day. It's as if a digital clock is incessantly running in her head—but she has never seen one. She is a remarkable young woman. And she has a remarkable family.

Ellen was born August 3, 1957, to Ory and Barbara Boudreaux in an Air Force base hospital near the station where her father was a career pilot. She was her parents' third child, following two daughters 11 years and 13 years older. Ellen was born two and one-half months early and weighed a mere 2 pounds. She was given oxygen for 12 days and subsequently developed retrolental fibroplasia. The inevitable scar tissue formed, leaving her completely blind. Doctors suggested the surgical removal of the eyes later in life for cosmetic reasons if the family chose to do so. After birth, her weight dropped to 1¾ pounds; her parents were told that she would not survive and that they should not name her, pick out clothes for her or make any plans. But Ellen, apparently determined then already, "screamed louder than any other children in the nursery," according to her mother, and that will prevailed. Ellen did survive and, ten weeks later, went home with her parents.

Ellen developed slowly. When she was 4 months old, the doctors confirmed what the parents had suspected—Ellen was blind. Ellen was 6 months old when her sister Nancy came running out to tell her mother that "the baby is singing." There was a cradle gym above Ellen that played Brahms' "Lullaby," and indeed Ellen was, at age 6 months, humming that song with the same precision and rhythm that has characterized all of her music since.

At about this time a new problem surfaced. Ellen would not stay in her crib throughout the night. When she awoke at 3:00 or 4:00 A.M., she would become terrified at being alone and she would climb over the side of her crib and scoot along the hall in search of another human being. The voyage usually ended in the room of her 13-year-old sister, who always made room for the little sister to whom she was deeply devoted. Ellen would stay there until morning, when it was time to turn on the bedside radio and sing.

Popular at about that time were Buddy Holly, the Everly Brothers, Frankie Avalon, Elvis Presley, Chubby Checkers and Jerry Lee Lewis, among others. Together Ellen and her sister would listen to the radio, and the sister would sing to Ellen. Now, some 25 years later, Ellen can not only sing every one of those "golden oldies" but she can play them perfectly on the piano or guitar with all the musical introductions and embellishments intact, reproducing uncannily the voices of Holly, Presley, Lewis and others.

Ellen was 4 years old before she walked. But once she began to walk it was with a superior spatial sense. From the very beginning she was aware of large objects, walls, fences and buildings from a distance of six feet or more and insisted on going to them and putting her hands on them. She found her way around the house barefoot by remembering where the carpet ended and the linoleum started. Her father says that, from those early days on, she has been able to walk in thick, strange forests without running into trees, sensing them by some kind of instinct. She is also keenly aware of the presence of any other person in the same room. Even walking barefoot on the carpet her mother is unable to conceal her presence from Ellen. As Ellen learned to navigate she made a constant little chirping sound, like her own form of personal radar.

At age 4 or 5 she became hyperactive to a severe degree and was constantly in motion. She moved around and around the perimeter of every room in the house, taking objects off shelves and out of closets, and piling them in heaps in the middle of the floor. She would tear, chew, smell and feel everything. Cabinets in the house had to be tied shut and even those would often be invaded once she untied the knots. She loved particularly her father's tools, especially the metal ones. She seemed driven to rhythm and would beat time on all metal and wood objects. Combing Ellen's hair in the morning was difficult because she would be beating on a wall. She loved the sound of metal clanging so much that she could never walk past a car without going over to bang on it. For a time it appeared that perpetual motion and hyperactivity would make it impossible for Ellen's parents to keep her at home. "I don't know how we did it," her mother says now. But they did do it and Ellen remained at home.

Psychological testing was performed on Ellen when she was 4½. On the Vineland Social Maturity Scale, her social I.Q. was approximately 40, which would suggest an estimated I.Q. of between 30 and 50. She vocalized but did not verbalize, follow directions or respond to requests. "She very skillfully avoided obstacles, had superior spatial memory and seemed to have a very educated touch. She can locomote with ease around a room and has a superior spatial memory. These favorable findings, however, are along a very narrow bent. The picture is one of a severely defective child who would have a very guarded prognosis. The question of the advisability of institutionalization should be very seriously considered in a case of this sort, both for the benefit of the child and the child's mother and siblings."

Physical examination in 1962 showed a small, hyperkinetic girl with obvious opacities of the lens of each eye and portions of the iris (pupil) attached and fixed to the lens. Laboratory studies, an electroencephalogram and skull X-rays were normal.

Ory and Barbara refused to accept this rather grim prognosis for their daughter and began to look all over the United States for a school system that could deal with Ellen's several handicaps, not just until graduation, but in adulthood as well. They found such a program in the San Juan Unified School District in Fair Oaks, California, just outside Sacramento. They moved there when Ellen was 8. She did extremely well in school and now is enrolled in the Starr King adult special education program of that same school district. She began speech therapy in

1983. At that time she had no verbal interaction or conversation skills. Her speech consisted of humming, mumbling, jumbled jargon, perseveration and echolalia. The only connected speech she did have was when she was singing words to the many songs she knew. Three years and 84 sessions later, Ellen now can name objects, can complete sentences, can answer questions, rather than just echo them, and has begun interactive speech in simple sentences.

A recent summary of her progress in speech therapy is insightful:

> Her phenomenal memory has been one of her greatest strengths. She was able to store previously presented auditory information. We taught her to not echo, to wait, and *then* echo or retrieve information. Once she could *wait* before verbally responding, she began to break through the echolalia and the perseverative loops that were barriers to meaningful communication. She already has stored vocabulary and appropriate word order as it was easily emitted, once she learned how to access it. She began to be less rigid and more playful during therapy. She had shown no sign of plateau; she *has* shown remarkable skills, abilities, and potential to develop meaningful communication.

Ellen's progress in language is certainly impressive and is particularly significant because, unlike in the case of Nadia, where it was felt that the sacrifice of her artistic skill was a necessary trade-off for the acquisition of language, no such trade-off has occurred. This fact is particularly optimistic for all savants.

For Ory and Barbara Boudreaux the decision to keep Ellen at home was easy; they never wanted to do anything else. But that path itself was not an easy one. Ellen's hyperactivity and destructiveness, and her perpetual motion and drive, were tremendously trying for a long time. So were her eating habits. In infancy she developed an extreme fear of ingesting any solid foods. She would panic and reject a single pea, for example, in a plate of mashed food. For 11 years of her life everything was blended, at home or away. This was but one of the obstacles and impediments to normal living that children such as this typically present.

That particular idiosyncrasy disappeared suddenly one day, when Ellen was 11, of necessity. While on a car trip with her parents and grandmother over a very remote route, Ellen, as well as everyone else, became famished. Since no restaurant could be found, the group stopped at a gas station/store, where only some milk, a banana and some biscuits were available. Ellen's mother gently pushed the banana into Ellen's mouth. The child was hungry enough that she ate it, followed by the biscuits and some cookies. Eating solid foods has not been a problem since. In fact, Ellen's eating too much is the problem now.

Ellen's musical skill and memory are prodigious. Her interest in music began early, as mentioned above—it was first noticed when she hummed Brahms at age 6 months. At about age 4 Ellen surprised her mother by picking out some tunes on a small electric organ. At age 7 a teacher advised her parents to "get this child a piano." They did and the music has poured forth ever since. Ellen now constructs complicated chords to accompany melodies she hears on the radio or the stereo. She transposes the orchestra and chorus of *Evita* to the piano with complex, precise chords. She reproduces the crowd and mob sounds with intense dissonances using both hands. It is an impressive, and lengthy, performance.

She taught herself the guitar by spending seemingly countless hours going up and down each string, memorizing the tones that each fingering produced and experimenting with chords. She now plays ballads and folk songs that have become the favorites of her classmates and her fellow campers on her annual excursion to a special camp. She is driven by and enamored of rhythm—of any type, form or origin. At age 9 she happened to tune the car radio to a classical music station playing a full hour of Wanda Landowska performing Bach on the clavichord. She was transfixed and the family was captive for the full hour of that performance because Ellen would not allow them to change the station.

There is no special, spectacular musical ability in Ellen's family, although her mother is deeply interested in music and has had extensive exposure to it. For years Barbara Boudreaux was General Manager for the Sacramento Symphony Orchestra. Often accompanying her mother to rehearsals, Ellen heard lots and lots of music. Her sisters, Cheryl and Nancy, have no special musical talent. Ory Boudreaux says his sister was an excellent singer who often sang publicly at church and other events.

Ellen has recently begun to improvise. Previously her music was entirely echolalic in nature, although spectacularly so. Now when she listens to almost any album she will begin to play chords with it, improvising very unusual but beautiful accompaniments. She will play what she has heard in one form, such as jazz, then in another style, perhaps classical. She will transpose rock and roll to a waltz form in three-quarter time. She is fascinated with radio and television commercials and will immediately transpose those to the piano as well.

Ellen's highly developed sense of timekeeping became evident at about age 8. To help Ellen overcome a fear of the telephone that she seemed to have at that age, her mother coaxed her one day to listen to the automatic time recording, or the "Time Lady." Ellen listened for about ten minutes and returned to her room where she mimicked what she had heard on the phone. She correctly understood the sequence of seconds, and when she came to "one fifty-nine and fifty-nine seconds," Ellen announced, "The time is . . . two o'clock." The mystery is that, during the ten minutes she had listened, there was no change from one hour to the next, and no explanation exists as to how Ellen knew to change the hour at the 59-minute, 59-second point. She had obviously never seen a clock, and neither the concept of time elapsing nor the workings of a clock had ever been explained to her.

Time, like music, is a vital part of her life now. At the right time each day she listens—regularly, obsessively and without fail—to the NBC national news, speeches by her favorite speaker—"President Ronald Reagan," Spanish language broadcasts, football games, each game of the Oakland A's baseball team, stock market reports and fundamentalist revival meetings. It is impossible to determine what, if anything, she understands from all these programs since, although she listens to them attentively, she never discusses anything about them.

Whether her impeccable sense of time came first and that is what drove her to the radio and the television at precise intervals, or whether she first loved the programs and the regularity of their schedules, her keen time sense remains a question, one to which we may never know the answer.

Some have explained the savant in terms of reincarnation. Barbara Boudreaux recalls that one day some friends who believe that to be the case asked Ellen to listen to a Mozart piece she had never heard before. Near the end they stopped the piece and asked Ellen to play it for them. She obligingly did and, according to the friends at least, continued to play the piece beyond the point at which they had stopped—"as if" she had heard the whole number—and played it just as Mozart had written it. They concluded that the only way she possibly could have known what to play after that point was if she had played it before in some earlier life: an explanation which no one can confirm or refute, but which is, nonetheless, an explanation held by some.

Ellen's parents have reported three instances of unusual perception on her part, which were described earlier in the section on extrasensory perception skills in Chapter 7.

Barbara and Ory Boudreaux are proud of their daughter, and with good reason. Their unconditional love for her is evident and bountiful. It never occurred to them *not* to accept her, with or without her talents. While her talent is appreciated it is not pivotal; they love her, not just her abilities. Ellen's sunny disposition reflects theirs. Focusing on assets and strengths in those around us rather than dwelling on negatives and handicaps is also a lesson learned from these extraordinary parents. Barbara Boudreaux recalls, not with anger but rather with forgiveness, an incident that occurred during those trying early days. Someone visiting the home commented to her, "You must wonder what terrible things you've done that God has punished you this way." "I don't feel that way at all," she calmly states, expressing charity and understanding toward people who feel that way. The only thing she felt in that instance was surprise that someone would actually voice that opinion aloud. It surprised me also.

Ellen, like the other savants, is astonishing—she is blind, with an I.Q. of 50, but with a remarkable musical talent. Some things, however, set her apart. First, she is female, a rarity among savants. Second, she has learned language in a systematic, formal manner, and there has not been a trade-off of talent and skill, as has been suspected in other cases. Third, her sense of rhythm is associated with an uncanny sense of time; surely the two must be connected, for music appears to be, as some have suggested, unconscious counting and that is what time is also.

Ellen continues to improve, to improvise and to expand not only her repertoire of songs but her repertoire of instruments as well. How far she will go remains to be seen, but at this juncture it looks like it will be a long way indeed. Her strong and loving family—their belief and their support—make it impossible to ignore the influence of positive nurturing when trying to answer the nature/nurture question here. However much of Ellen's deficiency and talent is rooted in nature, the supportive environment in which she has been raised has minimized her deficiencies and maximized her talents. To be both prodigious and handicapped is the striking contrast present in all savants, and Ellen represents that contrast vividly and sharply. Ellen is a fascinating example of that condition, but more importantly, she is an example that inspires optimism for the prospects of other savants.

10

Alonzo

May 1984 was a busy month for Alonzo Clemons. His work was featured in the National Art Festival for the Handicapped in Washington, D.C. He had tea on the White House lawn and met Mrs. Nancy Reagan. From there he went to San Francisco to appear on a television show, and then to Grand Junction, Colorado, where he showed his skills at a statewide art festival. Then it was on to Kansas City, Missouri, to participate in a benefit for handicapped people.

May 1986 was busy as well. The First Interstate Bank of Denver sponsored a world premiere exhibition of 30 of his bronze sculptures, showing the progression from a rough and primitive style to a smooth and elegant fine art. The highlight of the show was his greatest work, a life-sized piece entitled "Three Frolicking Foals." Commissioned by Trammel Crow for a project in Chicago, the sculpture had been completed in three weeks.

In three years Alonzo gained a national and international reputation, something that usually takes years and years for an artist to establish. His works, handled by the Driscol Gallery in Denver, now sell for an average of $350 to $3,000 each, with some prices as high as $45,000. Art critics are enthusiastic about his sculptures, the public is astonished, and professional artists proclaim them to be excellent.

Alonzo is one of the gentlest people I have ever met. He radiates a contentment that is contagious. He smiles a lot. His eyes light up with a fiery sparkle when he answers questions with his monosyllable replies. Relaxed, at ease and pleasantly convivial, he seems refreshingly free of pressure and drives, except one—the drive to sculpt. He is in perpetual motion as his hands gently, but relentlessly, sculpt animal after animal, turning lumps of clay into works of art. He can create a horse and colt in 20 minutes.

Alonzo is now 30 years old. Most of his works are animals, especially horses, which he dearly loves. Next to his bed are shelves filled with quarter horses and thoroughbreds, bulls, sheep and dogs. His favorite piece, one entitled "Courtship," depicts two lovely horses, one a mare and one a stud. To me his most touching piece is a beautiful statue of a colt entitled "You Light Up My Life," which Alonzo created for Leslie Lemke when he saw a videotape of Leslie singing the song of the same title.

The two savants exchanged gifts.

Alonzo sculpts from memory. For him one fleeting glimpse of any animal, whether at a zoo, in a book or on the television, is memory enough. From that flows a three-dimensional replica precisely accurate in every detail; every fiber, muscle and tendon is exactly as seen. He is a virtual copy machine. How he can translate into three dimensions a picture seen in only two dimensions remains a mystery. It is no puzzle to him though: "God gives talent," Alonzo explains.

Alonzo Clemons was born in 1956. His mother recalls that he was a normal baby, although she considered him a precocious child because he seemed to learn so quickly. Even as a tiny toddler he showed remarkable interest in and ability with Play Doh, almost as if he were born to have something in his hands. A fall at age 3 caused brain injury that resulted in markedly slowed development thereafter, poorly developed speech and an I.Q. measured at 40. He entered a special education facility at age 12 and presently lives in a group home for developmentally disabled persons in Boulder, Colorado. At age 25 Alonzo could barely count to 10 and could not handle money but was able to dress and feed himself, dust his room and catch the right bus to go to his job as a stable hand at a nearby ranch. There he would clean horse stalls and do housekeeping chores in the lounges.

Sculpting, even in childhood days before the injury, seemed for him almost obsessional. At one point, while he was in the residential facility he entered at age 12, it appeared that his obsession was getting in the way of his other learning—so much so that the clay was taken away to be used only as a reward for other behaviors designed more for his overall growth, particularly in speech and academic subjects. It was then that streaks of tar appeared in his bedding. Found beneath the bed was an entire menagerie of sticky, black animals Alonzo had sculpted from tar he had scraped from the school pavement with his fingernails.

Today that obsessive attachment is to microcrystalline wax, which he transforms into remarkable sculptures by the perpetual motion of his skilled hands and fingers. In a single sitting of one hour he can produce, for example, a horse, a gorilla and a wildebeest. He kneads and presses the clay with his hands to initially form the sculpture and then uses his fingers to create the finer features and his fingernails for the minute etching and markings that characterize his works. He uses one tool—an awl—on occasion. At the end of the day, and particularly at the end of a larger project, his hands and fingers show the wear and tear of constant pressure.

He remembers what he has seen only once and uses the picture in his mind as a model. He does not refer back to any photo or other prop; he can sculpt in the dark.

Alonzo has three normal siblings, an older brother and two younger sisters, none of whom has any special artistic talent.

The demand for Alonzo's work has grown so that he has been able to quit his job at the stable and now works full-time in a studio near his home.

In contrast to his skill is his handicap. His vocabulary is limited to several hundred words. His speech is impaired; for example, he often substitutes the word "yet" for "yes." There is little echolalia, but little spontaneous conversation either. He usually responds to simple questions with one- or two-word replies. When asked how he does his sculpture, he replies, "Hands" or "God gives talent." He loves to work quietly without conversation. He seems most at peace when he works silently, usually with a slight, very contented smile. He seems capable of tremendous concentration and exclusion of the persons around him, no matter how large the crowd. He is exceedingly proud of his works and likes to accompany admirers silently from piece to piece, wearing his shy but almost boastful smile, content and pleased with what he sees and what he shows.

Alonzo has never had a formal art lesson, and he probably never will; his parents, and Pam Driscol, who began handling his sculptures in 1983, have agreed not to tamper with his technique or his style lest either be damaged or destroyed. Yet, even in the absence of any such training, there has been a natural but dramatic progression from rather crude, static, highly accurate but relatively lifeless figures, to pieces full of life, motion and movement. This transition accelerated markedly when Alonzo, on the advice of Pam Driscol, began to visit the zoo to see animals in real life rather than just in photographs or on television. Quickly and obviously his work became more polished and showed more action and activity. His "Three Frolicking Foals" particularly shows this vitality and excitement.

As his art has enlivened, so has Alonzo. His vocabulary, while still limited, has expanded. His repertoire of daily living skills, such as tying his shoes or making his bed, has expanded as well. He is less shy, more spontaneous and better able to adapt to new situations. He is still unable to read or write, and perhaps never will, but his verbal communication and the nonverbal communication transmitted so beautifully and powerfully through his art both show development. His obsessive sculpting has not hindered him but has actualized him; rather than being an impediment to his other communication skills, it has enhanced them.

Alonzo is a prodigious savant. His sculpture is remarkable not because it is done by someone who is retarded; it is remarkable in its own right and would be spectacular no matter who the artist might be. Buyers of his work are astounded to find, during the purchase or sometime after, that the artist happens to be mentally handicapped. Sales of his work have passed the novelty stage, with over 500 pieces in collections worldwide. He has earned enough for the purchase and renovation of a home next to his parents', which he uses as a full-time studio. Alonzo's dream is to someday have his own horse and maybe a place in the country somewhere to keep it. It looks like an attainable dream.

Alonzo, like Leslie Lemke, uses his talents to benefit other handicapped persons. For example, in December 1987 Alonzo demonstrated his art in Charlotte, North Carolina, at the Mint Museum to benefit a non-profit, sheltered workshop for the handicapped in that community. At another benefit, for a Wisconsin camp for the handicapped, I had the rare opportunity to see two remarkable savants, Leslie and Alonzo, together in a concert/exhibit. Alonzo sculpted to Leslie's accompaniment, and the other handicapped persons and their families gathered around. It was an impressive and touching experience. Alonzo's soft smile and Leslie's mellow voice blended beautifully. The chance to view Alonzo's art and hear Leslie's music simultaneously was a rare, fortuitous circumstance for the audience and for me.

Alonzo and Leslie have had one other appearance together, along with their families, on *The Morning Show,* broadcast live from New York City in 1985. I had the good fortune to be there as well. It provided another most interesting interaction between them and their respective talents. Alonzo brought with him the "You Light Up My Life" piece he had sculpted as a tribute to Leslie's rendition of that song. Seeing the sculpture, and Alonzo's pride in having produced it, as Leslie played and sang the song is a moment I will not soon forget.

Particularly interesting about that show was the fact that, unlike so many clipped and edited pieces done for the typical five- or six-minute spot on the evening news, there was enough time from beginning to end for the show's hosts and audience to get to know Alonzo. Also, there was sufficient time to see Alonzo actually produce, step by step, a piece in a 30-minute time frame. There was no model, except in his mind. He barely looked up, staring at the piece seemingly with the same fascination with what was taking shape—an elephant—as the audience, even though he had done a hundred others before it. A mellow smile was present the whole time. He seemed oblivious, but tolerant, to the conversation and explanations surrounding him. He simply smiled, and sculpted.

When thirty minutes passed and the elephant was done, Alonzo was pleased. The audience was awestruck when he also showed them the horse and colt he had completed in the twenty minutes he waited in the green room for the show to begin.

"Where does that talent come from, Alonzo?" asked Regis, one of the hosts of the show.

"God gave me a gift," replied Alonzo.

"He's got such a lovely countenance. Is he always that sweet-natured?" asked someone from the audience.

"Yes he is, he's so sweet and loving," replied his mother. "He's one of the happiest people I've ever met," concluded Regis.

I agree.

THREE

GENIUS WITHIN US

Explaining the
Inexplicable

How do they do it? The question leaps up in the mind of anyone confronted with the paradox that is the savant.

The case descriptions in earlier chapters answer some questions about the savant. Who are they? They are people like George, Alonzo, Leslie and Ellen, who have spectacular islands of ability way out of proportion to their overall handicap. What do they do? They sculpt, they play music, they memorize, they calculate, they draw or they exercise one or more of various other talents that are remarkably constant and narrow considering the vast realm of human talents and skills. Why do they do it? For the same reason we do things we are really good at—we enjoy them, they satisfy us, they bring us praise and they provide reinforcement. The savants' skills are their "project." So much for the who, what and why. Comes now the question of how: how does a person of such obvious deficiency achieve such greatness in one limited area?

There have been about as many theories that have attempted to answer this question as there have been investigators. Many of the theories stem from the study of a single case, comprising "undemocratic" research that does provide useful information, but that also is often rather idiosyncratic and limited. The most objective and comprehensive overview of research into the etiology of Savant Syndrome was done by Dr. Jane Duckett for her doctoral dissertation, at the University of Texas at Austin, entitled "Idiot Savants: Super Socialization in Mentally Retarded Persons."[73] The significant research that culminated in that dissertation was also reported in part in 1977 in the *American Journal of Mental Deficiency.*[74] It will be discussed in more detail later in this chapter, but for now suffice it to say that, in Duckett's own study and in her review of all the theories previously proposed, no single finding or theory emerged that could explain *all* savants. She called for "extensive theory revision." Let us now review the theories that have been put forth thus far.

EIDETIC IMAGERY

The most frequently advanced explanation for savant abilities and skills is eidetic imagery. Unfortunately, although many authors use that term, there is confusion as to exactly what it means and what it includes, so comparing one report to another is difficult. Generally, however, two types of phenomena are included in the term "eidetic imagery."

In its purest form, the term is reserved for a rare and very specific memory function in which, after one has viewed an object or a scene, an intensely strong visual image persists when the object or scene is removed.[75] That image remains extremely vivid at the spot where the object was located and the location may even be scanned with eye movements, as if the object were still there. This intensely strong image must persist for at least 40 seconds for it to be classified as eidetic. Under this narrow definition, if a person views a picture on an easel and is still able to "see" it—at the point where it rested on the easel—after it is removed, he or she will be able to give exact details about the picture because the picture will still be visible to him or her. Analogous to this would be the use of the stop-action mechanism on a videotape deck that freezes an image for a time. In eidetikers, under this definition, that intensely vivid visual image persists for a while but then fades and cannot be recalled later with any greater accuracy than it could by an average person.

To test for the presence of eidetic imagery, the subject is presented with a blank grey easel on which pictures are placed for scanning and review for somewhere between 10 and 40 seconds. After a picture is removed, true eidetikers will report that they still see the picture on the easel (not in their heads), will scan the easel with discernible eye movements as if they are still actually looking at the picture and will be able to describe the picture accurately. In contrast to images of photographic memory, the image does not necessarily appear in its entirety and often changes or moves. Since the eidetic image is seen on an actual surface, by placing another stimulus on the screen (easel) one can test to see if the images actually compete with each other or whether they fuse. If, within the 40 seconds, a blue square and then a yellow square are put on the easel one at a time in front of a true eidetiker he or she

Blind Tom, the nineteenth-century musical prodigy (Culver
Pictures Inc.)

James Henry Pullen, the Genius of Earlswood Asylum, with his fully rigged man-of-war

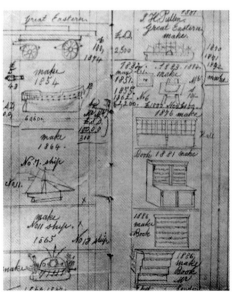

The first page of Pullen's notebook showing details of projects and (right) his illustrated yearly diary (1841–1873)

Pullen in old age in the naval uniform he liked to wear for ceremonial occasions

(all illustrations taken from *Mental Deficiency* by A.F. Tredgold, pub. 1914)

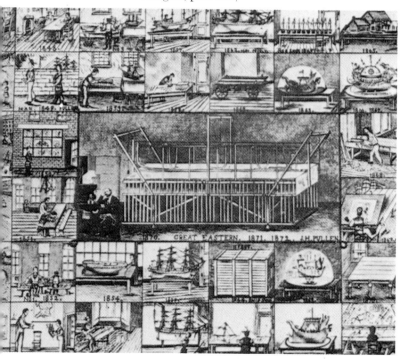

Leslie Lemke at the piano with his
remarkable foster-mother, May
(above)

Leslie can play other instruments
besides the piano and is keen to
develop his skills further (all
photographs © Chicago Tribune)

Leslie performing for the author, a
also in pub

Alonzo Clemons (right) and his
animal sculptures (Driscol Gallery,
Denver)

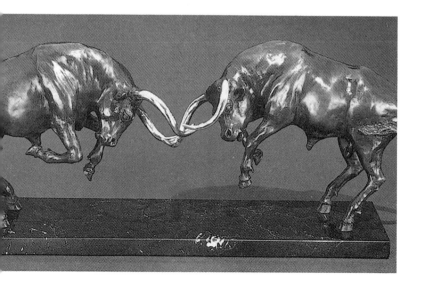

Stephen Wiltshire's first interpretation of Marble Arch, London, 1985 (Stephen Wiltshire)

Stephen Wiltshire photographed in 1988, aged fourteen (© Chris Marris)

Marble Arch as seen by Stephen in 1988 (Stephen Wiltshire)

The twins, Charles and George, whose speciality is calendar calculating (Bill Eppridge, Life Magazine © Time Inc.)

will see a green square, from the fusing of the two colors, whereas the non-eidetiker will see the color of the square actually on the easel. Some investigators therefore have used specific fusion tests to test for the presence of eidetic imagery in the savant.

The term "eidetic imagery" is also used by some authors to cover a related phenomenon called "visual image memory," which involves the ability to scan quickly and store, *for later recall,* vast amounts of extremely detailed and minute information. Popularly referred to as "photographic memory," this ability to "see" an image that is an *exact copy* of the original visual image is also rare. Visual image memory is extremely vivid and detailed but differs from the phenomenon described above in that the image appears "in the head" rather than at the site of the original stimulus and is a recalled image rather than an image that has persisted in uninterrupted fashion from the original stimulus.

While some researchers see these two phenomena—eidetic imagery and visual image memory—as qualitatively different from each other, psychologists Cynthia Gray and Kent Gummerman, after an extensive and critical examination of data and theories in this area, conclude that eidetic imagery is merely quantitatively different from visual image memory—the difference being simply that eidetic imagery is more vivid than visual image memory.[76] In the literature on savants, many observers comment on the extremely vivid and detailed memories in these persons and have used the term "eidetic" to differentiate that vivid and vast memory from ordinary memory function. While some have bothered to separate eidetic imagery into its two component parts as I have above, most have not, so in general the term in the literature reviewed here is used to cover both eidetic imagery, narrowly defined, and the broader phenomenon of visual image memory.

Eidetic ability is almost universally present in young children. The infant perceives direct stimuli in concrete terms (mother, bottle) and stores and retrieves only concrete images of such stimuli. During the course of a child's development the process of concrete visual perception expands to include the process of imagining, rather than just perceiving, and more adult memory, with the use of abstraction, conceptual thought and language emerging. Most investigators concerned with eidetic imagery see it as a developmental tool that decreases in importance as the child grows. Childlike memory is more concrete; adult memory contains more abstract ability.

Eidetic imagery is also present on a persistent basis in some forms of chronic brain damage. In those instances the term "palinopsia" (or sometimes "paliopsia") is used.[77] While palinopsia differs slightly from eidetic imagery in that the vivid image may persist for longer than 40 seconds or may recur at some future time, most investigators consider it to be a form of eidetic imagery. Palinopsia can also be present as a transitory phenomenon, lasting from days to weeks, in some instances of acute brain damage.[78]

Since eidetic imagery can be associated with brain damage, some researchers feel that the persistence of eidetic imagery in older children may be associated with particular forms of brain damage. Erol F. Giray and Allan G. Barclay describe 15 such brain-damaged children.[75] Elsa M. Siipola and Susan O. Hayden find eidetic imagery to be useful in differentiating brain injury as a cause of mental retardation from what they term a "familial"—or hereditary—pattern of retardation not clearly linked to specific brain injury or brain damage.[79] In their study they found 50 percent of the brain-injured retardates to be eidetic as compared to the more typical 6 percent seen by other investigators in patients with familial patterns of developmental disability. While subsequent investigations have not found the incidence of eidetikers in the brain-damaged group to be quite that high, they have, nonetheless, confirmed that association.

A. Dudley Roberts gives considerable attention to the presence of eidetic imagery in his case of a calendar calculator.[30] He carried out tests for the presence of eidetic ability and found such ability to be present with respect to calendar calculating as well as in other areas. He concludes, "The accumulated evidence points quite strongly toward eidetic imagery as an important factor in his day naming ability." In this case the calendar calculating skill was limited to a 30-year time span *backward* (1915–1945) and Roberts concludes that his subject had memorized calendars for those years and could recall them vividly and accurately through eidetic imagery. He notes that eidetic imagery usually fades after preadolescent years and is seldom carried into adulthood. Since his patient was very limited in the acquisition of a language, he concludes that the patient retained eidetic imagery as a substitute for language and that it served a useful purpose to him in calendar calculating. Of importance in this case, however, is the fact that this patient had encephalitis at 6 months of age and was a "quadriplegic spastic." The results of a pneumoencephalogram were markedly abnormal and confirmed a finding of considerable brain damage. A more likely explanation of the eidetic imagery in this case, then, is the patient's brain damage. The eidetic imagery may have, in fact, had very little specific association with the calculating calendar ability.

Identical twins George and Charles, the savant calendar calculators, were described by William A. Horwitz and his colleagues as having eidetic imagery. Yet, even those authors indicate that such imagery could not be the sole explanation for the skill because the twins' range of dates extended beyond known perpetual calendars.[26] Similarly, Oliver Sacks refers to the twins' eidetic imagery as their "immense mnemonic tapestry, a vast (or possibly infinite) landscaping in which everything could be seen, either isolated or in relation."[29] He felt that perhaps this prodigious power of visualization gave them also the potential of seeing the relations among entire constellations of numbers: "Could the twins, who seemed to have a peculiar passion and grasp for numbers—could these twins who had seen 111-ness at a glance, perhaps see in their minds a numerical 'vine' with all the number-leaves, number-tendrils, number-fruit, that made it up?" Sacks' speculation is provocative but certainly goes far beyond the usual definition of eidetic imagery.

Louise LaFontaine, in careful and comprehensive testing of five savant subjects, found that one of her calendar calculators possessed and made use of eidetic imagery.[56] This particular subject said he could "see yellow cards in his head." She concludes that, while eidetic imagery was an explanation for this one case, such a special sense could not account for subjects whose calendar calculating ranges extended into the future, for which no calendars were available. Her formal test data did not support eidetic imagery as being an explanation for all the savant abilities; thus, she concludes: "The present study has provided no strong support for any single explanation of the behavior of the idiot savant, and this may be the major value of such a study."

Dr. Martin Scheerer, Eva Rothmann and Dr. Kurt Goldstein conducted an in-depth, five-year study of one of their patients, a lightning calculator they call L., using a comprehensive and multifaceted test approach to determine the source of his skills.[21] Eidetic imagery was just one function for which he was tested. Using a series of seven tests for measuring visual responses, retention and imagery, they concluded that L.'s visualization and optic imagery were, in fact, subnormal. He seemed incapable of retaining and imagining things absent, and he appeared to use rote memory, as opposed to eidetic imagery, for the skills he exercised.

E. R. Jaensch and H. Menhel report a case in which they conclude that eidetic imagery did account for a calendar calculator's ability to give the day of the week or any date in the years 1920 through 1926.[80] For other years, the savant could answer correctly only if the questioner gave him the day of the week for any one date of the year in question. In specific testing for eidetic imagery in another calendar calculator, however, they found no indications of eidetic ability; recall of pictures was, in fact, poor in content and color.

Edmund J. Rubin and Sheila Monaghan cast doubt on eidetic imagery as being a universal explanation for the savant when they reported their interesting case of a 16-year-old, totally blind girl with calendar calculating ability.[37] The fact that she had been blind since infancy precluded the use of any visual aids, and her limited braille ability meant that no assistance was received through tactile means, such as the use of braille calendars. Obviously, the subject must have used a mechanism other than eidetic imagery to accomplish her feats.

The most systematic investigation of the role of eidetic imagery in the savant was Duckett's 1977 study.[73] For this very well-organized and comprehensive study, 25 institutionalized savants were matched with a control group of other, nonsavant retardates. Matching was based on chronological age, sex, I.Q. and length of institutionalization. All subjects were assessed in the areas of memory, creativity, visual memory imagery, eidetic imagery and cerebral dysfunction.

In Duckett's work, "visual imagery" means the recall in visual form of a previously stored image and the projection of that image upon an external surface, as measured by a picture description task. "Eidetic imagery" is defined as vivid, percept-like images that cannot be recalled in visual form after they have faded and is measured by a color fusion task, in which the subject must "see" green in order to demonstrate eidetic imagery. A single test, the symbol substitution test, was used to measure cerebral dysfunction or damage. Only two of the control subjects and none of the savants demonstrated evidence of visual memory imagery. One savant and one of the controls demonstrated eidetic imagery. This suggested that no real difference existed between the incidence of either visual memory imagery or eidetic imagery in the savants and the incidence in a matched control retarded population. Duckett concludes that eidetic imagery and visual image memory were, for all purposes, nonexistent in both groups and that their absence confirms her hypothesis that skills of savants cannot be explained by such imagery.

So what can one say about eidetic imagery and the savant? First of all, it does exist in some savants. Second, it does not, however, exist at a higher frequency in savants than in a similarly retarded, but nonsavant, group of individuals. Third, eidetic imagery exists in some forms of brain damage or cerebral dysfunction, particularly when such imaging is seen in older adolescents or adults. Fourth, eidetic imagery cannot be a universal explanation for savant skills because such skills, particularly calendar calculating, have been reported in blind individuals where eidetic imagery is not possible.

It is likely that, since many savants do have brain damage or demonstrate cerebral dysfunction, and since eidetic imagery is sometimes seen in such brain damage and cerebral dysfunction, the eidetic imaging, when present, is more a biological marker of that cerebral dysfunction than it is an explanation for savant abilities. Eidetic imagery, when it is present, is thus an effect or marking of idiosyncratic brain dysfunction rather than a cause of the savant's special skills and abilities.

INHERITED SKILLS

In 1931, two Ohio State University zoologists, David C. Rife and Laurence H. Snyder, criticized those psychologists who, they felt, had started off "clear headed" but had gone on a tangent of behaviorism, espousing that "any normal healthy child can be moulded to any desired pattern: artist or musician, recluse or social celebrity, craven or hero, fool or savant.[16] No very pertinent data have been presented for such a sweeping hypothesis." They felt strongly that the explanation of the savant lay in genetics. Mental retardation, they argued, was in most instances hereditary and so were special abilities such as music and art abilities. Therefore, "In the case of the feebleminded individuals showing marked special abilities, they had received purely coincidentally two sets of hereditary factors, those for feeblemindedness and those for special ability."

They sent letters to superintendents of institutions for the developmentally disabled throughout the United States asking for names of patients with mental handicaps and special abilities. They accumulated 33 cases: 8 musical, 8 mathematical, 7 artistic and 10 with various skills including mechanical ability and phenomenal memory. Nine savants were personally interviewed in their homes with their families present. Other cases were explored by correspondence with the institution staff and the families.

The cases included an 18-year-old male artistic savant with a mentally retarded father and an institutionalized brother, who had no drawing ability, and a normal brother with exceptional drawing ability. A second case was that of a 23-year-old male with special mathematical ability; he had a mentally retarded first cousin and a mother who was fond of and good at mental arithmetic. A third case involved inherited musical ability in the presence of acquired mental retardation following spinal meningitis at age 3. This 30-year-old man had a sister who was a gifted violinist, a paternal grandmother who had unusual musical ability as a pianist and two first cousins with exceptional musical ability. The researchers note, "The patient himself, in spite of his lack of mental ability, plays either classical music or jazz, with many variations. His ability is plainly inherent, and not the result of training." They go on to outline other cases, documenting special abilities among relatives as well as mental retardation among relatives. Some of those correlations were by indirect inference, for example: "An interesting case was that of a low grade idiot, unable to speak a word or dress himself. Yet when given an ordinary corrugated dust pan, he spun it rapidly, balancing it on the index finger. Other objects could be similarly spun, using either hand. His parents were both vaudeville actors." Reminiscent of Leslie and Ellen is their case of a 19-year-old blind, severely handicapped boy who played the piano by ear. "He plays anything he hears and is said to have perfect pitch. He has a feebleminded brother who has no musical ability, and a normal sister, who, though blind, plays the piano and composes music."

They draw several conclusions from their work. First, special abilities can develop in the presence of severe intellectual handicap "quite in the absence of training or instruction." Supplementary to that conclusion they found that where special abilities do occur "they seem to be definitely due to heredity, since they appear frequently in relatives of the patient's." They were struck as well by the fact that in individuals without these inherited special abilities, both normal and subnormal, training failed to bring out any indication of unique talent. They conclude that special abilities are inherited quite independently of general intelligence and that it is merely a coincidence when a person inherits both. Attacking their behavioristic counterparts they cite: "The fact that even feeblemindedness does not nullify the appearance of a special ability in those who inherit it, and that training is not essential for its appearance (although it would be, of course, for its complete development), coupled with the fact that even training fails to bring out such ability in other individuals, would seem to be a specific refutation of the principles of 'behavioristic' psychology." They finally soften their stand somewhat, however, by indicating that a radical position at either the hereditary or the environmental extreme is absurd and that "it is the interesting task of the geneticist and psychologist, working together, to solve the various personal equations for these unknowns."

In his case of a phenomenal memorizer Harold Ellis Jones emphasizes that while psychological factors such as compensation and reinforcement were important, they must be looked at in the light of genetics as well.[50] Henry H. Goddard, in his 1914 text *Feeble-Mindedness,* proposed that savant skills are genetically determined and that if an individual with such skills were not mentally retarded he or she would be a genius within the area of his or her skills.[81]

Dr. Abraham Brill expanded the usual definition of heredity to include not just the transmittal of constitution, talent and predilections from parent to child, but also a sort of collective unconscious, an actual body of knowledge, instincts and intuition inherited from ancestors much as lower animals inherit instincts and adaptive behaviors.[47] He states: "Our prodigies in a way resemble some of the lower animals insofar as they display in early life some instinctive knowledge like a prodigious memory." He offers as support for his ideas the lineage of his case, savant calculator S. Jungreis, whose family "supplied rabbis to the community for over 200 years" and whose paternal great grandfather, a rabbi, was called a "mathematical wizard." He cites also the case of the mathematical prodigy Pascal, who had a long and eminent line of mathematical geniuses as his forebears.

Jungreis, however, did not demonstrate his remarkable calculating skills until age 6, when they suddenly appeared; he lost those skills at age 9 when they vanished just as abruptly. To account for this, Brill, drawing on psychoanalytic and Freudian ideas about the unconscious and the psychosexual development of the personality, speculates that the death of Jungreis's mother and sister at a crucial phase of his psychosexual development "awakened and erotized his latent talent." It disappeared at age 9, Brill explains, because of the death of Jungreis's father, again at a particularly crucial stage in the psychosexual development of this particular individual.

However one views psychoanalytic theory and its relationship to and specificity for surges of abilities or energies in all of us, including savants, Brill paints a fascinating and thoughtful picture of the interaction of two kinds of unconscious in human development. Our *phylogenetic* unconscious is made up of instincts, traits and behaviors directly transmitted to a new member of the species by an ancestor. Our *ontogenetic* unconscious, in contrast, is made up of the individual's life experiences. Brill postulates that the inherited (phylogenetic) potential can lay dormant until "kindled" by some individual (ontogenetic) psychological happening. Another psychological happening can just as suddenly extinguish a talent or an ability.

Humans, then, are a composite of genetic and individual evolution. The end product is an interaction between both. Jungreis, according to Brill, was the end product of those two types of evolution, both of which contributed heavily to the presence of, and ultimately the disappearance of, the special talent. The concept that inheritence extends beyond personality traits and physical characteristics and includes the transfer of specific knowledge and skills, rather than just the potential to develop them, is a fascinating one. It is an appealing one as well, particularly when trying to explain how Leslie can "know" the rules of music or how George can "know" the rules of mathematics without having been exposed to them.

The savant, in my view, does argue for just such a transfer of knowledge and skills far beyond that generally subsumed under the term "inherited" or "genetic." Savants, as a group, may provide a ready population for the study of that possibility.

Duckett found special skills in some, but not all, of the relatives of the 25 savants she studied.[73] Dr. Bernard Rimland comments on the tendency of these skills to run in families, but LaFontaine found only one family member with special skills in 23 relatives of 5 very carefully studied savants.[41,56]

In view of all this, what is the role of genetics in producing Savant Syndrome? First, special abilities and mental retardation can be inherited as separate characteristics in certain instances; in some savants these two circumstances do occur together, coincidentally, and this can be genetically traced. Second, in other instances, however, such a genetic link cannot be clearly established, and therefore, like eidetic imagery, inherited skill is not a universal finding and cannot, by itself, account for all cases of this condition. Third, special abilities can be transmitted separately from retardation in normal individuals, and retardation can develop independently of hereditary factors—as a result of brain injury or brain disease, for example. Fourth, the emergence of special abilities in some savants is much more clearly linked to psychological factors than genetic ones; in other savants the psychological factors seem necessary, at least to kindle the genetic predisposition to special abilities. Finally, while in early research family backgrounds and heredity concerns were perhaps overemphasized, in recent research those factors have been approached too casually, and a better estimate of the contribution of heredity to the savant, while not total, could be made by giving more careful attention to genetic considerations.

In sum, it is not all nature, it is not all nurture. As with all of complex human behavior, the final result is an interaction of the two. Genetics, like eidetic imagery, cannot serve as a universal explanation of the savant.

SENSORY DEPRIVATION

Sensory deprivation falls into two categories: social isolation, such as solitary confinement, and sensory isolation due to faulty sensory input that results from conditions such as blindness, deafness or more global sensory deficits. The theory that savant abilities are based on sensory deprivation postulates that such social isolation or defective sensory input sensitizes the savant to minute changes in the environment and creates an intense concentration and preoccupation with trivial or bizarre endeavors such as memorizing obscure facts, counting, studying objects or almanacs for extended periods of time or engaging in mental arithmetic and calendar calculating.

Several investigators have felt that social isolation is an important, perhaps crucial, contributing factor to savant abilities. Dr. David Viscott highlights the social isolation and maternal deprivation in his case of Harriet in her early years: "The baby was ignored much of the time and with the exception of music, she was sensorily deprived."[18] Harriet, as you will recall, was kept in her crib day and night until almost age 2. Viscott points out: "If music became a wedge which separated Harriet from the other children and kept her from developing normally, it also became the only modality she was able to develop which allowed her to communicate her feelings to other people." Her exposure to music so early in life and her intense identification of music with the mother may have made music synonymous with the mothering figure, and her preoccupation with music may have been a way of re-creating the presence of her mother. This intense preoccupation gave Harriet her skill, and that skill then won her the praise and reinforcement that seems so integral to the development of many savants. In Harriet's case, the psychological factors were more than simply praise and reinforcement, in Viscott's view, since "her musical productions were designed not so much to communicate feelings as they were to engender love. Music did not serve to express her feelings abstractly, but became her only expression of what were limited and impaired feelings. Music seemed to become important to Harriet only if it made her mother love her."

Rubin and Monaghan report the case of R., a 16-year-old blind twin, who had been a virtual crib baby for the first three years of her life.[37] In addition to the sensory deprivation of complete blindness, there was social isolation during those first three years. These researchers attribute the savant abilities of this multihandicapped blind person to a number of factors, including some brain damage, but they feel that the social isolation was a significant contributing factor.

Generally, however, theories of sensory deprivation implicate a more biologically mediated disorder of perception due to blindness, deafness or other conditions of altered sensory pathways. Rimland particularly espouses this point of view, especially in the case of the autistic savant.[4] Citing a number of his own and other studies, he points out that, when a normal person sees something (visual input), that sensation touches off a whole variety of networking connections and associations within the brain that give that new stimulus meaning based on prior experiences. When I see a kitten, for example, I remember other kittens I have seen and I may recall the comfort of a gentle purr, may remember fondly a prior time associated with a kitten or may think of my grandchildren because they have a kitten. The one stimulus evokes a whole host of other, associated meaningful stimuli. The one stimulus provokes a sensory enrichment for me.

In Rimland's view, the autistic person lacks the ability to access those memories, those associations and those experiences of a prior time. Because of a fundamental biological defect, stimuli coming in are locked in a very narrow, closed loop or circuit, thus preventing the autistic person from realizing meaningful connections and enrichment that the rest of us regularly enjoy. While the impulse registers in the brain, it fails to broaden and draw on the rich network of similar impulses of the past which, in a normal person, give that impulse meaning and context. This failure to draw meaning and context from past stimuli sets up a form of sensory deprivation, which, according to Rimland, results from the ability to *apprehend* incoming stimuli but the inability to *comprehend* them. The closed loop results in an exceedingly narrow band of super-intense, indistractible, concentration.

This is sensory deprivation due to inability to broaden sensory input; the savant deals with only minute details in great specificity, with an inability to broaden scope or perceive stimuli in anything but an extremely narrow range. Rimland suggests that autistic savants perform their feats because of this pathological inability to broaden attention, which results in the closing out of external stimuli. The end product is intense mental energy devoted to internal preoccupations. The autistic child is thus hypodistractible and overfocused on certain internal processes. Rimland and D. A. Fein acknowledge that the neural mechanism involved in this selective faulty sensory modulation is still unidentified as to site, but they suggest that the hippocampus seems to play the crucial role in this sorting and attention process.[82]

Rimland refers to the "high fidelity" attention to certain details in the environment that many savants have, together with the inability to direct that attention to other matters. Normal persons have the capacity to deal with a broad range of potential stimuli and can choose, at will, from among them. Abstract thought can be substituted for more concrete attention; attention can be directed to particular stimuli and attention to stimuli can be fine-tuned, intensified or decreased. "The autistic child and the savant," writes Rimland, "do not have the option of deploying their attention to the narrow (physical) or broad (conceptual) ends of the spectrum, as the circumstances require. The adjusting knob on their tuning dial has come loose with the dial set at the narrow band, high-fidelity, physical-stimulus end of the range, so they are in effect locked into that attentional mode."[4]

In an earlier article Rimland describes this high-fidelity attention coupled with hypodistractibility thus:

Imagine exploring a dark cave with a variable-focus flashlight. You can broaden the light beam so you can study a stalactite with a focused beam of high intensity. We normals can control the breadth of the light beam—trading off breadth for intensity—at will. The autistic-savant child lacks this crucial trade-off capability. He must use a flashlight with a narrowly focused but intense beam, to explore the contents of the outer (extracerebral) world, as well as to search for relevant information in his own brain (intracerebral world). He is thus endowed with the capacity to deal with minute details in great specificity, but only at the cost of not being aware of the background or context of the detail, which to the normal brain imbues it with relevance and meaning.[41]

While applicable to the savant, it is in a much broader sense, this same attention defect that explains the behavior of all autistic children, not just the savant. It is simply heightened in the savant.

Edward Hoffman proposes that "the elimination or reduction of outer interfering stimuli to a minimum level is of major importance in the development of the idiot savant's abilities." He points out that individuals in extreme social isolation sometimes carry out mental calculation or exercises of rote memory as their way of adapting to that environment, and he theorizes that the savant does that also as one part of the development of those special skills.[36] An ability to sustain highly and narrowly focused concentration over long periods of time is the "special ability" seen in the idiot savant, according to A. Lewis Hill.[31]

Finally, Barry Nurcumbe and Neville Parker hypothesize, based on study of their several cases, that sensory deprivation, either from social causes (maternal deprivation) or from actual sensory input defect (deafness or blindness), creates a situation in which a child fails to develop the "inner controls against immediate drive gratification which are the basis of conceptual thought."[48] Lacking the ability to think conceptually, the damaged child thinks concretely. Concrete abilities hypertrophy and the child compensates for losses with extensive use of that which is left. This shows up as a rote memory ability but also, in their view, accounts for other savant skills as well. Once apparent, these skills are reinforced by other people and the praise and positive feedback awarded to the savant ensure the continuance of the phenomena. As an example, Nurcumbe and Parker report that, "One English idiot savant, a lightning calculator, was used in antiaircraft defense during World War I since he could produce answers to sums more speedily than others could by referring to logarithm tables." They reject rather forcefully genetic explanations, feeling that "there is deplorable tendency to explain many phenomena which cannot be readily understood as being genetically determined." The basic determinate of the idiot savant, in their view, is an atrophy or failure of the development of abstract thinking in the child "who would otherwise have been of normal intelligence." Maternal and sensory deprivation lead to excessive use of concrete thinking as a form of adaptation, thinking which is exaggerated by concentration on only a few kinds of repetitive behavior and skills, obsessional defenses and encouragement and reinforcement from others.

Sensory deprivation, whether from social isolation or biologic defect, like some of the theories outlined earlier, may more describe savant behaviors and attributes than explain or account for them. Certainly not all savants have been socially isolated—witness Ellen, Leslie and Alonzo, for example. In fact the child raised in relative isolation, or deprivation, seems to be the clear exception, for many savants experience the same general family and social network that most children enjoy.

Sensory deprivation of the very particular type described by Rimland in the case of the autistic savant may well be the defect or cause of infantile autism. I suspect it is, and his speculation regarding the cause of that condition overall is convincing and has become even more so as new data has emerged on the neuropsychology of autistic children. Yet, while it may explain infantile autism overall, it does not explain why savant abilities are found in some, but not all, of that population. Without question the incidence of savant skills in autistic children—one out of ten have such skills—is high as compared to the incidence in other groups. But the fact remains that nine out of ten do not. Therefore some other factor or factors must be independently at work in those who do have savant abilities.

Like the theories before, sensory deprivation does not provide an explanation that can encompass all the features of Savant Syndrome or explain all the savants. Other factors must be at work as well.

CONCRETE THINKING AND THE INABILITY TO REASON ABSTRACTLY

Numerous investigators have commented upon the inability of the savant to think abstractly, with reliance almost exclusively on concrete patterns of expression and thought. For some researchers, this failure in abstract ability has been viewed as an interesting and incidental finding, but others have defined it as the central defect in the savant and indeed the entire explanation of the condition.

This particular theory is most thoroughly explored by Scheerer, Rothmann and Goldstein in their comprehensive five-year study of savant L.[21] L.'s skills included calendar and lightning calculating, extended retention of numbers, the ability to spell words backwards or forwards orally or in writing, piano playing with perfect pitch and obsessive memorization and singing of opera in several languages. L.'s I.Q. was 50 on the Stanford-Binet. There was no family history of mental deficiency, although some musical skills and arithmetic ability apparently had occurred in relatives. The results of neurological examination, EEG, pneumoencephalograms and all other laboratory examinations were normal, with no demonstrable central nervous system abnormality.

The general defect here, which explains the savant in this view, is an impairment of abstract ability; there simply is none. L. could not understand or use language in a symbolic or conceptual manner and was unable to comprehend ideas, words, definitions or metaphors in any abstract sense. His speech was restricted to concrete, situationally determined, conditioned responses of a mechanical, automatic type. Such speech contains many stereotyped automatisms and generalities. This impaired abstract attitude displays itself also in a lack of social awareness and a general failure to be involved in interpersonal relationships. The savant develops into a well-trained "robot" with little ability to change with changing conditions; in the face of change or challenge, the savant holds to obsessive, stereotyped, concrete responses.

L. is described as having a superior acoustic memory but *subnormal* visual (eidetic) imagery. He could recite long speeches or sing complex arias with absolutely no understanding of them. He was unable to develop skills in a creative manner and was unable to learn intentionally by following instructions in a systematic manner. His memory was characterized not by retention of what he wanted to remember, but rather by the automatic registering of those things he was compelled to store, those things he seemed helpless to *not* retain.

A description of L. points out these characteristics: "Whereas he knows how many quarters and nickels are in 75 cents, he cannot explain why. Whereas after playing with a calendar, he suddenly knows the names of the weekdays for the months of the current and of the next year, he can never explain the 'how' and the 'why.' The direction of his talents becomes increasingly and abnormally concrete. His endowment creates an ability to remain specific but sterile."

This limitation to concrete thinking, with the natural human desire to achieve optimum capability, creates in the savant a continual expansion in his repertoire of these repetitive and narrow skills because "it is the only way he can come to terms with the world beyond his grasp." This concentration of skills and channeling of energies into such abnormally limited methods of retention and expression create abilities which on the surface seem miraculous. Yet, given the narrow outlets for the expression of these abilities, the abilities are not so astounding; according to Scheerer et al., "If any normal individual would be forced to indulge in nothing but L.'s memorial skills, he probably could accomplish the equivalent." These investigators observe that every human organism strives to achieve its optimum capability but a defective organism can exercise only those functions that nature permits him to develop. The idiot savant becomes a savant not in spite of a handicap—assuming the usual connotation of the word—but rather *because* of the handicap: "The term 'idiot savant' is self-contradictory; inasmuch as L. is 'savant' he is this because he is 'an idiot' and not in spite of it."

Using their explanation of the central defect in the savant, Scheerer and his colleagues then examine particular types of savant skills to apply that explanation to understanding those skills.

With regard to calendar calculating they look to Frank D. Mitchell's hierarchy of ability in understanding the great mental calculators of the past and present.[40] The first category of such nonsavant calculators are those who simply count: "The calculator thinks not of the arithmetical operations but of properties of numbers and of series, and the shortcuts he uses are of a relatively simple sort, showing no mathematical insight." This concrete, properties-of-numbers, noninsightful reciting of figures, rather than calculating of them, is reminiscent of Sacks' view of how twins George and Charles, the savant calendar calculators, "calculate": "Were they in some unimaginable way themselves 'seeing' primes, in somewhat the same way as they had 'seen' 111-ness or triple 37-ness? Certainly they could not be calculating them—they could calculate nothing."[29]

A second category of nonsavant calculators has a better developed knowledge of arithmetic and uses that knowledge to some limited extent rather than merely working unconsciously and concretely with numbers as objects. A distinction begins here, in this second category, between the calculators and the mathematicians. Mitchell explains: "The talent for calculation is generically rooted in a process of patterned groupings of concrete nature, be it orally, visually, or auditory-motor. The process can, but need not, develop into more abstract stages of arithmetical and mathematical understanding."

A third category of nonsavant calculators uses real mathematic ability and has the power to think in a distinctly algebraic manner and to discover and use ingenious shortcuts and symmetries. The savant calendar calculator uses rudimentary, primitive, concrete procedures based on elaborate systems of counting, treating numbers as objects and groups of objects, with no sense of relationships between them or any sense of more complex arithmetic systems. The mathematician calculator, on the other hand, understands arithmetic as an operation and algebra as a method of dealing with numbers and uses those operations and methods. The savant is a concrete calculator, not an abstract mathematician.

These same limits in abstraction ability lead to the kind of rote memory—concrete memory—that so characterizes savants of all types. The savant memorizes huge quantities of numbers, or words, or trivial facts, indeed a whole page in a foreign language, for example, with no sense or understanding of what those pieces of data or that language means.

This theory is finally summarized by Scheerer and his colleagues as follows: "We find then that an individual who is handicapped in abstraction and endowed in a particular field of performance shows a *sub*normal intelligence and an *ab*normal canalization of his endowment." The savant is driven to an abnormal degree and in restricted directions because those "endowments" are the only functions nature permits him or her given the inherent limitation of the savant condition. These functions become a coping mechanism that is limited to concrete devices and is channeled into atypical forms of expression and actualization: "A defective organism will cling tenaciously to those aspects of a situation and those features which make concrete, palpable sense to him, i.e., with which he can deal successfully. . . . therefore these aments retain easily what may appear senseless or peripheral or irrelevant to the normal observer. To the aments in question, however, this is the only 'sense' possible and pivotal in the experienced contents."[21]

Scheerer and his colleagues go to great lengths, indeed ponderous lengths, to describe accurately and document carefully this defect in abstract ability of the savant. They do that well, but they skirt the issue of the cause of that defect. "Whatever caused L.'s deficiency," they say, "no doubt can arise about its general nature." No attempt is made to speak to etiology; so while they may describe and define the nature of Savant Syndrome, they do not explain the cause.

Similarly, Nurcombe and Parker focus on the basic inability of the savant to think abstractly and highlight the retention of isolated islands of concrete ability.[48] They go one step further than description, however, and name maternal and sensory deprivation as important contributing causes to this crucial defect.

Walter A. Luszki, in his 1966 report of the performance of a deaf-retarded savant on the WAIS test, documents high-level concrete skills and impaired abstract abilities also.[83] He points out that, of all the subtests on the WAIS, the savant performed well on block design, which involves no semantic conceptionalization and no language characteristics of either a verbal or numerical nature. It is difficult, he admits, to separate out the effects of deafness from the intellectual defect here in explaining the high performance on this subtest as contrasted with so many poor scores on the other measures, but clear documentation of the abstraction defect does nevertheless exist.

This same finding surfaces again and again in research and reports on savants. It does seem to be an almost universal symptom or trait. It is probably best approached as that, as a symptom rather than a cause, and as a description of what occurs rather than an explanation of why it occurs. As a theory then, impairment of abstract ability does not explain the savant, but rather describes him. It is a valuable description, nevertheless, but must be left as that; questions as to causes need to supplement that useful description.

Let us search on.

COMPENSATORY ACTIVITY AND THE SEARCH FOR REINFORCEMENT

All of us enjoy doing that which we do well. Aside from any personal satisfaction our skills bring, the approval we get from others is important and acts as reinforcement and motivation to do even better. Some investigators feel that the reinforcement received by the savant for his or her special abilities is the foremost driving force behind these individuals. Other researchers, while recognizing the importance of reinforcement, feel that the more fundamental dynamic in the savant is a compensatory drive to develop skills in one area to offset major gaps and defects in others, much as a blind person develops superior acoustic acuity to compensate for the visual defect. In this etiologic framework the clue to the savant rests in the psychological, as opposed to biological, arena.

LaFontaine stressed positive reinforcement as a powerful motivator for the intense concentration, practice and skills seen in savants.[56] Duckett pointed to the fame her savants received in the institutional setting.[73] Hoffman also saw the importance of reinforcement, especially in institutions, commenting specifically that in the case of his savant "his mental feats are immensely socially reinforcing; he will receive a great deal of attention and interest that the normal retardate would not."[70]

Scheerer and his colleagues, as seen in the preceding section, highlight compensatory efforts, such as deliberate memorization, that savants make to offset the more generalized defect of impaired abstraction ability.[21] The savant uses reinforcement from others to meet needs for self-esteem. Jones proposes that the skills of his subjects were developed to compensate for inferiority they felt.[50] Dr. Ryuizaburo Shikiba indicates that the art of his subject was a direct search for relationships with others.[60] Viscott, in reporting what is clearly the most psychodynamic study of any savant, claims that his subject used music to try to gain her parents' approval and solicit their love.[18] S. B. Sarason and T. Gladwin point to the tremendous importance of special skills as a method of coping.[84]

Other psychological dynamics have been suggested as well. Jones feels that the phenomenal memorizing accomplished by his patient represents an unbreakable habit or a repetition compulsion in the patient's search for stimulation.[50] A. Fauville, taking a somewhat opposite stand, concludes that the special skill, rather than representing stimulation and thus a way to help the savant compensate and cope, is instead an unhealthy absorption in one particular area of behavior that leads to constant neglect of other types of behavior.[33]

Finally, Sarason points out that all the studies of the savant up to that time (1959) had overlooked the important role of parental influence and child-parent interaction in the development of this unique condition.[85] In Sarason's view, influence of the parents represented more than pure genetics, and while it was felt that parent personality was probably not the sole contributing factor in the development of Savant Syndrome, future studies, Sarason hoped, would address that issue as well as the issues of the interaction of unusual sensitivities in the savant and the influence of other environmental factors.

Certainly there can be no question that environmental, psychological and familial factors do impact on each savant in a unique way and help shape his development. What if Leslie had not come under the care of May Lemke? Or what if the staff *had* continued to try to stifle Alonzo's sculpting because he was spending too much time at it? Suppose Ellen's parents had seen her preoccupation with opera and music as a nuisance instead of a gift? But, while these factors—such as compensatory effort, reinforcement from others, repetition compulsion and parental influence—do help shape the final outcome in the savant, they do not, in my view, cause the condition. For if they did, then why wouldn't every developmentally disabled, or autistic, or brain-damaged individual be a savant or have savant skills? Why would savant skills be seen more frequently in males than in females, with such a constant regularity? Why would some patients who live in the same unit, in the same institution, and who are exposed to the same stimulation—or lack of it—develop savant skills when others do not? Surely every impaired patient would try to compensate and cope by using pathways and methods still available to them. Similarly, all such patients would crave, and benefit from, the reinforcement of those surrounding them. But, the incidence of Savant Syndrome is extremely rare, and the picture is very uniform, despite all sorts of different environments, families and surroundings.

The psychology, family and environment of the savant helps shape, but does not form, the condition. We need to look elsewhere—not for causes independent of psychological, familial and environmental factors but for additional causes.

ARCHITECTURE OF THE BRAIN

Some of the other theories regarding savant abilities rely more heavily on brain structure itself, particularly with respect to specialization of certain brain areas and structures for carrying out specific intellectual tasks. While generally this refers to right brain/left brain separation, more modern theories are concerned with even further subdivision of the brain into its component parts. Before proceeding into those theories, a brief overview of brain anatomy and organization will perhaps be useful.

The brain sits inside the solid skull (Figure 1), surrounded and cushioned by cerebrospinal fluid (CSF).

The largest part of the brain is the *cerebral cortex,* which is folded into numerous *convolutions* that entirely cover the lower centers of the brain. The cortex is divided into two *cerebral hemispheres,* right and

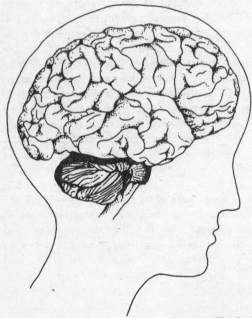

Figure 1. The Brain, Inside the Solid Skull.

left (Figure 2). Each hemisphere is subdivided into four *lobes—frontal, parietal, temporal* and *occipital* (Figure 3).

CSF flows, through some connecting channels, inside the brain itself, in chambers called *ventricles* (Figure 4). This cushion of CSF surrounds the entire central nervous system, including the spinal cord, and specimens of the fluid can be obtained for testing through use of a *spinal tap* (a procedure in which a needle is inserted between the bones of the lower back into the spinal canal and a small amount of cerebrospinal fluid is withdrawn for analysis). Prior to the development of *CAT scan* technology (Computerized Axial Tomography is a very high-reso-

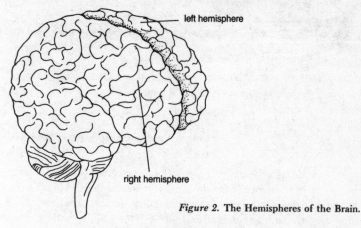

Figure 2. The Hemispheres of the Brain.

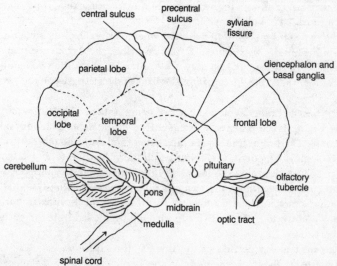

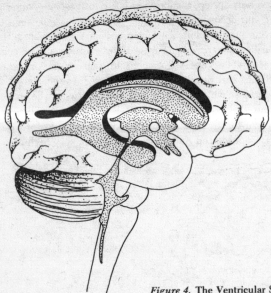

Figure 4. The Ventricular System of the Brain.

lution, computerized X-ray reconstruction of the brain or other organs), the only method available for detailed visualization of the brain was a procedure called the *pneumoencephalogram.* In this procedure air is introduced through a spinal tap and replaces the CSF, providing much more contrast on X-rays to the various brain structures than is possible with an ordinary skull X-ray.

The two cerebral hemispheres are connected to each other anatomically and neurally by a fibrous structure called the *corpus callosum* (Figure 5). An extremely rich network of circuits "wire" the two hemispheres together, transferring impulses back and forth between the two sides.

The human brain developed in three general stages. The oldest part of the brain, developmentally, is called the *brain stem,* or hindbrain (Figure 6). The brain stem is generally concerned with the most primitive biological functions, including respiration, heart rate and other vital processes. Running the length of the brain stem also, however, is the *reticular activating formation (RAF),* a general alerting system of the brain, which modulates and controls attention and alertness (Figure 7). Rich connections of the RAF run through the thalamus to the cerebral cortex.

The next oldest portion of the brain is the *midbrain,* sometimes referred to as the *diencephalon,* or the brain "between" the oldest

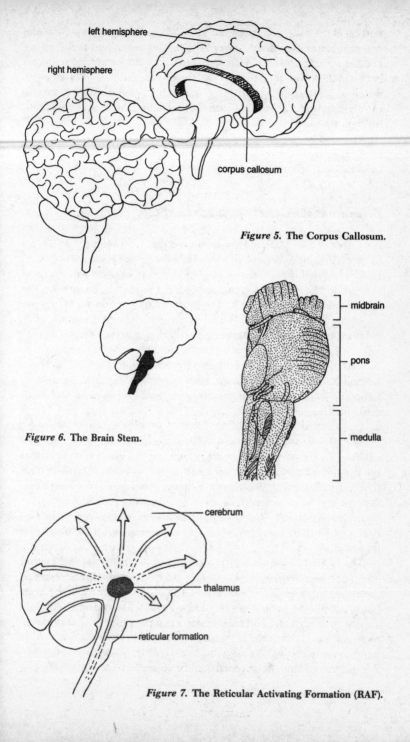

Figure 5. The Corpus Callosum.

left hemisphere

right hemisphere

corpus callosum

Figure 6. The Brain Stem.

midbrain

pons

medulla

cerebrum

thalamus

reticular formation

Figure 7. The Reticular Activating Formation (RAF).

portion of the central nervous system (CNS) and the newest section, the cerebral cortex, described earlier. The midbrain contains two very important structures: the *thalamus*, which is an important relay station between the lower brain centers and the cortex, and the *hypothalamus*, which regulates eating, drinking, body temperature and a variety of other important bodily processes, including hormonal functions, through the *pituitary gland*.

Attached to the hindbrain is another structure called the *cerebellum*. This structure generally controls balance, body position and movement in space (Figure 2).

RIGHT BRAIN/LEFT BRAIN SPECIALIZATION

A number of investigators have suggested that typical savant skills tend to involve abilities associated with right hemisphere functions. T. L. Brink, responding to Hoffman's behavioral explanation of mechanical abilities in the case of Mr. A., suggested that, while factors such as intense motivation, practice and reinforcement were no doubt of some importance in the savant, only a few individuals among the many retardates exposed to such factors actually developed savant skills.[71] Therefore, he held, such behavioral factors were not a sufficient explanation. Instead, Brink proposed that organic factors were responsible for these special abilities. Using his own case example—Mr. Z. (described in Chapter 7)—Brink suggests that those organic factors are intact right brain function and left brain damage, occurring together.

Brink notes that the left brain generally governs the use of language, mathematical computation and other orderly conceptual or abstract analysis. The right brain is generally superior in tasks involving spatial relationships, activities involving visualization and movement and skills such as mechanical ability. He notes that in the case of Mr. A., performance on tests of language skills was very low, whereas scores in testing of mechanical ability—right brain function—were very high.[70] He concludes, thus, that right brain/left brain organic factors explain that instance.

The case of Mr. Z. provided a unique circumstance of known and specific left brain damage, which resulted from a bullet track confined to that hemisphere. There was, at first, the expected right-side paralysis, but gradually the patient regained hearing and use of limbs with only a slight residual motor and sensory deficit on the right. With that partial recovery Mr. Z. was able to speak to a limited degree but was unable to write complete words or sign his name (as Mr. A. was able to do). Mr. Z.'s preserved and heightened ability to remember directions and routes, his enhanced spatial sense and his mechanical abilities were explained by Brink as being "traced to heredity, an undamaged right hemisphere, and, of course, sufficient motivation, practice and reinforcement." It seemed clear to Brink that, in this case, right brain/left brain factors were crucial and causal. Whether the right brain dominance here emerged as some sort of compensatory process to make up for damage in the left hemisphere, or whether the skills, inherited from the father who also had talent in these areas, simply emerged once out of the influence of the usually more dominant left brain, remained an unanswered question. In either event, right brain dominance linked to those skills seemed evident.

In his 1978 article on autistic savants, Rimland explored, even more fully, right brain/left brain considerations in explaining the special abilities seen so often in that group of patients.[4] Quoting some work by P. E. Tanguay, he points out that the special skills most often present in autistic children are those associated with right hemisphere functions and the absent skills are essentially left hemisphere activities.[86] At that point in time Rimland summarized left brain function as primarily the processing of verbal, logical, rational information in essentially linear or sequential fashion. The primary functions of the right brain, in contrast, were of a spatial, nonlinear and intuitive nature, according to him. Correctly cautioning that such hemisphere specialization is an oversimplification and not absolute, Rimland points to another important difference in the way the two sides of the brain function—the *simultaneous* nature of the right brain (immediate perception with few memory associations) and the *sequential* nature of the left brain (processing with interconnected memories and associations). In the autistic savant, simultaneous, "high-fidelity" imagery and function were found to be predominant, implicating that right brain activity was foremost.

The fact that mathematical and calculating skills, seemingly sequential left brain activities, are so common in the savant would appear to argue against such right brain/left brain dichotomy. In approaching that apparent discrepancy Rimland uses the example of Benj Langdon, the graduate student taught calendar calculating skills, to explain the role of the right brain in such functions. Langdon described a "migration" of abilities from conscious and systematic to unconscious and automatic after a period of very deliberate and conscientious study. Rimland states: "My hunch is that when this dramatic quantum change took place in Langdon's calendar calculating capacity, the site of processing migrated from his left hemisphere to some other point, quite possibly his right." This complex set of calculations thus became automated, and transferred from a sequential format (left brain) to a simultaneous format (right brain).

This is but the same phenomenon, in reverse, that I pointed out in Chapter 3, when describing the middle-aged woman who was a natural musician, able to play remarkably well by ear, and who lost that ability suddenly and totally when she began to study music systematically in order to become a better performer. Seemingly what had been usefully settled as a right brain, natural ability "migrated" (and was lost) when the skill was to be more systematically studied.

Right brain/left brain specialization is not as simple or as specific as originally proposed. Any skill or ability as complex as language cannot be a function of only one brain area or even one brain hemisphere. The cross connections and interactions between brain areas, cortical and subcortical, are numerous in number and location. With certain types of brain damage other areas of the brain, in the same hemisphere or on the opposite side, can be recruited for transfer of function and compensatory use. Techniques of brain mapping, which outline deep brain function rather than just cortical activity, show those vast interconnections and the intricate intercommunication between hemispheres and between areas in the hemispheres, superficial and deep.

Dr. Richard Restak, in his 1984 book *The Brain*, sums up most accurately and most clearly present-day knowledge about hemispheric specialization, which began with Dr. Paul Broca's description of the "language area" of the brain in the left hemisphere in 1861.[87] Based on a variety of studies involving split-brain research, PET scans of normal individuals doing a variety of cognitive or symbolic tasks, autopsy and neuropathological dissections and the use of radioactively tagged chemicals in animals, some contemporary conclusions regarding left brain/right brain function can be stated.

First of all, the left hemisphere is more involved than the right in language, speech and certain other motor skills, although these functions are not exclusively confined to the left side of the brain. The right hemisphere, in contrast, is generally more involved than the left in spatial tasks, visual-constructional skills and other performances that do not depend as heavily on verbal ability, for example, artistic or mechanical performance.

Second, regardless of the particular skill being tested, the strategy involved—cognitive or symbolic—also determines which side of the brain is being used. Thus the left brain has more to do with functions that use sequential, logical, symbolic (abstract) strategies and methods, such as reading or speaking, than with functions that use more simultaneous, intuitive, nonverbal (concrete) strategies and methods, such as painting, sculpting or constructing things. Restak states: "Division of the hemispheres into *symbolic-conceptual* (left hemisphere) vs. *non-symbolic directly perceived* (right hemisphere) avoids many oversimplifications." The right hemisphere can more easily derive meaning from concrete objects or events, while the left hemisphere is more involved, although not exclusively so, with symbolic language.

Third, to the extent that the right hemisphere is involved with language, it tends to be more involved with the emotional tone of speech—animation, enthusiasm or lack of it, expression and color—than with content and comprehension. Stated differently, the left brain is principally concerned with the production of speech (creating the thoughts and words), while the right brain is concerned with the emotional expression of that speech (intonation, inflection and accompanying emotion). Some investigators have modified or refined that view even further to suggest that the right brain is more involved with negative coloring of experience and language (including sadness, anxiety, anger and crying), and the left brain is more involved with positive emotions (such as happiness, joy and laughter). These hemispheric functions likely occur at lower, subcortical levels, and strict localization is even less precise than with some of the language and symbolic functions mentioned earlier. The subtle shading of emotional tone in language, as distinguished from the pure semantics, the words, of language, is called "prosody."

Fourth, and finally, some evidence has begun to emerge linking cerebral dominance to sex differences due to the prenatal influence of sexual hormones in the fetus on the developing brain. This concept will be explored further in Chapter 13.

The availability now of much more highly refined techniques for the study of brain function, cortical and deep, is providing more and more information about localization of skills in brain function. Split brain studies are no longer limited just to patients with lesions in the corpus callosum, the fibers that connect the two hemispheres of the brain, but can be done using catheters to supply anesthetic to only one half of the brain; testing for a variety of tasks and skills can then be accomplished. Certainly the newer brain flow studies, such as PET scans, which look at brain function rather than just structure, will provide massive amounts of data not just with respect to where certain tasks or skills are carried out in the brain, but also regarding how those areas change or interconnect with the use of different strategies in performing those tasks or skills.

While the data thus far does not support the earlier, simpler notions of right brain/left brain specialization—as if functions were entirely in the province of one hemisphere or the other—information gathered from studies using newer technology does point in the direction of some dominance of certain brain areas over others if one takes into account not just the task or skill per se, but also the strategies involved (cognitive or symbolic), the techniques involved (simultaneous or sequential) and perhaps even the emotions involved (prosody). It is premature, and overly simplistic, to classify Savant Syndrome as entirely a right brain/ left brain phenomenon; hemispheric specialization itself is much more complex than that. Yet, when one examines the correlations here between the types of functions that *tend* to be associated with one hemisphere or the other, and the types of symptoms and behaviors seen in the savant—simultaneous, concrete, high fidelity, spatial, intuitive— one sees a predominance of right brain function in this condition.

But unusual cerebral dominance, as seen in some brain diseases or lesions, is not the cause of that disease or lesion; rather it is a symptom. Similarly, in Savant Syndrome patterns of cerebral dominance are symptoms, or clues, to the disorder, not the disorder itself. They are promising clues, however, and are worthy of follow-up and explanation. Of the theories put forth by investigators to this point, that of right brain/left brain specialization is the most encompassing and comes closest to helping explain the seemingly inexplicable.

More about that later.

OTHER ORGANIC FACTORS

Biologic studies on the savant are sparse in spite of the fact that many investigators have suspected an organic, rather than a behavioral or a purely genetic, basis for the disorder. Horwitz alludes to a "specialized computer-like mechanism" and others as well infer some idiosyncratic brain circuitry in explaining the savant.[26] Until recently, however, the tools necessary to explore these ideas have been sparse, but some earlier findings are of interest nonetheless.

Autopsy Data

There have been four postmortem studies of brains of savants.

Down performed one such autopsy on his patient who displayed "the perfect appreciation of past or passing time." You will recall his description of the patient:

Gradually his response became less ready, and he would not or could not reply unless he was a little excited. He had to be shaken like an old watch, and then the time would be truly given. Gradually his health became enfeebled and the faculty departed. At an autopsy I found that there was no difference in his cerebrum from an ordinary brain except that he had two well-marked and distinct soft commissures [meaning unusual connections, or fibers, joining two areas of the cortex; it is difficult to know the exact significance of the finding but Down does note it].

Ireland conducted an autopsy in the "sad and mysterious case of Kaspar Hauser," who seemed to develop both his mental defect and special skill of superb memory from prolonged isolation and deprivation as a child and adolescent.[10] In fact, some felt that the diagnosis in this case should have been psychosis rather than retardation. The description is brief: "The skull was somewhat thicker than usual, and the brain rather small, but not quite overlapping the cerebellum, which was larger in proportion to the cerebrum. The tissue was found healthy, but the convolutions were broader and simpler than usual [perhaps signifying some atrophy or shrinkage of brain tissue in these areas]."[10]

Dr. F. Sano gave an extremely detailed sulcus-by-sulcus description of the brain of Pullen, the Genius of Earlswood Asylum,[13] who died at age 75. The brain showed marked arteriosclerosis and enlarged ventricles; arrested development of the central, temporal and frontal lobes with preservation of the occipital lobes; and less complex convolutional pattern on the left as compared to that on the right in the frontal areas. The corpus callosum was larger than expected. Sano postulated that the preservation of the occipital lobes, which is the visual reception area, due to arrested development in the other areas of the brain, accounted for Pullen's unusual visual and artistic skills.

Interestingly, in view of the current cerebral dominance theories, Sano did note *"a greater lack of development in the left than in the right hemisphere."* He commented that "some pathologic factors had reduced the brain mass, and especially had arrested the development of the central, temporal and frontal lobes. As is usually the case under such circumstances, the left side was more affected than the right."

Sano's observations in 1918 about left brain/right brain neuroanatomy and its significance are strikingly similar to the observations being made 70 years, and many savants, later. His speculation about some unknown pathological factor arresting the development of the central, temporal and frontal lobes on the left side and sparing the right side is hauntingly prophetic, as will be seen later in present-day research findings.

Finally, Dr. Walter Steinkopff describes postmortem findings in a male calendar calculating and musical savant with symptomatic right-sided epilepsy; there were no gross findings but there were microscopic changes in the right temporal area in the fourth and fifth cortical areas.[49] The significance of that finding in this case is difficult to assess because of the presence of epilepsy originating from that area.

The electroencephalogram (EEG), or brain wave test as it is sometimes called, is done by attaching small electrodes to the surface of the scalp with electrode gel and recording brain wave activity from various areas of the brain through those surface electrodes. The EEG records electrical activity of the brain just as an electrocardiogram (EKG) records the electrical activity of the heart from the surface of the body. The EEG, however, has not been particularly informative with respect to savants. EEGs on the twin calendar calculators were normal.[26] Steinkopff administered an EEG on his calendar calculator while the subject was calculating; cortical arousal was noted.[49] An EEG on Leslie Lemke was mildly abnormal with an excess of abnormal slow wave frequencies over the right mid-temporal areas, intermittent, but confined to that region. Drs. J. Griffith Steel, Richard Gorman and Jerry Flexman report a normal EEG in their 29-year-old autistic savant.[88]

In my sample of 280 patients with a diagnosis of Early Infantile Autism, EEG abnormalities were, as might be expected, more common in Group C—patients with documented brain damage.[5] In that group 60 percent of the patients who underwent an EEG showed abnormal findings, compared to 14 percent of the patients with classic Early Infantile Autism. Since savants are seen in both those groups, one may or may not find EEG abnormalities in any given savant. Without question in future studies the newer computerized tracings (C-EEG) will be more informative since they provide a much more sophisticated analysis of brain area interaction and have the potential for measuring subcortical activity rather than just surface cortical changes.

Rapid eye movement (REM) sleep patterns, it would seem, might be another interesting and useful area of inquiry with respect to savants since, as will be seen in detail in Chapter 13, REM sleep is thought to be associated with certain crucial memory functions. Since savants have unusual memory patterns, one might postulate that the findings of REM tests conducted on them would differ significantly from the findings of such tests administered to a normal population. Yet there has been only one examination of REM sleep in the savant. K. Z. Altshuler and D. R. Brebbia did all-night oculograms on the calendar calculating twins, George and Charles.[89] George, the brighter of the two (I.Q. 67), showed a higher-than-normal amount of REM while Charles (I.Q. 58) showed normal values. In view of earlier studies of developmentally disabled patients and studies of twins, one would have expected that both would have had lower-than-normal amounts of REM and that the pattern would have been the same for both of them. The authors speculate that in the future a more diversified sample of developmentally disabled patients will probably show the same wide distribution of REM patterns as seen in the normal population with no clear relationship between disease and REM. They felt that the REM findings here were not particularly informative regarding savant abilities and that the findings certainly did not explain those abilities.

Pneumoencephalograms

Before the availability of CAT scans and other high-resolution X-ray techniques, the pneumoencephalogram was used to look for certain kinds of central nervous system structural disease. In this procedure, with use of a spinal tap, air is used to replace spinal fluid so that various brain structures can be seen in greater contrast to each other than is possible when using conventional X-ray techniques.

In a 1975 study Drs. Stephen L. Hauser, G. Robert Delong and N. Paul Rosman analyzed the results of pneumoencephalograms conducted on 17 patients with Early Infantile Autism.[90] This is not a study of patients with Savant Syndrome as such, but 4 of the 17 patients did have savant skills in music or mechanical areas, and the high incidence of Savant Syndrome in Early Infantile Autism makes the findings relevant. In the study 15 of the 17 patients showed abnormalities involving the *left* temporal lobe and dilatation of the temporal horn in the *left* lateral ventricle. The increased width of the temporal horn was felt to reflect flattening and atrophy of the hippocampal contour on the left. There was a distinct deficiency of brain substance in the left cerebral hemisphere, although the authors felt there was probably bilateral disease present with only minor changes on the right. The researchers conclude: "The unusually frequent occurrence of left-handedness in our series also suggests that the major cerebral abnormality was left-sided and thus resulted in a 'taking over' of some motor and language functions by the right hemisphere. It may be useful to think of the lesion under discussion as asymmetrically bilateral."

The finding of left-side damage in these patients, coupled with specific lesions in the medial temporal structures such as the hippocampus and the amygdala, is especially pertinent, as will be seen later in relation to some more recent findings on cerebral lateralization and specialization.

CAT Scans

There is only one prior published report on CAT scan findings in Savant Syndrome. Steel et al. report that a CAT scan on their 29-year-old male autistic mathematical savant was normal.[88] Actually, however, this particular individual, while called a savant, had an I.Q. of 91 and was diagnosed as having infantile autism, residual state. The authors felt that this could be considered a case of Savant Syndrome because of marked overdevelopment of a single talent and severe deficits in verbal reasoning and social maturity.

Leslie Lemke, clearly a savant, did show CAT scan abnormalities (detailed earlier in Chapter 8). You will recall there was an area of defect or scarring in the frontal area of the brain, as well as some similar defect or scarring in the parietal and occipital lobes on the left. Questions were raised about the possibility of damage from either an earlier infection or perhaps some circulatory problems in these areas. In short, CAT scan results showed unequivocal left-side brain damage.

A 36-year-old profoundly retarded, blind, epileptic savant reported by Dr. Neil Charness, Jane Clifton and Lyle MacDonald has, like Leslie Lemke, remarkable musical skills.[91] His case will be reported in more detail in Chapter 13. He has a right-side paralysis of both the arm and the leg. A CAT scan shows clear left-side abnormality and an EEG shows excessive slow and spike wave activity over the left hemisphere. As with Leslie Lemke, there is unequivocal evidence of left-brain damage and dysfunction.

Neuropsychological Testing

Another way to detect organic brain dysfunction is through the use of detailed neuropsychological test protocols. These are much more extensive, precise and specifically tailored to locate and assess brain damage than earlier psychological test instruments. Leslie Lemke was given such a neuropsychological battery and a summary of those findings was outlined in Chapter 8. The overall impression was "Savant Syndrome with moderate mental retardation and severe impairment of verbal and nonverbal abstract reasoning skills." There was no question but that this protocol showed evidence of brain damage consistent with the EEG and CAT scan findings.

Steele et al. did a formal neuropsychological test battery on their subject using 13 subtests.[88] This individual, whose skill was in mathematics, did well in that area, as expected. The subject scored very poorly in tests of verbal abstract ability and in tests of verbal recall requiring associations. The researchers did find a high WAIS Verbal I.Q. but felt that it was due to concrete verbal memory. The subject did poorly on visual memory tests, and no special capacity for eidetic imagery was found. These researchers conclude that "an idiot savant is most likely an autistic person with inhomogeneous [scattered and selective, as opposed to general, damage uniformly affecting all areas of the brain] brain injury with preserved capacity for abstraction restricted to a single sphere of intellectual function." They determined that there was bilateral frontal lobe dysfunction with preserved posterior hemisphere abilities; however, the *preserved* functions "are especially those of the *right* posterior region."

Unfortunately, in larger-sample studies of the savant, the issue of organicity has not been consistently studied. LaFontaine did find, in her 5 carefully studied cases, that "in all the cases there is some evidence, in varying degrees, of some type of neurologically based difficulty."[56] Drs. Beate Hermelin and Neil O'Connor, in their 12 savant cases, have not reported any specific or systematic analysis of the presence or absence of organicity.[92] Duckett, in her analysis of 25 savants compared to a control group of 50 patients with developmental disabilities, attempted to use a symbol substitution scale to measure what she called "cerebral dysfunction."[73] She was unable to reach any firm conclusion from her tests on that particular scale and indicated "this writer is not aware of any instrument, method or equipment which assesses brain injury with complete accuracy in living subjects. . . . the best way to resolve the controversy regarding brain injury of idiot savants appears to be through autopsies."

Fortunately, newer techniques, such as the CAT scan and neuropsychological tests already available, and the PET scan and other brain mapping techniques becoming available, should provide an answer to the organicity question without waiting for autopsy data. As discussed, in the two cases where some reasonably useful postmortem data is already available (Sano[13] and Steinkopff[49]), organic changes were demonstrable. In the two cases where CAT scan information was available (excluding the case with an I.Q. of 91), clear left-side brain damage was present. If one adds to that the abnormal pneumoencephalogram findings of 15 patients in the study by Hansen et al. of 17 patients with Early Infantile Autism, which included some savants, the case for organicity as a consistent finding becomes compelling.[90] Emerging studies using more recent and more definitive techniques in larger samples should allow that initial impression to be confirmed, modified or refuted.

THE ENIGMA PERSISTS

So where are we with respect to the theories presented thus far? In a comprehensive review of these theories in 1974, and after very careful study of her five subjects, LaFontaine concludes "that there was no strong support for any single explanation of the behavior of the idiot savant, and this may be the major value of such a study. . . . the behavior of the idiot savant appears to be complex and truly difficult to comprehend."[56] She refers to the "mystery" of the syndrome. Duckett, in a 1976 review of theories and then in the report of her specific study of

25 savants, concludes similarly that no single theory to that point explained all savants. She asked for more study and referred to the savant as a "puzzle."[73]

And, now, where has this review left us? If one were to stop at this point with only these findings and these theories, the conclusion would probably have to be the same—that no single explanation surfaces and that more study of larger samples over a longer period of time will be needed. But new findings, new theories and new techniques of study have emerged.

Fortunately, we can go further now, and will, in the chapters that follow.

12

"Great Vigor of Memory"—in the Savant and in the Rest of Us

"I'll remember this day as long as I live," said George as he ended his interview with Morley Safer on the *60 Minutes* program of October 10, 1983. The startling fact is that he will—in full detail. This is in contrast to the rest of us, who will have trouble remembering what we did last Tuesday. "Great vigor of memory is often conjoined with a low order of intelligence," notes Dr. Forbes Winslow.[93] This is particularly, uniformly and spectacularly true in the savant.

While no single theory put forth thus far can explain all savants, there is one single trait that all savants do have in common. That trait is superior memory. Leslie Lemke has a seemingly endless repertoire of pieces that he has heard only once but can recall perfectly years later. Richard Wawro visits a marketplace in Poland and several years later paints from memory a picture of it—in exquisite and minute detail. Ellen listens to an entire opera once or twice and then sings it back without error. George remembers what the weather was on every day of his adult life.

Whatever diversity does exist in Savant Syndrome, remarkable memory—of a unique, uniform type—welds the condition together. Chapter 5 described a number of savants whose special skill is memory. Other savants have prodigious memory in addition to other talents. Indeed, the linking of special skills with special memory—in the presence of substantial intellectual defect—*is* Savant Syndrome.

Certainly I am not the first to be impressed with not only the remarkable memory of the savant, but also with the special nature of savant-type memory—automatic, mechanical, concrete and habit-like. The observations of Dr. Edward Sequin, who antedated Dr. J. Langdon

Down by two decades in the latter 1800s, should be mentioned here. Down, in his initial description of Savant Syndrome (noted in Chapter 5), comments on the extraordinary memory of the savant and uses the interesting term "verbal adhesion" to describe this peculiar and distinctive kind of remembering.[1] He states: "Memory of tune is a very common faculty among the feebleminded; they readily acquire simple airs, and rarely forget them. I have had one boy under my observation who, if he went to an opera, would carry away a recollection of all the airs, and would hum or sing them correctly."

Sounds familiar, doesn't it?

Dr. Alfred F. Tredgold notes, "In a considerable proportion of idiot savants, the gift is one of memory in some form or other, and of this, many interesting and remarkable examples have been cited."[12] He characterizes this phenomenal memory as being one of simple "automatic" forms: "There are many idiots who cannot speak a single word, and yet can hum a tune, which they have heard only once, with perfect accuracy. Other aments will reel off poetry almost ad infinitum, yet without any understanding of the sense of what they are saying, or even the meaning of the words."

In speaking of his patient Kirtie, Dr. Martin W. Barr states, "His memory is, indeed, phenomenal."[52] Kirtie repeats, after a single hearing, the words and music of all the popular songs he hears. He imitates and pantomimes. He repeats words and sentences in nine different languages. Barr characterizes this memory as "an exaggerated form of habit" and "obedience to suggestion, automatic, not volitional nor reflective," as seen in normal persons. "Thus in the act and in the echo he is simply a creature of suggestion," Barr concludes.

Dr. William W. Ireland refers to "imbeciles with unusually tenacious memories," and Dr. Wilhelm Griesinger comments on the "remarkable memory for places exhibited in certain idiots of low mental capacity."[10] Winslow observes, "Idiots have exhibited the faculty of retention to a remarkable extent, and men of very limited and circumscribed powers of reasoning and of most defective judgment have had memories distinguished for their tenacity."[93]

Dr. Harold Ellis Jones classifies phenomenal memory as a special ability and concludes that "the feebleminded show a high development of memory."[50] He characterizes the prodigious memory seen in a case of his as "an atypically focalized habit system." Dr. Macdonald Critchley uses the terms "exultation of memory" and "memory without reckoning"[32] to describe the phenomenon of savant memory.

Through the years these and other investigators have also noted that, contrary to the commonly held notion that memory and intelligence are generally linked, memory seems to operate as a separate system or variable in the savant and seemingly can develop separately from intelligence. Dr. Arthur P. Holstein, in discussing William A. Horwitz's description of the calendar calculating twins, sums that view up thus:

> It is interesting to speculate that perhaps the phenomenon of a type of memory which idiot savants have represents memory which in some fashion has developed separately from general intellectual ability as a part of the personality. This notion is not unusual since paranoid schizophrenics have an exquisite memory, and in a general way, they incorporate their memory ability into their personality. At any rate, the qualities of memory that George and Charles and the others exhibit are apparently not associated with any aspects of mental functioning associated with their intelligence of which they are impoverished.[26]

Recent studies by Drs. Beate Hermelin, Neil O'Connor and John Sloboda, who have available to them now a group of 21 savants, document the existence of superior memory in the savant and support the view that this memory is independent of more global intelligence.[22, 38] In both of two separate studies, one of 11 calendar-calculating savants and one of a musical savant, the researchers confirm the presence of such prodigious memory, but conclude that memory alone does not account for savant capabilities.

Finally, Joan Goodman presents her 1972 case of an autistic savant with calendar calculating skills and memorization abilities in the areas of geography, history, addresses, telephone numbers, maps, television trivia and movie trivia.[94] From childhood on, this savant was obsessed with the printed word, particularly in telephone books and encyclopedias. Digit span was at age level. There was a conspicuous concreteness and an impaired abstract ability. His measured I.Q. was 37 with a diagnosis of childhood psychosis (autism). His superior memory ability was clearly evident.

Goodman raises, in this case, the interesting possibility that her savant has, as suggested by Jerome Bruner, a failure in metabolism of short-term memory—a failure to forget—instead of an enhanced ability to remember. The savant, in such an instance, shows impressive long-term memory for what is usually short-term material for the rest of us, material such as phone numbers or assorted other trivia. There is, then, a conspicuous inability to forget and to erase. The insignificant facts remain and actually obscure or block pathways to more long-term, more typically associative memory.

In his foreword to Aleksandr Románovich Luria's 1968 book *In the Mind of the Mnemonist* Bruner notes that the memory of nonsavant mnemonist S., whom Luria describes in such detail, is full of particulars, but that S. lacks the ability to convert those details into more general concepts.[95] S. literally cannot forget. This failure to erase and process short-term memory, while impressive, produces a nonselectivity in remembering so that "what remains behind is a kind of junk heap of impressions." Thus in S., as in the savant, persistent concrete memory creates highly concrete thinking. Bruner accurately characterizes this kind of remembering as a failure of one aspect of memory and the hypertrophy of another.

Might this be the case in the savant? Might savants have an inability to forget rather than a special capacity to remember?

You will recall one behavior in Leslie Lemke that suggests this is a good possibility. In the challenge and request portions of his concerts, Leslie would store in memory any song or piece shouted out as a request by an audience member, and simply would not stop performing until every request was granted, no matter what the hour. Once given aloud, each request was in effect programmed in Leslie's memory and had to be fulfilled. If, by sheer necessity, the concert were to end, Leslie would continue at home that night to answer each and every request "entered" into his short-term memory. Otherwise, he would appear uncomfortable or seem to feel "unfinished." Those associated with Leslie have learned, now, to ask that requests be made only *in writing*.

A failure or inability to forget? It certainly seems so.

TESTS OF MEMORY FUNCTION IN THE SAVANT

While observations about memory in the savant have been very uniform, formal testing and documentation of that memory has been less consistent, principally because a variety of tests were used before more formal and standardized neuropsychological test batteries became available, and because subjects were studied individually rather than in groups.

Often, limited or fairly crude tests measuring functions or abilities such as digit span were used. Unfortunately, even the term "digit span" lacks a precise definition, and researchers do not always describe exactly what procedures were used in their particular test of that capacity. Typically, however, a subject is first given a series of random numbers, ranging from single-digit numbers to numbers with as many as nine digits, and is asked to immediately recall them. In some digit-span tests, such as the WAIS I.Q. subtest for that ability, described earlier, a second part of the test involves giving a series of numbers to the subject with instructions to recite that series backwards, rather than in the order given. If "874" were given in that portion of the test, the correct response would be "478." This function is referred to as "digit span backward." Digit span represents only one type of short-term memory, but testing for it can serve as a useful screening method. The major limitation in interpreting digit-span results in studies that reported them is the lack of standardization of the term. Recognizing the limitations of using digit span to measure memory, let us nevertheless begin with that.

Herman H. Spitz and Louise LaFontaine in 1963 reviewed reports of digit span in savants and noted that early reports gave contradictory results.[96] They note that the normal digit span for adolescents and adults with average and above average intelligence is 5 to 7 digits. LaFontaine had done an earlier study comparing digit span in a group of eight savants with digit span in a group of comparable educable retardates and in a group of eight nonretarded volunteers matched in age and sex to the savant group.[55] Analyzing that data further, Spitz and LaFontaine conclude that the digit span for the savant group was within the normal range $(6 + 1)$ in contrast to the limited digit span of nonsavant retardates $(3 + 1)$. About the savants they conclude:

> Although these retarded individuals display outstanding capacities of various types, they have one capacity in common: a digit span (and, by extension, an immediate memory span) which is within the normal range. If at least the capacity for immediate memory is normal, then the highly complex human brain—an unmatched computer even in a somewhat damaged or incomplete state—can be devoted largely to the development of some particular trait. That trait may be the memory span itself, or musical ability, or some other inherited trait which has somehow survived largely intact.

Digit span in Leslie Lemke was 7, or above average. Digit span in the autistic mathematical savant reported on by Drs. J. Griffith Steel, Richard Gorman and Jerry Flexman was 16, clearly superior.[88] Dr. A. Lewis Hill singled out digit span in a calendar calculator and found 5 digits forward and 5 backward.[31] Dr. Jane Duckett, in her study of 25 savants, with a matched control group of 50 retarded subjects, found an auditory digit span of 4.56 in the savant group as compared to 2.90 in the control group (statistically significant 0.001).[73] Digit span backward was 1.68 for the savant group and 0.58 for the control group (statistical significance 0.01). Results for visual digit span showed the same superiority of the savant group when compared to the control group.

But there is more to memory than digit span, and studies of memory function overall, more globally measured, are more significant. Certainly still the best study of overall memory in savants as a group, and in savants as compared to other retardates and to normal subjects, is

Duckett's 1976 work. She tested formally for three types of memory, with the hypothesis that a group of institutionalized savants would score significantly higher on these memory tests than would a control group matched for I.Q., age, sex and length of institutionalization. *Figural* memory, the capacity to remember pictures, was tested by using a series of animal figures. *Symbolic* memory was tested by using the Digit Span Test from the WAIS (the digits served as symbols in contrast to the actual images used in the subtest that measured figural memory). *Semantic* memory, the capacity to remember words as opposed to numbers or pictures, was tested using a series from a standard word-span test, the Meeker Semantic Memory Test.

The hypothesis was supported. The savants, as compared to the matched, institutionalized control subjects, were clearly superior in symbolic and semantic memory, although no differences in figural memory were found. Duckett also tested for the presence of eidetic imagery and visual imagery memory. Of the 25 savants only one showed eidetic imagery and none showed visual imagery memory.

LaFontaine, in her 1974 study of five savant subjects, found that on the Wechsler scales "the highest scores for all subjects were on memory type items, which are presumed to be measuring short-term memory."[56] Digit spans for these five individuals, incidentally, were 7, 6, 15, 11 and 8. There was no support for eidetic imagery in these individuals.

Steel et al. did administer a complete neuropsychological test battery to their subject.[88] On the Wechsler Memory Scale the subject scored in the 97th percentile but subtests showed this superiority to be nearly entirely localized to *concrete verbal memory*. There was no evidence of eidetic imagery. Leslie Lemke's neuropsychological test battery showed that "immediate attention and memory are relative strengths on this test. In the short-term memory test subarea, performance is approximately in the normal range." This area of formal functioning was in sharp contrast to severely impaired functioning otherwise, particularly with respect to abstraction abilities. The test showed clear evidence of preserved memory coupled with the ability to think only concretely.

In summary, observation of superior memory in savants has been confirmed by tests specifically measuring that ability. The memory is of a concrete, verbal type and seems to be a spared function that stands in contrast to otherwise markedly limited global intelligence. The memory, and the special talent it is associated with, are the hallmarks of Savant Syndrome.

WHAT IS NORMAL MEMORY?

To better understand the unique and distinctive memory function of the savant, let me summarize some of what we know about normal memory.

Human memory is enormously complex. Trying to understand it is like trying to grasp the concept of an infinite universe when we are accustomed to thinking in terms of boundaries and borders, or the concept of eternity when we are used to thinking in terms of things that begin and end. But we must understand memory if we are to understand us, because memory is more than simply remembering; it is, as well, the basic unit of thought and of creativity. It is the foundation on which these two higher brain functions are built.

The more I learn about computers, the more I stand in awe of the one we each have in our own skull. Where is there a computer a mere three pounds in size that can store somewhere between one hundred trillion (10^{11}) and 280 quintillion (2.8×10^{20}) bits of information—an entire lifetime of memories?[97] Where is there a computer that can not only store that massive amount of information but that can *independently* correlate, associate, analyze and actually create new insights and ideas from it? Where is there a computer that can truly learn, all by itself and on its own, without being programmed by some outside force to create that "learning"? Where is there a sophisticated computer that can run as long as 100 years without repair, needs no surge protector, never needs to be booted or formatted, replaces all its parts continually without loss of data and without down time and has its own built-in back-up memory such that it can lose up to 90 percent of its capacity and still not lose stored data?

Where is there a computer that can create Beethoven's Fifth or Brahms' Fourth? Where is there a computer that can dream? Where is there a computer that, while doing all of the above, can feel, or love, or care?

True, a computer can often do things more quickly than the brain, but when George was asked what day of the week it would be on June 6 in the year 91360 it took him less time than it took the computer to give that answer (it will be a Friday), and it took considerable time to program the computer so it could do that computation. The formula, hand-written, was a page and a half long. George had it in his head. We're not sure how it got there. As he said: "I've got a good mind, that's how I do it."

We understand the computer because we built it. But there is a great deal we do not understand about memory. Consider the method and durability of storage, for example, let alone how the material gets encoded in the first place. Is storage electrical? If so, then why aren't memories permanently destroyed during an epileptic seizure, which is truly an electrical storm in the brain—as can be witnessed by watching an EEG during a seizure? Or, if storage is electrical, why aren't memories permanently affected when a patient receives electroconvulsive therapy (ECT), during which time an electrical current is actually passed through the brain? If storage is electromagnetic in the same manner that storage of "memories" on tape or storage of data on a computer is, then why isn't memory permanently affected by a nuclear magnetic resonance (NMR) brain scan, during which the brain is subjected to tremendous magnetic fields? Try that with some tapes or discs. If storage by the brain is an actual physical storage, like grooves on a phonograph disc, how does that storage process take place, and why isn't there some clear evidence of that process in microscopic examination of the brain?

Those, and many more, are questions I guess we will need to leave for the future. What follows are some of the things we do know about human memory that may help us explain some of the differences between normal memory and savant memory, and thus provide some insight into Savant Syndrome.

SHORT-TERM AND LONG-TERM MEMORY

Short-term and long-term memory differ from each other not only in terms of duration, but also in the brain structures and circuitry used to process and to store information.

Short-term memory consists of images, thoughts or "bits" of data persisting for only a few seconds or, at most, several minutes. It is the type of memory used to retain a telephone number between the time one looks it up in a directory and the time one dials the number. Unless the number is "registered" in some manner by attention and mental marking of some type, in a very short time it naturally recedes and is not available for later retrieval. Short-term memory is generally limited to about seven bits of data, whether they are digits, words or other elements.

Long-term memory consists of those elements that are transferred from short-term memory into long-term storage. If, for example, you wish to transfer the telephone number you just looked up into long-term memory, rather than simply using it and forgetting it, it must be "encoded," marked or registered in some manner for filing in the brain for retrieval later. Such transfer and retrieval is aided by "chunking," or grouping, the bits of data together in some manner (194117761492 is recalled more easily by grouping the numbers as 1941, 1776 and 1492; 4149216110 is more easily remembered as 414 921-6110).

The term "intermediate memory" is sometimes used to describe memory longer in duration than that seen in short-term memory. The term "immediate memory" (iconic) is sometimes used to describe visual image memory that lasts only a tenth of a second or so. Other terms such as "recent [immediate and intermediate past] memory" and "remote [distant past] memory" are used as well. Whatever the terminology, however, the fundamental distinction—between a process in which items are perceived but discarded without entry into long-term storage (short-term memory) and one in which items are, by an active process, transferred into longer-term storage for later retrieval (long-term memory)—is maintained.

THE ANATOMY OF MEMORY

Given the capacity and the complexity of memory, it is no surprise that the anatomic structures involved in processing and storing items are numerous and that those structures are linked together by intricate circuitry. The following discusses some of those structures.

The Cerebral Cortex

Some memories are stored in the cerebral cortex (see Figures 2 and 3 in Chapter 11), which is the newest portion of the brain to evolve and is most developed in humans. Referred to sometimes as the "neocortex," or new brain, it has proliferated in man to cover almost entirely the more primitive and older portions of the brain, known as the "subcortex." Some of those subcortical structures are described here.

Cortical storage of memory images was dramatically documented, in 1963, in the work of Dr. Wilder Penfield, an eminent Canadian neurosurgeon.[98] Penfield was attempting to treat certain epileptic patients by surgically excising scarred areas of the brain that were serving as irritative sites and causing grand mal seizures. To locate these sites the surgery was done under local anesthesia with the patient fully conscious. This was possible because the brain itself has no pain fibers. Thus once the scalp and dura mater (the protective covering of the brain) were numbed with a local anesthetic the cerebral cortex itself could be stimulated painlessly with a tiny electrical probe under direct visualization. Such stimulation would create a certain response, depending on which area was being stimulated, that the patient could actually describe because he or she was fully awake.

When stimulated, some areas of the brain, such as the parietal lobe, would produce muscle movement in a limb or in some other area of the body. When other areas, such as the occipital lobe, were stimulated the patient would describe flashes of light. When the probe was put on certain areas of the temporal cortex, however, extremely detailed and often emotionally laden memories, which were otherwise inaccessible or at least had not been accessed for long periods of time, would come flooding forth. Some patients relived extremely vivid scenes from the past, including the sights, noises, smells or other sensations associated with those memories. Others heard specific pieces of music, which would recur in exact detail on stimulation of that same spot. Patients were startled by these buried memories, which emerged not just as a snapshot, but rather as a reliving of the event just as if the patient were actually there.

Penfield concluded from his work that the brain contains a permanent record of every experience we have had even though much of that experience is unavailable to us because we lack access to it. It is as if the brain were a gigantic videotape of a lifetime of recorded experiences; the tiny electrical probe acts as a miniature VCR, bringing those stored memories back to consciousness. Penfield's work suggests that those things we cannot remember are merely a myriad of memories we cannot access. Forgetting is not losing memories; it is not being able to locate memories.

The area most involved in memory retrieval using electrical stimulation is the temporal lobe, particularly that part of the temporal lobe lying closest to the brain's midline structures, with which it intersects and is richly connected. Most recent researchers, reflecting on Penfield's work, feel that what he demonstrated was not the existence of a finite, isolated, independent, sole site for each specific memory. Instead, they feel that the area stimulated contained only a partial representation of the particular memory, which was connected to and represented in other areas of the brain as well. Each such "memory" is likewise embedded in a system of richly intertwining neuronal connections, some of which extend to the surface of the cortex. When certain areas of the cortex are stimulated, therefore, certain memories are evoked. Penfield's work demonstrated that, clearly, the temporal cortex is involved in some memory storage and that there is stored memory, probably in large amounts, to which we do not regularly have access. Forgetting, therefore, is not a matter of memory decay, but rather a matter of imperfect access.

The Hippocampus

One of the subcortical structures closely attached to the cerebral cortex is the hippocampus (see Figure 8), so named because it appeared to resemble a sea horse (*hippokampos* in Greek) to the neuroanatomists who first described it. It is a curved structure intimately connected to the temporal lobe. There is one on each side of the brain. On pneumo-encephalograms it can be visualized as projecting into the floor of the lateral ventricle in each of the temporal horns. The hippocampus is one of the older, more primitive brain structures and is directly linked to the sensory inputs of touch, sight, sound, taste and smell. It is the first way station into the cortex for some sensations, such as smell, and a later substation for those sensory modalities that are not quite so directly connected. Vision, for example, makes several synaptic connections in its own circuitry before reaching the hippocampus.

The hippocampus is a critical structure in the transfer of short-term memory into long-term storage. This important function of this subcortical structure was most vividly documented by the extensively studied and reported case of H.M. In 1953, H.M. had surgery to correct a severe epileptic condition that had not responded to ordinary treatment with anticonvulsant medication.[99,100] When the part of the temporal lobe containing the hippocampus was surgically removed, from both sides of the brain, a striking, unique and incapacitating memory dysfunction, known as "anterograde amnesia," was produced. H.M. had had an excellent memory for everything prior to the surgery, but he could not learn anything new following the surgery.

While H.M. could remember the past up to the point of the surgery, no events or experiences thereafter could be put into long-term memory. Each such experience or stimulus was new to him when it initially occurred and each time it recurred, no matter how many times it recurred. He could remember a telephone number, for example, only

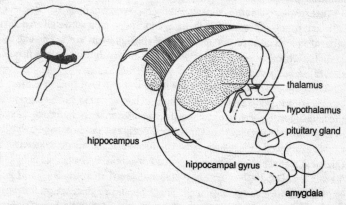

Figure 8. **The Hippocampus, Amygdala and Thalamus and Their Positions in the Brain.**

if there was absolutely no delay between his hearing it and reciting it back. Any delay at all caused loss of that information, no matter how hard H.M. tried to remember and no matter what devices or methods he tried to use to somehow transfer those digits into longer-term storage. H.M. was frozen in time to the point of the surgery. From then on he needed to relive and relearn each repeated experience as if he were facing it for the very first time.

It was a devastating disability. H.M. was fully alert, showed no general confusion and had full comprehension of everything going on around him (unlike most brain-damaged persons who show general confusion and disorientation whether or not they show memory defects). He could understand and laugh at a complicated joke or pun. Intelligence testing, except for subtests of intermediate memory, showed no impairment and a normal I.Q. He could name prior presidents and their accomplishments. Yet, while he knew he had a family and could even list their birth dates, he could not remember when, or if, they had visited and certainly could not recall what was said. If the doctor left the room, whether between daily visits or just to take a phone call, he had to reintroduce himself each time he saw H.M. because, in effect, H.M. had never met the doctor before.

When H.M. was told of his father's death, he was saddened and understood what had happened—for about 5 minutes. He then had no recollection of being told. He was unable to reminisce about anniversaries, birthdays or graduations in his family that occurred after the surgery because the memories on which such reminiscing would have relied were absent. Life was lived only moment upon moment, with no enduring connections between those moments. H.M. lived in a peculiar limbo of partial past tense and perpetual present tense.

Interestingly, some motor memory, specifically with respect to learning to mirror-write, was preserved, indicating some alternative or separate pathways for certain types of memory function. The existence of such pathways becomes important in understanding savant memory, as will be seen shortly.

The case of H.M. demonstrates several important findings. First, the hippocampus plays an important role in the sorting of information and the transferring of it from short-term to long-term memory. Second, even in severe memory disturbances, different kinds of memory function are affected differently, pointing to several pathways of storage and retrieval, rather than a single method or circuitry. In the case of H.M., memories prior to the surgery were unaffected and only the production of new memories was impaired. Short-term, pre-distractional memory was still present, as was memory for certain motor skills. Since different pathways exist for different kinds of memory, it is possible to have lesions or conditions that will show different kinds of memory impairment. Thirdly, the case of H.M. demonstrates, and animal studies confirm, that the hippocampus must be bilaterally destroyed or removed before the severe memory impairment H.M. experienced becomes evident.

Further convincing and conclusive proof of the role of the hippocampus in memory formation comes from another case, that of R.B., where actual autopsy findings in the brain serve as indisputable and precise markers of specific and localized hippocampal damage.[142,143] The case of R.B., reported by Dr. Stuart Zola-Morgan of the University of California School of Medicine in San Diego, is that of a 52-year-old male who had severe and unexpected blood loss (5,000 cc) following cardiac bypass surgery. There was shock and brain ischemia (loss of blood supply) for a period of at least one hour due to postoperative complications. Following that, R.B., like H.M., demonstrated a profound memory loss with anterograde amnesia.

The patient was described thus:

> He could not remember events of the preceding days or even sequences of three words just five minutes after learning them. Neurological exams confirmed the memory loss. Henceforth he was judged to have "severe impairment" on the Wechsler memory scale for the period following surgery. He reportedly asked physicians the same questions repeatedly and told the same story time after time. R.B.'s wife reported that her husband depended on her to keep telling him what was going on in his life from day to day. In spite of this circumscribed loss of memory, no cognitive or personality change was noted [overall I.Q. remained 111].

R.B. lived for five years after this brain injury, during which time there was essentially no improvement. A meticulous dissection of the brain was carried out (over 5,000 sections) in search of all areas where damage might be evident. Zola-Morgan reports that the only area of significant damage was in a particular area of the hippocampus field, called "CA 1," in the medial temporal lobe of that structure. Cells of a very characteristic type—"pyramidal cells"—are found in this particular area, and these cells were essentially destroyed in this case. These cells are particularly vulnerable to damage following ischemia, anoxia and trauma, and they appeared to be the sole area of significant injury in R.B.

The case of R.B. is of special significance because it correlates specific memory dysfunction with precisely localized damage *as confirmed by actual brain dissection.* The case of H.M., spectacular as it also is, relies on a surgical *description* of the area involved rather than actual brain dissection. Also, H.M. did have other severe brain dysfunction—intractable epilepsy—and it is difficult to confirm that damage existed only in the hippocampal area. The precise autopsy findings in the case of R.B. remove that doubt completely and demonstrate clearly what memory defects do result from lesions entirely in, and only in, the hippocampus.

The hippocampus is part of what is called the "limbic system" of the brain, an important subcortical network of connections between a variety of related structures that include, under the usual definition, the amygdala (described below), the hypothalamus and the pituitary gland. The hypothalamus regulates eating, water intake, sleep, body temperature, heart rate and other vital body functions. The pituitary gland is referred to as the "master gland" because it controls the various hormonal systems of the body. Together the parts of the limbic system are intimately involved in body homeostasis, survival (fight or flight) and certain emotional reactions. Some definitions of the limbic system include certain other subcortical areas as well but the ones listed here are the major components. The rich interconnection between the cortex and the limbic system is called the "cortico-limbic system."

The Amygdala

Another important subcortical structure in the anatomy of memory is the amygdala, which, like the hippocampus, is part of the limbic system. The amygdala is closely connected to the hippocampus and plays a particularly important role in using emotion to sort, encode and prioritize memories.

Emotion is a potent determinant of which memories are to be preserved and of the hierarchy in which they are to exist; thus emotion, storage and recall are intimately related, as any of our recollections will tell us. Memories that are highly emotionally laden in any direction—happy, sad, startling, terrifying—are most accessible and most available. Indeed, a particularly strong negative emotional encoding may make a memory very difficult to erase even though we may wish to do so. It is the amygdala that links emotion to experience and that sorts, codes and catalogues memory according to emotional tone and content. There are no human studies of specific amygdala injury such as the study of hippocampal injury in H.M., but in animal studies, lesions in the amygdala produce a loss of memory in which the animal does not experience fear in the face of predators.

The importance of emotion in encoding memory is exemplified by the vivid recollection all of us old enough to remember have of November 22, 1963, the day President Kennedy was shot. We all remember where we were and what we were doing when we heard that fateful announcement. The emotion we felt as a result of that startling tragedy differentiates that November 22nd from all the other November 22nds we have experienced in our lives. The emotional component encoded, through the amygdala, gives that memory a high priority, ranking it high in the hierarchy of memory accessibility.

The Thalamus and Reticular Activating Formation

Attention, like emotion, is a powerful determinant of what is remembered and what is forgotten. The greater the attention or arousal attached to an experience, the greater the likelihood that the experience will be remembered. Did I take my vitamin pill this morning or didn't I? If I paid some attention to that routine task I will remember. If I carried it out automatically or while I was distracted by other thoughts, I simply will not be able to recall it. If I want to store a telephone number in longer-term memory for later use, rather than just noting it long enough to dial it one time and then letting it lapse, I will need either to pay more careful attention to it or to use some mental marker or devices to try to remember those digits after the one-time use. Whether or not I can remember passing Beaver Dam on my way to Madison will depend on how deeply in thought I was along the way.

The thalamus (see Figure 8 earlier in this chapter), another subcortical structure in close proximity to the hippocampus and amygdala, is an important part of the arousal and attention system of the brain, particularly with respect to selective attention during learning. The thalamus serves a gateway function, helping us to focus attention on particular tasks. The posterior thalamus, especially on the left side of the brain, is involved in language function as well.[101] In fact, functionally distinct regions of the cortex are connected to the thalamus in such a direct manner that the thalamus will reflect the same asymmetry as the cortex, depending on which is the dominant hemisphere.

The thalamus connects extensively with the main arousal system of the brain, the reticular activating formation (RAF) (see Figure 7 in Chapter 11). The RAF is not a specific structure, but instead is a highly interconnected system of neuronal cells scattered throughout the brain and spinal cord. It modulates and controls the state of arousal in the organism. Rimland postulates that the RAF is the site of dysfunction in Early Infantile Autism, characteristics of which include attention defects, flattened emotional response and literal, high-fidelity, narrowband memory function—the same types of defects and memory function seen in many savants.[102]

Attention as a factor in memory becomes significant in trying to understand savant memory because the savant's ability for intense concentration—whether from a special ability to focus narrowly or a pathological inability to broaden that focus—is a consistent feature in Savant Syndrome. Dysfunction within attention pathways can affect savant memory in a predictable and consistent manner.

The thalamus and the RAF, as the modulators of attention and arousal, would appear to be implicated in both ability and disability in savants, as reflected by their unique memory. Just as the characteristic emotional flatness of savant memory points toward hippocampal and amygdala dysfunction, so the pathologically intense but narrow attention band in the savant, with attendant peculiar memory function, points toward problems in the thalamus and the reticular activating formation.

The Basal Ganglia

The basal ganglia (see Figure 9), also subcortical structures, are linked together in a loosely defined system and are responsible for very basic brain functions even more primitive than those associated with the cortex, the limbic system or the thalamus. The basal ganglia anatomically surround and lie just outside the more central and midline limbic system, and modulate some kinds of sensory input, particularly with respect to muscle movement, coordination and position. They, like the limbic system, serve as way stations for a variety of sensory inputs from the spinal cord and lower brain stem as these inputs travel to the cortex. These ganglia are intimately connected to the thalamus and amygdala and other structures in the limbic system. They are the structures in-

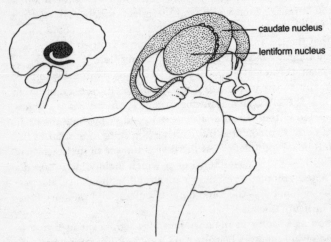

Figure 9. The Basal Ganglia.

volved in Parkinson's disease and certain other disorders of the motor system, but they also play an important role in receiving, sorting and coding sensory input on its way to cortical recognition and storage.

As early neuroanatomists cut through the brain they noted that the basal ganglia structures have a striped appearance due to the several kinds of grey matter they contain. These structures were named the "striatum," and consequently the basal ganglia are sometimes referred to as the "striatal complex." Mortimer Mishkin therefore refers to this particular subcortical-cortical circuit as the *cortico-striatal* system, in contrast to the *cortico-limbic* system described earlier.[103] These two different systems become important in understanding two different kinds of memory function in humans, and in particular the special kind of memory function the savant displays.

THREE KINDS OF MEMORY

Ancestral Memory

There are several kinds of memory. First, there is *ancestral* memory, composed of traits, skills, attributes and abilities that are inherited just as eye color, height, body build and many other physical characteristics are inherited. These are the various instincts and genetic unfoldings one sees in both animals and humans. Dr. A. A. Brill quotes Dr. William Carpenter in comparing savant Zerah Colburn and his calculating powers to Mozart and that composer's mastery of music.

> In each of the foregoing cases, then, we have a peculiar example of the possession of an extraordinary congenital aptitude for certain forms of mental activity, which showed itself at so early a period as to exclude the notion that it could have been acquired by the experiences of the individual. To such congenital gifts we give the name of intuitions: it can scarcely be questioned that like the instincts of the lower animals they are the expressions of constitutional tendencies embodied in the organism of the individuals who manifest them.[47]

Some families, and some members within those families, are musically inclined; others are not. Some families, or family members, are athletically inclined, and some are not. As mentioned in Chapter 11, a number of researchers, including Dr. Bernard Rimland, David C. Rife and Laurence H. Snyder and Brill, have pointed to the tendency of certain skills to run in families and perhaps to be an important contributor to Savant Syndrome.[4, 16, 47]

Memory traits, or certain kinds of memory strengths or weaknesses, tend to run in families as well, based on what I have seen in a number of patients. This differing ability or inability to remember names or faces, for example, seems to me to be a trait in the same manner as some people have a feeling for color coordination, and others do not, or other people have the ability to think like a chess player and others do not. Of course, training and discipline help improve performance in those areas, but an intrinsic superiority—a more natural ability or "intuition"—exists in certain persons and certain families. In my case, for example, my father had a particular difficulty in remembering names, especially first names, even of people who worked under him in the machine shop where he was foreman. We would meet them on the street and Dad would try to greet them by name, but it was often only after they had passed by that the name would finally come out. I have that same trait (or infirmity) even with people I have just been introduced to. Some may argue that it is a learned trait (or deficiency), but as I watch some of the unmistakable Treffert traits—posture, mannerisms and speech, as well as physical characteristics—unfold in my sons, as they have in my brothers, and my father and his brothers, the inheritance of these "inclinations," including those related directly to types of memory, seems unmistakable.

Ancestral memory no doubt contributes, in part, to the Savant Syndrome.

Cognitive and Associative Memory

There is a second kind of memory—*cognitive or associative*. Here the bits of experience in our present-day lives are processed and encoded, linked with other similar bits of information and then stored for later retrieval. This memory process involves the three R's—*R*ecognition, *R*etention and *R*ecall. Recognition involves sensory pick-up by sight, sound, touch, smell or any other sensation. Retention is determined by an attention, sorting and processing system using circuitry that involves, in particular, two subcortical structures, the amygdala and hippocampus, with actual storage occurring in a vast, interconnected network of neurons and synapses throughout the cortex and other subcortical structures. Retrieval is determined by accessing that huge storage network using a variety of associations, linkages and configurations that tap neural representations of similarly stored associations, linkages and configurations.

This is the kind of memory we use when we reminisce, when we read, when we learn, when we write and when we "think." This is the search and scan we do when we try to remember the little town we stayed in three years ago in Germany, when we scour our brain for the five-letter word that means compose, when we try to remember what we bought and the amount of the check we wrote but neglected to record and when we try to recall zip codes for Christmas cards.

Mishkin and his co-workers at the National Institutes of Mental Health, based on extensive research with primates and humans, refer to this kind of recognition, retention and retrieval as a *memory system,* as differentiated from a *habit system,* which will be described next as a third, and different, kind of memory.[104] Mishkin points out that this kind of memory uses circuits within a "cortico-limbic" system, relying heavily on the hippocampus and amygdala linkage to the cortex where the processed images are stored for later recall: "The content of the store is information or knowledge, and the process for which the system is responsible is cognition. In the terminology of other investigators, the memory system is responsible for episodic memory, vertical associative memory, declarative knowledge, and elaborative processing."

How is information entered into this memory system? Information from any one of the senses—smell, taste, touch, vision, hearing—enters as "bits" of data, e.g., as digits. The average capacity of short-term memory is about 7 bits of data. Sometimes these bits of data are linked together in our minds in "chunks" so that longer assemblies of them can be remembered more easily—much like a social security number is broken into smaller number groupings. Short-term memories last several seconds or, at most, several minutes. If we look up an unfamiliar telephone number, for example, we will probably remember it long enough to use it, but then we will forget it almost immediately unless, by paying some special attention to it, we encode and process it into long-term memory. That special attention may be repeating it to ourselves a number of times, using it repeatedly or using some mnemonic device to commit it to longer-term storage. "Making a mental note of it" is just that, paying some particular attention to an otherwise obscure fact or happening so that we do put it into longer-term storage rather than just letting it lapse and disappear.

Entering information into longer-term storage involves fairly complex circuitry. Each stimulus has several transfer sites on the way to long-term storage. Two critical sites are the hippocampus and the amygdala. Those stimuli that connect more directly with these two structures—notably stimuli of smell and taste—produce stronger recollections than do stimuli less directly connected to these structures—stimuli of vision and hearing. The hippocampus and the amygdala are both crucial components of memory circuitry, but the amygdala has a special function of linking emotional tone and memory together and is especially important in processing memories with a strong emotional component.

Emotion and memory are closely linked and emotional coding is a strong determinant of which memories are most strongly etched and most easily retrieved. As mentioned earlier, almost everyone remembers exactly where they were and what they were doing on November

22, 1963, at precisely the moment they learned that President Kennedy had been shot—that same day of any other year, before or after, is probably a blur or a blank, unless it held some other special significance for us. Other days of our lives that we can recall are often similarly determined by some strong emotional overtone, whether sentimental or scary, pleasant or tragic. While there are other mechanisms to enforce encoding, emotion is a powerful one, and much of what we easily and forcefully remember is because of the emotion attached to it—a birth, a death, a triumph, a disappointment.

It is interesting that the prodigious, automatic memory of the savant is devoid of emotion. It stores trivia without ranking for importance and stores music without feeling the music—automatically, mechanically and literally. It stores with incredible accuracy and depth but is narrow and limited in its scope. It clearly differs from memory in the rest of us.

"Habit" Memory

There is a third kind of memory, something Mishkin refers to as "habits."[104] In the case of H.M., described briefly above, even though a massive amnesia existed following surgery to remove the hippocampus bilaterally, H.M. could still be taught certain motor or procedural skills, as distinguished from verbal skills. In particular the ability to learn to mirror-write was documented, and despite the loss of memory in almost all other areas, H.M. could "learn" this skill—thus remember it—from session to session. One kind of memory was absent while another clearly was preserved.

Mishkin uses the term *noncognitive* to describe this third type of memory in contradistinction to *cognitive* memory. Others have made this same type of distinction but have used different terms, such as *procedural* ("how to") memory vs. *declarative* (fact) memory, or *automatic* vs. *effortful encoding* memory.

It is this noncognitive system that Mishkin refers to as "habits." Information is entered into the cognitive "memory" system through brain circuitry that involves the cortex, the hippocampus and the amygdala—Mishkin calls this system a "cortico-limbic system." Information is entered into the noncognitive "habit" system through a different neural circuitry, which involves the more primitive subcortical basal ganglia structures—Mishkin calls this system a "cortico-striatal system."

This "habit" system has certain attributes. It is more a system of conditioned reflexes than of conscious memory. Learning in this system is not one of recognition and use of associative memory; it is instead an automatic, conditioned response predicated on reinforcement of that response. It is an example of the classic stimulus-response model of behavioral psychology in contrast to the less automatic, conscious thought model put forth by cognitive psychology. Mishkin describes this habit system learning in considerable detail based on his careful animal studies thus: "The product of this process is not cognitive information but a noncognitive stimulus-response bond, that is, not a memory but a habit." He concludes, based on his studies, that "what is stored in the habit-formation system is not the neural representation of such items as objects, places, acts, emotions, and the learned connections between them, but simply the changing probability that a given stimulus will evoke a specific response due to the reinforcement contingencies operating at that time."

Mishkin and his co-workers tested this proposed habit system further, postulating it to be an earlier, more primitive system than the memory system that developed later phylogenetically. Also, this more basic habit memory develops earlier in the infant than the later-acquired memory system learning, pointing out again that two different systems are involved: "Whereas infants can readily acquire habits, they are seriously deficient in forming memories, presumably because the cortico-limbo-thalamic circuit that constitutes the memory system undergoes a relatively slow ontogenetic development."

The circuitry involved in the cognitive memory system is much more clearly established in both humans and animals than the circuitry involved in the habit system. Mishkin admits that the proposed neural pathways are not well defined as yet, but states that "the data from a number of sources point to the possibility that habit formation in primates and other mammals depends in large part on the second major cortico-subcortical system of the forebrain, namely, the cortico-striatal system. The striatal complex or basal ganglia is an obvious candidate from an evolutionary standpoint in that it antedates both the cerebral cortex and the limbic system in phylogenesis."[104]

This habit system of memory resembles the "memory without consciousness" so characteristic of the savant. Barr, ninety years ago, may have unknowingly delineated this system of learning when he described the phenomenal memory in his savant as "an exaggerated form of habit." "In the act, and in the echo, he is simply a creature of suggestion," Barr states.[52] The phrase "obedience to suggestion" and the description "not volitional nor reflective" certainly capture the essence of savant memory accurately, and both describe this "habit" system of learning as well.

Savant memory, I suspect, is just that—a highly developed, compensatory, noncognitive, alternative pathway developed to compensate for injury to or absence of the more usual and more frequently used cognitive memory seen in the rest of us. Savant memory is almost devoid of emotion, is automatic and nonvolitional, is certainly not reflective or highly associative and could well be the "habit" system described by Mishkin and his co-workers. The attentional defects in the savant, with the striking inability to broaden focus that results, likewise point toward injury or dysfunction in the more typical cortico-limbic circuitry; a cortico-striatal "habit" system may well be the naturally available alternative in the savant. It certainly is an intriguing and plausible explanation given the nature of that particular brain system, and given the particular way in which mind and memory operate in the savant.

We will return to that possibility in the chapters ahead.

SAVANT SYNDROME: A WINDOW TO THE MARVEL OF MEMORY

As I said at the beginning of this chapter, memory is exceedingly complex. I have tried to simplify it a bit and perhaps in so doing have not done justice to its complexity. But my purpose has been to bring to light that which seems crucial to understanding the marvel that is the memory of the savant.

The three memory systems described and their anatomical structures are not entirely distinct and discrete from each other. They exist in a neuronal web so intricate that they can operate both in conjunction with each other and separately. This morning as I shaved, carrying out that reasonably demanding routine without having to think about it, I also hummed a fairly complex (for me) song without having to think about it. Meanwhile I was composing this ending to this chapter in my head. Some intermixture of ancestral, cognitive and habit memory systems were all functioning in conjunction with each other, yet, simultaneously, those systems were functioning separately from each other as well. It will be a long time before we can figure that out in its entirety, if we ever can, but nevertheless, we have gained some understanding and clarification. I am convinced that savant memory, different as it is from memory in the rest of us, can, with careful study, provide some further interesting and useful insights into this most crucial, and wondrous, of human functions.

13

New Savants and New Findings

The mystery of Savant Syndrome, and clues to that mystery, continue to unfold. Careful studies of two new savants, along with exciting new insights into the development of cerebral lateralization and specialization, provide information that takes us further than we have been before in understanding this remarkable condition. What follows are descriptions of two musical savants, John and Eddie, and some helpful new findings regarding left brain/right brain function and specialization.

JOHN: A MUSICIAN WITH HANDICAPS

The uniformity of Savant Syndrome in its manifestations through the years is most striking. The resemblance between Blind Tom and Leslie Lemke, for example, who lived a century apart, is uncanny. The 1800s had Gottfried Mind and the 1900s, Richard Wawro. George and Charles startled audiences in 1985 with their mathematical prowess, as did Thomas Fuller in 1785. The similarity of a newly discovered savant, John, to Leslie Lemke, his contemporary, is likewise striking.

John, now 38, lives in an institution in Cedar Springs, Ontario, where he has been hospitalized since age 15.[105] He has four handicaps. He is blind. He is profoundly retarded. He has a severe spasticity and paralysis of the right arm and hand. And he is epileptic. Yet, like Leslie Lemke, he has great musical talent, displayed in his virtuoso singing and piano playing. Because of his right-side paralysis, he plays piano with just one hand, an astonishing feat.

John has been studied and described in careful detail by Dr. Neil Charness and his co-workers Jane Clifton and Lyle MacDonald at the University of Waterloo, in Ontario.[91] They refer to John as a "mono-savant"—a term they prefer to "idiot savant"—which they define as "a mentally retarded person with highly developed skills (and knowledge of) in one domain."

John's story is a familiar one. He was born three months prematurely, weighing 2 pounds, 2 ounces. He was given oxygen, as were all premature babies at that time, with the unfortunate result of retrolental fibroplasia and blindness. At about age 4, John developed epilepsy as well and has had approximately one grand mal seizure per month ever since, in spite of anticonvulsant medication. An electroencephalogram shows excessive slow wave and spiking activity in the left hemisphere and a CAT scan shows left hemisphere damage.

His verbal communication skills are very poor with frequent echolalia and perseveration. According to Charness et al. he has no concept of money, he is unable to tell time, and while unable to brush his teeth, shave or comb his hair, he can dress himself and wash his face and hands unassisted. "Although able to feed himself with a spoon with prompting, J.L. cannot tell when his bowl/plate is empty and he will continue to go through the motions of feeding himself."

John functions at a very low level intellectually. Because of that he was virtually untestable on the standard WAIS instrument, except for digit span. That was 5 forward, which, as with other savants, is at a normal level when compared to the severe deficits in other areas. On the Vineland Test for social maturity he showed the developmental level of a 2-year-old, making him one of the most severely impaired savants ever reported. The research description continues: "With respect to cognitive skills, J.L. is unable to discriminate correctly, through touch, a circle, square, and triangle, nor does he understand the concept of big and small."

According to his parents, John developed an interest in piano at about age 2½, which is about the same time that he first learned to walk and to speak, although his speech was largely limited to echolalia. He had no formal musical instruction, but spent hours and hours with his grandmother who played the piano for him and with him, encouraging him to sing along with her. John began practicing intensely, sometimes getting up in the middle of the night to do so. He would sometimes spend almost an entire day at the piano. By the time he was age 8, according to his parents, his talent was extraordinary, especially considering that he could only use his left hand. To deal with that obstacle he played bass with the heel or toes of his left *foot* until he had grown so that his size and weight prevented this. Since then, he has developed unique fingering techniques to play both the melody line and the harmony line for the piano and organ, although he must resort to "digital gymnastics" often to do so. Charness notes also that John "shows fine attention to rhythmic nuances, inclusion of embellishments, and attention to the dynamics of a vast array of different genres." In addition to piano and organ he plays melodeon and harmonica. He has perfect pitch.

Like other musical savants, John listens for hours to the radio and a variety of records. His musical repertoire is enormous and includes Broadway musicals, jazz, classical music, opera and popular music; he can sing and play for as long as eight hours without repeating a tune. He indexes songs by name as well as by sound. He can hum or sing words to the songs he plays and has much better verbal skills when singing than when speaking. Like Leslie Lemke, he imitates other instruments or vocalists, including one of Leslie's favorites, Louis Armstrong. John can change keys, can change styles of playing—from a waltz to ragtime, for instance—and can improvise or embellish, like Leslie and Ellen. Even though his language and communication skills are limited, he is a great mimic—his impersonations range from pop stars to opera greats. His family describes his absolutely lifelike renditions of the songs his grandmother sang to him, in the exact timbre, pitch and lilt of her voice and style.

John enjoys playing piano. In one instance, even after hours of testing he was reluctant to stop playing or to leave the room. Despite his obvious enjoyment in this area, John is emotionally very "flat" when engaged in other activities and interactions—although he has been known to display a sense of humor. His parents note that John enjoys the applause that a performance brings him, and according to them, "if an audience forgets to cheer, John will supply the applause himself." John regularly plays for the entertainment of his fellow patients at the center where he lives, and has become well known locally by giving concerts and playing organ at conventions and for church services. A newspaper article about him describes one of his concert performances thus: "The fingers of the player's left hand begin to move delicately across the keyboard. Tilting his head slightly to one side, he closes his eyes and smiles quietly to himself as he fills the air with the haunting strains of Beethoven's *Moonlight Sonata*. . . . the moment he sits down and plays with only his left hand, the severely disabled man is transformed into a supremely talented human being."

Because of John's ability to improvise, imitate other performers or instruments, transpose pieces from one key to another, change style and embellish elaborately, it does seem as if he has access to the rules of music in either some innate or some learned fashion. He does come from a family that is musically inclined. His mother's sisters were in a band, his uncle played the trumpet and his grandmother, according to Charness, played piano skillfully enough to give concerts.

Charness and his fellow researchers have worked with and tested John in careful detail to try to answer the fundamental question of whether his gift is one of simple mimicry—literal and eidetic—or whether he also has a cognitive sense of the rules of music? Does he use elaborate encodings of musical structure and musical knowledge, either there innately, from some kind of ancestral memory, or coded unconsciously from repeated and prolonged practice and performance?

To test that question two experiments were carried out. In the first test it was demonstrated that John's note span was between 5 and 8 notes. It was hypothesized that, if John's ability were more than simple or literal recall, he would be more sensitive to musical structure of the type skilled nonsavant musicians use and would be able to produce longer sequences of notes if the sequences were structured rather than random. Test results showed that John was sensitive to musical structure and that he was better able to reproduce structured patterns than random arrangements of notes.

The second experiment attempted to measure John's abstraction capability as opposed to his ability to simply play back passages literally and concretely. The researchers were able to document access to cognitive structures that code musical information; memory was not limited to concrete and sensory representations. Charness and his co-workers conclude: "The skill that J.L. exhibits in music is comparable to the skill that normally intelligent musicians develop. . . . it seems that intense practice, together with an intact neurological substrate for coding a musical symbol system, are sufficient to explain J.L.'s performance." Recognizing that so few mentally retarded individuals acquire such a high level of skill, they further conclude that certain personality characteristics, in addition to the underlying neural circuitry, are necessary to create the fortuitous circumstance of the savant.

Their equation for this musical savant then would look like this: brain injury + prodigious memory + neural circuitry that allows encoding into and access to a cognitive sense of musical systems + intense practice and repetition = the musical savant. There is remarkable memory to be sure, but it is more than memory. Drs. Neil O'Connor and Beate Hermelin asked the same question about the calendar calculators: Is it math or is it memory?[38] It is neither, or it is both. That makes savant skills all the more complex, and all the more challenging to explain.

Eddie is a 7-year-old musical savant who came to national attention as a result of an article in *The New York Times* on January 7, 1987.[106] According to Eddie's mother, at age 3 he began to play a toy piano after listening to the radio and to records. Now age 7, Eddie plays a full-size piano and has a vast musical repertoire that includes songs such as Glenn Miller's "Boogie Woogie," Thelonius Monk's "Blue" and Beethoven's "Fur Elise." His piano teacher states, "Eddie has a great memory and if you sing a melody to him, he will anticipate the predictable pattern of the melody and add four-part harmony." Early in his life Eddie had been handicapped by severely limited vision caused by cataracts, but those were removed at age 6 and he has since begun to learn to read notes. As his musical prowess has developed so has his language. He has gone from being entirely nonverbal to being able to create original sentences in English and Spanish. This is reassuring and is in contrast to Nadia, the autistic savant, who allegedly lost her artistic skills as she developed language.[58]

Eddie has been studied in considerable detail by Dr. Leon Miller of the University of Illinois at Chicago. Miller describes this savant in two articles, in which he discusses specifically melody span and sensitivity to tonal structure.[107, 108]

Medical history shows that the child's mother had rubella during her first trimester of pregnancy and that failure-to-thrive syndrome was present during the child's first year of life. Congenital cataracts were removed at age 4, resulting in corrected vision of 20/200. There is left-ear deafness. "Social and adaptive skills, as measured by the Callier-Azusa scale, given at 5 years, were quite variable but generally delayed, ranging from a 12-month level for social development to a 40-month level for daily living skills." Eddie began to walk at about age 4, and there was very little vocalization when he was an infant or a young child. At age 5½ speech was limited to single words or simple phrases and was primarily echolalic. Eddie has never had any formal musical training.

Miller's first study was done when Eddie was age 5½ and attending a school for multiply handicapped. Miller set out in a formal and systematic manner to test whether the skill exhibited by this savant was limited to literal renditions of commonly heard melodies or whether it showed sensitivity to more general characteristics of standard musical structure. He used as stimulus materials 24 short piano pieces, from various music instruction books, which consisted of 4- to 16-bar melodic lines with varying degrees of harmonic accompaniment. The pieces, which included examples from each of the major and minor diatonic keys, were melodies that represented a variety of styles and tempos. The reproduction of this music by the subject was tape-recorded and carefully analyzed with measure-by-measure comparison to the original. Miller concludes: "While the performance exhibited by this savant indicated considerable skill in remembering brief musical passages, the memory did not represent a literal nonselective repetition of all notes heard. . . . it shows impressive sensitivity to the rules governing composition, particularly the role of different notes in determining (diatonic) key structure." Miller felt that this experiment showed a knowledge of structural rules not limited to examples provided from earlier experiences and that it indicated an implicit knowledge of musical structural rules.

Miller followed up that study with a number of specific experiments to determine the nature of melody-span memory in the savant as well as the variables affecting that melody-span memory. His goal was to learn why some savants play back certain kinds of musical pieces more accurately and exactly than they do other pieces, as had been reported by Sloboda, Hermelin and O'Connor in 1985, as well as by other researchers.[22] In the first of the follow-up experiments, groups of note strings of varying lengths were constructed and played on a piano, and Eddie's responses were tape-recorded for further analysis. Results showed that his memory was less than perfect; he rarely could remember note strings of more than 7 notes. This, of course, is very similar to the results of digit-span studies by Herman H. Spitz and Louise LaFontaine.[96] The fact that strings of randomly selected notes were less well remembered than strings with certain musical structures led Miller to conclude that memory, in this instance, was not literal or eidetic but rather showed sensitivity to general characteristics of musical structure.

In his second follow-up experiment, Miller, rather than using just isolated strings of notes, used some note strings that had an accompaniment consisting of a musical chord sounded for two beats before and after the string of notes itself. In some instances the chord was in the key signature of the string of notes (consistent context); in other instances it was in a distantly related key (inconsistent context). Results showed that the accompaniment did very little to help the subject remember the strings of notes; however, when inconsistent context was provided performance deteriorated considerably. Miller concludes from these findings that Eddie's talent does depend on being able to perceive the overall structure of music (rather than on just using literal memory) and that harmony (or context) is important in the total recall that this savant displays.

In the third follow-up experiment, single notes were played in groups of three or four, rather than being played randomly at a regular pace. Such grouping of notes (chunking strategy) did produce better results than the nongrouping of notes and did help in overall recall and performance, although it did not bring the savant subject to the level of accomplished nonsavant musicians.

From all these experiments Miller drew two important conclusions. First, he concluded that there was a general sensitivity to the length and key signature of pieces heard. If memory was eidetic or only literal, such sensitivity would not have affected recall. Second, he found that the phenomenal memory shown by Eddie involved an ability to encode notes by incorporating them into and linking them to meaningful structures in long-term, cognitive memory. This points up also that savant memory here could not be explained on the basis of eidetic or literal recall only; there must be reliance on other types of memory function as well.

Eddie's memory shows access to musical structure and knowledge much as the memory of calendar calculators shows access to the "rules of mathematics," which are either inherited or are formed by some unconscious algorithms through extensive and repeated practice. Leslie, John and J.P., the subjects studied by Sloboda, Hermelin and O'Connor, all show this same ability.

Yet, Miller points out, many questions remain. He suggests research into the speed of encoding and strategies for subsequent retrieval since both of these are often critical to memory-span performance. Secondly, he is puzzled as to the source of the implicit knowledge of harmony that is available to the musical savant. Finally, he notes that, while the repertoire of savant music is quite varied, certain styles and preferences seem to predominate. He questions whether some intrinsic limitation exists, or whether the preferences simply reflect exposure. He suggests studies using wider ranges and types of music.

I am certain that such studies will follow, but the case histories of John and Eddie, so carefully studied and documented now, make it clear that the memory of the savant, remarkable in its span, depth and fidelity, is not just a tape-recorder slave to what is played or heard. It can also access a store of material that exists as a result of either some kind of ancestral or inherited memory, or an unconscious encoding—a memory without reckoning—that develops simply from practice and repetition. Eidetic imagery, compensatory drives, narrowed attention span, limited concrete thinking and impaired abstract ability cannot, singly or collectively, explain John or Eddie. None of these answers either the question of how the savant does what he does or the question of why. The new information that follows may help us answer both.

In February, 1987, the BBC aired a programme on the Savant Syndrome entitled 'The Foolish Wise Ones'. One segment featured a then twelve-year old autistic boy, Stephen Wiltshire, drawing from memory on camera a remarkably accurate sketch of St Pancras station which he had visited for the first time only briefly several hours before. As the camera recorded, he quickly and assuredly drew the elaborate and complicated building exactly as he had seen it with the clock hands set at precisely 11.20, the hour he had viewed them. There were hundreds of calls and letters to the BBC following that broadcast seeking a source to purchase originals of Stephen's astonishing work. That initial interest and then a sustained demand for the drawings led to the publication of an entire volume of Stephen Wiltshire's works entitled *Drawings*, (London, J.M. Dent & Sons Ltd, 1987).

In the introduction to *Drawings*, Sir Hugh Casson, former president of the Royal Academy, says of Stephen: 'Happily, every now and then, a rocket of young talent explodes and continues to shower us with its sparks. Stephen Wiltshire – who was born with severe speech difficulties – is one of those rockets.' He then describes the artistic brilliance further: 'His sense of perspective seems to be faultless....I've never seen in all my competition drawing such a talent, such a natural and extraordinary talent that this child seems to have...[Stephen] is possibly the best child artist in Britain.'

Stephen concentrates almost exclusively on architecture. He provides exact, literal renditions of any building, no matter how complex, and in fact he seems to prefer the especially intricate. He views buildings, in person or from a photograph, and retains an exquisitely precise and detailed image for later recall and drawing. Additionally, he can sense and draw a building, no matter how complex, with a three-dimensional perspective from a two-dimensional drawing or photo.

Like other savant artists, Stephen's work depicts exactly what he sees without embellishment, stylization, or interpretation. He makes no notes; impressions are indelibly and faithfully inscribed from a single exposure for later recall and he draws swiftly, beginning anywhere on the page. Thus, like Alonzo Clemons and Richard Wawro, his remarkable artistic ability is linked to an equally remarkable memory.

At the age of ten Stephen drew what he called a 'London Alphabet', a group of drawings from Albert Hall to the London Zoo with structures such as the Houses of Parliament and The Imperial War Museum in between. An exquisite sense of perspective is demonstrated in a drawing he labels 'Looking down the lift shaft and stairs', and his drawing of

Buckingham Palace is an extraordinary example of Stephen's intricacy and accuracy.

Stephen Wiltshire is, by any standards, an extraordinary artist, but what about his handicap? Stephen started attending the Inner London Education Authority complex needs school at the age of four, as an extremely withdrawn and almost mute child. He existed in the world of his own so typically described in autistic youngsters. He was distant, preoccupied, had little or no eye contact and often roamed about the classrooms aimlessly, sometimes staring for long times at pictures, then suddenly dashing from room to room. He would absorb himself for long periods of time with scribbling on scraps of paper.

In school he did learn to read and began to immerse himself for hours in books on architecture and travel. Simultaneously he developed some language but it has remained difficult and sparse. He is characterized by the headmistress of the ILEA school as having a 'gentle personality, humour and curious dignity'. Overall he is described as eminently likeable and it is obvious that far from detracting from his general development, his art has seemingly aided it. While some seemed to fear that the acquisition of language and other skills might, like Nadia, rob him of his genius, this is not the case at all. Instead, like Leslie Lemke and Alonzo Clemons, Stephen's special skills and overall social development have progressed simultaneously, apparently step by step. The blossoming of his genius has coincided with a blossoming of his personality.

Stephen's father was killed in an accident when he was three years old and he lives with his mother and sister in London. He enjoys pop music and has a remarkable memory for the many tunes that he hears. He has moved on now to a secondary school and he speaks of wanting to be an architect and some day designing his own buildings. A trust has been established from his commissions to make such training possible and exhibitions of his drawings such as that sponsored by the Royal Incorporation of Architects of Scotland, for example, have contributed to it. Stephen's would-be peers, who sponsored that exhibition, gave his drawings a high endorsement, terming them, as they surely are, 'drawings of architectural excellence'.

When I learned about right brain/left brain specialization in medical school lectures, the concepts were not as advanced as they are now, but the results of stroke on language when the injury was on the language-dominant side rather than the nondominant side were obvious and predictable. The real-life significance of cerebral lateralization came thundering home to me, however, the first time I encountered that clinical concept in a patient. It was during my internship. A patient had been admitted with headache. He was an extremely interesting person, a writer who loved his work. He loved to read as well, and his fund of knowledge about a whole variety of topics was as broad as it was deep. Language, spoken and written, was his love and his livelihood.

The patient was right-handed. X-rays showed a tumor in the right hemisphere which, considering the patient's age and the configuration of the tumor, was most likely a glioblastoma multiforme, a malignant and usually lethal form of cancer. There was one hope, however. Since the tumor was on the right—and therefore in the nondominant hemisphere—the entire right half of the brain could be removed *without* having the patient lose useful language. There would be, of course, the inevitable motor paralysis on the left, but at least language function would be spared. If the tumor had been on the left such a procedure, because of the inevitable loss of language, would not have been considered.

Some of us have faced hard decisions in our lives, but few of us, I suspect, have had to face a decision of this magnitude or one requiring such enormous courage. My patient had two choices: probable death from his brain tumor *or* surgery that might lengthen his life but that would ensure paralysis of half his body. He knew he would go into the operating room whole and come out paralyzed.

He chose the hemispherectomy. The tumor was found to be malignant upon biopsy, as suspected, and the procedure was carried out. I wondered, aside from the resulting paralysis, what effect the surgery would have on overall memory or intellectual functioning. Here was a reader and a writer—someone depending entirely on those skills. What would be left?

I was startled to find, during our conversations following surgery, that I could not detect any postoperative change. The paralysis was there, certainly, as predicted, but the patient's memory, language and thought processes, at least as could be detected in conversation and without formal testing, did not seem to be defective. That was long before much of the present-day material about right brain/left brain specialization had been written, but it left an impact on my mind, at least, that such specialization is not absolute and that ample cross-representation, or copying, or some similar process must occur. One of the first lessons in learning to use a computer or word processor with memory is to *always* make a back-up copy before emptying data in working memory into storage memory. Maybe this cross-representation is just that simple, a survival mechanism built into brain function.

My point, then, is this: While the term "left brain/right brain" is used liberally and loosely, even in the new, sophisticated studies discussed hereafter, cerebral lateralization and specialization is complex, not absolute, and cannot be reduced to concepts as simple as right brain skills and left brain skills. At best one can talk about cerebral dominance for certain functions, rather than cerebral exclusivity, recognizing the tremendous complexity of the human brain. I put forth that caveat, before looking at these fascinating new studies, to underscore that explanations of the savant phenomenon in terms of right brain/left brain functions, as if those functions were that discrete or that separate, need to be interpreted in terms of the complexity of central nervous function.

AN EXCITING NEW FINDING—"THE PATHOLOGY OF SUPERIORITY"

Norman Geschwind and Albert Galaburda, in the book *Cerebral Lateralization,* have provided, I feel, extremely important insights and information applicable to Savant Syndrome.[109] Within their work, as will be seen, are clues not only to why savants have the type of skills they have, but also to why the incidence of Savant Syndrome is so much higher in males than in females. Their work also provides clues as to the type, and site, of central nervous defect and dysfunction that produce this condition. Their work is most easily understood by looking at a series of their hypotheses and their findings. Elements of their work that are important to the explanation of Savant Syndrome are as follows:

(1) The human brain is asymmetrical even in fetal life. There is a natural, demonstrable and regular asymmetry that favors the left hemisphere, particularly the temporal lobe, in all humans, which exists not as a hereditary trait, but as a fundamental given in human anatomy. There are a number of reasons, from an evolutionary standpoint, why this is so, and this same asymmetry is reflected in the animal kingdom. This actual anatomic asymmetry is easily documented and has been reflected in scientific literature for years under the term "cerebral dominance" (with the left hemisphere being "dominant" in most persons). This dominance is, however, as much an actual anatomic one as

a functional one. It is not genetically determined in the usual sense, but rather it is a regularly recurring anatomic reality that is reflected already in the fetal brain.

(2) Hemispheric dominance is not a matter of an active, dominant, major hemisphere vs. a passive, nondominant, minor one; rather, each hemisphere is superior in certain functions. For example, the left hemisphere is generally dominant for language and manual skills and the right, for spatial and musical abilities.

(3) Dominance is not limited to cortical structures but is reflected in some subcortical structures as well.

(4) The left hemisphere develops later than the right in the fetus and therefore is at greater risk from prenatal influences for a longer period of time.

(5) One of these prenatal influences is a male-related factor, probably circulating testosterone, which can slow cortical growth and impair neuronal architecture and assembly in the more vulnerable left brain, causing an actual neuronal migration, enlargement of the right hemisphere and a shift of dominance to the right brain. In the case of a male fetus in utero, fetal gonads produce testosterone in high quantity; in fact, during some periods of intrauterine life fetal levels can reach those of adult males. While the female fetus is also exposed to some testosterone, from the maternal circulation, almost all of that is converted to estradiol in the placenta and it therefore does not have the same effect on the cortex as circulating testosterone has in the case of a male fetus. Data on both animals and humans support the existence of hormonal effects on the cortex, including this male-related influence on the growth of certain cortical regions.

(6) When this shift of dominance to the right brain occurs, it produces anomalous (a pattern differing from the standard form) dominance favoring talents associated with right brain skills (the kind of skills seen in savants). This shift is associated with the same disproportionate male-female sex ratios seen in dyslexia, delayed speech, autism, stuttering and hyperactivity. It also accounts for the higher incidence of left-handedness in males in general.

(7) A "pathology of superiority" is created wherein compensatory growth occurs in some portions of the brain (right brain) as a result of poorer development of or actual injury to other brain areas (left brain).

(8) Testosterone affects the growth of many other tissues as well, including those of certain immune systems of the body, and creates in males a disproportionate susceptibility to certain immune disorders.

With respect to Savant Syndrome, Geschwind and Galaburda point out that superior talents of a right hemisphere type are often associated with learning disorders, and many autistic children have "dramatically isolated islands of superior behavior." They point out as well that "high right hemisphere talents are common in dyslexics and their families." They explain these islands of ability as a "pathology of superiority," that is, compensatory growth leading to superior development of some portions of the brain as a result of poorer development of other portions.

The data, from a wide variety of human and animal studies, that support these findings, and the clinical correlations between these findings and Savant Syndrome as well as other conditions, is impressive but too detailed to outline here. But these hormonal effects on brain structure, particularly with respect to the cortex, offer considerable promise in explaining male predominance in Savant Syndrome and the predominance of right brain skills. While a compensatory shift to right brain dominance is certainly not a new idea, earlier theories could not explain why injury occurred so much more frequently in males; this finding accounts for that difference.

In summary, applying this information to the savant, the scenario develops in this way: Fetal brain asymmetry favors the left hemisphere, and its particular functions, in all humans. However, in the fetus the right hemisphere develops completely before the left hemisphere does. Because of its later development the left hemisphere is more vulnerable for a longer period of time to a number of prenatal influences. One such influence can be actual injury to the brain from a variety of prenatal causes. In such a case there is an interference with normal cortical architecture on the left and a neuronal migration to and assembly in the right hemisphere. This, of course, can occur in either males or females. Another such influence, even in the absence of injury, is a male-related factor, probably circulating testosterone, which can also slow cortical growth on the left and produce this same neuronal migration to the right, with actual enlargement of the right hemisphere, and a shift of dominance to the right side. In either event, right-side skills, of the type seen in the savant, predominate.

If at the time of birth, or at any time thereafter, injury to the left side occurs, this same compensatory shift to the right side can take place; such a shift in dominance would favor typical right brain skills.

This explanation accounts for the type of skills usually seen in the savant (right brain), accounts for the higher incidence of Savant Syndrome in males and is consistent with the clinical findings, and the CAT scans and postmortems where those have been done, that regularly point toward and implicate left brain damage or dysfunction.

In looking at savants, in both the past and the present, one is struck by the number who were born prematurely—Leslie, Ellen, George, Eddie and John, to name a few. In his 1964 book Dr. Bernard Rimland notes the possible contribution of certain prenatal influences to the etiology of infantile autism and reviews the numerous studies pointing to a relationship between prenatal and perinatal injuries and a variety of developmental and behavioral problems.[102]

The phenomenon of a massive brain cell death in humans just prior to birth is well established and commonly accepted.[110] Geschwind and Galaburda summarize it thus: "In all species studied, neurons are formed in excess, and many die when they fail in the competition to form connections."[109] According to this view there are many more brain cells than can possibly make connections, perhaps as a survival mechanism, and once pregnancy is nearly complete those cells that have not made connections, and thus are not necessary, become part of this massive prenatal brain cell die-off.

Geschwind and Galaburda point out that when left brain injury occurs *prenatally,* prior to the neuronal cell die-off, there is still a large reservoir of right brain neurons (which otherwise would be discarded) available to accommodate a neuronal shift to the right hemisphere; the shift occurs easily, and the right side of the brain actually becomes enlarged compared to the left side. Right hemisphere skills predominate, and in some instances, Savant Syndrome occurs. While this same shift can occur postnatally, it is more difficult and less complete because of the lack of excess neurons that are present prenatally. This is consistent with the finding that premature birth is commonly reported in savants, particularly in prodigious savants.

Another researcher, Dr. Brent Logan, Director of the Prenatal and Infant Education Institute in Snohomish, Washington, has been very interested, from a somewhat different perspective, in the phenomenon of massive neuronal cell die-off in humans prior to birth. He proposes to use that prenatal plentitude of neurons by introducing learning *before* birth to maximize connections and interactions between brain cells which, according to his research, would prevent some of that massive cell die-off.[111]

A considerable body of knowledge about learning before birth has begun to emerge. In a review of this theory, Logan points out that, between the tenth and eighteenth weeks of life, formation of new neurons, or nerve cells, is at its highest. At the end of this formation the maximum number of brain cells is reached.[112] What follows is a phase of profuse proliferation of connections (synapses) between nerve cells (neurons) as the cells themselves enlarge, the connecting arms (axons) elongate and the branches (dendrites) at the end of those axons grow rapidly larger. There follows a massive brain cell die-off that affects as many as ninety percent of the brain cells where no such connections have occurred. Charlotte M. Mistretta and Robert M. Bradley state it this way: "During neuronal development the processes of cell division, migration, growth, differentiation and death all take place. Depending on when the organism is exposed to a particular modification of its usual early sensory experience, any one of these ongoing processes could be affected. It has often been suggested that one of the least complex ways to modify the developing nervous system would be through the process of cell death."[113]

Prenatal stimulation, using a variety of largely auditory techniques, is being proposed by some as a way of enhancing and accelerating the development of neuronal synapses and connections. Presumably, by using the excess neurons to establish more connections, one can prevent what is seen by some as a wasteful brain cell die-off. Dr. Logan summarizes the desired process as "promoting the brain's most important growth—dendritic arborization, axonal myelination, synaptic site selection—so that massive neuronal depopulation penultimate to birth becomes significantly reduced while the surviving cells are strengthened from exercising impressive input."

A number of investigators have suggested various possible in-utero stimuli, ranging from the spoken word to classical music, to be systematically used by the mother during the pregnancy. Logan takes this a step further and uses a tape recorder device on the abdomen of the mother to play a variety of taped heart sounds that conform to prenatal and maternal heartbeat parameters. He reasons that if these sounds, which are ordinarily heard and experienced by the fetus, are merely doubled, the synaptic connections and cell preservation may be doubled as well. He uses, then, a cardiac curriculum (heart tones) for this prenatal university. He cites, as evidence of success, a wide variety of reports showing very gifted or markedly precocious children with accelerated learning, unusual artistic talents and elevated I.Q.s.

The theory, and application, of this ingenious approach—"Learning Before Birth"—is much more extensive and detailed than can be presented here. This is a new area of inquiry and endeavor, and only time will tell whether there is a firm basis to this theory based on a neurological fact of life (or death). Rigorous testing and documentation are needed. Yet, these separate accounts of a phenomenon that does regularly occur—massive brain cell die-off just prior to birth—may have some interesting implications for understanding Savant Syndrome. Geschwind and Galaburda would see this in terms of a convenient and fortuitous reservoir of brain cells that can be recruited to offset left brain damage in certain instances to produce right brain compensatory dominance. Or might it be, as Logan's work suggests, that the savant is the beneficiary of some kind of unusually rich prenatal imprinting that prevents, at least in some areas, an otherwise massive brain cell die-off, or else simply enhances cell counts, resulting in prodigious ability in selected, but narrow, areas?

These findings raise interesting questions about the role of prematurity in the etiology of Savant Syndrome. Does premature birth in some manner set up a different condition, and outcome, of brain cell die-off, as compared to a full-term birth? Does the blindness so often seen in conjunction with premature birth leave whole areas of cells to be recruited for other talents and skills because, with lack of visual input, cells are available that would otherwise be used for sight? Is there a unique vulnerability and sensitivity of some of these not-yet-discarded cells in the premature child to high-level oxygen, producing in them, as in the retina, change and damage that leads to the idiosyncratic functions and circuitry unique to the savant?

These fascinating questions await tremendously important answers in the future.

TO SLEEP, PERCHANCE TO FORGET

Remember the magic slate you wrote on as a child? As soon as it was filled you could lift the plastic sheet and it would be clear again. If you didn't clear the slate periodically the impressions would all become a blur and would be indistinguishable from each other.

How are the brain's impressions—which result from the thousands of stimuli that enter the brain each day—kept from becoming a gigantic, indistinguishable blur? Does the brain have its own "plastic sheet"? Some say we clear the slate when we dream. Clearing the slate is, perhaps, the purpose of dreaming.

This theory is advanced by Francis Crick, Nobel laureate for his work on DNA, now with the Salk Institute, and a collaborator, Graeme Mitchison, of Cambridge, England.[114] They propose that the function of dream (rapid-eye-movement, or REM) sleep is "reverse learning," in which some cell assemblies, the networks of memory, are strengthened (and thus saved), and some are weakened (and eventually erased). This is the brain's method of consolidating some daytime impressions for retention, and fragmenting others so they can be discarded. Through this process, information is reclassified and reordered during sleep, thus preventing the brain from becoming hopelessly blurred like the unpurged magic slate. They provide some interesting observations and information in support of this explanation of the purpose of dreaming and REM sleep.

Two kinds of sleep in animals and in man have been well delineated. In man, rapid-eye-movement (REM) sleep occurs for about 1 to 1½ hours of the sleep cycle, alternating with non-REM sleep, which takes place in four stages of increasing depth. Almost all dreaming is done during REM sleep. If deprived of REM sleep, subsequent sleep shows a catch-up phenomenon of REM cycles in persistent quantity, pointing toward the necessity of that sleep state. During REM sleep, outside sensory input is largely excluded and the cortex and other forebrain areas are periodically and widely stimulated by brain stem impulses that work as what has been called a "dream state generator."[115] At the onset of REM sleep, cells in the lower brain stem, specifically the pons, begin sending signals to the higher brain centers. These are ultimately distributed widely over the cortex. According to Crick and Mitchison, these brain stem impulses are random, unconscious and nonspecific. Being such they are most likely to excite equally random and nonspecific networks, as opposed to more organized and entrenched cell assemblies. In some as yet unknown manner there is a clearing—reverse learning—and weakening of these more random, "noisy" or static cell connections that results in a strengthening of the more established and useful cell assemblies. This random stimulation of relatively unconnected circuits accounts for the bizarre and random quality of most dreams that we recall, if we recall any at all. The researchers suggest: "In REM sleep we unlearn our unconscious dreams. We dream in order to forget."

Crick and Mitchison postulate that were it not for the clearing and cleansing function of REM sleep, the cortex would either have to be tremendously larger, or would become inoperative with clutter and unwanted "parasitic" modes of behavior and connections. Most mammals, including man, demonstrate REM sleep—the curious exception is the spiny anteater found in Australia, which, correspondingly, has a disproportionately huge, almost unwieldy cortex. It is suggested that the spiny anteater "needs such a large cortex because it cannot tune it up by the process of reverse learning." The researchers cite work by other investigators who, working with other natural and artificial neural networks, have used the concept of reverse learning to further enhance stored memories and suppress superfluous ones.[116]

The fact that REM activity is more frequent in the fetus and the newborn than in the older child and the adult requires some explanation. If dreams are related to clearing day-to-day experiences, one would expect to see less REM sleep in the relative sameness of intrauterine life. There are two possible explanations. First, the increased REM state in the fetus is due to the tremendously increased number of neurons prior to the massive neuronal die-off that takes place just before birth, or second, this lower brain stem stimulation serves a different function in the fetus and the newborn, that is, it acts as a generator of impulses to stimulate the synaptic activity so crucial to neuronal growth and proliferation and to the ultimate sparing of neurons (since it appears that those neurons ultimately affected by cell die-off are those for which neuronal connections have not been established).

Findings in much of the work with artificial cell assemblies done by other investigators correlates with this interesting theory of memory consolidation and clearing. However, some other investigators, actively working in the field of dream research, point out some of the shortcomings of this theory as the total explanation of REM sleep.[117] It does not explain, for example, the new learning or "Aha" experiences that sometimes occur in each of us during sleep, nor does it explain the recurrent dreams or the more coherent, meaningful dreams that we sometimes have and remember. Further work to refute, confirm or modify this intriguing theory continues.

All of this is of interest regarding the savant because, as pointed out earlier, there is some evidence that the phenomenal memory of the savant may be due to a failure to forget, rather than a unique ability to store and retrieve. There has been only one study of REM sleep in the savant, the study by Drs. Kenneth Z. Altshuler and Robert Brebbia cited in Chapter 11.[89] In that study of the calendar calculating twins, REM sleep was at above normal levels in the more intelligent of the two savants and at a normal level in the other. Thus both had REM levels *above* that expected in view of their limited I.Q.s (REM activity is generally lower in mentally defective persons than in persons of normal intelligence). The higher than expected levels of REM sleep in these two savants can be interpreted in several ways. If the theory that REM activity acts as an eraser is correct, finding higher than expected levels of such activity here would argue against the failure-to-forget explanation for the savant. If, however, REM sleep has an entirely different function, then this finding is still unexplained. Further sleep studies in savants could be informative on this point and need to be carried out.

There is no question that cortical clearing and cortical purging, like lifting the plastic page on the magic slate, has to occur at some point; otherwise, our cortexes would have to be absolutely massive, like those of spiny anteaters, if we were to function at all. For all the reasons outlined, it seems likely that REM sleep does that work. We probably do dream to forget, to clear and to rid ourselves of "static," and in the absence of dreaming, as REM deprivation studies demonstrate, we might well become disorganized and fragmented with cortical overload and peculiar brain function. Sleep may do more than refresh and restore us; sleep, particularly the REM phase, may well provide the time and be the activity we require to keep us sane and lucid.

Obviously this view of the purpose of dreaming is very different from more traditional Freudian or psychoanalytic theories, wherein dreaming is felt to be psychologically, rather than physiologically, necessary. In these older and more commonly accepted dream theories, the content of dreams is not random but very purposeful, highly symbolic and emotionally charged. Difficulty in remembering dreams is not because of the nature of the process, but rather represents purposeful and deliberate repression of content for psychological reasons. Far from being meaningless and chaotic, dreams carry specific messages and can be interpreted. They are drawn from cortical storage of life experiences and emotions. They are not, in relation to memory function, a sorting, cataloging and discarding process; rather, the "memory" process is one of active censorship by certain portions of the personality (superego) over other parts (id).

Dreams, in the newer theories outlined above, serve quite a different physical housekeeping function; content is incidental and haphazard, and stimuli emanate from subcortical areas, having little relationship to psychological meaning. In these newer views inability to remember our dreams is not a function of higher level censorship but is simply due to having both sensory input and output shut down for a bit while the slate is cleared. There is no conscious/unconscious struggle, only a cortical cleansing by a convenient and purposeful subcortical impulse.

Which view is right? They probably both are in part. Advocates of the purely psychological model have trouble explaining the uniformity and regularity of REM state; they also have difficulty explaining the documented increased REM state in the fetus and the newborn and the presence of REM activity at all in animals. Advocates of the purely physiologic model have trouble explaining those experiences we all have wherein some dream content *is* meaningful, insightful and relevant. We do remember some of our dreams and when we do we find that, while some are bizarre, some also are quite remarkable, complex and creative. More work needs to be done in reconciling these two very different views. Perhaps further sleep research and comparisons between sleep in persons of normal intelligence and sleep in savants can—given the very different nature of savant memory function and the role of the REM state in memory function—provide valuable information with respect to this very basic function of the brain.

BLINDNESS, MENTAL DEFECT AND MUSICAL GENIUS—
AN INTERESTING, RECURRENT TRIO

Looking first at Dr.'s Trelat's 1861 case of "an imbecile born blind, affected with rickets, and crippled, who had great musical talents," then at Blind Tom and finally at present-day musical marvels such as Leslie, Ellen and John—all described earlier—one can clearly see that the association of retardation, blindness and musical genius has occurred with a frequency that is conspicuous and disproportionate considering the odds of such a trio of traits occurring together. In a detailed review of 15 musical savants, Charness pointed out that 6 cases had this particular constellation of traits.[91] His case of John brings that total to 7 out of 16. That is an uncanny percentage when one considers the rarity of blindness and the rarity of Savant Syndrome. That these traits should be linked with this frequency, and occur together with musical genius, makes this triad a curious and spectacular confluence.

What produces this unlikely but interesting association?

Reviewing these cases more closely, two additional factors surface. First, the blindness is often that of retrolental fibroplasia, and second, there is almost always a history of premature birth.

Retrolental fibroplasia was first described and so-named in 1942.[117] As the normal fetus develops, some portions of retina are well vascularized but other portions are only partially vascularized as late as the 30th or 31st week of gestation. Therefore, when a child is born prematurely prior to the 31st week, part of the retina contains mature blood vessels and capillaries and other parts still have an immature vasculature. In retrolental fibroplasia the vascular bed of those portions of the retina still developing at the time of birth proliferate extensively and wildly soon after the child is born; most children born with this condition are born prematurely. This uncontrolled and unnatural capillary growth finally erodes into the vitreous fluid of the eye, forming fibrous tissue that ultimately detaches the retina from the back of the eye, resulting in total blindness. In some instances, as in the case of Leslie Lemke, it results in glaucoma as well, requiring surgical removal of the eyes. Dr. Arnall Patz provides the most detailed description of this pathological process and its devastating outcome.[118] This condition is limited usually, although not always, to infants born prematurely at about 6 months and weighing 3 lbs. or less. The retina is most vulnerable at about the 6th month of gestation, and in the prematurely born infant this eye condition, when it occurs, begins 3 to 5 weeks after birth.

For a number of years following its discovery, the cause of this disorder remained a mystery. Then in 1951 a clear causal association was made between it and the use of high-concentration oxygen in the newborn nursery, particularly with premature babies.[119] Careful control and monitoring of O_2 levels in newborn nurseries was immediately instituted and the incidence of the condition declined precipitously. Unfortunately, many premature youngsters born before these curbs on oxygen use in premature infants were instituted developed retrolental fibroplasia with subsequent blindness.

A number of studies of blind children with retrolental fibroplasia have shown a disproportionately high incidence of mental retardation, behavioral problems and especially infantile autism in these individuals. In a study of 24 patients with retrolental fibroplasia, Drs. Lauretta Bender and Karl Andermann found that twenty-two were mentally retarded; in her report she lists a number of other studies where the incidence of mental retardation ranged from 30 percent to 50 percent in children with retrolental fibroplasia.[120] W. R. Keeler points out the frequent occurrence of infantile autism in patients blinded from retrolental fibroplasia and raises the question of whether some vascular capillary process similar to that which occurs in the retina might occur elsewhere in the brain and lead to the characteristic autistic symptoms seen in his group.[121] Of the 60 children with retrolental fibroplasia studied by J. Cohen, 30 percent were retarded, compared to an expected incidence of 3 percent in the general population.[122] Interestingly, 10 percent of his sample scored in the superior range of intelligence.

The question arises as to whether the high incidence of mental defects in these blind children is linked directly to retrolental fibroplasia or whether those defects might simply be the accompaniment, in a nonspecific sense, of prematurity, a variable that these children also have in common. Cyril E. Williams notes that, whereas the incidence of serious mental defect in premature children is about 4 percent to 10 percent, the incidence of such mental defects in children with retrolental fibroplasia is about 10 percent to 40 percent, and at least 50 percent of children discharged as "ineducable" from special facilities for the blind in England had retrolental fibroplasia.[123] He concludes that, while prematurity may be a contributor to mental defect in children with retrolental fibroplasia, there is such a high and specific correlation between retrolental fibroplasia and mental defect—a correlation different from that seen in either prematurity or other types of blindness—that a special connection must exist.

Another question of course is whether blindness itself is responsible for the development of savant skills such as music as a trade-off to that particular sensory deficit. That seems unlikely as an explanation for several reasons. First, the vast majority of blind children do not develop such a compensatory talent, so it certainly is not a universal explanation.

Second, Keeler found that a large number of children with retrolental fibroplasia developed autism (savant skills are fairly common in children with such symptoms), while none of a control group of 18 patients blinded from other causes developed this disorder.[121] If blindness from any cause is solely responsible for savant skills, the proportion of savant skills in those blinded from all causes should be the same. That, however, simply has not been my experience, nor is that the experience reflected in the literature on Savant Syndrome. The incidence of savant skills is disproportionately high in persons where retrolental fibroplasia is the cause of the blindness, as compared to the incidence in persons whose blindness is attributable to other etiologies. It appears that either retrolental fibroplasia is *directly* linked to infantile autism because both illnesses result from the same process, which in each case affects a different area of the central nervous system, or retrolental fibroplasia, at least, serves as a biological marker of autism, even though the specific causes of the two conditions differ.

Rimland also notes a high incidence of premature children, some of whom develop retrolental fibroplasia, among those with Early Infantile Autism.[102] He suggests there may be a direct link between the high level of oxygen administered at birth (hyperoxia) and the autism, as well as a link between the oxygen and the retrolental fibroplasia itself. Even in his nonblind cases of autism there was "an unusually high incidence of children administered oxygen soon after birth or in early infancy." Such use of oxygen was almost always because of premature birth. While acknowledging that, certainly, the majority of autistic children have not received oxygen at birth—thereby indicating that autism can develop from other causes—Rimland cites studies that show wide variations in blood oxygen levels at the time of birth in normal or premature infants not exposed to supplemental oxygen. This, he feels, makes hyperoxia still an etiologic possibility in Early Infantile Autism.

Why are high levels of oxygen harmful to premature infants and particularly to the retina? And what is the association of these high oxygen levels to mental defect and, more particularly, to Savant Syndrome?

When the premature infant breathes in the high-concentration oxygen, the capillaries in the area of the immature retina that is still developing markedly constrict. For reasons still unclear, the more mature retinal vessels in the better developed areas of the retina are not nearly as vulnerable to this vasoconstriction. It is the newer and smaller capillaries that seem to react severely and uniquely to the high O_2 levels. This vasoconstriction produces relative undernourishment and damage to the less developed, vulnerable areas of the retina, and secondary proliferative or compensatory overgrowth occurs, producing obliteration, scarring, detachment of the retina and then blindness. Rimland, and others, speculate that perhaps some still-developing, equally vulnerable *other* area of the brain may, like the retina, suffer this same vasoconstriction and relative anoxia with resultant brain damage and brain dysfunction. Rimland suggests that the area affected may be the reticular activating system. To date there is no specific evidence implicating this specific subcortical area of the brain, but animal studies have shown deleterious effects of high-concentration oxygen on certain other areas of the brain such as the cortex. The mechanism, corresponding to that in the retina, for such proposed injury and resulting cortical or subcortical damage would be the same—vasoconstriction of immature vessels in developing neuronal tissue and resulting undernourishment and damage to those sensitive structures. Such damage can be easily directly observed in the retina, even as it develops, in both man and animals by direct visual inspection through an ophthalmoscope. That unfortunately is not possible with other areas of the brain.

I suspect that where the spectacular and consistent triad of blindness, mental defect and musical genius exists, there is neuronal damage—equivalent to that in the retina of persons with retrolental fibroplasia—in some localized and well-defined structures of the brain. Most likely these are subcortical structures, such as the hippocampus and the thalamus. Oxygen use in the case of premature birth may contribute to neuronal damage by producing some vasoconstriction in these vulnerable areas, just as it produces vasoconstriction in the retina, but cases in which oxygen was not used rules out oxygen use as the sole cause. The possibility even exists that the brain damage in patients with this trio of traits is even more precise and involves (or spares) those areas with special significance for musical ability and musical memory.

It is possible that the same mechanisms that affect the retina injure the localized brain areas. It is also possible that the retrolental fibroplasia itself, the result of special vulnerability to oxygen, may simply be a marker of some accompanying specific type of brain damage or dysfunction in these patients, with neither the eye defect nor the oxygen administration causally linked to Savant Syndrome. In either event, the linkage of retrolental fibroplasia and this particular form of Savant Syndrome needs to be especially studied and explored.

There will be continued opportunity to do so. Since the discovery of the link between oxygen level, prematurity and retrolental fibroplasia, O_2 levels in the newborn nursery have been rigorously monitored. For a period of time in the 1950s and 1960s the number of cases of retrolental fibroplasia (and perhaps the number of cases of Savant Syndrome, since these two conditions are so closely linked) fell precipitously. In the past ten years, however, neonatal intensive care units have made premature birth survival much more possible at lower and lower birth weights. While high-concentration oxygen is no longer routinely administered to premature babies, it is being administered—knowing full well the risks, and accepting those risks—to those premature babies where infantile respiratory distress syndrome requires O_2 as a life-saving measure. With this new exposure, some cases of retrolental fibroplasia are beginning to occur again. However, because it is now recognized earlier, extremely close monitoring of eyeground changes is preventing resultant blindness in more and more cases. Still, this new circumstance may have implications with respect to the development of Savant Syndrome even in the absence of blindness itself, for all the reasons mentioned above.

So, study of the linkage between retrolental fibroplasia and Savant Syndrome needs to proceed. Such study will provide, I am convinced, information and clues more consistent, more visible and more available than will the study of any other savant cases or groups of savants.

It is an answer, in my opinion, in search of discovery.

ASPERGER'S SYNDROME

In 1944 an Austrian psychiatrist, Hans Asperger, described a condition in which persons with rather severe psychiatric impairments show some exceptional skill or talent far out of proportion to overall intellectual ability. Usually the skill would involve an extraordinary capacity for memorization.[144] He named the condition "autistic psychopathy." The constellation of symptoms in what has now come to be known as *Asperger's Syndrome* is, in most ways, indistinguishable from what Dr. Leo Kanner had named "Early Infantile Autism" at approximately the same time.[3] Kanner's work and terminology have been incorporated into the worldwide literature on this topic whereas, until recently, Asperger's work was largely confined to the German psychological and psychiatric journals. Therefore, the term "Asperger's Syndrome" is less familiar than "Early Infantile Autism." Debate continues as to whether there are essential and distinctive differences between these two conditions or whether they are simply variants of the same disorder. Whether they are the same or not, the fact that savant skills are so frequently highlighted in accounts of Asperger's Syndrome makes it important to summarize here what has been written about that condition.

The best review of Asperger's Syndrome is a 1981 article by Dr. Lorna Wing of the Institute of Psychiatry in London.[145] In that article she reviews Asperger's original cases and then adds 34 cases of her own. From her accounts of those two groups of cases comes the following composite picture of such patients: Males outnumber females approximately 6:1. Speech is often delayed, and when it does appear, it is repetitive, vocal intonation is monotone and there is a conspicuous absence of the use of first person pronouns. Nonverbal communication is flat, with little facial expression; the patient often seems to "stare through" persons rather than make direct eye contact. Social interactions are severely restricted, naive and peculiar. Repetitive activities are preferred and engaged in at length; there is resistance to change and intense attachment to particular possessions. Motor coordination is particularly poor, patients are clumsy and posture and gait are peculiar. There is excellent, often prodigious, memory with intense preoccupation and mastery of one or two subjects of interest, such as bus schedules, sports statistics or historical trivia, sometimes to the exclusion of learning in all other areas. Language overall is rather limited except in the area of special ability. Conversation related to that area can be expansive, pedantic and seemingly scholarly but shows little grasp of the meaning of the words put forth so liberally. Even these dissertations tend to be carried out by rote.

As can be seen, many of the symptoms of Asperger's Syndrome—withdrawal, peculiar language, concreteness, preoccupation with sameness, flatness of affect, etc.—are exactly the same as those of Early Infantile Autism. Indeed the majority of the symptoms in the two conditions are identical. However, several somewhat distinctive features of Asperger's Syndrome do appear in the accounts of that condition. Those include: (1) clumsiness and poor motor coordination (features that, ordinarily, are not particularly noticeable or typical in autistic patients); (2) a higher level of social functioning than seen in autistic patients but still with bizarre, peculiar and naive social interactions; (3) the use of facile, expansive language in one or two favorite subject areas but with no grasp of the meaning of the words used (in contrast to the mutism or globally impaired speech so often characteristic of autism); and (4) an average or above average measured I.Q.

It is the normal or above normal I.Q. that has kept Asperger's Syndrome from being regularly referenced in the literature on the savant. Asperger, in fact, believed that his patients were of high intelligence but gave no I.Q. scores to confirm that impression. Approximately 80 percent of the cases reported by Wing were of average or above average intelligence. Yet, despite high I.Q. scores, Asperger's Syndrome does show the combination of substantial mental handicap, islands of exceptional talent and prodigious memory that so characterizes Savant Syndrome. Hence its inclusion here.

Among those describing this disorder there is no clear consensus on whether it is a form of adult schizophrenia, a personality disorder called "schizoid personality" (a diagnosis Asperger favored), or whether it is a variant of, or a gradation of, Early Infantile Autism.[146] I favor the latter. Many of these patients seem, from descriptions given, to be autistic patients—now adults—who are functioning at fairly high levels. Other investigators agree with that assessment.[147] The patient of Dr. Griffith Steel and his co-workers described in detail in Chapter 11, who those researchers call "an autistic mathematical idiot savant," fits into this category; the patient's I.Q. was measured at 91.[88]

Dr. Terrie Moffitt, of the University of Wisconsin–Madison Department of Psychology, and her colleague Denise Stevens, of the Beckman Research Institute of the City of Hope, provide an in-depth description of a patient with Asperger's Syndrome and a report of detailed neuropsychological testing on that patient, who they carefully followed from age 4½ to age 34.[148] The patient, A.C., has an exceptional mathematical ability. He did not speak until age 5½, and several doctors gave a diagnosis of autism. When the patient was 9 it was noted that he was obsessed with numbers and showed a remarkable memory for them. He left school at age 18 and became a rubbish collector. As an adult A.C. was given a diagnosis of schizophrenia—paranoid schizophrenia by one psychiatrist and schizotypal personality disorder by another.

His mathematical ability is described thus: "When asked to square any number between 1 and 10,000 he could do so in an average of 21.46 seconds. . . . A.C. could add, subtract, multiply and divide 2-, 3-, 4-, 5- and 6-digit numbers with great ease and rapidity. . . . One of his favorite pastimes was to begin with a number within viewing distance, for example, a license plate number or telephone number, and then multiply two smaller numbers together whose resultant was the larger number in view." He can decimalize numbers easily; he decimalized 1/851 in 126.28 seconds, giving as his answer a number with 66 decimal places. His mathematical ability, like that of other savants, extends well beyond that which could be attributed to memorization only. According to Moffitt and Stevens, "A.C. appeared to have learned a repertoire of mathematical shortcuts and rules that aided him in his calculations," yet he is unable to comprehend more abstract math such as calculus.

Moffitt and Stevens provide a good description of a typical patient with Asperger's Syndrome:

> A.C. presented as a bizarre, eccentric individual. He was very poorly groomed, unkempt, odorous, and painfully inept in interpersonal situations. He was somewhat obese, with an odd lurching gait and hunched posture. He had peculiar mannerisms, massive facial tics, and often giggled inappropriately. . . . phrases were repeatedly emitted in stereotyped fashion without connection to the social context, resembling

verbal tics. He engaged in lengthy and pedantic disquisitions on favorite subjects, oblivious to the interpersonal signals of boredom from the listener. . . . he habitually engaged in acts such as searching through rubbish bins on a main street for scraps of paper on which to write number games. [His mathematical prowess is described above.]

Detailed neuropsychological testing showed an I.Q. of 99 on the WAIS–R, with the greatest strengths shown on the arithmetic and digit-span subtests. On a 20-word memorization test (where 5 to 9 words is the average performance), A.C. scored 17. He achieved a perfect score on the WAIS–R digit-span subtest, leading to the conclusion that "auditory verbal recall memory appeared to be exceptional." Results of testing for abstraction and reasoning ability were normal, but not exceptional—the subject's performance was insufficient to explain his remarkable calculating achievements. In tests of nonverbal visuospatial skills the subject made errors suggestive of "a concrete cognitive style and difficulty integrating visual information holistically." Formal tests of executive function (judgment) showed no notable deficits in spite of a clinical history of poor judgment and social impairment.

A.C.'s excellent memory alone, Moffitt and Stevens conclude, cannot account for his remarkable mathematical skill. Nor can that skill be explained on the basis of a cognitive understanding of mathematics because he seems to have no grasp of, or ability to use, mathematical principles and knowledge in areas outside his one area of number expertise. Instead, his skill, like that of all savants, goes beyond memory and reasoning ability and somehow encompasses the numerous mathematical formulae and rules he uses within his area of skill but otherwise can neither understand nor apply.

Interestingly, the researchers speculate, based on the case of A.C. and on neuropsychologic studies of other persons with Asperger's Syndrome, that in these cases there may be a defect in the functioning of the *right* hemisphere of the brain and a relative superiority of *left* brain verbal skills. This, of course, is just the opposite of what is usually seen in savants, particularly those with prodigious abilities, and presents some intriguing research possibilities for comparing Asperger-type savants with those showing more classic Early Infantile Autism or mental retardation.

In summary, Asperger's Syndrome is another condition in which savant skills are seen in a rather severely handicapped population; however, in this condition the population is psychologically handicapped and has average or above average intelligence as measured by I.Q. testing. The psychological handicaps are so global and pervasive overall, and so similar to those of Early Infantile Autism, that some researchers suspect that Asperger's Syndrome is merely a variant of Early Infantile Autism with higher than usual verbal function preserved. If that is the case, the relatively high frequency of savant skills in Asperger's Syndrome should not be unexpected, for there is a high incidence of those skills in Early Infantile Autism as well. The neuropsychologic finding of possible right brain deficiency—with left brain superiority—in patients with Asperger's Syndrome deserves further study, to uncover implications this finding might hold, not only with respect to understanding Savant Syndrome but also with regard to understanding the etiology of what I believe to be two subtypes of Early Infantile Autism. I am sure that work will proceed.

14

How Do They Do It?

When Leslie Lemke plays, or Alonzo sculpts, or George computes, the first reaction of those observing is pure astonishment. What follows, almost invariably, is the question, "How do they do it?" To see or hear a savant perform is to experience cognitive dissonance—one part of our intellect is observing what is certainly real and clearly happening, while another part is telling us, based on prior experience, that it's not possible.

Some explain savant ability by saying that it needs no explanation—that it's a miracle. Well, a miracle, according to my dictionary's definition, it is, in that it is "a wonderful happening that is beyond the *known* laws of nature." That is what this inquiry is all about, trying to uncover laws of nature that can explain the savant phenomenon.

Understanding a miracle does not detract from the wonderment of it. We have had many miracle drugs, for example, that were just that—a miracle—when they came on the scene. I remember the miracle of penicillin, which began eradicating otherwise fatal infections. I remember polio vaccine when it was a miracle, before it became commonplace. I remember the miracle of antipsychotic drugs such as Thorazine, when they were first introduced in my hospital and how they began controlling and eradicating hallucinations and delusions in patients who formerly had been treated with only sedatives and had been put in physical restraints. Each of these miracles was the answer to the prayers of many. Yet they worked within the laws of nature, just as birth and death do. Every birth is a miracle to me. That doesn't mean we should not try to understand everything we can about genetics, obstetrics and pediatrics. To leave all of that alone, or to leave alone all that we have learned about infectious disease and psychosis from studying how penicillin and Thorazine work, would be to prevent more miracles from happening.

Regarding the savant, some have expressed to me the feeling the opinion that we ought to leave this remarkable phenomenon alone— because it is a miracle and should be left as such. But in my practice of medicine I see miracles regularly—patients who should not recover but who do; a cure when the odds are so heavily against one; procedures that, in some patients, work way beyond usual expectations. There is nothing sacrilegious in trying to understand such miracles occurring within the laws of nature so that we can try to extend them to help other persons as well. Just as we gain knowledge about some of nature's laws from clues uncovered through the use of "wonder" drugs or uncommon cures, so we can learn about ourselves and about some other laws of nature from the uncommonness of the savant.

Studying savants has made them no less wondrous or miraculous to me. Indeed, my awe and appreciation of them and how their condition came to be continue to escalate. But so has my cognitive dissonance grown, which propels me to keep on studying them. And that is, I think, one of the purposes of miracles—to propel us to study the laws of nature, as wonderful and as intricate as they are. Science is not sacrilegious. Rather, it has always produced, at least in me, a deeper appreciation for the marvelous, vast scheme of things and how that scheme came to be.

So, one explanation of savantism is that it's a miracle. But let us not leave it at that.

George has an explanation also. He says, "I've got a good brain, that's how I do it." We really cannot leave it at that either.

What follows is an explanation based on our present understanding of this complex and curious phenomenon. I hope that in a short time we will understand much more.

A SPECTRUM OF SKILLS

While the various skills savants show fall into a narrow range, considering all the skills in the human repertoire, the degree of ability involved in those skills is quite broad and ranges from fairly limited to prodigious. Seeing even simple abilities in a profoundly handicapped youngster is sometimes as striking as seeing more complex talents where the backdrop of disabilities is not nearly as severe. On our children's unit at Winnebago, for example, the islands of intelligence—even in that population—ranged from one patient's uncanny skill—and solo talent—for assembling complicated jigsaw puzzles (even with the picture face down) to another patient's dual accomplishment—the memorization of an entire city's bus system *and* the memorization of encyclopedic historical knowledge.

I have used the terms "talented savant" and "prodigious savant" to differentiate between two skill levels. These skill levels are arbitrary, of course, and there is no clear cutoff point between the two, no litmus test to absolutely distinguish one from the other.

In general, talented savants are individuals who have skills and abilities that are remarkable when viewed against the handicap but that would not be spectacular if seen in a normal individual. Talented savants are, obviously, much more common than prodigious savants. Abilities in this group range from one single skill to multiple skills. Musical talent is by far the most common ability in this category, and while memory—usually tied to a fairly extended repertoire of pieces— is quite good, it is not as striking or as uniform as in the prodigious savant. Many of the savant skills reported in the medical literature are skills of talented savants, since almost any facility or program for the developmentally disabled will have within it several of these persons with varying degrees of noticeable skills.

Prodigious savants also have skills and abilities that are remarkable when viewed against the handicap, but those skills would be spectacular even if seen in a normal person. This condition is much less common; in fact, it is extremely rare. The literature does not really distinguish between these skill levels, and the designation "savant," or more often "idiot savant," is used quite liberally, often without qualification as to specific I.Q. level and almost always without specification as to skill level. This makes it difficult to make meaningful case comparisons.

Recognizing that the savant spectrum lacks definitive boundaries, I have found, in my review of the entire world literature on this topic over the past century, about 100 known prodigious savants, using the definitions above. Certainly there may have been some unreported prodigious savants, but I do not believe that the number would be large. Bear in mind that I am reserving the term "prodigious savant" for those persons whose skill would be *spectacular* even if seen in a *normal* person. That is a high qualification to meet. Using that same definition for the prodigious savant, there are few (perhaps only 12 to 15) such persons living *presently* worldwide, to my knowledge, and most of those are described in this book. There may be some living at the present time who have not been reported, but, again, I doubt that number would be very large. Most of the reports on this topic in both the scientific and popular literature, however, have come only from the U.S., England, France, Japan and Germany. Savants, including prodigious savants, would not be expected to be limited to just those countries and continents. One can expect to see the same narrow band of skills distributed over a similar spectrum of disabilities no matter what the country of origin.

The question often arises as to whether there may be hundreds, if not thousands, of savants, particularly talented savants, not yet identified or discovered, or perhaps not yet "created" simply because no May Lemke or her equivalent has seen or nurtured the genius hidden within some handicapped person. That may be true to some extent for the talented savant. Some natural optimists may well come upon some undiscovered and untapped talent lying in certain handicapped persons, and through their optimism, faith and effort cause that talent to blossom and grow. From what I have seen, however, I do not feel that savant ability lies in every handicapped person any more than musical talent lies in every normal person. I also do not believe that the number of unidentified savants is in the thousands. Some undiscovered talented savants do exist and slowly surface through the untiring efforts and caring of those around them. Stories of such discovery and nurturing are always touching and inspirational.

But I doubt, in the case of the truly prodigious savant, that the special ability remains hidden. The talent and force of the prodigious savant is, I believe, so strong that it naturally surfaces even in the absence of a discoverer. Just as Alonzo *must* sculpt—and *had to* even when the clay was taken from him—so Leslie *must* play and George *must* compute. The talent can erupt suddenly and can be astonishing in contrast to extreme handicap. Recall A. Dudley Robert's case, described in Chapter 3, in which there was a measured I.Q. of 8, absence of language with communication limited to nodding yes or no, a word comprehension of 7 words and yet the ability to calendar calculate.[30] Those around the prodigious savant can motivate, help shape, reinforce and hurry along a talent, but it is either there or not there. The spectacular talent of the prodigious savant is extremely rare. Fortunately for us, the beneficiaries of these remarkable gifts, prodigious savants do come along once in a while and do share their mighty talents with us—talents that astonish us and, I think, teach us about ourselves.

The beginning of wisdom is to call things by their right names. The distinction between the talented savant and the prodigious savant is important because I think the mechanisms of their respective conditions and the ways in which those conditions came to be are different. For that reason we will separate them from here on.

MECHANISMS IN THE TALENTED SAVANT

In the talented savant some skill or group of skills stands in noticeable contrast to mental handicap, but such skills would not be considered spectacular if seen in a normal person. For this group some of the earlier theories, as outlined in Chapter 11, probably provide a sufficient explanation, particularly those theories having to do with genetic and psychological factors.

Talented savants are the kinds of savants described by David C. Rife and Laurence H. Snyder, for example, in their 1931 analysis of 33 cases from a number of institutions in the U.S.[16] The levels of musical talent, mathematical ability or drawing skill in their savants were conspicuous, but not spectacular. Strong family histories of related abilities were evident and the talents surfaced without, necessarily, any special training. Rife and Snyder's conclusion that in these instances, and others like them, individuals can inherit a "special ability" independent of general intelligence seems justified and sufficient. Prodigious memory need not be an accompaniment of these skills. This circumstance of some particular, conspicuous talent—whether athletic ability, artistic skill or mathematical prowess—occurs in normal persons as well.

Examples of individuals with such inherited skills who have been spared from a more global intellectual or mental defect are fairly easy to find. One patient of mine had the single isolated skill of being able to write with both the right hand and the left hand simultaneously, with one hand writing out the first half of a word while the other hand wrote out the second half of the word. In writing the word "California," for example, the patient would simultaneously write "Calif" with the left hand and "ornia" with the right hand on a blackboard. Another patient was an extremely gifted artist, whether he used his left or right hand. He drew equally well with either hand—which hand he chose to use would depend on the phase of his illness—in spite of marked mental disturbances and autistic behavior. The skills in these two individuals appeared to be innate and natural and existed as islands surrounded by a sea of disability. The studies by Rife and Snyder, Dr. Bernard Rimland and Dr. Jane Duckett give support to an inheritance mechanism in some savants since these researchers all found that the talents of many of the savants they studied were accompanied by a strong family history of the same trait.[16, 41, 73]

In some instances, then, heredity is a sufficient explanation for the talented savant. In other cases psychological factors such as compensation or reinforcement predominate or coexist. There is little doubt that the attention, the positive feedback and, in some instances, the notoriety that the special ability brings to the savant is highly reinforcing. In that sense the savant is no different from the rest of us, who also delight in having some special talent and being praised for it. As pointed out in Chapter 11 on this theory of savant skills, many authors have outlined even more specific psychodynamics, such as a search for love and self-esteem, an attempt at coping, a search for approval or an attempt to compensate in one area to offset deficits in another.[18, 21, 50, 60, 84] Drs. LaFontaine, Hoffman and Duckett focus on the importance of such psychological factors, particularly in the institutional setting where many of the talented savants are found.[56, 70, 73] Certainly on our children's unit at Winnebago one could see the special attention such skills brought from staff, visitors and families. Our little lad who could make free-throws with the unerring accuracy of a pitching machine— and with about as much emotion—regularly demonstrated his special skill and had performed for many, many visitors. It brought him special attention. Our resident trivia historian on the unit took great pride in his ability and derived a good deal of status from being able to remind each of us, each day, how many things he could recall about that day in history and how few we were able to recite. The attention, astonishment, praise and positive reinforcement that these skills always elicited helped build feelings of self-esteem, importance and worth.

One final biological factor seems important in explaining the talented savant. That factor is impaired abstract thinking coupled with an attention defect. Concrete thought patterns linked with inability to broaden focus results in unusually intense concentration within an exceedingly narrow range. In such instances there is little symbolic thought but there is high fidelity recall. Such concentration, and the muting of both external and internal stimuli, result in an inordinate capacity to tolerate boredom and repetition. The savant can engage in seemingly interminable repetition, repeating the same behaviors again and again or poring intensely and endlessly over the same written materials, such as bus schedules, compilations of sports statistics or almanacs. While most of us would tire of these activities, or at least be distracted by something external or internal, not so with the savant. This is particularly true of autistic patients, who will spend literally hours being fascinated by one spinning object, or some strings, or gazing at a single picture or a printed page. I view such behavior as the result of a biologic defect but, as pointed out in Chapter 11, some observers see even this type of behavior as being psychologically compensatory in nature or as resulting from psychological or social deprivation.

Whatever its cause, this factor contributes, along with the others outlined above, to the acquisition of the rather narrow, but remarkable, skills seen in talented savants.

In the case of talented savants the question "How do they do it?" can be answered, at this time, this way: Several factors are operative. In some instances inherited talent or special aptitude exists separately from deficiencies in general intelligence. In other instances special abilities are used as psychological mechanisms to compensate for more global defects or to gain approval, praise and a sense of worth. In still other instances impaired abstract thinking, coupled with an attention defect characterized by inability to broaden focus, creates intense concentration locked on skills within a very narrow band. All three of these factors can operate within the same individual or they can operate separately. Positive reinforcement provides motivation for constant practice, repetition and display of these skills. Memory is often enhanced within the narrow areas of ability but is not as expansive or consistent as in the prodigious savant.

MECHANISMS IN THE PRODIGIOUS SAVANT

Inherited skills, compensatory drive to offset other limitations, a striving for recognition and reinforcement from praise are certainly important factors in the case of the prodigious savant, as they are in the case of the talented savant. But there is more. Specific, special and unique biological and neurological factors join with psychological and genetic dimensions to produce the rare, but spectacular, phenomenon of the prodigious savant.

First there is the "pathology of superiority," described in detail in Chapter 13. Left hemisphere damage—either from actual brain injury before, during or after birth, or from impaired and slowed cortex development from the influence of testosterone in the case of the male fetus—results in faulty cell assembly on the left and a compensatory neuronal migration, enlargement of the right brain and shift of dominance to the right brain. Pneumoencephalographic studies, CAT scans and other neuropsychological studies on prodigious savants thus far confirm this type and location of actual central nervous system damage. The particular kinds of skills seen in the savant are those characteristically associated with right cerebral dominance.

A second, related organic factor is unusual and idiosyncratic memory circuitry; the prodigious savant uses a highly developed, noncognitive, "habit" memory as the alternative pathway to compensate for injury or absence of the more usual and more frequently used cognitive memory seen in the nonsavant. The memory function associated with this unusual alternative pathway is more automatic than volitional, has a paucity of emotion attached to it, is not reflective or highly associative and is very deep but also very narrow, with focus placed on concrete, high fidelity, nonsymbolic storage and retrieval. These characteristics are associated with a particular subcortical network in the brain—the cortical-striatal system—which is recruited in this instance, as in the case of right brain recruitment to offset left brain damage, to compensate for damage in the more usual and ordinarily used cortico-limbic system. Such a shift in reliance from the cortico-limbic system to the cortical-striatal system explains not only the unique memory function of the savant but also the impaired ability to broaden focus, the intense depth but narrow width of concentration abilities and the limited repertoire of skills so characteristic of the savant. These particular deficits point toward impairment not only in cortical structures, but in subcortical areas as well, particularly in hippocampal and amygdala structures. Thus hemispheric (right brain/left brain) specialization must be considered as involving more than cortical areas. Pneumoencephalographic studies, of autistic patients at least, confirm such changes in these subcortical structures.

A third mechanism appears to be involved in the prodigious savant. The talented savant can, with constant repetition and practice, create sufficient coding so that some unconscious algorithms develop (although he will have no understanding of them). However, in the prodigious savant, access to the rules of music or rules of mathematics, for example, is so extensive that some ancestral (inherited) memory must exist to account for that access. Such memory, in these individuals, is inherited separately from general intelligence.

Once the skill is established in the prodigious savant, intense concentration, obsessive repetition, reinforcement from display of these special abilities and an unstoppable drive to use them produce the rare, characteristic and spectacular picture seen in this type of savant.

The unusually frequent triad of blindness, retardation and musical genius may, in prodigious savants, point to a special neuropathology in which certain portions of the brain, indeed the same areas as those outlined just above, suffer the same kind of damage as the still-developing retina sometimes suffers in premature infants, particularly those who receive oxygen in excess. Whether the same oxygen that leads to retina damage and retrolental fibroplasia also leads to actual brain damage remains to be seen; it is also possible that the retrolental fibroplasia is simply a marker of brain damage incurred in a manner different from the way the retinal damage occurred. If these two conditions are causally linked, as I believe they are, then there should be an excess of prodigious savants born in that period of time when oxygen was used too liberally in premature infants, just as there is an excess of individuals born in that period who developed retrolental fibroplasia. While prodigious savants who are not blind do exist, and while some blind prodigious savants did exist before oxygen was routinely used in premature infants, the association of blindness and savantism is simply too regular and too frequent not to be causally connected.

A final postulation may serve as a partial explanation of special capacities in the savant. This postulation, which needs exploration, but is extremely difficult to confirm, suggests the possible association of prematurity in the savant with prevention of massive early neuronal cell die-off and recruitment or retention in some manner of these otherwise discarded cells. Since presumably this process would occur in all premature infants, and not all premature infants are savants—certainly not prodigious savants—this postulation may, at best, provide only a partial answer, but it is nonetheless worthy of further exploration.

In summary, with respect to the prodigious savant, the question "How do they do it?" can be answered, at this time, this way: In the prodigious savant there is a disruption of typical left hemisphere functions resulting from either prenatal influences—particularly hormonal effects on the cortex from circulating fetal testosterone—or prenatal or subsequent brain injury with compensatory migration and dominance, then, of right hemisphere functions. That abnormality, coupled with idiosyncratic hippocampal/amygdala/forebrain circuitry, probably resulting from those same influences or injuries, produces the characteristic cluster of symptoms, capabilities and defects—and especially the unique memory—found in the prodigious savant. The predilection for particular right brain skills and abilities is a reflection of compensatory cortical migration and neuronal rededication, and the predilection for simultaneous, high fidelity, nonsymbolic and literal memory function is a reflection of compensatory reliance on what can be called "habit memory" to offset defects in cognitive memory.

In both the talented savant and the prodigious savant, concreteness and impaired abstraction abilities are locked within a narrow band, yet constant repetition and practice can produce sufficient coding so that access to some noncognitive structures or unconscious algorithms can be automatically developed and used. In the prodigious savant, however, some genetic factors may also be operative since practice alone cannot account for access to extensive "rules of music" or "rules of mathematics," which seems innate in these individuals.

Once savant skills and memories are established, intense concentration, practice, compensatory drives and reinforcement play major roles in developing and polishing them. The suspected intermix of neurophysiologic, genetic and psychologic factors in this unique brain dysfunction is not new, but technology now available is providing an opportunity to better study and understand the actual components—especially the neurophysiologic components—of this dysfunction.

SAVANT SYNDROME: A COMPLEX AND WONDROUS EQUATION

Savant Syndrome, thus, rests on a three-pronged tripod of (1) unique brain function and circuitry, (2) acquired and sometimes inherited abilities and (3) motivation and reinforcement. In the case of the talented savant, motivation from someone who cares deeply and who earnestly cheers on and praises the savant, together with all the reinforcement that comes from that caring, encouragement and praise, is relatively more important than idiosyncratic brain circuitry, although right brain skills do predominate and memory is remarkable. In the prodigious savant—and this is an arbitrary designation based on a spectrum with no absolute cut-off points—clear left brain damage with compensatory right brain dominance exists, along with damage to lower brain centers, accounting for the prodigious memory of an automatic, relatively emotionless, tremendously deep but exceedingly narrow type, which is so characteristic of the prodigious savant. This specific kind of cortical and subcortical brain damage and dysfunction dominates the total clinical picture of the prodigious savant, but as with the talented savant, motivation from a believer and reinforcement from an appreciative audience can be tremendously important. The talented savant can be—but is not necessarily—the beneficiary of some inherited talents. Sometimes in these individuals the special skills result from persistent repetition and untiring effort to replace lost abilities with compensatory new ones. In the prodigious savant, however, the skills are so spectacular, and the inherent access to the rules and "language" behind those skills so extensive, that there must be, at least as part of the reason, a genetic endowment that somehow is preserved apart from, and that exists separately from, overall intelligence, which is always compromised, sometimes severely so.

While savant ability sometimes emerges as artistic talent, it most often takes the form of musical talent. The occurrence of music, mathematics (including calendar calculating) and outstanding memory as the most commonly seen special abilities must be more than coincidental. Some say that music is simply unconscious counting, and therein may lie the link between the seemingly disparate skills of music and math. The fact that memory, math ability and music ability are so closely linked in the savant condition must mean that they are closely linked in the brain itself, in view of the special type and location of central nervous system dysfunction in savants, particularly in prodigious savants. This is but one of many, many clues to understanding normal brain function that study of this unusual condition of central nervous system dysfunction is likely to unlock. I am convinced that in understanding how savants work, we can better understand how we work.

Science has had a good look—indeed a sophisticated, high-resolution, extremely detailed look—at brain *structure*. It has not, however, had such a detailed look at brain *function*, except indirectly, until recently. Knowing whether brain structure is intact in the savant is not enough. Of equal, if not more, importance is the ability to answer the question, "Are those structures working correctly?" Even with limitations in technology thus far, however, we have been able to put together some insightful and useful early answers to the question of "how savants do what they do"—answers that have been presented in this chapter. Much more information, and more complete answers, will be forthcoming from new technology and new inquiry. What lies ahead in that search, and what might that search mean not only for the savant but also for the rest of us?

15

And What of
the Future?

Everything we know about health we have learned from the study of disease. Throughout the history of medicine and healing man has sought to understand dysfunction in order to restore and maintain normal function. Careful study of brain dysfunction in Savant Syndrome can propel us further ahead than we have ever been in learning about normal brain function and the central nervous system, particularly memory. New technology just now available will make this possible. What follows may seem rather like a quantum leap from where we are at present, but then, all of the marvels of present-day medicine, both diagnostic and therapeutic, seemed like quantum leaps when they were first predicted.

This chapter looks at the process within the savant and its implications for the future. The following chapter will look at the savants themselves. The unique and remarkable memory function of the savant, using alternative circuitry and pathways as it does, provides, I am convinced, an opportunity to study those special pathways and to apply knowledge about them. Here I want to explore how the knowledge we gain from the savant can perhaps be ultimately used, harnessed and applied to improve normal brain function or help impaired brain function.

A PACEMAKER FOR THE BRAIN

Most likely, forgetting is not memories lost but rather memories not located. You and I, like the savant, have a tremendous amount of material recorded on the disc of our lives in our heads. We simply cannot access most of it most of the time. Dr. William Penfield's tiny electrical probe touching the temporal lobe and hippocampal areas, as described earlier, gave vivid evidence of memories stored but ordinarily inaccessible. My patient under sodium amytal recalled a trip taken years before in enormous detail—including each and every stoplight—when a particular area of her memory was "touched" with this chemical probe. She, and dozens of my other patients, under the disinhibiting influence of sodium amytal, have been recipients of a whole cascade of "forgotten" images and impressions that intrigue, amuse or startle the patient when repeated to him or her upon awakening. An outpouring, under hypnosis, of locked, hidden or simply inaccessible memories gives a further hint of all that we have stored, compared to how little we recall. Our dreams, when we recall them, are filled with images we would have sworn we had forgotten because they simply had not been part of our conscious self for a long, long time. Those dreams—sometimes so real that we awaken startled, or laughing, or crying—carry not just images but often the very smells, the sounds, the feelings of fear or fright or the exhilaration of delight and excitement that has occurred in the situation in our dream. We awake wondering "Where did that come from?" It came from the tremendous storage disc of 10 billion neurons that we call our brain.

Then, going on about our duties and tasks the following day, we cannot remember where we left our keys, whether we mailed the letter or left it in the car or what the date is without repeatedly looking at our calendar watch. While we find it difficult to recall our son's zip code as we try to address a letter to him, even though we have written it many times before, we can think, create, deduce, solve a multitude of complex problems and answer a variety of difficult questions. We pick data from here and there in our mind and put it together in some new way, just as I have picked words from here and there in my head to put together this sentence, this chapter and this book. Thus, our memory is so vast horizontally but so shallow vertically—"a mile wide but a millimeter deep," as one of my friends cynically summed up a local politician. In contrast, the savant memory is so deep, but so exceedingly narrow.

Savant memory is very different from ours. Although a vast multitude of events and data from an entire lifetime is faithfully recorded in my brain—just as the weather that occurred on every day of George's adult life is recorded in his brain—I doubt I have access to more than a minuscule amount of that data. Our memories are like huge libraries in which large numbers of books, especially those poorly circulated and rarely checked out, are misfiled or misplaced. The books have not been destroyed or discarded. They are there *somewhere*. The problem is in locating them. Savant memory is somewhat different—it uses alternative filing systems that give access to more of those books than the single system we depend on most of the time. Granted, I can do some things, particularly with cognitive memory, that George cannot, relying as he does on his more literal "habit memory." If savants rely chiefly, by necessity, on habit memory circuitry to achieve the depths of their prodigious memory—compared to us, who rely heavily on cognitive memory with its limitations—then by better understanding that alternative memory circuitry in the savant we can perhaps learn ways to tap it in the rest of us to give us better recall of that which we access so poorly.

Tapping and harnessing brain circuitry seems like an outlandish idea at first. I remember, though, seeing movies of some of the work of Dr. Robert Heath at Tulane University in the late 1950s, work no longer possible because of human research ethical issues now being debated. In these procedures, a patient who suffered severe rage episodes had, with his consent, a tiny wire implanted into that area of the brain that was producing these catastrophic, uncontrollable outbursts. These rage episodes began with a strange feeling that the patient could identify at the onset. When the patient experienced that feeling, an aura of sorts, he would push buttons attached to his belt that were connected to the tiny electrical wires implanted in the specific area of his brain producing these outbursts. A small current then would temporarily disrupt activity in the affected area and the rage episode would be aborted. Rather than an uncontrolled outburst, a calm, which was clearly visible in the film, came over the patient. The film showed a dramatic demonstration. The patient, and those around him, were tremendously relieved.

That same approach has application in the treatment of more classic epilepsy. Seizures have been characterized as an electrical storm in the brain, and all one has to do is watch an EEG during a seizure to confirm that characterization. Presently, epilepsy is treated primarily by using medication to calm the entire central nervous system to prevent those electrical outbursts from occurring. There are side effects to the medications used, however, particularly unwanted sedation. A more sensible and rational approach, since the seizure is basically an electrical event, is to abort the seizure in the same manner as the rage attacks were aborted in Heath's patient—by administering a small electrical current to the affected areas of the brain via an implanted electrode. Some work using this targeted, more effective approach is already under way in the treatment of epilepsy.

Such an electrode implant is a pacemaker, not of the heart, but of the brain. With a pacemaker, an electrode implanted on the heart itself, within its electrical conducting system, either paces the heartbeat at some predetermined rate or is programmed to operate only when the heart is having its own electrical storm, a condition called "ventricular fibrillation," which, if not treated, is fatal. Just as a tiny current can abort an electrical storm in the brain, it can do the same in the conducting system of the heart. Cardiac pacemakers are a very efficacious and logical approach to such problems and have become quite common. Unheard of a decade or so ago, they fall into the "so what else is new" category now. I suspect it will be the same with brain pacemakers in the decades ahead.

The brain is basically an electrical organ, in which electrical activity is generated, and is mediated chemically through neurotransmitters. An analogous mechanism can be found in a battery, an electrical device in which electrical potentials are produced through chemical reactions, as they are in the brain. Since the brain is an electrical organ, it makes most sense, when the technology is available, to treat a wide variety of disorders through direct electrical intervention in those brain centers affected, rather than depending on less specific, less targeted and less effective medication approaches. Electrical stimulation can be a direct attack on what is fundamentally an electrical problem in the brain.

By understanding the unique alternative circuitry of memory that appears to exist in the savant—and I believe we will be able to do just that with the newer technologies now available—we may then be able, ultimately, to access and activate that same circuitry, which also exists in each of us, to enhance recall and retrieval from the tremendous store of information we each have, but tap so poorly. Harnessing such circuitry with brain pacemakers sounds 2084-ish, and carries a variety of serious overtones. To me, however, it is no less possible, nor any less desirable, than preventing ventricular fibrillation in the heart or aborting an epileptic seizure in the brain. We are a long way from that day, but the savant provides, I feel, a rare window of opportunity through which to study memory circuitry in a manner otherwise not possible. I envision the day when, through the use of exceedingly precise and complex technology, we will be able to "pace" memory circuitry in some manner to allow enhanced retrieval of the myriad of memories we have stored but recall incompletely, or with difficulty, or not at all.

Such access would be welcome. It would be nice if I could recall portions of *Gray's Anatomy* that I once memorized so laboriously, without essentially having to begin over again when I need to know that material for some licensure test years later. While each and every bit of information from that early memorization is not necessarily still there—some sifting, sorting and discarding of information may occur in the brain, as was pointed out in Chapter 12—it is amazing how much does come back upon a refresher reading years later. It is *not* as if I am reading the material for the first time. I truly have been there before, and my mind, by doing some gentle prodding, reminds me of this. It is like the experience of revisiting a shopping mall in a distant city that you have not been to in 10 or 12 years. If, just before revisiting that mall, you were asked to describe the location of certain stores in it, you could not do so. However, the moment you step inside the mall again you pick up clues that then stimulate stored but well-hidden memories, and slowly, but clearly, you remember being there before and you remember the location of those shops as if you had been there only yesterday. To be able to recall the German I once knew so well, or the pharmacology I had learned so completely—rather than having to seemingly start over when, years later, I refer back to those skills or topics— would be such a time-saver. The learning may be a bit easier the second time around, but if we could access our huge stores of knowledge with even a fraction more facility, through enhanced retrieval, it would be a gigantic advance and fantastic time-saver. With that added time we could learn more new things rather than continually relearning—or at least reactivating—things we already know but cannot remember.

NEWER TECHNOLOGIES

Much of this expected discovery, and ultimate application, depends on emerging methods and techniques. What is this new technology?

Until recently, studies of brain function have been indirect and not nearly as available or detailed as studies of brain structure. One way of studying brain structure is by using CAT scans, which are essentially very high resolution, serial slices of the brain that show central nervous system anatomy extremely well. The CAT scan is a clear advance over the skull X-rays of the past, but it is still only a picture of brain structure and, by itself, tells nothing about brain function. Certainly the existence of structural abnormality is important and crucial information, but many brain disorders are disorders of function, not of structure. There can be severe amnesia, for example, or florid psychosis, with no anatomic abnormalities. This is true of many other organ systems as well. For example, a CAT scan of the liver may show an entirely normal profile. But there can be severe dysfunction of the liver, or even liver failure, in the absence of CAT scan abnormality.

Magnetic Resonance Imaging (MRI) uses intense magnetic fields to produce extremely detailed images of surface and deep brain structures. The resolution is even higher than that of the CAT scan, and because MRI is less impaired by bony skull than CAT scans are, it differentiates the various layers of grey and white matter of the brain more clearly and outlines these soft structures with striking clarity. This capability allows certain subcortical brain centers to be delineated as well, and in that regard, MRI is a clear advance over CAT scan technology. Nevertheless, MRI is still only an outline of brain structure and does not measure, delineate or assess brain function.

Pneumoencephalography has largely been replaced by these two techniques because of their safety, ease of administration and lack of discomfort for the patient as compared to the older pneumoencephalographic procedure. It, too, is limited to viewing structural changes in the central nervous system, although it does delineate some subcortical structures fairly well and has provided some useful information about these brain areas in autistic patients and some savants.[90]

The PET (Positive Emission Tomography) scan, a technique available since the early 1980s, does begin to assess brain function rather than just brain structure. In this procedure a radioactively tagged substance such as glucose or some related material is injected into the subject and then tracked by instruments that chart the course of utilization of the tagged compound. By using special substances that accumulate in proportion to use, a dynamic, colored, composite map of the brain *as it acts* is obtained. A graphic and highly visible picture of the brain in action can be seen and assessed as the patient performs various tasks and responds to various kinds of stimuli. With the use of standardized tasks, brain metabolism in different subjects with a variety of central nervous system disorders can be compared, and qualitative and quantitative function in various areas of the brain can be charted and compared. Such activity is not limited to surface areas only, and subcortical activity can be charted along with cortical changes. Since PET scans are generated from within the brain as it works, they provide a dynamic mosaic— of dynamic interactions between the different brain areas—that changes in response to specific stimuli and standardized tasks.

There have been no PET scans on savants as of yet. The procedure is costly, requires fully informed consent, is invasive, is lengthy and requires considerable understanding and cooperative participation in fairly detailed procedures. PET scans are available only in a few research settings, and the standardized tests usually involve visual concentration tasks which, of course, limit the tests' usefulness with blind individuals. Some PET scan findings comparing normal subjects and autistic patients will be outlined a bit later in this chapter.

A related method of studying brain function, rather than only brain architecture, is by a technique known as "Regional Cerebral Blood Flow" (RCBF). In this technique, the pattern of blood flow in the brain, rather than glucose utilization, is used to measure cerebral activity in the various regions of the brain. It is much easier to use than PET, and because it is much less expensive, it is more readily available; the only disadvantage is that, because of limited resolution, or clarity, the images produced are not yet as detailed or precise as in PET scans. One method of using this technique is SPECT (Single Photon Emission Computed Tomography) scanning to trace the distribution of a radioactive substance[123] (I labeled diamine), which is distributed in normal brains proportional to blood flow itself. This requires an injection, and therefore the procedure is invasive. By using Xenon-133, however, which can be *inhaled* rather than injected, the procedure is much more acceptable and much more easily administered. By assigning colors to "hot" or "cold" areas of activity, depending on differential blood flow, a dynamic, colored picture of the brain *as it works* can be mapped. Areas of the brain can be compared to, and contrasted with, each other within the same patient under varying conditions, or maps of patients with different symptoms or findings can be compared. Work is being done to improve resolution of the image, and once this is achieved, this technique should be generally available compared to PET which, because of expense and complexity of procedure, will remain more limited in its availability.

Finally, another developing form of new technology is the computerized electroencephalogram (C-EEG). While this technique is limited much more to surface cortical activity, computer analysis of complex EEG waves can, nevertheless, provide statistical probabilities as to what a specific composite of wave forms means. Rather than being represented by mere pen and ink tracings, the activity is displayed in brain maps, much like PET scans, that point out statistical variations between areas. Some computerized EEG analyses measure brain electrical activity generated while the subject is at rest or doing various tasks, while others measure evoked potentials (a stimulus is provided and its impact is measured on the computerized brain map). By applying a standard stimulus to various subjects, sometimes information can be obtained from the evoked potential EEG that otherwise would not be available from an ordinary tracing. The computerized EEG allows not only an analysis of qualitative changes in tracings and wave forms but also a complex quantitative analysis, in which these images are displayed in color-coded fashion to reveal dysfunction or variations from normal. This technology is in its infancy but is rapidly being assimilated into neurologic and psychiatric research and practice. It is so new that there have been as yet no such tracings on savants. The advantage of the C-EEG over the PET scan is that it is noninvasive, uses no radiation, is much less costly and is administered much more easily. These newer tracings are being done in a number of medical centers now. Because they are not limited to only a few research settings, as are PET scans, some tracings on savant subjects should be soon forthcoming and will perhaps provide new information and insights.

PET SCAN FINDINGS AND IMPLICATIONS
FOR SAVANT SYNDROME

As just mentioned, there have been no PET scans done on savants as yet, but several studies using this new technology have interesting implications for understanding Savant Syndrome:

PET Scans, Music and Musicians

Dr. John Mazziotta and his colleagues, Michael Phelps and Richard Carson, at UCLA School of Medicine in Los Angeles, California, have produced several findings of considerable interest in documenting the different ways the brain processes verbal, as compared to musical, stimuli.[124] They did PET scans on 20 male subjects, all right-handed, between the ages of 21 and 28. Standardized tasks were presented to the subjects and the PET scans were compared. The tasks included: (1) a verbal stimulus consisting of listening to a Sherlock Holmes detective story; (2) a musical stimulus consisting of listening to a series of individual chords with complex harmonic composition (these chords—from the timbre subtest of the Seashore Measure of Musical Talent[125]—either were identical or differed in their harmonic composition, and subjects were asked to discriminate between the chords and communicate their response by tapping a microswitch); and (3) a second musical stimulus, the tonal memory subtest from the Seashore Measure, consisting of a series of tone sequence pairs (subjects were asked to distinguish those that were alike from those that were different sequentially).

While subjects listened to the verbal story, there were diffuse metabolic changes in the *left* hemisphere, along with bilateral activation of the transverse and posterior temporal lobes. Some activation was seen in the *left* thalamus as well, in contrast to no such activity on the right in that structure. This PET scan finding correlates, then, with the commonly held view that verbal or language stimuli are processed principally by the left, or dominant, hemisphere.

In contrast, the response to musical chords showed bilateral parietotemporal activity and diffuse *right greater than left* fronto-temporal *asymmetries.* This finding correlates with the generally held view that music, at least of this type, is more of a right hemisphere activity.

The researchers then took some of the subjects and divided them into two groups: a musically sophisticated group, whose members used analytic strategies with considerable visual imagery (playing by sight), and a musically naive group, whose members used subjective, nonanalytical strategies (playing by ear), especially in processing the musical stimuli. Musical sophistication was defined as having the ability to read music and being either active professionally in the musical arts or well versed in musical listening skills. Analytic strategies, in contrast to nonanalytic, were defined as the use of specific and highly organized visual imagery (often actually "seeing notes" in the mind while playing or listening to music). Using these criteria on the tonal subtests, it was found that hemispheric dominance varied depending on whether the listener was an analytic, musically sophisticated subject or a nonanalytic, musically naive subject. Analytic, musically sophisticated listeners, who use considerable visual imagery, showed an asymmetry favoring the *left* temporal areas, whereas nonanalytic, musically naive listeners had *right greater than left* fronto-temporal asymmetries. Thus, the same musical stimulus—in this case, tonal sequence—is processed differently by the brain, in terms of hemispheric dominance, depending on whether an analytic or a nonanalytic strategy is used and on whether the listener is musically naive or musically sophisticated.

Several findings here are of interest with respect to the savant phenomenon. First, there is general confirmation that verbal and language skills (which are generally poor in the savant) are left brain dominant. Second, certain musical skills (which are generally good in the savant) tend to be right brain dominant. Third, with some musical skills cerebral dominance is determined by which strategy is employed. Savant Syndrome, in general, tends to be associated with nonanalytic strategies using a minimum of high visual imagery skills. Although in many instances savants are accomplished performers, they usually play "by ear" and are musically unsophisticated, in the terminology of this study. That this type of musician tends to use the right brain predominantly for these musical skills would correlate with what we know about left brain/right brain integrity in, at least, the prodigious savant.

I outline this study not as the definitive explanation of the savant, certainly, but because it points up the kind of information we can get about brain function by observing it *directly as it functions* with a variety of stimuli and tasks. As the technology improves, as it surely will, we will be able to study more and more brain structures, including subcortical structures, and outline actual circuitry. As studies such as this begin to use standardized memory tasks as the stimuli, perhaps we will be able to trace—and ultimately enhance, in the manner I have suggested—the circuitry of memory.

The PET scan begins to provide some knowledge, and promise, in that direction. I am certain, with the burgeoning technology in this fascinating area, much more will follow, and relatively quickly.

Delineating Subcortical Activity

A second report by Mazziotta and his co-workers points up the value of this technology in delineating subcortical as well as cortical activity in the savant. Study of subcortical activity is so critical to understanding memory circuitry because memory is dependent on these lower brain centers.[126] This particular study evaluated PET scan response to visual (white light) stimuli and to the same auditory stimuli used in the study reported just above. In this project the thalamus, the caudate nuclei and the lenticular nuclei, all subcortical structures, were visualized. This study is important because it "is the first to demonstrate in normal subjects the participation of subcortical structures in auditory and language information processing."[126]

In this particular work bilateral activations occurred with verbal stimuli, but only the head of the left caudate was activated when subjects used visual imagery as a strategy to identify tonal sequences. Thus, verbal imagery and tone-linked visual imagery were not handled identically by the brain, but rather they transversed different pathways, involved different brain structures, and were associated with different patterns of dominant hemisphere involvement.

The significance of this work—beyond these findings, as important as they are—is the fact that here is a technique that can study cortical *and* subcortical structures and can do so in normal subjects while those subjects carry out standardized tasks. Mazziotta reflects this view point thus:

> Since most of our knowledge of human brain function has been derived from lesion studies where large segments of the neuronal apparatus have been damaged, the resultant conclusions may not reflect the normal state of brain physiology. Noninvasive positron CT studies using physiologic stimuli may produce an entirely new set of rules to use in exploring normal brain function. It is not necessarily true that observations gained over the last century in patients will be wholly substantiated by noninvasive studies in normal subjects. In fact, positron CT results may vary substantially from pathological-clinical data. Whatever the outcome, positron CT should provide new and previously unobtainable information about the biochemical and physiological basis of human cerebral function.[127]

PET Scans and Autistic Patients

While no PET scans have been done on persons specifically identified as savants, in several studies PET scans were carried out on adult patients who had been diagnosed as having childhood autism and on 15 age-matched control subjects.[128] No single abnormality in the autistic subjects emerged as a consistent finding, although there was a generally higher glucose metabolic rate in all areas of the brain, a loss of normal right-side elevation of metabolic rate in certain frontal areas, and scattered areas of extreme relative metabolic rates in certain cortical areas and basal ganglia. Since no single defect was consistently present, the presence of scattered defects suggested an organic etiology but one of a heterogeneous, nonuniform type.

Dr. Monte Buchsbaum and his staff at the University of California/ Irvine also carried out PET scans on adults who had been diagnosed as having autism during their childhood.[129] In this study high-functioning adult autistic patients were compared to 13 age-matched control subjects. In the autistic patients there was a loss of the *right greater than left* cortical and thalamic asymmetry that one would expect to see given the particular attentional task both groups were exposed to (one which, interestingly, both groups did equally well on). In all 7 autistic patients, but in none of the 13 control subjects, the PET scans showed brain regions with significant deviation from normal values. In 6 of the autistic patients there was such an area in the frontal lobe, and in 4 of the autistic patients, abnormalities were seen in the basal ganglia. Buchsbaum concludes that "this variable pattern of hypofunction is consistent with heterogeneous etiology" but differs enough from PET scan data in schizophrenic patients to suggest that autism is a process different from schizophrenia.

Most investigators postulate that there is, in autistic patients, subcortical pathology coupled with cortical dysfunction, since it appears that cortical damage alone would not produce the characteristic picture seen in childhood autism. In the autistic patients in this study some 42 subcortical areas were available for comparison but only 2—the right posterior ventrolateral thalamus and the right putamen—showed decreased relative glucose utilization. Of particular interest with respect to the savant phenomenon is the absence of differences between the autistic and control groups in the hippocampal areas "in light of the well-developed rote memories of autistic patients." The author concludes from this that "the data are consistent with normal memory function or with superior memory shown by autistics being mediated by other yet unidentified structures which might show metabolic elevation during memory processing." My interpretation of that finding, and my speculation concerning it, is that the "other yet unidentified structures" are the alternative memory pathways described earlier, particularly those having to do with "habit" memory.

A very precise refining of diagnostic categories and their subtypes in the group of patients more loosely called "autistic" in the scientific literature will cause specific subgroups with uniform etiologies to emerge. PET scan technology, measuring subcortical as well as cortical function as it does, can perhaps help identify and sort out those categories as the technique becomes even more refined and the sample sizes become larger. Hopefully, at some point PET scan data will be available on savants as a subgroup. It is my speculation that savants—particularly prodigious savants, fairly narrowly and rigorously defined—are sufficiently uniform in etiology that correspondingly uniform PET scan findings will be seen. The PET scans may particularly highlight left cortical damage and dysfunction coupled with identifiable subcortical damage and dysfunction. Memory circuitry may be significantly and consistently different from that of normal persons and may be distinguishable as well from the memory circuitry of other brain-injured persons who do not have the characteristic constellation of pathology that is unique to the savant.

The uniformity of central nervous system dysfunction and the unique memory circuitry in the savant will serve as a useful contrasting pathway and network against which normal memory can be studied, undoubtedly accelerating our knowledge perceptibly. From knowledge about how memory works, then, can come mechanisms by which it can be enhanced. I happen to think the means of enhancement will chiefly be electrical.

MATTER OVER MIND: THE MEMORY-EXPANDING DRUGS

The search for a drug to improve memory, like the search for the perfect aphrodisiac, has seen promises that have been outnumbered by disappointments. Through the centuries a variety of herbs, potions and compounds have been highly touted as brain refreshers and restorers. I remember as a child being told to eat fish because it was "brain food." A compendium of these compounds and their histories, from the tonics of the 1860s to the mind expanders of the 1960s, would fill an entire book. There is not room enough here to look at this fascinating area exhaustively, but a brief overview will give an idea of where we are now and where we are going in the discovery and design of drugs to repair, restore or enhance memory.

Throughout most of human history, more effort has been expended in the search for products to alter mood than for substances to enhance memory. In fact, the early substances that did have any useful impact on memory did so as a side effect to the basic function of altering mood, attention or arousal. In 1917 Lashley set forth on one of the first scientific efforts to test memory-improving drugs with formal, experimental methodology.[130] He found that, in rats, small amounts of strychnine and caffeine resulted in some improvement in learning and memory. However, as with so many of the substances used before and after that experiment, the improvement seen was due to some arousal effect or some effect on concentration, sensory acuity or attention, rather than an effect directly on memory processes themselves. The recent surge of interest in the etiology and treatment of Alzheimer's disease has created an intensive search for remedies for that condition. As a spinoff of that effort, new products have come forth, with potential not only to repair ailing memory, but to expand normal memory as well.

Drugs to improve memory and cognition in normal persons, and to improve memory or at least impede memory loss in diseases such as Alzheimers, are now known as *nootropics*. While a number of these drugs have been in use in Europe for some time, in the U.S. they are only being used in research settings at the present time. Their usefulness is based on their broad effects on a number of physiologic mechanisms in the brain.

This chemical approach to restoring or enhancing memory focuses on neurotransmitters and is different from the electrical approaches mentioned earlier, which focus not on substances, but on circuitry. That there should be these two simultaneous and parallel approaches is not surprising since, as pointed out earlier, the brain is an organ that uses chemical reactions to do its work of generating and transmitting electrical impulses. The basic units of this chemical reaction are the neurotransmitters. There are numerous such neurotransmitters in the brain, but several are of particular interest in the matter of memory and memory enhancement and have been the most extensively studied thus far.

Acetylcholine is the neurotransmitter that has received the most attention and probably holds the most promise. The crucial role of this substance in normal memory function has been repeatedly documented. The ability of the brain to synthesize this substance diminishes with age, and lowered levels are correlated with memory deficits. Depletions of enzymes important in the production of this substance have been noted in regions of the brain implicated in Alzheimer's disease. It is not surprising, then, that there have been attempts to improve memory in patients with memory defects, and indeed in normal subjects as well, by administering products that increase acetylcholine in brain tissue. Some of these products presently contain choline, arecoline and piracetam. Lecithin has also been suggested for use as a memory enhancer, but unfortunately, neither choline nor lecithin is transmitted very effectively from the blood to the brain and there is controversy about the effectiveness of these substances when taken orally, even in large doses. Some feel that combining products—particularly choline with lecithin, and choline with piracetam—may increase absorption by the brain above what is absorbed when these substances are administered separately.[131]

Physostigmine, particularly when combined with lecithin, has been shown to improve memory in some Alzheimer's patients. It works by slowing what is a natural breakdown of acetylcholine in those areas of the brain affected by Alzheimer's disease. Vasopressin, or a related compound, DDAVP, has shown some usefulness in patients with memory diseases and in normal subjects.[131] However, these two latter substances may work by heightening arousal or increasing attention, rather than by directly affecting memory, since vasopressin even as a natural substance is present in larger amounts in the thalamus and amygdala (structures associated with arousal and attention) than in the hippocampus. Several newer research products, such as MSH/ACTH 4-10, CI-911, pyritinol and 3-HMC, are being explored in research settings.[131]

Two memory-enhancing substances have been of particular and somewhat sensational interest recently. The experimental drug THA was found to be useful in 16 of 17 Alzheimer's patients, in some instances dramatically so.[132] An accelerated program to test that compound began at a number of medical centers in the U.S. in early 1987. Problems with toxicity to the liver halted those trials in the summer of 1987, but already a related compound, HP-029, has been developed in the hopes that it will have the same beneficial effects without posing risks to the liver. A multi-center test program for that compound began in early 1988 and will last for two years. HP-029, like many of the substances above, works by inhibiting an enzyme that destroys acetylcholine. It is not a cure for the disorder, but it does hold some promise for control of the condition. The other drug, Vinpocetine, is currently being studied at eight centers in the U.S. as a treatment for dementia following stroke where there has been significant memory impairment. This substance is already available for use in Japan, Europe and Latin America. Animal studies show that it has considerable effect as a memory enhancer—or a "cognitive activator," as the drug company conducting these studies prefers to call this compound. Trials of this product, in an eight-center U.S. study, in patients with Alzheimer's Disease have shown good initial results, and FDA approval for more general use is being sought.

Sometimes it is the troubling side effects of medications—rather than the beneficial effects for which they are prescribed—that provide leads to understanding the cause and pathophysiology of certain diseases. Certain antipsychotic drugs, for example, produce Parkinson-like symptoms and from that iatrogenic production of dysfunction we have learned a good deal about the etiology of Parkinson's disease. Several of the ultra-short acting benzodiazepine drugs, used for relief of anxiety and induction of sleep, have the peculiar and isolated side effect of anterograde amnesia.[133] This is a form of memory loss, or more accurately a lack of memory formation, in which everything that occurs from the time the drug is administered cannot be recalled. Patients have reported to me that, after taking the very short acting sleep-inducing medication triazolam, they have engaged, for example, in rather lengthy phone conversations that they could not recall the following day. At best that can be embarrassing; at worst, when some major decisions have been made by phone, that can be dangerous.

A series of similar incidents, following the use of triazolam for insomnia, was reported in the *Journal of the American Medical Association* in January 1988.[149] In one instance, a 29-year-old physician took a small dose of triazolam at bedtime and the following morning took a three-hour train trip to a distant city, completed work on some complex papers and returned home with no recollection of the trip; ticket stubs and a copy of the papers allowed him to reconstruct the trip. A 44-year-old professor traveled to an adjacent state one morning after a bedtime dose of triazolam, gave a two-hour lecture and slide presentation to 200 people and "came to" at 12:20 P.M. the following day to find herself at lunch with 12 strangers. She had no recollection of anything that had occurred during the 14 hours between the time she took the sleeping pill and 12:20 P.M.; her lunch companions told her that the lecture went well. A 46-year-old woman took a bedtime dose of triazolam, but instead of falling asleep at 11:00 P.M., she told her family (who could sense nothing wrong) that she was going to bake a cake. The following morning, on awakening, she found a "beautiful almond cake" that she had made from a recipe she had never seen before. She had no recollection of having baked the cake.

The fascinating circumstance here, from a research point of view, is that the anterograde amnesia reported in each of these instances occurred in the *absence* of the severe sedation, confusion or disorientation that usually accompanies such global memory loss. Instead, actions during each of these amnestic episodes were deliberate, complex and purposeful. These cases show striking similarity to the hippocampal memory loss of H.M and R.B., as detailed in Chapter 12, with anterograde amnesia occurring in the presence of otherwise intact central nervous system function. Significantly, however, the disability from triazolam is temporary and chemically induced, while the difficulty in H.M and R.B. was permanent and induced by demonstrable and irreversible brain damage.

Probably the most common type of anterograde amnesia is the alcoholic "blackout," in which a person simply does not recall, after a certain point, where he was, whom he was with, what happened or where he left the car. This type of amnesia is heavily colored by the sedative effects of alcohol and widespread other effects on the brain. The triazolam effect, in contrast, is much more precise, interferes only with transfer from very-short-term memory to long-term memory and is an almost pure culture model of disrupted memory consolidation without impairment of memory retrieval. This externally induced, limited, transient anterograde amnesia provides a rare opportunity to study human memory consolidation and retrieval processes more clearly.

As with many side effects—such as the hair growth caused by one of the major antihypertensive drugs, which is now being marketed for that side effect—the particular, peculiar side effect of triazolam and other drugs like it is being put to good clinical use: These drugs are being given before surgery or unpleasant chemotherapy treatments, so that the patient does not remember any of the unpleasantness, anxiety or pain associated with those procedures. While some of this effect is simply dose-related, as with alcohol, the specificity of this reaction in contradistinction to the reactions of so many other products used without this side effect leads to the natural conclusion that some unique and targeted neuropathophysiology is at work here and is worthy of much more vigorous and intense investigation. This is a lead well worth following, for from study of this memory impairment may come useful information about memory enhancement.

The preceding is not an exhaustive list of substances under review, but it does point out some of the rationale for efforts in this approach to memory enhancement and some of the activity being carried out. Because of the tremendous interest in the treatment of Alzheimer's disease alone, there is a quickening interest in these compounds. Whether these drugs will live up to their advance billing in terms of effectiveness, and whether they will turn out to be safe, remains to be seen. In any event, a useful spinoff of the accelerated studies of these drugs will be a better understanding of memory process from the neurotransmitter standpoint and, ultimately, application of that knowledge. From this research will come not only a better understanding of central nervous system disease but also a better understanding of normal memory and of methods for achieving memory enhancement in normal persons.

The search continues, then, for a compound that can demonstrate *matter over mind*. With techniques now available to investigate and alter brain chemistry in specific and exacting locations in the brain, research in the next five years should easily eclipse all the work of the last fifty.

A significantly different and new approach to restoring function in some brain diseases, both in animals and in man, could conceivably have application for memory repair or even memory enhancement. As with brain pacing, this methodology raises as many ethical issues as it has scientific obstacles, but nevertheless it is already in use in man in at least one major brain disorder—Parkinson's Disease. The procedure involves transplanting cells into an area of damage in the brain and letting the newly implanted cells take over the work of the dead or dying neurons. This technique is more accurately termed a "brain graft," or "brain implant," rather than a "brain transplant" since only a quantity of tissue, and not an entire organ, is being replaced.

Parkinson's disease occurs when cells in the substantia nigra, a sub-cortical area of the brain, die and stop producing a crucial neurotransmitter in that structure, dopamine. As those cells cease to function, the tremor, gait, posture and ultimate neuro-debilitation of that disorder appear and progress. In animals, implantation of dopamine-secreting neurons from fetal brain tissue of the same species into the substantia nigra area of the brain has reversed the condition. The implanted cells sprouted new fibers, resembled the original cells in neurophysiologic activity and did indeed secrete dopamine. This is a most important and exciting finding for restoring brain cell function in damaged areas, but the use of human fetal brain tissue as the source of brain graft material raises serious and complex ethical questions.

As a result, an alternative brain graft procedure has been developed for use in humans for the treatment of Parkinson's disease. This procedure, adrenal-brain autotransplant, is based on the fact that certain cells in the human adrenal gland—chromaffin tissue cells—also produce dopamine, the neurotransmitter in short supply in Parkinson's disease. By transplanting these cells from the patient's adrenal gland into the substantia nigra area of the brain of the same patient dopamine production can be restored. A 1986 report outlines the rationale, technique and results in four Swedish patients on whom this procedure was carried out between 1982 and 1985.[134] Improvement did occur, but it was short-lived. In 1987 a team of Mexican neurosurgeons reported achieving longer-lasting results by grafting the adrenal tissue into the lateral ventricle of the brain near the head of the caudate nucleus, rather than in to the substantia nigra itself. This procedure ameliorated most signs of Parkinson's disease in two relatively young patients (35 and 39 years old).[135]

Such adrenal-to-brain grafts, while not commonplace as yet, are being done in at least five medical centers in the United States, as well as in other centers throughout the world. The procedure received a great deal of publicity in July 1987 when Muhammad Ali told reporters he was considering undergoing that procedure after conferring with a Mexican neurosurgeon who had already completed the procedure 18 times.

There is a very significant problem inherent in adrenal-to-brain grafts, however. The procedure requires two major simultaneous operations—abdominal surgery to obtain the adrenal gland tissue and brain surgery (craniotomy) to transplant the tissue. Since most patients with Parkinson's disease are elderly, these two operations performed simultaneously are associated with high mortality in this age group and have a relatively poor success rate. Therefore, in 1987 the Mexican neurosurgical team mentioned earlier implanted grafts of human fetal tissue, which involves only one operation (craniotomy), in two patients with Parkinson's disease.[150] One patient received fetal substantia nigra and the other received fetal adrenal medulla tissue, both from a fetus of a spontaneous abortion (miscarriage) in the thirteenth week of pregnancy. In both cases objective improvement in the symptoms of Parkinson's disease was evident. The surgeons conclude: "If long term follow-up of these patients demonstrates sustained medical improvement without complications, the use of fetal tissue as donor grafts may prove superior to autografting in Parkinson's disease."[150]

Experimental transplantation of fetal nerve tissue in rats reversed the equivalent of Huntington's Chorea, a disease seen in humans in which injury to a specific brain area results in severe and debilitating tremors.

Investigators looking at the promising results of brain implants, in both animals and humans, and their possible application in the treatment of several diseases already believe that the use of fetal tissue for brain grafting could open the door for treatment of other brain diseases, including Alzheimer's disease. There is hope that the fetal tissue needed for brain implants ultimately will be able to be grown by tissue culture techniques in the laboratory, thus bypassing some of the difficult ethical questions raised in using fetal cells from aborted fetuses.

As can be seen, there are very significant obstacles associated with transplant procedures—obstacles that must be overcome before any wide application can be envisioned. Rejection reactions and all the other problems inherent in tissue transplantation apply here, to say nothing of the sizable ethical issues, such as what the source of neuronal cells for transplantation will be. More significant than the tissue transplants themselves, then, at this point, are the discoveries and insights *behind* them that do offer a much wider application to brain injury, brain dysfunction and, perhaps even, someday, memory enhancement.

What are those discoveries? Until recently, it had been generally accepted that neuronal tissue did not regenerate—that once cell death had occurred there was no way to reverse or repair that damage. This brain transplantation work rests on significant and startling observations otherwise. In this work—which began with the implantation of small bits of brain tissue from rat fetuses into the irises of the eyes (outgrowths of actual brain tissue) of adult rats—brain tissue is grafted on brain tissue. In the transplanted tissue one can actually view, under an electron microscope, the neurons *growing new fibers*, spreading into adjacent areas and functioning as operating neuronal cells. Particularly if the tissue is implanted next to other neuronal tissue, growth is spurred on once the graft "takes" and rapid proliferation follows. The transplanted cells, and the new growth from them, function as effectively, in the new location, as original neurons.

An allied finding is equally significant. Retinal tissue implanted into sightless eyes of rats not only grew, but grew *in the proper direction*, seeking out the visual centers of the brain and bypassing other possible connections.[134] In still other experiments implanted fetal *cortical* tissue also sought out its correct neuronal targets.[134] Such targeted migration of neurons is exactly the process that apparently occurs in Savant Syndrome, as pointed out in Chapter 14, as right brain areas are recruited and the proper pathways established after left brain injury. This finding is important in neurologic rehabilitation also, as will be seen in the next section.

These two important findings—transplanted neuronal cell growth and growth that is targeted toward specific neuronal connections—have obvious implications for the future. The possibility of using transplanted neuronal tissue to restore normal function in damaged areas of the brain, where restoration was formerly thought to be impossible, holds hope for the treatment of a variety of conditions, not just memory defects. While it may be true that dead brain tissue does not regenerate, it can be effectively replaced through the use of these procedures, and certain functions can be restored. Beyond the possibility of treating defect and disease—in the even more distant future and subject to the same very sizable technological and ethical obstacles—lies the possibility that memory enhancement, rather than just memory replacement, might be attempted. Much remains to be seen. Yet, transplantation is promising, not just in relation to the possible direct effects of brain grafting, but also in relation to possible new discoveries or developments based on these exciting new findings about neuronal growth and regeneration.

REROUTING AND RECRUITMENT: REPAIR BY DETOUR

In some instances there is an alternative to tissue transplantation for correction of central nervous system damage and dysfunction. This alternative is based on the same important finding that all is not necessarily lost when damage or cell death occurs in some portions of the central nervous system. You will recall that retinal tissue implanted into sightless rats not only grows, but grows in the correct direction, seeking out the visual centers in the brain and bypassing other possible connections. The same is true of implanted fetal cortical tissue.

The ability of some central nervous system tissue to grow, and to do so in a targeted manner, is useful in some brain-injured persons where the brain, by this process, *reorganizes* itself to compensate for damage. This capacity, known as "brain plasticity," is the basis of an important new concept that replaces the older, more pessimistic concept that once neuronal tissue was damaged nothing could be done to replace it and that little ability existed in the central nervous system to functionally compensate for the loss.

Yet case reports, formerly quite rare but now more common, tell of instances where patients have made unexpected and remarkable recoveries after massive brain destruction from stroke or other injury or disease. In all such cases the patients accomplish this—just as savants develop their abilities—through consistent, tedious, persistent repetition of movement or processes, coupled with exceedingly intense motivation and perceptible, measurable feedback. Progress is extremely slow, but if the motivation and practice can be sustained, the improvement can, in some instances, be remarkable.

A case that came to my attention was that of a 52-year-old woman who had a left brain CVA (stroke) with the expected right-side paralysis and severe language deficits. Her family was told that she would probably be bedridden for the rest of her life. She had no speech and could communicate only by blinking her eyes. After a year in a nursing home with no progress, the family brought the patient home, paralyzed and unable to speak. A physiotherapist began to work with her and taught her family how to carry out motions and exercises on a daily basis. After twelve months the patient was able to crawl, but not able to stand or walk. Her family began to teach her the alphabet again, just as one would teach a child. She slowly learned to count again as well. After three years, she was able to walk, although with a decided limp. She lived for years after her stroke and died at age 75. In the interim she was able to live in her own home with her husband, cook and do household chores. She continued to show aphasia when using nouns, but otherwise her mental activity and language were intact and clear.

Instances of such compensatory brain repair, based on brain plasticity, are no longer considered medical rarities. Such repair occurs in certain patients equally disabled from central nervous system damage and insult. Because progress and movement are initially imperceptible, at first motivation depends on feedback that patients get from electrical measuring devices attached to nerve and muscle. Such neuromuscular retraining programs depend on the capacity of the brain to reorganize itself, to sprout new targeted growth from still undamaged neurons and to reroute that new growth around damaged areas in a compensatory manner. Constant repetition, resulting from intense motivation, feedback and reinforcement, can produce, in some instances but not all, the desired change—and this is due to central nervous system plasticity. The scenario sounds familiar after studying the savant, and it is, because the process, at least in the prodigious savant, is one and the same, although it results from a different cause and occurs at a different age.

The concept of brain plasticity is reshaping the field of neuro-rehabilitation, which is putting to work now, and will in the future, some of the advances we have already made in understanding central nervous system function and dysfunction. Insights from studying the savant will propel that knowledge and progress along even further and more quickly. While the brain may not be able to totally regenerate and repair itself, its ability to reorganize that which is still viable can result, in some instances, in achieving what otherwise would have been virtually unexpected. While the brain is highly specialized, it is not so fixed in that specialization that it cannot, in some ways, substitute and compensate.

That is a hopeful new view for many persons where hope otherwise seemed dim.

MIND CONTROL—A GIANT CAVEAT

A colleague of mine, as part of his Psychiatry Board Certification examination some years ago, interviewed a patient, about whom he would be questioned by the examiners. When my colleague asked the patient why he was in the hospital, the patient replied that it was because someone had implanted wires in his head and was controlling his mind. Hearing that account, my colleague made a diagnosis of schizophrenia, based on what sounded like a well-defined delusional system. He was wrong. Unfortunately he had failed to ask the patient to *show* him the wires, which were covered by a baseball cap and thus inconspicuous. It was no delusion. The patient did have wires in his head. He was involved in a project being carried out at the clinic in which the staff was controlling his mind, or at least a part of it, with a tiny electrical current, applied through an implanted electrode, that aborted otherwise severe rage episodes.

Mind control! It is the prospect of that which raises so many serious and searching ethical questions when it comes to research on the brain. I remember reading somewhere about an experiment in which a donkey had a solar cell strapped to its forehead and an electrode implanted in the pleasure center of its brain, connected by a wire to the solar cell. The donkey would walk toward the sun and would thus be rewarded by the activation of its pleasure center. At worst this experiment has all sorts of ominous extrapolations. Suppose such a center is located in man—and such pleasure receptors do exist, as has been shown in research work with drugs such as cocaine. Perhaps, then, we could all literally be "plugged in" someday and, like the donkey, carry out tasks, requiring only activation of our pleasure centers, instead of a paycheck, to spur us on. Or, even more portentous, suppose some higher authority, like the government, wanted us all to think in some particular, uniform way and had electrical access to our brains through which it could exert thought control.

That is the ominous side of the coin. But suppose the opposite were to occur. Suppose that electrodes placed in some brain centers—like the brain pacemakers I proposed earlier—could control the tremor of Parkinson's disease, could abort an epileptic seizure or could short-circuit a devastating rage attack. The question then is, as with nuclear energy, can we be sure technology and such power will only be put to "good" use? And who defines "good"? Watching what cocaine can do in activating the pleasure centers in man and in animals gives one pause. Yet a direct electrical approach may be the most rational and hopeful one in the treatment of a number of diseases and dysfunctions of the brain. Can such technology be channeled in only appropriate ways? Can we have the good without the bad?

Work with animals has shown the precision with which electrode placement can be carried out in the brain. There are presently in use techniques for implanting a tiny, tiny probe into *single* neurons of some species to discover how those neurons function. If we discover how they function, we can probably also learn how they can be influenced. By ablating certain small centers in the brain of some animals we have learned a great deal of what those centers do, and extrapolations of that knowledge have been useful in designing treatments for some human disorders. Stimulation of those centers in animals has produced some revealing insights as well, particularly as work has proceeded on the pleasure centers of the animals. Applying that work to humans involves ethical issues that do not seem to be as crucial with the kidney, the pancreas or the heart.

Heart transplants do raise some ethics questions. For instance, who gets one if donated organs are in limited supply? But issues such as that would pale in relation to the searing questions that would be raised if ever there was such a thing as a complete brain transplant. That day seems far, far away, yet already we are "transplanting" certain types of cells experimentally in the treatment of Parkinson's disease and some postulate that such a technique might be useful in Alzheimer's disease as well. Suppose there were such a thing as a brain transplant. One of the most fundamental of the serious questions that would then pour forth would be the one raised by Dr. Richard Restak, in his book *The Brain*, and by others: When a brain transplant is performed, does the body receive a new brain or does the brain receive a new body?[87] In other words, who are we really? Is there more to the mind than the brain? Is there more to an individual than a collection of ten billion neurons and a trillion connections among them?

Penfield devoted 40 years of his life to studying the brain. He began his career with the assumption that the brain and the mind were the same unitary entity. He concluded his career with these words:

> There is no good evidence, in spite of new methods, such as the employment of stimulating electrodes, the study of conscious patients and the analysis of epileptic attacks, that the brain alone can carry out the work the mind does. I conclude that it is easier to rationalize man's being on the basis of two elements than on the basis of one. . . . no scientist should begin thus, nor carry on his work with fixed preconceptions. And yet, since a final conclusion in the field of our discussion is not likely to come before the youngest reader of this book dies, it behooves each one of us to adopt for himself a personal assumption (belief, religion), and way of life without waiting for a final word from science on the nature of man's mind. . . . science has no such answers.[120]

I agree that science does not have that final answer. It is for that reason that the kinds of findings I envision resulting from study of the savant and the ultimate application of those findings will need to be debated in an arena larger than the laboratory or the examination room. As we move toward brain pacemakers, as we inevitably will—and must if we are to rationally and effectively intervene in some disorders—the ethical issues will need to be examined with the same vigor and precision that will be required in the examination of the brain itself. I raise those issues here, not to try to solve them, certainly, but to point out that some of the necessary research is on hold right now because of procedural impediments and limitations—obstacles that are about to be dissipated by new leaps ahead in techniques and knowledge. Study of the savant will add to those steps forward. The pace of progress will quicken technologically and we will need to keep pace with that progress in our ethical debates and resolutions.

There is one final caveat, perhaps the ultimate protection from ourselves in this treacherous, but promising area of brain research: Can the brain entirely analyze itself? Our brain can, no doubt, ultimately understand how the liver, the heart and the spleen work, but is there some intrinsic, inherent *in*ability of the brain to transcend itself sufficiently to understand itself? While there is much we can unravel, and have already, about the complexity of the wondrous organ we call the brain, there seems, inevitably, a point at which the brain cannot go enough outside itself and above itself to provide all the final answers.

Perhaps that is not an obstacle but rather a safeguard that protects us from ourselves. I'm not sure. But, nevertheless, none of that should prevent us from moving ahead in trying to understand what we can about brain function, and I think study of the savant can contribute to that understanding. We do need to move carefully and cautiously, however, into some uncharted areas that border on mind and thought control. I hope that the ethics and safeguards applicable here will be explored with the same vigor and careful scrutiny we give the brain itself so that they can be safely in place not after but simultaneously with the explosion in technology and application that is upon us.

The question of mind control is a crucial one. It is an area in which the mind and the brain (if they are not indeed one and the same as some believe and as Dr. Penfield concluded at the end of his career) need to come together on a common ground as if they were.

16

A Smoother Pebble

> I do not know what I may appear to the world; but to myself I seem to have been only like a boy on the seashore, and diverting myself in now and then finding a smoother pebble or a prettier shell than ordinary, whilst the great ocean of truth lay all undiscovered before me.
>
> —Sir Isaac Newton

After 25 years of observing savants, and after studying virtually all that has been written about them this past 100 years, I too feel like the boy on the beach fascinated with the smoother pebble, the one that is different enough from all the other pebbles to stand out, to be noticed and admired. The savant is a smoother pebble on a beach where all the other pebbles look much more alike. Meanwhile, an entire ocean of truth, waiting to be discovered, lies in the background. I have suggested some of the things that might be in that ocean, and how we might discover them. Let us, in this final chapter, take a closer look at the pebble itself—its specialness; some of the forces that have helped give it its unique shape; how we can study and admire it without forfeiting its individuality; and how we can be sure that, in a world that seeks so intensely to have all the shapes the same, we not only appreciate this different shape just as it is, but do so without requiring it to change so it is exactly like all the others.

A patient of mine described the pressure to conform, the parental and societal expectation to be just like everyone else, somewhat differently. She characterized herself as being "an oval soul on a round planet." She described that predicament this way:

We live on a round planet, so we assume that all the planets are round like the one that we live on. But God looks out over the universe and sees all kinds of planets—round one, square ones, oblong ones, oval ones and a whole variety of shapes. They are not all round like I learned in science class. What happens before you are born is that God then sorts your soul out. If you have a round soul, He puts you on a round planet; if you have a square soul He puts you on a square planet; and if you have an oval soul He is supposed to put you on an oval planet. In my case He made a mistake. I've got an oval soul and He put me on a round planet. The school, my parents and even you, Dr. Treffert, keep trying to file my soul round like everyone else's. I'm decomposing in school and when I graduate I'll simply give up my seat to some new starry-eyed cadaver-to-be.

Ultimately, I am glad to say, this patient was able to keep the shape of her soul and still become the productive, contributing, comfortable person she has turned out to be. The filing, scraping, sanding and stomping on her soul stopped and she turned out quite all right. She took a bit of a different direction than her parents had wanted, but now they too are satisfied with the outcome. It was not always that easy, but my patient persisted confidently and ended up with a shape that was her very own, a shape a bit different than those around her, a smoother pebble also. But it was her own.

The temptation with the savant is to file or scrape a bit—benevolently surely—to shape the soul, or the pebble, to make it more like all the others. With Nadia, this resulted in a "curious cure," as Nigel Dennis points out—"a genius with her genius removed."[59] Similarly, Oliver Sacks appropriately questions the price paid by George and Charles, the calendar calculating twins, for whom quasi-independence and "socially acceptable" daily living skills seemed the dubious trade-off for what had been "the chief joy and sense of their lives."[29]

Having witnessed the families of Leslie, Alonzo, Ellen and some others interacting with the specialness of their savants, I see that, fortunately, the picture of a trade-off need not be painted so definitely, so harshly or so inevitably. Like an adult delicately teaching a child to ride a bicycle, their families have known when to hang on and when to let go. They have been able to provide for their loved ones both roots *and* wings, just as we try to do for ours. Those families have been, for me, a study in what unconditional positive regard—and that is what love is—really means.

To see May Lemke's intense pride in a child who was imperfect and impaired; to see Ory and Barbara Boudreaux's quiet contentment when Ellen sings; to see the "that's my boy" gleam in his Mom's eye when

Alonzo sculpts; and to hear Mary Larsen's gentle "I told you he would" boast when Leslie began to improvise—to see all of that is to see love in action and to see what love can do.

So much of our love is conditional, predicated on what those close to us *do* rather than on what they *are*. A patient put it this way: "If I fail in what I do I fail in what I am." There might be a special temptation with the savant to zero in on only what they do and to overlook their overall specialness and uniqueness. Watching the families in action, as I have had opportunity to do, has shown an overall acceptance that is not limited to the special ability or talent. When Richard Wawro and his father celebrate the completion of another painting, they display the same pride and fervor that they did in the first such celebratory ritual hundreds of paintings ago. The embrace and the gestures are more than a commemoration of another painting—they are a poignant and persuasive outpouring of joy, belief and unconditional acceptance of what Richard is, not just of what he produces. May and Mary look beyond and over Leslie's handicaps and see his strengths and wholeness, not his disabilities and gaps. With the Boudreaux family and Ellen, and the Clemons family and Alonzo, it is the same. They focus not just on what Ellen or Alonzo *do*, but also on what they *are*—special, unique, extraordinary people with souls shaped a bit differently than the souls of others. But in those special shapes lies particular beauty, like the beauty of a smoother pebble one might find on a beach.

Whatever questions of a scientific nature might be answered by looking at the savant, they are equaled or excelled by lessons in caring, belief, determination, appreciation and acceptance that the savant and their families can teach us.

THE QUESTION OF EXPLOITATION

Sometimes I am asked whether having the savant give a concert, or host an exhibition, or even just demonstrate some special talent to visitors on the unit at the hospital, might be some sort of exploitation.

I don't think so. There have been, in the past, accounts of such exploitation or at least of someone's conclusions regarding those accounts. The most often quoted instance is that of Blind Tom, the slave's son described in Chapter 2. His "master," Colonel Bethune, took Tom on concerts throughout the world, promoting him as the Blind Genius and "everywhere he went, his concerts were hailed as artistic triumphs, and in London alone a series of performances netted his mentor an estimated $100,000."[15] Bear in mind that that was in the *first* year alone and was in the 1850s, when such a sum of money had significantly more value than it does even today. After the death of his mentor, Tom stopped playing; he died in 1908, lonely and alone. On the face of it the scenario suggests exploitation. Yet, as one reads the accounts of Blind Tom's concerts, the enthusiastic vigor, fervor and mission-like zeal with which he carried out his "project" comes through, just as it has with many, many performers of the past, impaired or not, and just as it does with many modern-day savants.

It is clear that Blind Tom loved to play. Having him do so, in and of itself, is not exploitation any more than having an athlete who loves to play the game, play. What Colonel Bethune did with the money, and what portion of it went for the ongoing or future care of Blind Tom, are questions of propriety, I suppose, but there is no way available to settle these questions beyond the versions of that remarkable story available to us, and they give no definitive information in that regard. The fact that Blind Tom died lonely and alone, and that he stopped playing after the death of Colonel Bethune, speaks not of exploitation in this regard, or even dependency; in my opinion, it speaks only of attachment, affection and loss.

Leslie Lemke loves to perform, whether to an audience of two or two thousand—or just for himself. Alonzo loves to sculpt and cannot be kept from it. Ellen loves to sing. It does bring her praise, to be sure, but she does it principally because it is her project. While an appreciative audience helps, she does not depend on it. So the performing, whether private or with wide visibility, cannot be, by itself, exploitation.

But what about other effects from that visibility? Might that be the form that the exploitation takes? There was an interesting large-scale study done on the effects of prominence and performance on a group similar to the savant in that the decision about their performing was made initially by others, usually their parents. This group is the so-called Quiz Kids, who in the 1940s became a household word through their then high visibility. Here a group of precocious children, most of whom relied on memory, interestingly, as their mainstay skill, were put by their families before an entire nation on the radio each week. In the book *Whatever Happened to the Quiz Kids?* Ruth Duskin Feldman, herself one of those performers, looked at the perils and profits of growing up gifted under that circumstance.[136] Feldman wanted to write her book about "the Quiz Kids who came out all right," to contrast with the portrait painted, in a book entitled *Working,*[137] of a Quiz Kid who had been one of the first and foremost at age 7 but who was a refugee at age 39. Feldman concludes: "Reporters and photographers poking you and knocking you around and asking ridiculous questions. As a child you can't cope with these things. I was exploited. I can't forgive those who exploited me." The reassuring fact is that most of the

Quiz Kids did turn out all right, and in fact, many continued to excel.

The theme that runs through the stories of these gifted performers, particularly those unaffected by this public visibility and adulation in their vulnerable growing years, is the same theme that has been evident in the savants I have been privileged to work with, and in their families and caretakers—a bedrock appreciation of the person, not just the special endowment, and an acceptance of what that person is, not just what he or she can do. In one portion of her book Feldman asks 16 ex-Quiz Kids to give advice to parents of gifted children on how to handle the special potential in such children, as well as the special problems that occur. The advice given is the antithesis of exploitation: spend time with them—money and presents do not make up for company and companionship; use praise, avoid criticism and do not typecast them; give opportunity but do not push; accept them joyfully as they are; realize that the gifts are the child's, not the parents'; don't become ego-involved in how the youngster uses the gifts; offer opportunities for independence; leave time for loafing; let them do what they choose to do; keep them challenged for *their* satisfaction; be sensitive.

That is sound advice for any child rearing, but it is particularly applicable when dealing with the potential hazards of raising a specially gifted child at either end of the intelligence spectrum, for whom a talent or endowment can bring public attention, notice and visibility. From what I have seen and read, the families and caretakers of savants are, in general, doing the right things and doing them for the right reasons. Some families choose to remain more private and less visible chiefly because that is their style. Others want to share the talent more widely—sometimes to inspire other handicapped persons, sometimes as a mission to share a "miracle" and sometimes to simply share the marvel and appreciation of artwork or music that is beautiful in its own right, not just because the artist is handicapped.

That there is money or remuneration, in some instances, attached to those efforts is not in and of itself exploitive or even necessarily a circumstance prone to exploitation. Some of the families I have seen, and many who have written to me, see such opportunity simply and only as one mechanism to insure funding of some sort for adequate, comfortable and personal care after the principal caretakers, usually the family, are no longer there. Others see an opportunity for the handicapped person to support himself or herself, something that builds self-esteem in *each* of us, handicapped or not. In other instances it helps offset costs of care in families of limited financial circumstances where institutionalization or placement of some other sort might otherwise be necessary.

So as far as exploitation by the family is concerned, I have not seen it. That is not to say it could never occur, or has never occurred. Leslie Lemke has had offers to perform in Las Vegas like one might perform in a sideshow at a county fair—offers that his family regards as entirely the wrong thing for entirely the wrong reason. His, and all the other caring families like his, see to it that such offers are refused.

Most of what Leslie Lemke does is for modest or little remuneration. Numerous appearances through the years—at schools, prisons, nursing homes and the like—have been for free. Appearances at churches will sometimes, and not always even then, have a freewill (pass-the-plate) offering. Those appearances that do generate funds usually barely offset the expenses of travel, food and lodging, if they do even that. Occasionally a group will donate another piano (he does wear them out) or some other item like a chair or an exercise bike for Leslie's use. Some appearances may have ticket sales with proceeds going to an association for retarded persons or some such group. In those few instances when there is some money left over, it goes to the Miracle of Love Ministries to help offset the cost of handouts, book markers or other materials used for that ministry.

If there has been any exploitation of Leslie, it has not been by the family, but *of* the family in having May Lemke agree to certain movie, video and other arrangements before she was knowledgeable about such arrangements or properly advised. Some of the fairly sizable proceeds from those endeavors should have gone to the trust fund for Leslie's future care.

Alonzo Clemons has also been able to generate some income from his sculptures, which are handled by the Driscol Galleries in Denver, Colorado. Some of his pieces, such as the *Three Frolicking Foals,* have been sold for as much as $45,000. That particular work was purchased not because the sculptor was handicapped, but because it was a "beautiful piece of sculpture," according to the buyer. There is no reason, then, that he, like any other skilled artist, should not be compensated for his work. Sales of pieces such as that, along with sales of 500 or so other works of his, have produced enough revenue so that a place could be purchased next to his parents' home to serve as his personal studio. Alonzo is very pleased about that. To those who support "normalizing" the handicapped to bring them into the social mainstream, Alonzo is a gleaming example of how, in some instances, life can be "normalized" for the mentally handicapped. That hardly qualifies as exploitation.

Alonzo's world premier exhibition was sponsored by First Interstate Bank of Denver, Colorado, on May 19, 1986. A portion of the proceeds of that event were used for yet another purpose—to set up the Fund for the Study of Savant Syndrome through the Charitable, Educational and Scientific Foundation of the State Medical Society of Wisconsin.

Projects will include establishment of a clearinghouse for information about Savant Syndrome, assembly of the most complete collection of written and audio-visual materials on this topic and, eventually, a symposium of those clinicians, academicians and researchers from throughout the country, and perhaps the world, who share knowledge, interest and insight with respect to Savant Syndrome.

In summary, having a savant use his or her special skills and abilities, whether in the living room, on the hospital unit, on stage or before a camera, if he or she wishes and is willing to do so, is not exploitation.

"Accept them joyfully as they are" suggests one of the ex-Quiz Kids as her antidote to exploitation. From what I have seen and studied, the families, caretakers and professionals who surround the savant do seem to appreciate the special skills as but one part of the specialness of the savant. Indeed, savant skills are built, and flourish, on repetition and positive reinforcement. The savants I have seen love to use their skills, just as the rest of us do, to gain a sense of achievement, pride and satisfaction. If they can please, surprise or even astound others while enjoying themselves, so much the better. Why should we, or would we, deprive them of that?

CREATIVITY AND EMOTIONS—SOME ADDITIONAL TRADE-OFFS

Savant skills, while spectacular in some isolated areas of functioning, do have a price—considerable impairment in other areas. Sometimes those impairments are global. Caring persons around the savant, however, manage to overlook those areas, or at least manage not to focus totally on them, and are able to appreciate that which is present rather than regret that which is absent.

As with most trade-offs, those in Savant Syndrome have their pluses and minuses. Startling recall skill—habit memory—in the memorizing savant is substituted for the broader, cognitive memory skills available to the rest of us. In the musical savant an enormous musical repertoire of an echolalic type exists without the ability to carry out more varied types of playing. Some of those types of trade-offs have already been described. Two other areas of trade-off should be mentioned. The first is creativity.

Is the savant creative?

In my experience, not very. In almost every instance the savant echoes, rather than creates. That has generally been the experience of others who have worked with the savant as well, beginning with Dr. Alfred F. Tredgold, who observed that "the talents of these persons lie chiefly in the direction of imitation, and they have no capacity for originating."[12] I suppose that really doesn't matter very much, however, when one sees or hears what savants *can* do—the fact that their wondrous performances are echoes or copies, rather than original creations, seems a minuscule consideration. But it does raise some interesting questions about the relationship of creativity to intelligence and the interface between creativity and memory.

There is no uniformly agreed-upon definition of creativity. Philosophers, psychologists, neurophysiologists and others argue about what it is and where it resides. But while not yet precisely defined, it can be fairly easily described, since most would agree that creativity as a process, or creativeness as a personality characteristic, consists of these types of components: originality; inventiveness; flexibility; fluency; openness to change and new ways of doing things; ability to visualize, conceptualize and abstract; sensitivity; self-awareness and self-disclosure; and impatience with the status quo, the ordinary and the routine. These are traits in short supply in most savants, who show, rather, considerable inflexibility, lack of ability to abstract and conceptualize, constricted emotion and, usually, a very strong tendency toward routine and sameness. While the repetitive abilities seem limitless, originality and inventiveness are usually quite limited.

At its simplest, creativity is the ability to produce something new. How does the savant do at that?

There are only two studies that have formally investigated creativity in the savant. One tested for that element in savants, as compared to nonsavant retarded subjects, and the other tested for that same variable in savants, as compared with a matched control group of persons with normal intelligence.

Using the Torrance Thinking Creative with Pictures Test, Dr. Jane Duckett compared 25 savants to a matched control group of retarded subjects.[73] Savants did not differ significantly on this measure of creativity from the nonsavant retarded sample. The scores for *both* groups, savant and nonsavant, were very low, although those scores did indicate "that retardates have some measure of creativity." Those findings are consistent with the widely held consensus that creativity is generally related to, an indicator of, and correlated with overall intelligence. It is not surprising then to find low creativity scores in persons with low I.Q. levels overall, including the savant.

The second study is that of Hermelin, O'Connor and Lee. The compositional and improvisational skills of five musical savants were compared to those same skills in a matched control group of six normal children who had musical training over a period of two years but had not been exposed in any formal sense to compositional or improvisational instruction.[152] All five savants were male; three were blind; the mean age was 34; and I.Q.s ranged from 50 to 69 with the mean I.Q. 59. Six children, with an average chronological age of 13, were used as a control group, rather than adults, because the only comparable adult group in terms of talent would have been professional musicians who would have had some exposure to formal training in composition and improvisation. Such adults would have been inappropriate controls since none of the savants had received any such education.

Five tasks were used to test for what was called "musical inventiveness," graded on a scale of 1 to 5 for each task. The tasks were as follows: 1) continuation of a hitherto unknown tune after a portion of the tune was played; 2) invention of a new tune; 3) invention and production of an accompaniment to a new tune played to the subject; 4) invention simultaneously of a new melody and accompaniment; 5) improvisation over a twelve-bar blues sequence played for the subject. Three other measures were used to rate "musical competence": (1) general sense of timing and rhythm, (2) degree of complexity of musical inventiveness and (3) ability to produce a well-balanced musical sequence in terms of modulation and production of regular phrase length.

On the tests of musical inventiveness the savant group was superior to the control group. Similarly, on the tests of musical competence the savants were superior to the control subjects, showing a better sense of timing, better balance and more complexity. The researchers attribute some of this difference simply to the fact that music was the savants' only endeavor and preoccupation, to which they devoted seemingly endless hours and energy, while for the control group music was but one of many activities in their lives. Hence, motivation and sheer familiarity with music accounted for some of the heightened abilities of the savants. But even allowing for that factor, savants, according to these investigators, showed a capacity to improvise *and* create music—activities that are consistent with a fairly high level of cognitive sophistication with regard to music. This ability extended beyond mere reproduction or mimicry of music played to them.

Dr. Hermelin and her co-workers conclude that this study confirms the findings of their earlier studies: that there exists in each person a series of separate intelligences, of which music is but one, rather than a single, consistent intelligence level that permeates all the skills and abilities of the individual. With respect to music, that intelligence can encompass *some* creativity and improvisation in addition to mimicry. They go on to point out, however, that studies by others have found that such creativity *does* operate within some finite boundaries fixed by intelligence level overall. Those studies have demonstrated that, while a separate and spared musical intelligence can exist side by side with some severely impaired other areas of intelligence in the same person, creativity is one attribute that is limited in scope by overall level of intellectual ability. Hermelin and her colleagues state: "Thus an interaction between general intelligence and intelligence-independent abilities must be assumed, and the idiot savant not only demonstrates the existence of such intelligence-independent abilities, but he likewise suggests that the degree to which these abilities are realizable is probably constrained by the general level of his cognitive processing capacity."[151]

My experience with the savant parallels the findings of these two studies—improvisation within fairly repetitive and restrictive constraints is much more common than creating something entirely new; and the ability to create something entirely new, when it is present, is really very restricted and suffers from a more global limitation that seems to be present whenever there is an impairment of overall general intelligence. While there are some savants—such as Dr. David Viscott's patient, Harriet—who have shown a high level of creativity, most savants show either little or no creativity.[18]

Hermelin makes the distinction between composing and improvising quite clearly:

> A clear distinction exists between the act of reproducing existing music and the production of new musical ideas. But a further distinction can also be made between composing entirely new music and the addition of improvisations to existing composition. As distinct from composition, where the ideas themselves have to be produced, improvisations are subject to definite constraints which arise from the initial musical theme and from the structure and style of the piece on which the improvisations are to be based. The improviser thus provides an embellished harmonic or melodic section without essentially changing the characteristic framework of the given piece of music. One type of music in which improvisation plays a central part is jazz. The question asked here is whether persons of below average intellectual status can invent music within the constraints which are inherent in improvisation, and whether they can also compose new music.[151]

A detailed analysis of savant improvisational ability was carried out by Hermelin and her co-workers, who did a note-by-note musical comparison of the improvisations done by Leslie Lemke and those done by a professional musician of normal intelligence after both had heard the same two compositions.[151] The two pieces of music used were the same ones described in a study in Chapter 2—Grieg's lyric piece (Opus 47, No. 3—"Melodie") and Bartok's atonal composition ("Whole-Tone Scale," Book V, *Mikrokosmos*). The comparative analysis looked at variables such as the number of times the theme was repeated, the frequency with which the tonal center of the piece was preserved, how often transitions from one key to another were inserted and how frequently elaborations and cadenzas were inserted. In response to 46 bars of the Grieg piece Leslie produced 215 bars of improvisation and the musician produced 95 bars; in response to 27 bars of the Bartok piece Leslie produced 100 bars of improvisation, as compared to 87 bars of improvisation by the musician.

On the Grieg piece both subjects adhered to and repeated the theme frequently and closely. Leslie differed in his improvisations by using remote keys more frequently, by inserting transitions from one key to another more often and by using musical flourish and embellishment to a much greater extent. Leslie's improvisations were described as "virtuoso embellishments" that did, however, show "a considerable degree of musical inventiveness and pianistic virtuosity." His style of improvisation was "extravagant, flamboyant and expansive" while the professional musician retained much more of, "Grieg's rather sparse texture and melodic shape." The musician's improvisation was "simple, reflective, contained and restrained." The researchers conclude that "both subjects' attempts at improvisation show a high degree of generative musical ability, and what distinguishes them from each other is not so much a differential degree of musicianship but rather their own, different musical preferences as well as their respective personality characteristics."

In contrast to this considerable difference in improvisational style on the Grieg piece, the improvisations on the Bartok piece by Leslie and the professional musician resembled each other closely. Leslie and the musician both remained in whole tone scale most of the time and both retained the general sense of timing that the piece contains overall. Both pianists used few transitions from one key to another, and there was a virtual absence of cadenzas or embellishments in both improvisations. Hermelin and her co-workers attribute this similarity in improvisation to the musical constraints of the particular piece, which both subjects respected and found themselves bound by and adherent to.

Leslie's improvisations, while they were longer, richer and more elaborate, still reflected the basic structure and tonal characteristics of the original pieces, and as had his improvisations in earlier studies, they demonstrated remarkable access to the "rules of music." This rich store of musical knowledge is clearly independent of I.Q. since, while the professional musician and Leslie shared those same musical "rules," as was reflected in their improvisations, they showed marked differences in general intelligence. Both Leslie and the professional musician showed musical generative ability, to the extent that improvisation allows, and both, in their improvisations, reflected the structural characteristics *and* constraints of the two pieces of music.

This study points out that not only do savants access specific cognitive stores of information (as opposed to having simple eidetic recall) in their remarkable memory operations, but they also call on that same store of information for generative or creative processes, at least in their improvisation. But improvisation operates within clear constraints and does not represent free-form creative genius. In the final portion of their report on this study, the researchers in fact conclude that the talents of savants, while remarkable, "fall short of those which underlie the achievements of true creative genius." They speculate, based on general findings about the relationship between intelligence and creativity, that a certain complexity of "multi-stage mental architecture" is a prerequisite for the emergence of a "profoundly original idea" and that the savant probably lacks all of that architecture, as well as what the researchers term "cognitive efficiency" in accessing that architecture. Speaking of creating "truly novel ideas," the study concludes: "If idiot savants are barred from this process, it may be because, if not intelligence, then intact and fully intergrated cortical and subcortical systems, which are lacking in those with profound mental handicaps, may be a necessary though not a sufficient requirement for the manifestation of generative, expressive and executive abilities at their highest levels."[151]

In general, savants echo rather than create, and mimic rather than invent. This in no way detracts from the enormity of their skills; it is a qualitative difference. While Leslie Lemke has more than a tape-recorder memory in that he can improvise extensively, his improvisations—which he generates from the vast lexicon of music that he is somehow, marvelously, able to tap—are still variations on a theme. He is still not creating something entirely new, using the ordinary definition of creativity. Alonzo does not do free-form sculpture, and Richard Wawro does not do impressionistic art. Alonzo's sculptures are *exact*, to the fiber, reproductions based on his remarkable recall. Richard's paintings incorporate some interpretation, but they too are quite literal, astoundingly so in terms of the time elapsed from when scenes get imprinted and when they are remembered.

Nothing is absolute, and one can sometimes see some low levels of creativity in the savant. But in general, the trade-off is less inventiveness and creativity for remarkable literal recall, storage and retrieval, sometimes linked with a vast musical or mathematical lexicon, based on a unique kind of nonsymbolic, high-fidelity memory function. This is important because it may provide a fortuitous opportunity to further study, in a circumscribed manner, the fascinating and important interfaces of creativity, intelligence and memory. In the face of such a trade-off, we must be content with the way the savant is, and not require him or her to change, or hope for more. It is enough that savants have such remarkable skills; we should not require them to be more creative as well. The savant is one of those cases in which we need not file, scrape or sand the soul to give it a different shape than it naturally and necessarily has.

EMOTIONS IN THE SAVANT

There is another major area of trade-off in the savant, also with its pluses and minuses—the area of emotions. Savants are typically rather constricted emotionally. What they do and say seems to have little excitement, passion, sentiment or feeling attached to it. As I just pointed out, the concept of creativity extends beyond creating new *things* and embodies, as well, certain personality *traits,* such as flexibility, openness to change and new ways of doing things, self-awareness, self-disclosure and impatience with the status quo. Since the savant has limited creativity in terms of acts or productions, it is not surprising that the same limitation applies to personality traits, including emotion. Dr. Richard Restak points out that such emotional constriction may be due to lack of creativity in the savant, since at least certain kinds of creativity are dependent on "heightened ability to 'get in touch' with the emotions, not just the images of the past."[87] Savants may, thus, miss some of the nuances of life that the rest of us experience with our wider range of feelings.

Being able to feel deeply and experience the nuances of life is a double-edged gift. One cannot feel the pain of loss without having first felt the warmth of love. The same heightened sensitivity that makes some persons cry at the hurt of being criticized allows them to cry as well at the exhilaration of an especially beautiful sunset. Those steeled to criticism are probably equally steeled to the beauty of sunsets. To feel ostracized one must experience what it feels like to belong. To feel boredom one must have had a sense of involvement. To feel distant requires having been close.

The emotional flatness one sees in the savant likewise exists in both directions. They are denied access to (or protection from, depending on which feeling it is) the peaks and valleys so characteristic of human emotion. Leslie has cried, but has done so infrequently. Alonzo is quietly proud but never intensely exhilarated. In the descriptions of almost all the savants by so many observers, certain words keep recurring: flatness, lack of spontaneity, obsession with sameness, compulsivity, shallowness, distance, uncommunicativeness and passivity. There have been some exceptions. The Genius of Earlswood Asylum is described as having had some angry outbursts in a "fit of passion" and even as having had some "amorous feelings" that alternated with sullenness when his overtures were rebuffed.[12] But even Harriet, who did experience some depression and some glee, according to Viscott's detailed description of her emotional landscape, was characterized by him overall as "constricted, impassive and defensive." Of her music, where she seemed able to express some feelings, Viscott says: "Her performance lacks some of the luster and responsiveness that could be expected from one who has spent so much of her life involved with music. While many of the works she plays evoke emotions which coincide with her own the level of feeling she expresses seems somewhat shallow and childlike; but that is not to say that it is not genuinely felt by her. It is as if her musical expression, while real, is superficial and imitative."[18]

Range of emotion, like range of creativity, is severely limited in the savant. This may be partly due to intellectual defect overall, rather than being some trait intrinsic to the savant, for it takes a certain cognitive awareness (for better or worse) to feel envy, guilt, suspiciousness, self-sufficiency, conceit, fulfillment, exaltation, despair and most of the rest of the emotions—good and bad—in the broad range of human emotion. But the uniform constriction of emotion seen in the savant seems to be somewhat heightened and special, beyond that which would be attributable to overall intellectual impairment. In my view, it results from certain limitations imposed on the savant by the unique neural pathways and particular type of memory function the savant has, all of which has been discussed in earlier chapters. In short, the same biologic, central nervous system factors that impair creativity excursions in the savant impede emotional excursions as well.

Such a trade-off of emotion has its advantages and disadvantages. I have never seen a savant experience performance anxiety before giving a concert or an exhibit; I certainly have seen it in others. Critics don't count in the minds of savants, who frankly don't care what anyone else thinks of their work—they love it the way it is. I haven't seen despair in this group, or pessimism, or cynicism, or feelings of inadequacy, all attitudes we can heap on ourselves because we are able to feel a bit more keenly. It is a trade-off. Many savants seem almost boastful of their talents, as well they should be; they are not embarrassed to express pride in their achievements because they have none of the false modesty that our polite society imposes upon us.

The contentment, the simple satisfaction and the unabashed childlike pride of the savant, and the gentleness with which the savant views us, are refreshing, and at times enviable. To Leslie, visiting the White House and playing for the President is no more or less important than playing at the local nursing home. Intimidated by and in awe of no one, the savant is just as pleased to see a child admiring his sculpture as the television commentator for the evening national news. No nervousness, no second guessing, no feelings of inadequacy. There may be a paucity of emotion, but there is a purity of emotion as well. No games are being played; there is no jockeying for position, no manipulation.

Alonzo is one of the most mellow people I have ever met. His gentleness, his quiet contentment and his smile are infectious. He seems so unspoiled. What he lacks in vocabulary he makes up for with spirit and the sparkle in his eyes. A walk with him through one of his exhibits is likely to be mostly silent, punctuated perhaps with a few simple words. But there is a communication nonetheless, one can feel it. It is the kind of silence that speaks.

Leslie also is largely silent, except when he plays. He too is gentle and unspoiled. He can be a bit more temperamental at times, as Mary can confirm, particularly when he is tired or when his routine is hurried or different. His joy, energy and enthusiasm, however, are unmistakably evident when he is playing and singing.

Ellen is busier and more hyperactive still. Like a kitten, she does show some affection, but usually on her terms and on her schedule. There is a purity in her spirit and her energy as well. Like Leslie, she never "practices." Each song is a new event, a performance, in and of itself. Why practice? For whom? The rest of us practice to first perfect so that we can please. But if the pleasure is in performing for oneself rather than necessarily pleasing others, and if one can get satisfaction just from doing, without feeling a tiring compulsion to do it exactly right, then every tune can be a new, vital happening. Nothing is wasted or worthless, imperfect or not.

A trade-off? Yes, there is an emotional flatness to savants. They lack the peaks and intensity of feeling that the rest of us have. They are unlikely to cry at a sunset or shout at a championship game. In that sense they miss a lot. But they are content, as a group, with themselves and with what they do. They don't seem to envy someone who does it better, or has it better. They like "their song." While they don't feel the peak of ecstasy, they don't feel subjective despondency either. While they don't recognize or relish fame like we do, they don't experience the self-doubt or self-effacement that a considerable many of us do. As with all trade-offs, this is not altogether bad. While none of us would prefer, I am sure, to substitute our full range of feelings, the good and the bad, for the type of emotional flatness and constancy the savant displays, there is still much they can teach us about simplicity and about contentment, two items in short supply in many of us.

ELIMINATE THE DEFECT OR TRAIN THE TALENT?

Just as there are many theories on the cause of Savant Syndrome, there are a number of viewpoints as to the best approach to the education, training and treatment of savants to allow them to have lives as productive, as independent and as fulfilling as possible given their severe handicaps. At the core of the controversy is a basic question framed succinctly a half-century ago by Arthur Phillips, a special education teacher, when he wrote about his "talented imbeciles": "The problem of treatment comes next. The question that arises is one of method, whether it is better to try to eliminate the defects or train the talents. Theoretically, this question is unsettled. Some educators incline to the view that a child should be given what he does not like and be kept from doing what he does like. If he has artistic ability and does not like arithmetic, give him arithmetic."[45]

Phillips answered his own question regarding his pupil, Earl, who had shown mechanical ability as his "excess of one ability over other abilities": "This method will not succeed here. Earl does not like reading and arithmetic and he has no ability to do either. He has no trainability in academic things. There is no alternative but to develop his personal talent."

That answer is still applicable and is, in my view, the correct one. Fortunately, however, it is not a question of *either* training the talent *or* eliminating the defect; rather, it is merely a question of which to concentrate on first. Now, some 50 years after Phillips faced this issue, there is ample evidence, I feel, that with appropriate approaches, understanding and relentless patience on the part of those working with the savant, talents can be trained and, as a part of that training process, some of the other defects will be lessened, albeit not altogether eliminated.

Many of the cases reported in this book make that point forcefully. Some staff members tried to keep Alonzo from his "obsession" with clay because it got in the way of his concentrating on "more useful" things. However, rather than keeping Alonzo *from* "useful things," his sculpting became the key to his becoming more social, more communicative and more self-sufficient. Because May Lemke literally immersed Leslie in his area of ability, music became for him a tool that he would use to become more interactive, more independent and more involved. While he is obviously still impaired, that impairment has been lessened by his musical obsession. The obsession does not impede further growth and development; indeed it provides a mechanism for growth. A mathematical savant in Chicago turned his obsession with memorizing numbers into remembering zip codes and now sorts mail faster than anyone else in the post office where he works. He too had been encouraged by some to put his mind to more useful things than memorizing random numbers. Like most savants, even if he wished to, he could not do otherwise.

A convincing case for "training the talent" is that of a woman named Temple Grandin, whose autobiography *Emergence Labeled Autistic* recounts her "emergence" to date from childhood autism with many of its severe impairments.[140] While Temple Grandin is not a savant (her I.Q. is above average), her childhood symptoms of severe obsessiveness, fascination with spinning objects, lack of speech until age 3½, refusal to be held, isolation and a variety of the other hallmarks of the autistic child speak of severe impairment at that age. She describes her mind as being "completely visual" with a remarkably heightened sense of spatial visualization and mechanical ability. Like many savants, she has severe difficulty with abstract thinking and can think only in terms of visual similies (she can comprehend the concept of "human relationships" only in terms of actually seeing a glass door in her mind—that is, the door must be opened gently; if you kick it, it will break). She handles numbers by actually seeing them in her head in horizontal rows, which she reads from left to right.

Grandin describes her unusual, unrelenting obsession with the cattle chute, a device used to calm livestock, which she quite accidentally discovered was calming to her when she crawled into one as a child. Without interference from those around her to "eliminate" this bizarre preoccupation, it led her into the field of livestock equipment design, for which she is now internationally recognized. President of her own company, she is completing her Ph.D. in animal science from the University of Chicago. Some of the signs of autistic behavior are without question still present. But there has been a remarkable emergence nonetheless.

Dr. Bernard Rimland, in my opinion the world's foremost expert on autism in children, was at first skeptical that Grandin could have, as an adult, completed a doctoral program and become a world authority in her field after having been such a handicapped child; perhaps the diagnosis was wrong. But when they met, he had this reaction: "Her voice and her unusually direct manner persuaded me that she was a recovered (or recovering) autistic. . . . When she arrived, a tall, angular young lady, obsessed with squeeze machines and cattle chutes, I was convinced that she had diagnosed herself correctly."

The relentless obsessiveness and other stereotypical behaviors Grandin showed as a child were as intense as those shown by many savants, at least those with autism, and there is a lesson here on the question of eliminating the defect or training the talent. Her first-hand advice is this: "Too many therapists and psychologically trained people believe that if the child is allowed to indulge his fixations, irreparable harm will be done. I do not believe this in all cases. . . . Certain traits are beneficial." She is proof that that is so.

In his foreword to Temple Grandin's book, a teacher of hers, William Carlock, indicates that there is more to the recipe for teaching and treating such persons than just "training the talent." His advice contains some of the other essential elements: "Temple had demonstrated there is hope for the autistic child—that deep, constant caring, understanding, acceptance, appropriately high expectations, and support and encouragement for what is best in him will provide a base, from which he can grow to his own potential." Temple is an example of how important those ingredients are as well.

A visit to a most unusual university provides more insight into the question of training the talent or eliminating the defect. The school is Hope University—UNICO National College, in Anaheim, California. It is the only fine arts college in the world set up specifically and only for the gifted mentally retarded. The major sponsoring charity for this university has been UNICO National, an Italian-American service organization. Its student body of 38 gifted mentally retarded persons provides striking examples of what can happen when one does "train the talent." When they have completed their secondary education, persons with retardation who have great interest in music, art, dance or drama are encouraged to arrange a visit to the campus as prospective students.

The founder and mainstay of this special university is Doris Walker, a remarkable woman who, along with her carefully chosen staff, instructs, trains, nurtures, encourages and loves these students. A group called HI HOPES, which began in 1972, has carried the message and inspiration of this school all over America and to a number of foreign countries. The group consists of nine members. One of the original members, Paul, is without doubt, a prodigious savant. Blind in addition to being retarded, he has a mellow, unforgettable baritone voice, sings in five languages, shows prodigious memory and plays drums magnificently. Tim has cerebral palsy in addition to mental retardation, yet he is a concert pianist who gave concerts in the U.S. and Europe before joining HI HOPES in 1986. Two other HI HOPES members, Gary and Ron, show great talent in playing, especially keyboards and stringed instruments. They are both able to play many compositions and songs from memory, to learn new ones quickly, and to change arrangements and insert chords and concepts from various sources with ease. When playing together, Paul, Gary and Ron seem to follow each other's spontaneous inspirations almost instinctively. Others in the group have a variety of musical skills and a spectrum of abilities, ranging from talented to prodigious.

We were fortunate to have HI HOPES give a concert in Fond du Lac in the summer of 1985 when I had a chance to meet the members of this gifted group, along with the "leader of the band," Doris Walker. It was a most entertaining and uplifting evening during which they shared their sincerity, enthusiasm, musical talents and well-deserved pride in what they, individually and as a group, had been able to accomplish.

Whether a particular member might be considered talented or prodigious is of little consequence to their leader. Each, as should be, is special and important in his or her own right. Such unconditional acceptance, love, nurturing, belief, praise and reinforcement is provided for each and every member of Hope University by Walker and her staff.

The staff agrees that, given the talents of all of the students, an academic subject is best learned through the medium of the arts. The arts underlie all subjects of the curriculum at Hope University and infuse the teaching of them. For instance, a student may receive individual voice, theory and instrument lessons, but music may also be used to teach reading, math and money skills. Working separately or as a class, students may write their own songs to learn the rules of spelling. Drama class may include role playing in numerous areas, such as acceptable behaviors, appearance and conversation. Guided imagery with music and art may be used to stimulate imagination. A student's individual decision as to what the class will do in an arts activity helps to develop leadership skills. Practice, rehearsal and performance are used to reinforce these areas.

In a class setting one activity may be used for a variety of objectives. A song can be danced to by some; the words of which are being learned by others; while more are thinking of new rhythms, chords, melodies and arrangements for the song. Using the students' strengths in the arts helps learning in areas that are difficult for them. But whatever the topic learned, the learning is a success for every student, with acceptance of every person's weaknesses and strengths.

It is *special* education at its finest. A student's talent is used to draw him or her out and serve as a pathway to more function, more independence and more self-worth. The school philosophy stresses "whole person" development and the performing groups "allow the students to showcase their talents and, in addition to entertaining their audiences, prove that there are hidden talents among our handicapped citizens that need to be discovered, trained and nurtured." There one can see, on a single campus, the full range of savant abilities, and it is an encouraging sight.

The goal, then, in dealing with the special skills of the savant—

bizarre, monotonous and impractical as they might be—is not to eradicate them. It is, rather, to patiently and creatively put them to good use without fearing that in so doing overall development will be harmed or impeded. Quite to the contrary, such skills become a mode of expression through which others can reach and interact with the savant, and consequently those skills lead to the development of other related skills and human communication. The skills serve as a window to the world for the savant, and they serve as a window to the savant for the rest of us. Training the talent can diminish the defect.

THE ULTIMATE TRADE-OFF: MUST THERE BE ONE?

The biggest fear for those involved with savants is that somehow, in working with them, we will cause them to lose their special abilities. If the talent is in some way compensatory for deficiency, by improving the area of deficiency, will we lessen the proficiency? Nadia is often cited as the most tragic example of such a dreadful trade-off. But working *with* savants has to be separated from working *on* them. Working with them means nurturing, tending and encouraging them, and providing them with a whole palette of options to choose from rather than making all the choices for them. It means buttressing strengths and minimizing deficits. Working on them, in contrast, means being presumptuous enough to make what, in our judgment, are all the right choices for them. It means requiring, rather than hoping; giving commandments instead of making suggestions; pushing rather than leading; and filing, scraping and sanding the shape of their souls so that they become more like us, and stay less themselves.

K. Motsugi, in writing about the successful efforts to tap the skills and potential of the Japanese savant artist Shyoichiro Yamamura, summarized those efforts this way: "The secret in developing Yamamura's talent was to share his spirit."[138] Dr. Akira Morishima quotes another talented teacher, Takashi Kawasaki, who reached much the same conclusion through working with another Japanese savant artist:

> Yamamato's art activities are
> not for praise
> not for his skills
> He enjoys drawing and art production
>
> Other's criticism
> It's nothing for him
>
> Why does he draw and produce?
> It is his life
> It is his spirit.[63]

Sharing that spirit and shaping it are two quite different ventures. For Nadia, the gift of genius was but a brief one—it lasted from ages 3½ to 6½. Such a sudden appearance and disappearance of a skill also happens in other savants, in other prodigies who are not savants[42] and in normal children who, are, for only a time, especially talented at some skill or adept in some area of knowledge. Some of us may remember or may have been told about our own brief flicker of precociousness, or may have witnessed that in our children, where some rather exceptional musical memory or drawing skill appeared, but then vanished. Try as one might in later life, one cannot recapture it.

Thus there are several ways of looking at what happened to Nadia. Perhaps there was some link and a consequent trade-off of savant skills for language and for socialization, as some have suggested. Or, possibly that skill disappeared just as abruptly as it appeared, as such skills sometimes do, without any causal link to teaching or to therapy. Or perhaps the cessation of her talent was a reaction to the illness and death of her mother when Nadia was 8. After all, the talent spontaneously developed when Nadia was "overjoyed" by her mother's returning from the hospital after a 3-month bout—her first—with that illness. The loss of that talent could have been a reciprocal, depressive reaction to that original joyful beginning.

My feeling is that the sudden disappearance of that prodigious skill was not causally linked to either the therapy or the mother's illness and death. Any temporal relationships that existed were merely coincidental. The talent came, and it vanished, like similar talents in other savants, and like similar brief flurries of talent in childhood in some normal children. In the case of Leslie Lemke, however, whom I know and have observed, there has been a phenomenal growth between 1974 and the present—not only have his musical skill and repertoire increased markedly, but his vocabulary, social skills and ability in the simple skills of dressing, eating and toileting have risen dramatically. Musically, he has even begun to improvise, instead of just copy, and he is a more polished performer, more animated and even witty at times. He smiles more, ambulates better and, in general, seems to be having a better time of it than he did before. With all those gains and all the input and work of those around Leslie, with all that "therapy" and all that teaching, there has been no disappearance, not even a diminution, of his spectacular savant skills. In fact, those skills, like Leslie himself, have grown even further.

Alonzo Clemons has grown also, not just as an artist, but as a person. He too is more animated, more spontaneous and more communicative. There has been no trade-off here. Success, I am glad to say, has not spoiled him. He is as mellow and as gentle as before. Ellen too speaks more, socializes more and functions more independently with no diminution or disappearance of precious savant skills. She reaches out more. At summer camp each year she plays guitar, leading her fellow campers in song and in spirit—creating quite a different picture of relatedness than the one that existed several years ago before school and before speech therapy.

These and the many other such instances described in this book are reassuring for those who fear that the price of progress is a regression of savant abilities. It is not.

Nadia lost her magnificent drawing ability in spite of, not because of, efforts to help her. Why is that important? Because the recorded experience with Nadia could make us timid or apprehensive about working with the savant to encourage, to reinforce, to present opportunities and possibilities, to coach, to cheerlead and, yes, even to teach. To teach in the best sense of that word—by sharing and reinforcing savant spirit rather than requiring, demonstrating rather than demanding and complimenting rather than criticizing, remembering all the while that the gifts and talents are those of the student, not the teacher. By actualizing all the potential of the savant we do not run the risk of destroying him or her if we can appreciate and value, as we should with everyone, not just what they do—and they do a lot—but what they are as special and unique individuals.

If we can do that—and I have seen many families, therapists and teachers who can—we take no huge risks with the savant; we only enhance the opportunities and possibilities to see a soul unfold a bit further, to blossom and become, just as we wish for ourselves. Certainly we should wish no less for those marvelous geniuses among us, who, if we permit them, can teach us something about the genius that I believe resides as well in each of us.

* *

> If we do not change our direction, we
> are likely to end up where we are headed.
> —Chinese Proverb

What I have tried to do in this book is to change our direction somewhat from that in which we have been headed in dealing with and understanding the savant. The savant should not continue to be viewed only as an astonishing anomaly—an "out-lier," to use the term in vogue at present—who briefly engages, astounds or entertains us. Instead, we need to pause for a more in-depth look not only at the condition the savant has, but at the savant himself. We can learn a great deal from the savant about the brain and its marvelous intricacy. From that knowledge can come methods of tapping some of the buried capability that I am convinced lies in each of us, particularly in the area of memory.

But we can learn a great deal about human potential from the jarring contradiction, the magnificent coexistence of deficiency and superiority, that is Savant Syndrome. We can learn that handicap need not necessarily blur hope and that stereotyping and labeling serve only to obscure, in a pernicious manner, an individual's strengths. We can learn the difference between paucity of emotion and purity of emotion. From the families, teachers and therapists of the savant we can learn that, in dealing with people who have problems, sometimes severe ones, it is not enough to care *for* those people, we must care *about* them as well. We can learn that there is a difference between sharing the spirit and shaping the spirit. We can learn how to work with a differently shaped soul—to understand, to actualize and to appreciate it—while still respecting its uniqueness.

This change in direction begins with changing the name of this unusual circumstance from "Idiot Savant" to "Savant Syndrome." The idiot savant is not an idiot in any scientific, colloquial or classical sense; all the term does is mislead and stereotype. A syndrome is a regularly recurring constellation of symptoms and traits, and that is what this spectacular condition is. From there we can separate the talented savant from the prodigious savant and learn, then, something about memory, genius and creativity that applies not only to them, but to us as well.

But I don't want to try to summarize the savant in these few remaining paragraphs. There has been too much hurried, clipped summarization already in one-minute segments on the evening news or two-column stories in the Sunday supplement. I wrote this book to try to do justice to these extraordinary people and the spectacular condition they have, looking at them in some depth, from both a scientific and a humanistic point of view.

Dr. Edward Sequin, writing about the savant in 1866, said: "To explain the physical and physiological mysteries of such human beings is beyond the present power of any known science."[8] About that same time, in 1873, Dr. Walter Kempster, the first superintendent of Winnebago Mental Health Institute nearly a century before I met my first savant there, wrote: "The results attained in the past one hundred years are certainly gratifying, and should stimulate us to carry forward the good work, constantly endeavoring to advance the interest of the people in whose cause we are engaged, so that, when the record of the next hundred years shall be written up, it may be said of us, that our eyes were not altogether blinded, or that, with the light we had, our opportunities were not unimproved."[141] Hopefully, persons looking back on our efforts to understand the savant a hundred years from now will be able to say the same about us—that our eyes were not altogether blinded; that, with the light we had, opportunities did not go unimproved.

There has been a century of observations since Sequin and Kempster.[153] I have been party to those observations for a quarter of that time. I started my own observations with a scientific curiosity and a spirit of inquiry that I still have. But that curiosity and spirit have grown to encompass a firm belief that in this condition lie clues to our own nature. And, beyond that, I have gained intense appreciation, admiration and awe for these special people and their equally special families. They can inspire us as well as teach us.

If my journey, as I have recorded it, brings you to those same insights and to that same appreciation, and if at the same time it slightly redirects the course we have been taking, then I shall have succeeded.

About the fact that this condition exists at all, and that it is even possible, George says: "It's fantastic I can do that."

It truly is.

Bibliography

1. Down, J.L.: *On Some of the Mental Affections of Childhood and Youth.* London, Churchill, 1887.
2. Dostoyevsky, F.: *The Idiot.* New York, The New American Library, Inc., Signet, 1969.
3. Kanner, L.: Early infantile autism. Journal of Pediatrics 25:200–217, 1944.
4. Rimland, B.: Savant capabilities of autistic children and their cognitive implications. In Serban, G. (ed.), *Cognitive Defects in the Development of Mental Illness.* New York, Brunner/Mazel, 1978.
5. Treffert, D.A.: Epidemiology of infantile autism. Arch. Gen. Psychiat. 22:-431–38, 1970.
6. Wing, J.K.: *Early Childhood Autism: Clinical, Educational, and Social Aspects.* New York, Pergamon Press, 1966.
7. Hill, A.L.: Idiot savants: rate of incidence. Percept. Mot. Skills 44:161–62, 1977.
8. Sequin, E.: *Idiocy and its Treatment by the Physiological Method.* New York, Kelley, 1971 (originally published 1866).
9. Binet, A.: *Psychologie des Grands Calculateurs et Joueurs d'echecs.* Hachette, Paris, 1894.
10. Ireland, W.W.: *The Mental Affections of Children.* Philadelphia, P. Blakiston's Son & Co., 1900.
11. Witzmann, A.: Remarkable powers of memory manifested in an idiot. Lancet, pp. 16–41, June 5, 1909.
12. Tredgold, A.F.: *Mental Deficiency.* New York, William Wood, 1914.
13. Sano, F.: James Henry Pullen, the Genius of Earlswood. Journal of Mental Science 64:251–67, 1918.
14. Podolsky, E.: *Encyclopedia of Aberrations.* New York, Citadel Press, 1953.
15. Goldensen, R.M.: *Mysteries of the Mind.* New York, Harper & Row, 1976.
16. Rife, D.C., and Snyder, L.H.: Studies in human inheritance VI: a genetic refutation of the principles of "behavioristic" psychology. Hum. Biol. 3:547–59, 1931.

17. Minogue, B.M.: A case of secondary mental deficiency with musical talent. J. Applied Psychology 7:349–57, 1923.

18. Viscott, D.S.: A musical idiot savant. Psychiatry 32:494–515, 1969.

19. Anastasi, A., and Levee, R.: Intellectual defect and musical talent: a case report. Am. J. Mental Deficiency 64:695–703, 1960.

20. Owens, W.A., and Grimm, W.: A note regarding exceptional musical ability in low grade imbecile. Educational Psychology 32:636–37, 1941.

21. Scheerer, M., Rothmann, E., and Goldstein, K.: A case of "idiot savant": an experimental study of personality organization. Psychology Monograph 58:1–63, 1945.

22. Sloboda, J.A., Hermelin, B., and O'Connor, N.: An exceptional musical memory. Music Perception 3:155–70, 1985.

23. Revesz, G.: *The Psychology of a Musical Prodigy.* London, Kegan Paul, Trench, Trubner, 1925.

24. Hermelin, B., O'Connor, N., and Lee, S.: Musical inventiveness of five idiot savants. Psychological Medicine 17:685–94, 1987.

25. Rothstein, H.J.: A study of aments with special abilities. Unpub. masters thesis, Columbia University, 1942.

26. Horwitz, W.A., Kestenbaum, C., Person, E., et al.: Identical twin-idiot savants—calendar calculators. Am. J. Psychiatry 121:1075–79, 1965.

27. Horwitz, W.A., Deming, W.E., and Winter, R.F.: A further account of the idiot savants: experts with the calendar. Am. J. Psychiatry 126:160–63, 1969.

28. Hamblin, D.J.: They are idiot savants—wizards of the calendar. Life 60:- 106–8, March 18, 1966.

29. Sacks, O.: *The Man Who Mistook His Wife for a Hat.* New York, Perennial Library, 1985.

30. Roberts, A.D.: Case history of a so-called idiot-savant. J. Genet. Psychology 66:259–65, 1945.

31. Hill, A.L.: An investigation of calendar calculating by an idiot savant. Am. J. Psychiatry 132:557–60, 1975.

32. Critchley, M.: *The Divine Banquet of the Brain.* New York, Raven Press, 1979.

33. Fauville, A.: Un débile mental calculateur prodige. Revue belge Pédagogie 17:338–44, 1936.

34. Byrd, H.A.: A case of phenomenal memorizing in a feeble-minded Negro. J. Applied Psychology 4:202–6, 1920.

35. Rosen, A.M.: Adult calendar calculators in a psychiatric OPD: a report of two cases and comparative analysis of abilities. J. Autism & Developmental Disorders 11:285–92, 1981.

36. Hoffman, E.: The idiot savant: a case report and review of explanations. Ment. Retard. 9:18–21, 1971.

37. Rubin, E.J., and Monaghan, S.: Calendar calculation in a multiple-handicapped blind person. Am. Jour. Ment. Def. 70:478–85, 1965.

38. O'Connor, N., and Hermelin, B.: Idiot savant calendrical calculators: math or memory? Psychological Medicine 14:801–6, 1984.

39. Hermelin, B., and O'Connor, N.: Idiot savant calendrical calculators: rules and regularities. Psychological Medicine 16:1–9, 1986.

40. Mitchell, F.D.: Mathematical prodigies. American Journal of Psychology 18:61–143, 1907.

41. Rimland, B.: Inside the mind of the autistic savant. Psychology Today 12(3): 68–80, August, 1978.

42. Smith, S.B.: *The Great Mental Calculators.* New York, Columbia University Press, 1983.

43. Scripture, E.W.: Arithmetical prodigies. Am. J. Psychology 4:1–59, 1891.

44. Tredgold, R.F., and Soddy, K.: *Textbook of Mental Deficiency,* 10th ed. Baltimore, Williams and Wilkins, 1963.

45. Phillips, A.: Talented imbeciles. Psychological Clinics 18:246–55, 1930.

46. Wizel, D.A.: Ein Fall von Phenomenalem, Rechentalent bei einen Imbecillen. Archiv. f. Psychiatrie, Bd. 38:122, 1904.

47. Brill, A.A.: Some peculiar manifestations of memory with special reference to lightning calculators. J. Nerv. Ment. Dis. 92:709–26, 1940.

48. Nurcombe, M.D., and Parker, N.: The idiot savant. J. Amer. Acad. Child Psychiatry 3:469–87, 1964.

49. Steinkopff, W.: Extraordinary calculating capacity of an imbecile patient: report on follow-up and autopsy. Psychiatrie, Neurologie and Medizinische Psychologie 25:107–16, 1973.

50. Jones, H.E.: Phenomenal memorizing as a special ability. J. Applied Psychology 10:367–76, 1926.

51. Parker, S.W.: A pseudo-talent for words, the teacher's report to Dr. Witmer. Psychological Clinics 11:1–17, 1917.

52. Barr, M.W.: Some notes on echolalia, with the report of an extraordinary case. J. Nerv. Ment. Dis. 25:20–30, 1898.

53. Downey, J.E.: A case of special ability with below average intelligence. Journal of Applied Psychology 10:319–21, 1926.

54. Cain, A.C.: Special isolated abilities in severely psychotic young children. Psychiatry 33:137–49, 1970.

55. LaFontaine, L.: The idiot savant: ten case studies. Unpub. Ed. M. thesis, Boston University, 1968.

56. LaFontaine, L.: Divergent abilities in the idiot savant. Unpub. Ed.D. dissertation. Boston Univ. School of Educ., Boston, 1974.

57. Goodenough, F.: *Measurement of Intelligence by Drawings.* New York, Harcourt, Brace and World, 1926.

58. Selfe, L.: *Nadia: A Case of Extraordinary Drawing Ability in an Autistic Child.* New York, Academic Press, 1978.

59. Dennis, N.: Portrait of the artist. New York Review of Books 25:8–15, 1978.

60. Shikiba, R., ed.: *Works of Kiyoshu Yamishita.* Tokyo, Nihon burai burat, Bungei Shunju Shinsha, 1957.

61. Lindsley, O.: Can deficiency produce specific superiority: the challenge of the idiot savant. Exceptional Children 31:225–32, 1965.

62. Morishima, A.: His spirit raises the ante for retardates. Psychology Today 9(1):72–73, June, 1975.

63. Morishima, A.: Another Van Gogh of Japan: the superior work of a retarded boy. Exceptional Children 41:92–96, 1974.

64. Morishima, A., and Brown, L.F.: An idiot savant case report: a retrospective view. Mental Retardation 14:46–47, 1976.

65. Morishima, A., and Brown, L.: A case report on the artistic talent of an autistic idiot savant. Mental Retardation 15:33–36, 1977.

66. Fairholme, E.G.: *The Animal World.* January, 1909.

67. O'Connor, N., and Hermelin, B.: Visual and graphic abilities of the idiot savant artist. Psychological Medicine 17:79–80, 1987.

68. Blank, J.P.: I can see feeling good. Reader's Digest, 127(762):98–104, 1985.
69. Becker, L.A.: *With Eyes Wide Open* (Documentary film). Austin, Texas, Creative Learning Environments, 1980.
70. Hoffman, E., and Reeves, R.: An idiot savant with unusual mechanical ability. Am. J. Psychiatry 136:713–14, 1979.
71. Brink, T.L.: Idiot savant with unusual mechanical ability: an organic explanation. Am. J. Psychiatry 137:250–51, 1980.
72. Bergman, P., and Escalona, S.: Unusual sensitivities in very young children. The Psychoanalytic Study of the Child 3:333–52. New York, International Universities Press, 1949.
73. Duckett, J.: Idiot savants: super-specialization in mutually retarded persons. Unpub. doc. dissertation. University of Texas—Austin, Department of Special Education, 1976.
74. Duckett, J.: Adaptive and maladaptive behavior of idiot savants. Am. J. Mental Deficiency 82:308–11, 1977.
75. Giray, E.F., and Barclay, A.G.: Eidetic imagery: longitudinal results in brain-damaged children. Am. Jour. Ment. Def. 82: 311–14, 1977.
76. Gray, C.R., and Gummerman, K.: The enigmatic eidetic image: a critical examination of methods, data, and theories. Psychological Bulletin 82:383–407, 1975.
77. Bender, M.B., Feldman, M., and Sobin, A.J. Palinopsia Brain 91:321–38, 1968.
78. Lessell, S.: Higher disorders of visual function: positive phenomena. In Glaser, J., and Smith, J. (eds.), *Neuro-Opthalmology, Volume III, Symposium of the University of Miami and Bascom Palmer Eye Institute.* St. Louis, C.V. Mosby, 1975.
79. Siipola, E.M., and Hayden, S.D.: Exploring eidetic imagery among the retarded. Perceptual and Motor Skills 21:275–86, 1965.
80. Jaensch, E.R., and Menhel, H.: Gedachtnishleistung eines schwash-sinnigen eidetikers. Psychiat. Neurol. Schr. 30:101–3, 1928. (See "Feats of memory in a feebleminded man," Psych. Abs. 2, 1928, #2702.)
81. Goddard, H.H.: *Feeble-Mindedness.* New York, Macmillan, 1914.
82. Rimland, B., and Fein, D.A.: Special talents of autistic savants. In Obler, L.K., and Fein, D.A. (ed.), *The Exceptional Brain: Neuropsychology of Talent and Special Abilities.* New York, Guilford Press, 1988.
83. Luszki, W.A.: An idiot savant on the WAIS? Psychological Reports 19:603–9, 1966.
84. Sarason, S.B., and Gladwin, T.: Psychological and cultural problems in mental subnormality: a review of research. Genet. Psychology Monograph 57:3–290, 1958.
85. Sarason, S.B.: *Psychological Problems in Mental Deficiency.* New York, Harper and Brothers, 1959.
86. Tanguay, P.E.: A tentative hypothesis regarding the role of hemispheric specialization in early infantile autism. UCLA Conference on Cerebral Dominance, 1973.
87. Restak, R.M.: *The Brain.* New York, Bantam Books, 1984.
88. Steel, J.G., Gorman, R., and Flexman, J.E.: Neuropsychiatric testing in an autistic mathematical idiot-savant: evidence for non-verbal abstract capacity. J. Amer. Acad. Child Psychiatry 23:704–7, 1984.
89. Altshuler, K.Z., and Brebbia, D.R.: Sleep patterns and EEG tracings in twin idiot savants. Diseases of the Nervous System 29:772–74, 1968.

90. Hauser, S.L., Delong, G.R., and Rosman, N.P.: Pneumographic findings in the infantile autism syndrome. Brain 98:667–88, 1975.

91. Charness, N., Clifton, J., and MacDonald, L.: A case study of a musical mono-savant: a cognitive psychological focus. In Obler, L.K., and Fein, D.A. (ed.), *The Exceptional Brain: Neuropsychology of Talent and Special Abilities.* New York, Guilford Press, 1988.

92. Hermelin, B. and O'Connor, N.: The idiot savant: flawed genius or clever Hans? Psychological Medicine 13:479–81, 1983.

93. Winslow, F.: *Obscure Diseases of the Brain and Mind* (p. 586). London, 1863.

94. Goodman, J.: A case of an "autistic-savant": mental function in a psychotic child with markedly discrepant abilities. J. Child Psychiatry 13:267–78, 1972.

95. Luria, A.R.: *The Mind of a Mnemonist* (p. viii). New York, Basic Books, 1968.

96. Spitz, H.H., and LaFontaine, L.: The digit span of idiot savants. American Journal of Mental Deficiency 77:757–59, 1973.

97. Hunt, M.: *The Universe Within.* New York, Simon and Schuster, 1982.

98. Penfield, W., and Perot, P.: The brain's record of auditory and visual experience. Brain 86:595–696, 1963.

99. Milner, B., Corkin, S., and Teuberl, H.L.: Further analysis of the hippocampal-amnesic syndrome: 14-year follow-up study of H.M. Neuropsychologia 6:215–34, 1968.

100. Milner, B.: The memory defect in bilateral hippocampal lesions. Psychiatric Research Reports 11:43–58, 1959.

101. Graff-Radford, N.R., Eslinger, A.R., Damasio, A.R., et al.: Nonhemorrhagic infarction of the thalamus: behavioral, anatomic and physiologic correlates. Neurology 34:14–23, 1984.

102. Rimland, B.: *Infantile Autism: The Syndrome and Its Implications for a Neural Theory of Behavior.* New York, Appleton-Century-Crofts, 1964.

103. Mishkin, M., and Petri, H.L.: Memories and habits: some implications for the analysis of learning and retention. In Squire, L.R., and Butters, N. (ed.), *Neuropsychology of Memory.* New York, Guilford Press, 1984.

104. Mishkin, M., Malamut, B., and Bachevalier, J.: Memories and habits: two neural systems. In Lynch, G., McGaugh, J.L., and Weinberger, N.M. (ed.), *Neurobiology of Learning and Memory.* New York, Guilford Press, 1984.

105. McKeague, P.: He is blind, retarded—and a virtuoso. The Miami Herald, February, 25, 1986.

106. Epstein, N.: A boy's music offers a view of how idiot savants learn. The New York Times, January 17, 1987.

107. Miller, L.K.: Developmentally delayed musical savant's sensitivity to tonal structure. Amer. J. Mental Deficiency 5:467–71, 1987.

108. Miller, L.K.: Sensitivity to tonal structure in a developmentally disabled musical savant. The Psychology of Music 15:76–89, 1987.

109. Geschwind, N., and Galaburda, A.M.: *Cerebral Lateralization: Biological Mechanisms, Associations, and Pathology.* Cambridge, Mass., MIT Press, 1987.

110. Hamburger, V., and Oppenheim, R.W.: Naturally occurring neuronal death in vertebrates. Neurosci. Commentaries 1:39–55, 1982.

111. Logan, B.: The ultimate preventive: prenatal stimulation. Eighth Con-

gress of the International Society for the Study of Prenatal Psychology, Badgastein, Austria, September 27, 1986.

112. Logan, B.: Learning before birth: the cardiac curriculum. First Developmental Enrichment Conference of the Infant Stimulation Education Association, UCLA Center for the Health Sciences and Georgetown University, Costa Mesa, California, March 14, 1986.

113. Mistretta, C.M., and Bradley, R.M.: Effects of early sensory experience on brain and behavioral development. In Gottlieb, G. (ed.), *Studies on the Development of Behavior and the Nervous System.* New York, Academic Press, 1974.

114. Crick, F., and Mitchison, G.: The function of dream sleep. Nature 304:111–14, 1983.

115. Hobson, J.A., and McCarley, R.W.: The brain as a dream state generator: an activation-synthesis hypothesis of the dream process. American Journal of Psychiatry 134:1335–48, 1977.

116. Melnechuk, T.: The dream machine. Psychology Today 17(11):22–34, November, 1983.

117. Terry, T.L.: Fibroplastic overgrowth of persistent tunica vasculosa lentis in infants born prematurely. Amer. J. Ophthal. 25:1409, 1942.

118. Patz, A.: The role of oxygen in retrolental fibroplasia. Pediatrics 19:504–25, 1957.

119. Campbell, K.: Intensive oxygen therapy as possible cause of retrolental fibroplasia: clinical approach. Med. J. Aust. 151:2–48, 1951.

120. Bender, L., and Andermann, K.: Brain damage in blind children with retrolental fibroplasia. Arch. Neurol. 12:644–49, 1965.

121. Keeler, W.R.: Autistic patterns and defective communication in blind children with retrolental fibroplasia. In Hoch, P., and Zubin, J. (eds.), *Psychopathology of Communication.* New York, Grune & Stratton, 1958.

122. Cohen, J.: Study of children blind from birth for effects on behavior and learning. Factor 3, 9:8 (Oct.), 1962.

123. Williams, C.E.: Retrolental fibroplasia as associated with mental defect. Brit. J. Ophthal. 42:549–57, 1958.

124. Mazziotta, J.C., Phelps, M.E., Carson, R.E., and Kuhl, D.E.: Tomographic mapping of human cerebral metabolism: auditory stimulation. Neurology 32:921–37, 1982.

125. Seashore, C.E., Lewis, D., and Sactveit, J.G.: Seashore measures of musical talents. New York: Psychological Corp. 1, Series B, 1960.

126. Mazziotta, J.C., Phelps, M.E., and Carson, R.E.: Tomographic mapping of human cerebral metabolism: subcortical responses to auditory and visual stimulation. Neurology 34:825–28, 1984.

127. Mazziotta, J.C., Phelps, M.E., and Halgren, E.: Local cerebral glucose metabolic response to audiovisual stimulation and deprivation: studies in human subjects with positron CT. Human Neurobiology 2:11–23, 1983.

128. Rumsey, J.M., Duara, R., Grady, C., Rapoport, J.L., et al.: Brain metabolism in autism. Arch. Gen. Psychiatry 42:448–55, 1985.

129. Buchsbaum, M.S., Siegel, B.V., Wu, J.C., Hazlett, E., et al.: Attention performance in autism and regional brain metabolism rate assessed by positron emission tomography (in press).

130. Lashley, K.S.: The effects of strychnine and caffeine upon the rate of learning. Psychobiology, 1:141–70, 1917.

131. Storfer, M.D.: *The Human Memory*. New York, The Foundation for Brain Research Publications, July, 1984.
132. Summers, W.K., Majovski, L.V., Marsh, G.M., Tachiki, K., and Kling, A.: Oral tetrahydroaminocridine in long-term treatment of senile dementia, Alzheimer's type. New England Journal of Medicine 315:1241–45, 1986.
133. Scharf, M.B., Saskin, P., and Fletcher, K.: Benzodiazepine-induced amnesia: clinical and laboratory findings. Journal of Clinical Psychiatry Monograph Series 5(1):8–13, 1987.
134. Kiester, E.: Spare parts for damaged brains. Science 86, 7(2):33–38, 1986.
135. Madrazo, I., Drucker-Colin, R., Diaz, V., et al.: Open microsurgical autograft of adrenal medulla to the right caudate nucleus in two patients with intractable Parkinson's disease. New England Journal of Medicine 316 (14):831–34, 1987.
136. Feldman, R.D.: *Whatever Happened to the Quiz Kids?* Chicago, Chicago Review Press, 1982.
137. Turkel, S.: *Working*. New York, Pantheon Books, 1972.
138. Motsugi, K.: Shyochan's drawing of insects. Japanese Journal of Mentally Retarded Children 13(4):44–47, 1968.
139. Binet, A., and Simon, T.: Application des méthodes nouvelles au diagnostic de niveau intellectuel chez des enfants normaux et anormaus d'hospice et d'école primare. L'Année Psychologique 11:245, 1905.
140. Grandin, T., and Scariano, M.: *Emergence Labeled Autistic*. Novato, California, Arena Press, 1986.
141. Kempster, W.: Second annual report to board of trustees, Northern Hospital for the Insane, Winnebago, Wisconsin, 1876.
142. Memory Center in Hippocampus? Medical Tribune, July 2, 1986, p. 6.
143. Zola-Morgan, S., Squire, L., and Amara, D.: Human amnesia and the medical temporal region: enduring memory impairment following a bilateral lesion limited to field CA1 of the hippocampus. Journal of Neuroscience 6(10):2950–67, 1986.
144. Asperger, H.: Die 'autistischen Psychopathen' im Kindesalter. Archiv für Psychiatrie und Nervenkrankheiten 117:76–136, 1944.
145. Wing, L.: Asperger's syndrome: a clinical account. Psychological Medicine 11:115–29, 1981.
146. Van Krevelen, D.A.: Early infantile autism and autistic psychopathy. Journal of Autism and Childhood Schizophrenia 1:82–86, 1971.
147. Bosch, G.: *Infantile Autism*. D. Jordan and J. Jordan, trans. New York, Springer-Verlag, 1970.
148. Stevens, D.E., and Moffitt, T.E.: Neuropsychological profile of an Asperger's Syndrome case with exceptional mathematical ability. Clinical Neuropsychologist (in press).
149. Letters to the Editor: "You don't have to be a neuroscientist to forget everything with triazolam—but it helps." Journal of the American Medical Association 259(3):350–52, 1988.
150. Madrazo, I., Leon, V., Torres, C., et al.: Transplantation of fetal substantia nigra and adrenal medulla to the caudate nucleus in two patients with Parkinson's Disease. New England Journal of Medicine 318(1):51, 1988.
151. Hermelin, B., O'Connor, N., Lee, S., and Treffert, D.: Intelligence level and musical improvisation ability (in press).

152. Hermelin, B., O'Connor, N. and Lee, S.: Musical inventiveness of five idiot-savants. Psychological Medicine 17:685–694, 1987.
153. Treffert, D. A.: The idiot savant: a review of the syndrome. American Journal of Psychiatry 145:563–572, 1988.
154. Selfe, L.: *Normal and Anomalous Representational Drawing Ability in Children.* London, Academic Press, 1983.
155. Hermelin, B., and O'Connor, N.: Spatial representations in mathematically and in artistically gifted children. British Journal of Educationa Psychology (in press).

Appendix

Enquiries regarding referral resources, or requests for other information about handicapped persons with special skills, can be addressed to:

The National Autistic Society
276 Willesden Lane
London NW2
England

The International Autistic Research Organization
49 Orchard Avenue, Shirley
Croydon CR0 7NE
England

Association for Autistic Children
115/396 Scarborough Beach Road
Osborne Park
Western Australia 6017
Australia

Autistic Association
41 Cook Street
Forestville, New South Wales
Australia

Autistic Association
3 Fisher Street,
Myrtle Bank, South Australia 5064
Australia

Institute for Child Behavior Research
4182 Adams Avenue
San Diego, California 92116
USA

Enquiries regarding more information on Savant Syndrome can be directed to:

Darold A. Treffert, M.D.
Brookside Medical Center
481 East Division Street
Fond du Lac, Wisconsin 54935
USA

Information regarding Leslie Lemke concerts can be obtained from:

Miracle of Love Ministries
8099 Grant Road
Arpin, Wisconsin 54410
USA

Information regarding Alonzo Clemons's works can be obtained from:

Driscol Gallery
555 17th Street
Denver, Colorado 80202
USA

Information regarding Richard Wawro's works can be obtained from:

Dr Laurence A. Becker
Creative Learning Environments
507 Park Blvd
Austin, Texas 78751
USA

Information regarding Stephen Wiltshire's works can be obtained from:

J.M. Dent & Sons Ltd
91 Clapham High Street
London SW4 7TA
England

Index

A, 70–1
A, Mr, 93–4, 154
abstract reasoning, 144–8
AC, 212–14
Addis, Barnett, 52
Akira Morishima, 84, 85, 269
Alonzo, *see* Clemons, Alonzo
Altshuler, Kenneth Z., 160, 202
Alzheimer's Disease, 111, 238–9, 243
AM Chicago, 98, 108
American Association for Mental
    Deficiency, xxviii, 113
American Journal of Mental Deficiency,
    49, 131
American Psychiatric Association, xxviii,
    36
amnesia, 240–1
Anastasi, Anne, 24–5
Andermann, Karl, 207
arithmetic, *see* calculators
artistic ability, 79–91, 194–5
Asperger's Syndrome, 210–14
autism, *see* Early Infantile Autism
autopsies, 158–9, 199

Baekkelund, Kjell, 108–9
Barclay, Allan G., 134
Barr, Martin W., 9, 71–2, 166
Becker, Laurence, 90
Bender, Laurette, 207
Bergman, Paul, 96
Bethune, Thomas Greene, 5, 16–19, 20,
    30, 31, 82, 111, 187, 206, 252–6

Billy, xviii
Binet, Alfred, xxvii, 6, 46, 67
Blind Joe, 20
Blind Tom, *see* Bethune, Thomas
    Greene
blindness, xi, xxvi, 19–20, 49–50, 140–4,
    148, 206–10
Boudreaux, Barbara and Ory, 116–22,
    251–2
Boudreaux, Ellen, 20, 97, 100, 116–22,
    131, 138, 144, 149, 165, 200, 206, 251,
    253, 264, 270–1
Bradley, Robert M., 199
brain
    capacity, xiii
    damage, 133–4, 136, 141, 199
    electrical probes, xxii, xxiv, 227
    electrodes, 228–30, 247
    function, xii, 225
    implants, 242–4
    repair, 245–6
    structure, xiii, xxi–xxii, 14–15, 42–3,
        150–4, 154–8, 158–9, 173–81,
        197–9, 225; amygdala, 178–9; basal
        ganglia, 180–1; cell death, 200–2;
        cerebral cortex, 173–4;
        hippocampus, 174–8; left brain/
        right brain, 94, 114, 154-8, 196–7;
        reticular activating formation,
        152–3, 179–80; thalamus, 179–80
Brain, The (Restak), 156, 248
Brebbia, D.R., 160, 202
Brill, Abraham A., 60–2, 138–9, 181

Brink, T.L., 94–5, 154–5
British Association for the Advancement
  of Science, 80
Broca, Paul, 156
Brown, Louis, 84, 85
Bruner, Jerome, 167–8
Buchanan, James, 17–18
Buchsbaum, Monte, 236
Buxton, Jedediah, 57–8
Byrd, Hiram, 46–7, 76–7

Cain, Albert C., 77
'Can Deficiency Produce Specific
  Superiority' (Lindsley), 83
Carl, 77–8
Carlock, William, 267
Carlyle, Thomas, 15
Carpenter, William, 181
Carson, Richard, 233
CAT scans, 42, 151, 161–2, 188, 199,
  221, 230–1
'Cats' Raphael, The', see Mind, Gottfried
CBS Evening News, xxiii, 107
Cerebral Lateralization (Geschwind/
  Galaburda), 197
calculators: calendar, 7–8, 10, 36–54,
  134–5, 136, 144–6; lightning, 4, 7–8,
  10–11, 55–67, 135, 144–6, 212–14
Casson, Sir Hugh, 194
C-EEG, 232
Charcot, Jean Martin, 6
Charles (twin), see George and Charles
Charness, Neil, 162, 188–90, 204
childhood schizophrenia, xix, xx, xxvii
chorioretinitis, 38
Clemons, Alonzo, xxiii, 100, 108, 123–7,
  131, 144, 149, 194, 195, 215, 218, 251,
  252, 253, 255, 262, 264, 265, 270; and
  Leslie Lemke, 124, 126
Clifton, Jane, 162, 188–90
Cohen, J., 207
Colburn, Zerah, 181
Columbian Centinal, 56
compensatory activity, 148–50
concrete thinking, 144–8
creativity, 256–62
cretins, 9
Crick, Francis, 202–5
Critchley, Macdonald, 45–6, 64–5, 68,
  76, 166
Cronkite, Walter, xxiii, 107

David, xvii–xviii, 68

deafness, xxvii, 14, 140–4
Delong, G. Robert, 161
Dennis, Nigel, 81, 251
developmental disability, xx, xxvii
Diamandi, Pericles, 6
Digit Span Test, 167, 168–70
directional sense, 98–9
Divine Banquet of the Brain, The
  (Critchley), 64
Donahue, xxiii, 107–8
Dostoevsky, Fyodor, xiv, 11
Down, J. Langdon, 3–5, 7, 8, 10, 14, 45,
  53, 58–9, 68, 71, 95–6, 98, 158, 165–6;
  Lettsomian Lectures, 3–4; Syndrome,
  3, 8
Downey, June E., 75–6
dreaming, 202–5
Driscol, Pam, 125, 255
drugs, 237–41
Duckett, Jane, 131–2, 136, 140, 148,
  163–4, 169–70, 219, 220, 257

Earl, 92–3, 265
Early Infantile Autism, xviii–xix, xx–xxi,
  8, 32–3, 77, 79, 142, 161, 200, 207,
  210–14, 235–7; defined, xxvi–xxvii
echolalia, 71, 79, 105, 120; defined,
  xxviii
'Echolalia' (Barr), 71–2
ECT, 172
Eddie, 191–3, 200
education, 265–9
EEG, 160–1, 162, 172, 228, 232
eidetic imagery, see memory
Eimland, Bernard, 52–3
Ellen, see Boudreaux, Ellen
Emergence Labeled Autistic (Grandin),
  266
emotions, 262–4
EN, 28, 29
epilepsy, 228
Escallona, Sibylle, 96
ESP, see extrasensory perception
exploitation, 252–6
extrasensory perception, 96–7

Fauville, A, 46, 149
Feeble–Mindedness (Goddard), 138
Fein, D.A., 142
Feldman, Ruth Dukin, 253–4
Fleury, 64–5
Flexman, Jerry, 160, 169, 170
Freud, Sigmund, 139, 205

Fuller, Thomas, 55–7, 187
Fund for the Study of Savant Syndrome, 255

Galaburda, Albert, 197–9, 200, 201
Gary, 267
Gentleman's Magazine, The, 57
George (calculator), xxiii, 63–4, 68, 108, 131, 139, 171, 215–16, 218, 227, 228, 275
George (ESP), 96
George and Charles (twins), xi, 36–42, 44, 47, 52, 67, 96, 134, 146, 160, 165, 167, 187, 249
Geschwind, Norman, 197–9, 200, 201
Giray, Erol F., 134
Gladwin, T., 149
Goddard, Henry H., 20, 138
Goldstein, Kurt, 26–7, 135, 144–8
Goodenough, Florence, 79
Goodman, Joan, 167
Gordon, 68–70
Gorman, Richard, 160, 169, 170
Grandin, Temple, 264
Gray, Cynthia, 133
Great Mental Calculators, The (Smith), 55, 64, 66
Griesinger, Wilhelm, 166
Grimm, Walter, 26
Gummerman, Kent, 133

Hamblin, Dora Jane, 39
Hansen, 163
Harriet, 21–4, 31, 141, 259, 263
Hauser, Kaspar, 159
Hauser, Stephen L., 161
Hayden, Susan O., 134
Heath, Robert, 228
Hermelin, Beate, 28–31, 50–2, 53, 86, 163, 167, 190, 193, 257–60
Hero-Worship (Carlyle), 15
HI HOPES, 267–8
Hill, A. Lewis, 44–5, 47, 143, 169
HM, 175–8, 184, 240
Hoffman, Edward, 48–9, 93–4, 95, 143, 148, 154, 220
Holstein, Arthur P., 38, 167
Horwitz, William A., 36–42, 44, 96, 134, 158, 167
Hoskins, Eugene, 46–7
Howe, Dr, 11
Huntington's Chorea, 243
hydrocephalus, xxviii, 84

Idiocy (Sequin), 5–6
Idiot, The (Dostoevsky), xiv
idiot savant: defined, xxvi, 3
'Idiot Savants' (Duckett), 131
In the Mind of the Mnemonist (Luria), 167–8
Inaudi, Jacques, 6
inherited skills, 137–40
IQ, 38; defined, xxvii–xxviii
Ireland, William W., 7, 68, 166
Island of Genius, An (film), 115

Jaensch, E.R., 135
Jarvik, Lissy, 36–42
Jeremy, xi
John, 187–90, 193, 200, 206
Jones, Howard Ellis, 68, 73, 138, 148, 166
Journal of Applied Psychology, 68
Journal of Genetic Psychology, 42
Journal of Mental Science, 14
Journal of the American Medical Association, 240
JP, 193
Jungreis, S., 60–2, 139

K, 73–5
Kanner, Leo, xviii, xx, 8, 208; Early Infantile Autism, xviii, 8, 210
Keeler, W.R., 205, 206
Keller, Helen, 14, 15, 105
Kempster, Walter, 272, 275
Kennedy, John F., 178–9, 184
Kenneth, xi–xii
Kestenbaum, Clarice, 36–42
Kirtie, 71–2, 166
Kiyoshi Yamashita, 82–3

L (calculator/musician), 26, 144–9
LaFontaine, Louise, 77–8, 135, 148, 149, 163, 169, 170, 218
Lancet, The, 7
Langdon, Benj, 52–3, 54, 155
language, 9; verbal adhesion, 68, 166
LaPlant, Robert, 112
Larsen, Mary, 105, 111, 113, 252
Lashley, K.S., 237
Lee, Sara, 31, 255–8
Lemke, Joe, xxiii, 103–15
Lemke, Leslie, xi, xxii–xxiii, 20, 68, 98, 100, 103–15, 131, 138, 139, 144, 149, 160, 162, 165, 168, 169, 170, 187, 189, 193, 195, 200, 206, 215, 218, 251, 252,

Lemke, Leslie (*cont.*)
253, 255, 259–60, 261, 262, 263–4,
270; and Alonzo Clemons, 124, 126;
CAT scan, 162
Lemke, May, xxii, xxiii, 103–15, 149,
218, 251, 255
Leslie, *see* Lemke, Leslie
Levee, Raymond, 24
lightning calculators, *see* calculators
Lindsley, Ogden, 83, 85
LN, 31
Logan, Brent, 200, 201, 202
Luria, Aleksandr Romanovich, 167
Luszki, Walter A., 147

MacDonald, Lyle, 162, 188–90
Maudsley, Dr, 10, 73
Mazziotta, John, 233, 235
mechanical ability, 92–5
Medical Society of London, 3
Meeker Semantic Memory Test, 170
memory, 9–10, 20–1, 50–1, 54, 61–2,
165–86, 227; anatomy, 173–81;
ancestral, 181–2; cognitive and
associative, 182–4; concrete verbal
memory, 170; drugs, 237–41; eidetic
imagery, xxvi, 132–7, 170; expanding,
237–41; feats, 4; figural, 170; habit,
184–6; long-term, 172–3, mnemonists,
68–78; normal, 171–2; palinopsia,
133–4; photographic, xxvi, 132–7;
picture lexicon, 86–8; semantic, 170;
short-term, 172–3; symbolic, 170;
tests, 168–70
Menhel, H., 135
meningitis, 20–1
Mental Affections of Children (Ireland),
7
Mental Deficiency (Amentia) (Tredgold),
8–11
mental retardation, xx, 19–20; defined,
xxvii–xxviii; chorioretinitis, 38;
primary amentia, 14
Michelle, 96–7
microcephalus, xxviii
Miller, Leon, 191–3
Millie, 77
Mind, Gottfried, 9, 86, 88, 187
mind control, 246–9
Minogue, Blanche M., 20–1
Mishkin, Mortimer, 181, 183, 184–6
Mistretta, Charlotte M., 201
Mitchell, Frank D., 52, 146

Mitchison, Graeme, 202–5
mnemonists, 68–78. *See also* memory
Moffitt, Terrie, 212–14
Monaghan, Sheila, 49–50, 53, 135–6,
141
Morning Show, The, 126
motor functions, 9
Motsugi, K., 267
Mozart, W.A., 7, 23, 24, 28, 121, 181
MRI, 230–1
Muhammad Ali, 243
musical ability, xi, xxvi, 4, 10, 16–35, 79,
187–93, 206–8, 217, 233–5

Nadia, 79–82, 90, 111, 119, 195, 251,
270, 271
neuropsychological testing, 162–3
New York Evening Journal, 61
Newson, Elizabeth, 79–82
NMR brain scan, 172
NP, 28–31
Nurcombe, Barry, 63–4, 143, 147

Obadiah, 59
O'Connor, N.O., 28–31, 50–2, 53, 86–8,
163, 167, 190, 193, 257–60
ontogenetic unconscious, 139
Oliver, Perry, 16
*On Some Mental Affections of Childhood
and Youth* (Down), 3–5
Osty, Dr, 65
Owens, William, A., 26

palinopsia, 133–4
Parker, Neville, 63–4, 143, 147
Parker, Sarah Warkfield, 68–70
Parkinson's Disease, 239–240, 242, 243
Parsons, Oscar, 52
Pascal, Blaise, 139
Patz, Arnall, 206
Paul, 267
Penfield, Wilder, 173–4, 227, 248–9
Person, Ethel, 36–42
PET scans, 156, 157, 231–7
Phelps, Michael, 231
'Phenomenal Memorizing' (Jones), 68
Phillips, Arthur, 59, 69–70, 92–3, 265
photographic memory, *see* memory
phylogenetic unconscious, 139
pneumoencephalography, 42–3, 152,
161, 221
Podolsky, Edward, 19
prenatal learning, 200–2

prodigious savant, 219, 221–4
'Pseudotalent for Words, A' (Parker), 69
Psychological Abstracts, 83
Psychology Today, 52
Ptacek, Louis J., 112
Pullen, James Henry, 5, 11–15, 86, 92, 159

R, 49–50, 141
RB, 177–8, 238
RCBF, 231–2
reasoning, 144–8
Reeves, Russell, 93–5
reinforcement, 148–50
REM sleep, 160–1, 202–5
Restak, Richard, 156–7, 248, 262
retrolental fibroplasia, xxvi, 49, 104, 117, 206–10
Revesz, Geza, 28, 29
Rife, David C., 20, 62–3, 137, 181, 219
Rimland, Bernard, 32, 96, 99, 140, 141–3, 155, 181, 200, 208, 209, 219, 266
Roberts, A. Dudley, 42–4, 54, 134, 216
Ron, 265
Rosen, Arnold M., 47
Rosenberg, Harold, xiv
Rosman, N. Paul, 161
Rothmann, Eva, 26–7, 135, 144–8
Rothstein, H.J., 33–4
Rubin, Edmund J., 49–50, 53, 135–6, 141
Rush, Benjamin, 55–7
Ryfe, David C., 77
Ryuizaburo Shikiba, 83, 148

S, 167–8, 242–5
Sabine, 60
Sacks, Oliver, 40–3, 67, 135, 249
Safer, Morley, xxiii, 108, 165
Sano, F., 11, 12, 14, 15, 159, 163
Sarason, S.B., 149
Sartre, Jean-Paul, 115
Savant Syndrome: defined, xxv–xxviii, 94, 131–64, 224–5; memory and, 165–86
Scheerer, Martin, 26–7, 135, 144–8
schizophrenia, *see* childhood schizophrenia
Scripture, E.W., 57, 58, 66
Selfe, Lorna, 79–82
senses, 9
sensory deprivation, 140–4

sensory discrimination, 95–6
Sequin, Edward, 5–6, 11, 12, 13, 14, 16–19, 70–1, 165–6, 272, 275; 'idiotic genius', 5
Shyoichiro Yamamura, 85, 269
Siipola, Elsa M., 134
Simon, Theodore, xxvii
60 Minutes, xxiii, 53, 108, 165
Sloboda, John, 28–31, 167, 193
Smith, Steven B., 55, 64, 66, 67
Snyder, Laurence H., 20, 62–3, 77, 137, 181, 217
Society for Psychiatry and Neurology, 45
Soddy, Kenneth, 59
sodium amytal, xxiv, 227
SPECT scan, 232
Spitz, Herman H., 169
Stanford-Binet test, xxvii, 113, 145
Starr King program, 118
Steel, J. Griffith, 160, 161, 169, 170
Steinkopff, Walter, 65–6, 159, 163
Stevens, Denise, 212–14
strokes, 245
Sullivan, Anne Mansfield, 105

Tactual Performance Test, 113
Takashi Kawasaki, 84, 269
'Talented Imbeciles' (Phillips), 59, 69
talented savant, 217–21
Tanguay, P.E., 155
Terman tests, 75
testosterone, 198
Textbook on Mental Deficiency (Tredgold/Soddy), 59
That's Incredible, xxiii, 107
Tim, 267
time sense, 97–8
Tony, xviii
Torrance test, 257
Tredgold, Alfred F., 8–11, 13–14, 19, 59, 68, 72–3, 86, 95, 166, 256
Trelat, Dr, 10, 20, 204

UNICO National College, 267–8

verbal adhesion, 166
Vineland Social Maturity Scale, 118, 188
Viscott, David, 21–4, 141, 259, 263
Voisin, Jules, 95

Walker, Doris, 267–8
Wawro, Richard, 88–91, 165, 187, 194, 252

Wechsler scales, xxvii–xxviii, 113, 147, 162, 168, 170, 188
Whatever Happened to the Quiz Kids? (Feldman), 253–4
Whinfrey, Oprah, 98, 108
Williams, Cyril E., 207
Wiltshire, Stephen, 194–5
Wing, Lorna, 210–11
Winslow, Forbes, 10, 73, 165, 166
With Eyes Wide Open (film), 90
Witmer, Lightner, 69
Witzmann, A., 7–8, 45, 68
Wizel, D. Adam, 11, 59, 60

Woman Who Willed a Miracle, The (film), 115
Working (Turkel), 253
World Health Organization, xxviii
'World's Champion on Memory', 75–6

X, 20–1

Yoshihiko Yamamoto, 84

Z, Mr, 94–5, 154–5
Zola-Morgan, Stuart, 177

Rites of Spring
The Great War and the Birth
of the Modern Age
Modris Eksteins

'Always provocative and often stunning . . . a fascinating narrative of World
War I and politics'
WASHINGTON TIMES

On May 29, 1913, near riot broke out in the Parisian audience for the first
performance of *The Rite of Spring*. Stravinsky's powerful, discordant music
and Nijinsky's frenzied, almost brutal choreography were intended to shock,
and shock they did like no other artistic event before or since. *The Rite of
Spring* shook the Establishment and started an urgent and irrevocable
movement towards newness and purification in Art and intellectual life. Yet
more shocking, however, was the Great War, which began only fifteen
months later. The horrifying and unprecedented scale of its carnage resulted
in almost universal revulsion and reinforced the overwhelming urge for
change and renewal.

In *Rites of Spring*, Modris Eksteins has written a dazzlingly original and
penetrating work of cultural history showing how these two momentous
events have shaped our contemporary sense of self. He argues that the Great
War's slaughter swept away the old order and ushered in the individualism,
collective violence and mass culture of our age, and he identifies, in
Stravinsky's dance of death, a potent symbol for the world today in which
the struggle for freedom has paradoxically produced the power of ultimate
destruction.

Rites of Spring avoids the linearity of conventional histories to offer startling
new insights. Concluding in Spring 1945 with the suicide of Hitler in his
bunker beneath Berlin, it takes the significant political, cultural and social
events of those times and links them together in a symbolic chain to sum up
the whole of our turbulent century and to reveal to us who we are, what
values we adhere to and how we came to be.

'An immensely stimulating book, explaining much that has seemed confused
and contradictory in our troubled century, and it deserves to be widely read.'
Michael Howard THE TIMES LITERARY SUPPLEMENT

'Rich in intellectual challenges . . . full of insight.'
DAILY MAIL

'Belongs on a bookshelf with Paul Fussell's *The Great War
and Modern Memory*.'
NEW YORK TIMES

BLACK SWAN

A SELECTED LIST OF NON-FICTION
FROM BLACK SWAN

☐	99160 0	**FIRE FROM WITHIN**	*Carlos Casteneda* £4.99
☐	99332 8	**THE POWER OF SILENCE**	*Carlos Casteneda* £3.95
☐	99364 6	**VIDEO NIGHT IN KATHMANDU**	*Pico Iyer* £4.99
☐	99243 7	**CONFESSIONS OF A FAILED SOUTHERN LADY**	*Florence King* £3.99
☐	99376 X	**REFLECTIONS IN A JAUNDICED EYE**	*Florence King* £3.99
☐	99337 9	**SOUTHERN LADIES AND GENTLEMEN**	*Florence King* £3.99
☐	99377 8	**WASP WHERE IS THY STING?**	*Florence King* £4.99
☐	99405 7	**1933**	*Philip Metcalfe* £5.99
☐	99143 0	**CELTIC DAWN**	*Ulick O'Connor* £4.95
☐	99367 0	**THE RIGHT STUFF**	*Tom Wolfe* £5.99
☐	99366 2	**THE ELECTRIC KOOL AID ACID TEST**	*Tom Wolfe* £4.99
☐	99370 0	**THE PAINTED WORD**	*Tom Wolfe* £3.50
☐	99371 9	**THE PUMP HOUSE GANG**	*Tom Wolfe* £4.99